PSYCHOANALYSIS: THE VITAL ISSUES

VOLUME I

Psychoanalysis as an Intellectual Discipline

PSYCHOANALYSIS: THE VITAL ISSUES

Volume I: *Psychoanalysis as an Intellectual Discipline*

edited by

JOHN E. GEDO, M.D.
Chairman, Fiftieth Anniversary Celebration Committee,
Chicago Psychoanalytic Society

and

GEORGE H. POLLOCK, M.D., Ph.D.
President,
Chicago Institute for Psychoanalysis

EMOTIONS AND BEHAVIOR MONOGRAPHS
Monograph No. 2

edited by
The Chicago Institute for Psychoanalysis

INTERNATIONAL UNIVERSITIES PRESS, INC.

New York, New York

Library of Congress Cataloging in Publication Data
Main entry under title:

Psychoanalysis as an intellectual discipline.

(Psychoanalysis ; v. 1)
Papers presented at a conference held in Chicago,
Nov. 6-8, 1981, and sponsored by the Chicago Psycho-
analytic Society and the Institute for Psychoanalysis.
Bibliography: p.
Includes index.
1. Psychoanalysis—Congresses. 2. Developmental
psychology—Congresses. 3. Psychoanalysis—Philosophy—
Congresses. 4. Creative ability—Congresses. I. Gedo,
John E. II. Pollock, George H. III. Chicago Psycho-
analytic Society. IV. Chicago Institute for Psycho-
analysis. V. Series.
RC500.5.P79 1983   vol. 1 [BF173] 150.19′5   83-26432
ISBN 0-8236-5385-4
ISSN 0734-9890

Contents

PART IV: ON THE EPISTEMOLOGY OF PSYCHOANALYSIS

Contributors

MICHAEL FRANZ BASCH, M.D. Training and Supervising Analyst, Chicago Institute for Psychoanalysis; Attending Psychiatrist, Michael Reese Hospital and Medical Center, Chicago; Clinical Professor of Psychiatry, Pritzker School of Medicine, University of Chicago.

DAVID BEVINGTON, PH.D. Professor, Department of English Language and Literature and the College, The University of Chicago.

DAVID A. FREEDMAN, M.D. Training and Supervising Analyst, Houston/Galveston Psychoanalytic Institute; Professor of Psychiatry, Baylor College of Medicine.

JOHN E. GEDO, M.D. Training and Supervising Analyst, Chicago Institute for Psychoanalysis; Chairman, Fiftieth Anniversary Celebration of the Chicago Psychoanalytic Society.

MARY M. GEDO, PH.D. Chicago writer and critic.

MARK J. GEHRIE, PH.D. Graduate, Chicago Institute for Psychoanalysis; Assistant Professor (Research Associate) Department of Psychiatry, University of Chicago School of Medicine.

ARNOLD GOLDBERG, M.D. Attending Psychiatrist, Michael
Reese Hospital, Chicago; Training and Supervising
Analyst, Chicago Institute for Psychoanalysis; Clinical Professor of Psychiatry, Pritzker School of Medicine, University of Chicago.

WILLIAM I. GROSSMAN, M.D. Training and Supervising
Analyst, The New York Psychoanalytic Institute;
Clinical Professor of Psychiatry, Albert Einstein Col-
lege of Medicine.

WAUD H. KRACKE, PH.D. Associate Professor of Anthropology, University of Illinois-Chicago; Research
Graduate, Chicago Institute for Psychoanalysis.

DONALD N. LEVINE, PH.D. Professor, Department of So-
ciology and Committee on Analysis of Ideas and
Study of Methods, and Dean of the College, The
University of Chicago.

JOSEPH D. LICHTENBERG, M.D. Editor-in-Chief, *Psychoanalytic Inquiry*; Faculty, Washington Psychoanalytic
Institute and Baltimore-D.C. Institute for Psychoanalysis.

GEORGE MORAITIS, M.D. Training and Supervising Analyst, and Member of the Faculty, Chicago Institute
for Psychoanalysis; Member of the Faculty, Department of Psychiatry, Northwestern University.

HENRI PARENS, M.D. Training and Supervising Analyst
(Adult and Child Analysis); Research Professor of
Child Psychiatry, The Medical College of Pennsylvania; Director, The Early Child Development Program, MCP-EPPI.

GEORGE H. POLLOCK, M.D., PH.D. President, Chicago Institute for Psychoanalysis; Professor of Psychiatry,
Northwestern University; President, Center for Psy-
chosocial Studies, Chicago.

BARBARA S. ROCAH, M.D. Training and Supervising Analyst, Chicago Institute for Psychoanalysis.

LEO SADOW, M.D. Training and Supervising Analyst, Chicago Institute for Psychoanalysis; Clinical Professor of Psychiatry, University of Illinois College of Medicine.

MARK R. SCHWEHN, PH.D. Assistant Professor of Humanities, Committee on General Studies in the Humanities, The University of Chicago.

MELFORD E. SPIRO, PH.D. Presidential Professor of Anthropology, Department of Anthropology, University of California, San Diego.

SAMUEL WEISS, M.D. Training and Supervising Analyst, Chicago Institute for Psychoanalysis; Clinical Associate Professor of Psychiatry, University of Illinois College of Medicine.

Preface

The 1981-1982 academic year marked the fiftieth anniversary of organized psychoanalysis in Chicago. Among the year-long series of activities that served to celebrate the occasion, one of the most extensive was a scientific conference on November 6-8, 1981, co-sponsored by the Chicago Psychoanalytic Society and the Institute for Psychoanalysis. Aptly entitled "The Vital Issues," this symposium brought together many of the most productive psychoanalytic thinkers and academicians concerned with depth psychology currently active in this country. Despite a few regrettable omissions, the roster included almost everyone from the Chicago psychoanalytic community presently engaged in scientific work.

From the inception, the organizers hoped to evoke a body of original scientific work that would merit publication in a commemorative volume. The success of the conference is underscored by the fact that we now present the proceedings in two volumes, in spite of our inability to include certain contributions previously committed for publication elsewhere. Our editorial task has consisted of arranging the material at our disposal into coherent, topically organized books; we have not attempted to pass judgment on the scientific merits of individual contributions because we feel that the conference deserves to be permanently recorded as a whole; it is a collective statement of the vital debates and enduring consensus within contemporary psychoanalysis.

The shape of these two volumes has been crucially affected by the circumstance that many of the most outstanding contributors to the symposium whose presentations focused on the issues of psychoanalytic theory could not make their papers available to us. As a result, instead of adhering to the thematic divisions of the conference program, we have opted to organize the material on the basis of an entirely new schema. Our first volume deals with the interrelationships between psychoanalysis and other intellectual disciplines; the clinical theory of psychoanalysis and its applications form the subject matter of the second volume. Subsections within these major topics will be introduced by briefer essays; some of these were also presented in some context at the conference, others have been prepared specifically for this publication.

This first volume presents four aspects of psychoanalysis as an intellectual discipline. Part I on the origins of motivation deals with our roots in neurobiology and developmental psychology, and with the complex question of the use of data from infant observation. A second topic addresses the problems of interdisciplinary collaboration itself in its various permutations; these are illustrated here through examples from the sphere of the social sciences. Next, we offer a section on studies of the course of human life, here focused on certain vicissitudes of creativity. And the last aspect of psychoanalysis we consider is the philosophy of its theory construction.

We would like to dedicate this collection to the memory of our many psychoanalytic predecessors in Chicago.

THE EDITORS

Part I

The Origins of Motivation

Introduction

BARBARA S. ROCAH, M.D.

Psychoanalytic developmental psychology is part of an effort to advance psychoanalysis as a general psychological theory of human behavior. The study of the origin of motivational structures is a complex aspect of developmental psychology that requires investigation of inherent factors in the infant as well as discovery of the ways in which they are patterned into conscious or unconscious goals we call motivations. Drs. Basch, Freedman, Lichtenberg, and Parens have widely different approaches to this complex topic. My introduction consists of a historical-conceptual review of advances in psychoanalytic developmental theory in which I attempt to locate the investigative directions of the contributors to this section.

Freud's theory of motivation has been summarized by Rapaport (1960). Instincts were the universal inherent factor in humans that acted upon a hypothetical closed system, termed the mental apparatus, that governed human behavior. An instinct was conceptualized by Freud (1915) as being on the frontier of mind and body. It was the psychical representative of stimulation originating in the organism which made a demand upon the mind for work in consequence of its connection to the body. This was a totally psychological concept of motivation, not a biological concept. This concept asserted that the laws governing human behavior mediated through the mental apparatus could be studied without reference to molecular, physiologic, or neural processes.

Freud developed three instinct theories which postulated that all mental occurrences must be built on the interplay of forces of the elemental instincts which he described in 1905 and 1911 as sexual vs. self-preservative instincts, in 1914 as narcissism vs. object libido, and in 1920 as life vs. death instincts. Until 1911 Freud asserted that all instincts were regulated by the pleasure principle. This was a physicalistic principle of tension discharge, not a reference to experiential pleasure or pain. The pleasure principle was modified in the course of development by the infant's capacity for delay of gratification in accordance with the demands of reality. Freud (1911) termed this the reality principle.

This model of tension discharge was based on a reflex-arc physiology. It was reformulated in 1920 as the constancy principle which Freud aserted was the most elemental principle of human existence. This principle, the dynamic manifestation of which Freud termed the death instinct, described the inherent tendency of matter to return to an earlier inorganic state. This state was interfered with by evolutionary forces that overcame inherent inertia and changed matter into organic life, and finally into mental life. The death instinct was hypothesized as the motive for behavior that was beyond the pleasure principle manifested in repetition compulsions.

Freud's (1905) instinct theory, the libido theory, contained within it a theory of the relationship of instinct to external reality as well as a developmental theory of motivation. The aim of the sexual instinct was the discharge of tension upon a suitable drive object. The infant first awoke to the world of real objects as a consequence of the failure of hallucinatory wish fulfillments, and the imperative need for satisfaction of instinctual drive. As development progressed, sexual energy was displaced over time from oral to anal to phallic zones until the infantile sexual instincts were organized into genital primacy at the time of the Oedipus complex. The component instincts were subjectively patterned by a complemental series which described the interaction of the inherent instinct with environmental and constitutional factors. The component instincts that remained fixated at a prodromal stage, through repression, became pathogenic predispositions to later neurotic symptom formation.

Freud (1915) asserted that an instinct was represented in the mind by an idea or an affect. Affect was not regarded as a motive for behavior until 1926 when Freud asserted that anxiety or guilt was a signal that mobilized the organism to defense or flight. Growth was measured by the appearance of restraint systems that evolved from conflict between the instinct and reality. With the development of the structural theory in 1923, Freud postulated that psychic energy was contained through ego defenses, secondary thought processes, as well as through the child's internalization, in the superego, of drive-restraining relationships with external objects who frustrated the child's wishes.

Freud's complicated theory of psychic determinism which I have just summarized was radically challenged in some aspects by Hartmann (1937). He asserted that not all internally determined behavior was instinctually motivated. He postulated the conflict-free sphere of the ego, consisting of the ego apparatuses of primary autonomy which guaranteed infant adaptation and coordina-

tion with the environment. These apparatuses were
defined as inborn maturational capacities for perception,
learning, intention, object conceptualization, thinking,
memory, locomotion, language, and productivity. Hartmann emphasized the role of the environment in development which he defined as "average expectable" when
it functioned as the appropriate environmental releaser
of the apparatuses of primary autonomy. The average
expectable environment was both a biological and a social
concept. He differentiated between a state of adaptedness
which obtained between the organism and the environment that was favorable to both, and the process of adaptation that brought about that state. Through the
infant's use of the apparatuses of primary autonomy
Hartmann could postulate achievement of a state of
adaptedness without needing to postulate infant awareness of goal or purpose. His work on the problem of adaptation not only raised adaptation to the level of one of
the five metapsychological assumptions of psychoanalysis, but also defined self-preservation as an ego function
rather than an ego instinct. His emphasis on the non-
conflictual origins of psychic structure and goals involving relationships with others expanded the theory of
motivational structures and pathogenesis to include the
process of adaptation mediated by inborn autonomous
factors and environmental factors, as well as drive.

  Parens (1973, 1979, 1983) takes up the question of
motivation for adaptation which he feels Hartmann left
unanswered. Parens (1973) asserts that psychoanalytic
observations of infants engaged in sensorimotor activity
reveal that this behavior is motivated by an inherent
nondestructive trend in the aggressive drive. He dis-
agrees with Hartmann's 1948 assertion that noninstinctual energy fuels these activities since the ego, the agency
of drive neutralization, is not formed until 6-8 months.

In Parens's view, destructiveness is not inherent in the aggressive drive but is secondarily acquired from excessive frustration.

Parens's radical revision of Freud's death instinct theory is not the only psychoanalytic research influenced by Hartmann's work. Other investigators have been concerned with the way in which behavioral regulation within the infant-caregiver system becomes psychological regulation and motivation in the infant. This genre of research focuses on the transactions between what are regarded as two biological systems: the infant and the caregiver. Three developmental models have emerged which describe the ontogeny of infant integrative and differentiating mechanisms: continuity models, discontinuity models, and genetic field theories.

Works which emphasize continuities in development describe epigenetic sequences of organization of experience derived from infant-caregiver transactions. Early organizations that do not differentiate between self and other are superseded by more complex organizations, but early ones remain potentially active. A. Freud (1965) isolates developmental lines that appear continuous throughout childhood and beyond which indicate functional organizations of drive at various discrete points in the life cycle. Mahler (Mahler, Pine, and Bergman, 1975) describes stages in a separation-individuation process that chart the development of autonomy in an infant over the first two years of life. Basch (1975) describes a holistic schema of brain-ordering functions and genetic epistemology. This schema outlines a range of potential behaviors that are available to an individual in response to life experiences that are dependent upon the phylogenetic unfolding of ordering capabilities.

Discontinuous models describe not only how new competencies arise in the infant, but qualitative changes as well. In contrast to linear, continuous models in which more complex development is thought to arise from primitive precursors, discontinuous models describe the maturation of separate independent variables which are eventually synthesized into new competencies in a manner proscribed by the genetic code. Kagan (1974) has described intellectual development in this manner; Spitz (1959), Emde, Gaensbauer, and Harmon (1976), and Freedman (1979) have studied affectual development and object representation from this perspective. Freud's (1905) theory of the diphasic course of sexual development is another example of a discontinuous theory of development.

In both the continuous and discontinuous models behavior is regarded as goal directed and purposeful toward increasing adaptedness. Adaptation is accomplished through more complex repetitions of emerging competencies in new combinations. Purpose is inferred from the infant's action rather than from hypothetical symbolic wish fulfillments. The subset of goals to achieve adaptedness is described as an inherent property of biological organisms (Weiss, 1949, Piaget, 1967). Various internal "motives" for progressive adaption have been suggested, such as incomplete assimilation and accommodation cycles (Piaget, 1936), effectance motives (White, 1959), pattern matching and information sorting (Steckler and Carpenter, 1967; Basch, 1977; Stern and Shapiro, 1981), the resolution of discrepancies (Kagan, 1974), and the resolution of oscillating tendencies (Sander, 1975). It is important to ask, however, whether the inference of purpose defines a behavior as motivated? Do we consider, in other words, the process of the infant establishing competent and effective phylogenetic and ontogenetic programs for survival, self-preservation, and maintenance of biological order and organization within the infant-caregiver system as motivated behavior?

The third model that describes the ontogeny of integrative and differentiating mechanisms in the human is genetic field theory. Spitz (1959) is one of the most prominent names associated with this model. Spitz's (1959) complex field theory permitted the study of events that took place in synchrony. He took a complex position that gave equal weight to intrinsic drive, object relationships, and conflict-free maturational forces within the infant as the codeterminants of the regulatory, integrative, and differentiating exchanges within the infant-caregiver system. Spitz describes three qualitatively different organizations of infant object awareness that emerge discontinuously. These organizers reflect the synthesis of instinctual, memory, perceptual, reality-testing, and communication systems in the infant as well as the development in the infant of the capacity for directed behavior. In his concept of critical phases he describes the specificity of environmental meshing with infant organizers that permit integration of these synthetic organizations within the totality of the infant's functioning. Emde, Gaensbauer, and Harmon (1976) and Freedman (1979, 1982, 1983) have utilized Spitz's genetic-field-theory approach in their developmental research. Freedman (1982) has emphasized that motivation cannot be accounted for by Freud's universal postulate of dual drives. Following Loewald (1971) he states that the observation of children who are sensorily impaired, or who are raised in extreme environmental conditions, demonstrates that the emergence of ego functions and drive organization are products of experience, not inborn factors. What is inborn is neurophysiologic brain functioning, the maturational base of psychobiologic behavior. Freedman states that drive, affect, and object awareness are autosynthetic products that develop discontinuously according to a genetically coded timetable from the infant's nonreflective, presymbolic psychobiological activity. Furthermore, in his view, this psychobiological activity does not become patterned into motives without critical affective nutriment from the environment.

Whereas in Freedman's view motives develop from the decisive effect of the environment on clusters of maturational forces within the infant, affect seems to be one inborn apparatus that has a decisive motivational effect on the environment. Stern and Shapiro (1981) demonstrate that the infant is "prewired" to tune into the mother's face and voice attentively. Fraiberg's (1971) and Freedman's (1979) work with blind infants who become autistic demonstrates the hazards for infants who are unable to tune into mother in this attentive fashion to induce maternal bonding. Spitz's (1945) hospitalism research and Engel's (Engel and Reichsman, 1956) and Dowling's (1977) research on infants with esophageal atresia point to the critical loss of function in the infant in the face of constitutional and acquired deficits in the infant's capacity to engage the environment affectually. Steckler and Carpenter (1967) describe a perceptual-affective system through which the infant can autonomously regulate his receptiveness to incoming stimuli. The infant can "tune in" and motivate the environment to engage in more exchanges, or can "tune out" the environment and initiate avoidance behaviors.

The most comprehensive and radical statement about affects as the inherent factor that shapes object relations and determines later motivational structures is made by Basch (1976, 1983). He states that it is the transformation of experience by the infant into affective qualities that determines motivations which can be autonomously repeated. Affect, in his view, is the original organizer of experience before there are cognitive knowing and cognitive frames of reference. The recognition that affective knowing is a precursor to cognitive discursive knowing places, in Basch's view, the proper perspective on early behavior as a continuous determinant of later behavior. The infant's capacity to engage the environment nonreflectively through physiognomic expressions that are read by the environment as affects compensates for the infant's motoric helplessness by permitting communication at a distance. There is, in Basch's view, a seamless web between this nonreflective presymbolic experience and later symbolic affectual experience, as it is described by Freedman (1979). Under these presymbolic conditions the object is a psychobiologic functional object, not a represented object, nor a target for the infant's wishes. The object is part of an open system between the infant and the caregiver who ministrates to the infant's needs for tension reduction, stimulation, information feedback, etc. Sander (1975) believes that it is through this interactional communication and repetitive interpretive feedback by the psychobiologic object that the infant becomes differentiated and synthesis is accomplished.

In conclusion, the developmental research that I have briefly reviewed implies that the infant-caregiver system is a complex, functional bidirectional system that leads to successive states of more sophisticated adaptedness between the two partners. The investigators whose work has been mentioned vary in their opinion about whether the infant's activity in this process is motivated, and how psychobiological activity is transformed into psychological activity. Psychological motivation is regarded by most investigators as those symbolically patterned predispositions to action toward cognitively differentiated others or inanimate goals.

The process of adaptation describes the interactional

matrix wherein the infant's inherent, subjective predispositions to action become differentiated, organized, and integrated. The study of adaptation also offers a way of biologically defining the influence of object relations on an individual's evolving goals of attachment, and need satisfaction within a context of mutually satisfying conditions for both partners. This developmental perspective in psychoanalysis which describes the effect of internalized object relations as a motivational template for future behavior raises a number of questions. (1) We do not know the hierarchical ordering of regulatory principles that determine the patterning and internalization of these early transactions involving the caretaker and infant. Freud's hypothesis of tension relief has been expanded, through developmental research, to include information seeking, affect, repetition, and reversal of passive into active rhythmicity as other regulatory possibilities. (2) We do not know how early experience with others acts as an organizer of future encounters: continuously, discontinuously, or at critical periods in the development of an individual. Emde (1981a) in a critical review of this aspect of developmental research suggests that we are at a great disadvantage when we attempt to deduce the internal experience of infants or reconstruct it from psychoanalytic work with adults and children. Reconstruction presents development as linear and continuous which may be inexact. (3) Though developmental research is a predictive tool, we do not have the means to predict what aspects of the infant's experience within the infant-caretaker system will become subjectively and symbolically patterned into meaningful wishes. We have no way of knowing the fate of those experiences which do not acquire symbolic representation. Lichtenberg (1978, 1983) refers to Gedo's (1979) discussion of this complex problem: "If behavior receives its first regulation in a presymbolic form, do some of these behaviors, especially maladaptive ones, persist? If so, do we not encounter them in a psychoanalysis and need to broaden our means of recognizing, and interpreting these behaviors without symbolic representation?" Lichtenberg answers affirmatively. He believes that these behaviors can be comprehended through analytic scrutiny of what he terms body problem-solving behavior in patients. These are nonreflective, presymbolic perceptual registrations in memory of experience before affective-cognitive level of representation has been reached. He gives three examples from patients of behavior that in his view is without symbolic representation or logic. Engel's (Panel, 1979) report on how his patient Monica fed her own child in a manner that paralleled the unusual circumstances of her own infancy is another example of this presymbolic registry that motivates future action. Lichtenberg believes that although these body problem-solving behaviors may become incorporated into later fantasies they enter into psychopathology as independent variables that pertain to that unrememberable and unforgettable sector of human experience. Psychoanalysis offers a postdictive approach to these problems that complements the predictive tools of developmental research.

REFERENCES

Basch, M. (1975), Toward a theory that encompasses depression: revision of existing causal hypotheses in psychoanalysis. In: *Depression and Human Existence*, ed. E. J. Anthony & T. Benedek. Boston: Little, Brown, pp. 485–535.
—— (1976), The concept of affect: a re-examination. *J. Amer. Psychoanal. Assn.*, 43:29–68.
—— (1977), Developmental psychology and explanatory theory in psychoanalysis. *The Annual of Psychoanalysis*, 5:229–268. New York: International Universities Press.
—— (1983), Response to Dr. Freedman, In: *This Volume*, New York: International Universities Press, pp. 39–52.

Dowling, S. (1977), Eleven esophageal atresia infants. *The Psychoanalytic Study of the Child*, 32:215-256. New Haven, Conn.: Yale University Press.

Emde, R. (1981a), Shaking of the foundations: Changing models of infancy and nature of early development. *J. Amer. Psychoanal. Assn.*, 29:179-220.

——— (1981b), Toward a psychoanalytic theory of affect. II: Emerging models of emotional development in infancy. In: *The Course of Life*, ed. S. Greenspan & G. Pollock. Washington, D.C.: U.S. Department of Health and Human Services, vol. 1, pp. 85-112.

——— Gaensbauer, T., & Harmon, R. J. (1976), Emotional expression in infancy: A biobehavioral study. [*Psychological Issues*, Monogr. 37]. New York: International Universities Press.

Engel, G., & Reichsman, F. (1956), Spontaneous and experimentally induced depression in an infant with a gastric fistula. *J. Amer. Psychoanal. Assn.*, 4:428-451.

Fraiberg, S. (1971), Intervention in infancy: A program for blind infants. *J. Amer. Acad. Child Psychiat.*, 10:381-405.

Freedman, D. (1979), The sensory deprivations: an approach to the study of the emergence of affects and capacity for object relationships. *Bull. Menninger Clin.*, 43:29-68.

——— (1982), Of instincts and instinctual drives: Developmental considerations. *Psychoanal. Inquiry*, in press.

——— (1983), The origins of motivation. In: *This Volume*. New York: International Universities Press, pp. 17–38.

Freud, A. (1965), *Normality and Pathology in Childhood: Assessments of Development*. New York: International Universities Press.

Freud, S. (1905), Three essays on the theory of sexuality. *Standard Edition*, 7:125-248. London: Hogarth Press, 1953.

——— (1911), Formulations on the two principles of mental functioning. *Standard Edition*, 12:213-226. London: Hogarth Press, 1958.

——— (1914), On narcissism. *Standard Edition*, 14:67-104. London: Hogarth Press, 1957.

——— (1915), Instincts and their vicissitudes. *Standard Edition*, 14:117-140. London: Hogarth Press, 1957.

——— (1920), Beyond the pleasure principle. *Standard Edition*, 18:3-66. London: Hogarth Press, 1955.

——— (1926), Inhibitions, symptoms and anxiety. *Standard Edition*, 20:77-178. London: Hogarth Press, 1959.

Gedo, J. (1979), *Beyond Interpretation*. New York: International Universities Press.

Hartmann, H. (1937), *Ego Psychology and Problems of Adaptation. J. Amer. Psychoanal. Assn.*, Monogr. 1. New York: International Universities Press, 1958.

—— (1948), Comments on psychoanalytic theory of instinctual drives. In: *Essays on Ego Psychology*. New York: International Universities Press, 1964, pp. 69-89.

Kagan, J. (1974), The form of early development: continuity and discontinuities in emerging competencies. *Arch. Gen. Psychiat.*, 36:1047-1054.

Lichtenberg, J. (1978), The sense of the object. *J. Amer. Psychoanal. Assn.*, 27:375-386.

—— (1983), Infancy and the psychoanalytic situation. In: *This Volume*, New York: International Universities Press, pp. 57–87.

Loewald, H. (1971), On motivation and instinct theory. *The Psychoanalytic Study of the Child*, 26:91-128. New York: Quadrangel Press.

Mahler, M., Pine, F., & Bergman, A. (1975), *The Psychological Birth of the Human Infant*. New York: Basic Books.

Panel (1979), Monica: A twenty-five year longitudinal study of the consequences of trauma in infancy, G. Engel, reporter. *J. Amer. Psychoanal Assn.*, 27:107-127.

Parens, H. (1973), Aggression: a reconsideration. *J. Amer. Psychoanal. Assn.*, 21:34-60.

—— (1979), *Development of Aggression in Early Childhood*. New York: Jason Aronson.

—— (1983), Toward a reformulation of the theory of aggression and its implications for primary prevention. In: *This Volume*. New York: International Universities Press, pp. 87–114.

Piaget, J. (1936), *Origins of Intelligence in Children*. New York: International Universities Press, 1952.

—— (1967), *Six Psychological Studies*. New York: Random House.

Rapaport, D. (1960), *Psychoanalytic Theory of Motivation: The Collected Papers of David Rapaport*, ed. M. Gill. New York: Basic Books.

Sander, L. (1975), *Infant and Caretaking Environment: Explorations in Child Psychiatry*, ed. E. J. Anthony. New York: Plenum Press, pp. 129-165.

Spitz, R. (1945), Hospitalism. *The Psychoanalytic Study of the Child*, New York: International Universities Press.

—— (1959), *Genetic Field Theory of Ego Formation*. New York: International Universities Press.

Steckler, G., & Carpenter, G. (1967), A viewpoint on early affective development. In: *The Exceptional Infant*. Vol. 1: *The Normal Infant*. Seattle: Special Child Publications, pp. 163-189.

Stern, D. & Shapiro, T. (1981), Psychoanalytic perspectives on the first year of life: Establishment of the object in the affective field. In: *The Course of Life*, ed. S. Greenspan & G. Pollock. Washington, D.C.: U.S. Department of Health and Human Services, vol. 1, pp. 3-128.

Weiss, P. (1949), The biological basis of adaptation. In: *Adaptation*, ed. J. Romano. Ithaca, N.Y.: Cornell University Press.
White, R. W. (1959), Motivation reconsidered: the concept of competence. *Psychol. Rev.*, 66:297-333.

1

The Origins of Motivation

DAVID A. FREEDMAN, M.D.

William Harvey (1651) wrote, "Nature is nowhere accustomed more openly to display her secret mysteries than in cases where she shows traces of her workings apart from the beaten path; nor is there any better way to advance the proper practise of medicine than to give our minds to the discovery of the usual law of nature by careful study of rarer forms of disease. For it has been found in almost all things that what they contain of useful or applicable nature is hardly perceived unless we are deprived of them or they become deranged in some way" (p. xx).

I cite Harvey because he lends authority to an approach to the study of development which I have found fruitful. I refer to the observation of the maturation and development of individuals who, because of some vicissitude in very early life, do not fall into the population of the normally endowed. Whether because of a congenital or an early acquired somatic deficit, or because of the nature of the environmental circumstances under which their early years have been spent, these individuals' early life experiences are outside the range of the average and

17

expectable. To this extent the study of their development serves as a check on those inferences we draw from the observation of physiologically intact youngsters who are being reared under "normal" circumstances. I specify development because I have been at some pains to exclude individuals with evidence of a congenital central-nervous-system defect. In this way I have attempted to differentiate between the effects of gene-determined maturational events in the organ of the mind and the modes of their expression. These latter necessarily reflect the environmental circumstances in which new, maturationally determined potentialities emerge. Otherwise stated, I assume that maturation proceeds without development but that development always implies an underlying maturational process.

I became interested in this approach as a result of having had the opportunity to observe a number of youngsters who were either victims of the pandemic of retrolental fibrous dysplasia or who, for other reasons, were born blind. These children, as has been noted many times, show a remarkable propensity to develop a syndrome that closely simulates the autistic psychosis of childhood. In the course of my observations several additional striking facts emerged. These underscored, for me, the potential usefulness of the study not only of the congenitally blind, but also of the victims of other tissue and environmental vicissitudes during very early life.

In the first place, an autistic-like psychosis is by no means always present in the congenitally blind. The incidence is, indeed, extremely high; 25 percent, as compared to a small fraction of 1 percent in the general population, is a conservative estimate. At the same time many youngsters are less seriously afflicted, and there are, in addition, blind children who seem to develop with little or no evidence of major psychological difficulties.

Much like a gene factor of limited penetrance, blindness only increases its victim's vulnerability to an autistic outcome; per se it is not the cause.

Secondly, it is specifically lack of vision which makes these youngsters vulnerable to a psychotic outcome. Victims of congenital deafness do not manifest a similar vulnerability. The incidence of major psychotic disturbances is no greater among the deaf than it is in the general population.

Thirdly, the opportunity to observe a number of victims of environmental deprivation and parental neglect as well as a review of the literature on neglected and feral children make it clear that a significant proportion of these youngsters present with a clinical picture which bears a much greater similarity to that of the congenitally blind than to that of the deaf. At the same time, when sufficient detail is available, it appears to be possible to correlate the vulnerability of members of this group to specific aspects of their traumatic experience.

Given the prevalence of autistic phenomena among the blind, their absence among the deaf, and, in particular, the "in-between" status of the environmentally deprived, it seemed to me that a closer scrutiny of these populations might contribute to the understanding of the early processes which lead to the development of a differentiated psychic structure—i.e., one equipped with such functional characteristics as the ability to be aware of and to enter into relations with others, the ability to establish internalized representations of others, and the capacity to engage in purposeful goal-directed behavior. I believe the evidence I have to present supports the hypothesis that these various abilities—which are basic to virtually all psychology—emerge over time in relation to one another, and as a result of the ongoing maturational and development process. Otherwise stated, as I interpret them, my observations do not support the assumption of inborn instinctual drives which both shape and are shaped by the individual's life experience. While it is certainly true that each individual is born with gene-determined and anatomically defined potentialities and limitations, these only define a range of potential variability with which he is endowed. How within this range specific psychologically meaningful characteristics emerge is the question at hand. This, I propose, is a developmental issue. Indeed if one is to be consistent with Freud's (1915) definition of an instinctual drive, he must conclude that drive, self, and psychic structure must develop *pari passu* out of the interplay of the maturing organism and its evironment. Freud, it will be recalled, proposed that instinctual drives[1] are characterized by the four defining characteristics: source, impetus, aim, and object. Of these, at least two (aim and object) imply some degree of self awareness, and the ability to differentiate self from non-self.

II

I turn now to a brief review of some aspects of the maturation and development of the neonatal and infantile central nervous system. The dramatic changes that the brain undergoes during these periods are illustrated by the following slides. Figure 1, from the work of Yakovlev

---

[1] Much of the confusion that characterizes this aspect of psychoanalytic theory derives from the translation of the German *Trieb* as instinct. This has led to a failure to maintain a clear distinction between the behavioral expression of fixed patterns of neural activity—e.g., micturition, respiration, the sham rage of animals with hypothalomic lesions, and other automatisms—and goal-directed, purposeful behaviors which may utilize such fixed patterns. In keeping with the glossary definitions (Moore and Fine, 1967), I refer to the former as Instincts and the latter as Instinctual Drives.

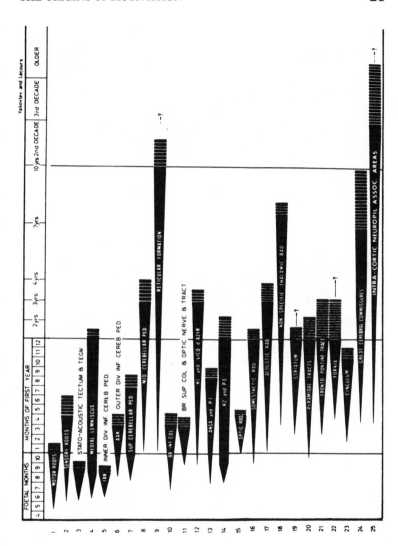

FIGURE 1. Adapted from Yakovlev and LeCours (1965). Courtesy of Blackwell Scientific Publications Limited.

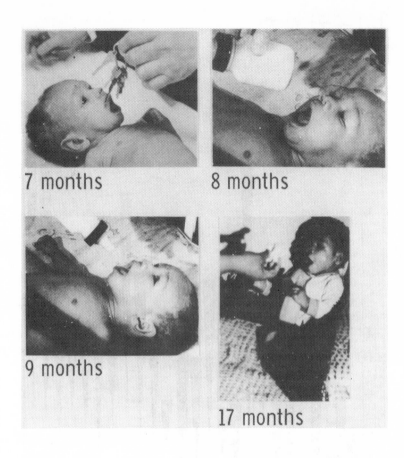

FIGURE 2. From Perry and Freedman (1973). Courtesy of the Association for Research in Nervous and Mental Disease, Inc.

and LeCours (1965), illustrates the time sequence of myelin deposition in the indicated pathways. It is probably the case that myelin deposition is an entirely maturational phenomenon, i.e., it follows a timetable which appears to be independent of the environmental ambience. Thus, an environmentally deprived youngster whom I had the opportunity to follow until his death when he was 23 months old (Perry and Freedman, 1973) showed age-appropriate myelinization despite the fact that he could not crawl and had not developed even rudimentary hand/eye coordination (Fig. 2). Although, as this case demonstrates, the presence of myelin in a pathway does not insure neurologic and, therefore, psychologic functioning, the evidence of the demyelinating diseases makes it clear that in its absence functioning is impossible. It is, in other words, a necessary but not a sufficient condition for the efficient transmission of nerve impulses and, therefore, for psychological functioning which is, after all, a manifestation of the activity of the nervous system.

In the light of this consideration, it is particularly noteworthy that both the age at which myelin deposition begins and the time lapse between the inception and completion of the process vary enormously from neural system to neural system. Specific brain functions and, therefore, the psychological functions that they subserve emerge independently from one another and follow idiosyncratic maturational and developmental time courses. Our mental abilities, it would appear, develop piecemeal rather than across a broad front, and our perceptions of ourselves and others are the products of a synthetic function. Thus, the congenitally blind individual may have well-developed auditory and haptic internalized representations of external objects despite his total lack of a visual representation. This was well documented by von

Senden (1931), who described the sequelae of surgery for congenital cataracts. The acquisition of sight often proved to be a mixed blessing. Immediately after surgery none of these individuals was able to use visual cues to identify objects which they could readily recognize by touch. For many the incapacity proved permanent. More recently Justin Call (1980) has observed that "the infant comes to know his mother by "littles," as an oral mother, as a vocal mother, as a holding mother, etc. (p. 273).

Figure 3, from the work of Conel (1935-1959) illustrates a more complex aspect of the problem. When Conel published this work, and for much of the time since, it was and has been widely believed that changes in the richness and density of neural processes are also the results of maturational changes. The increasing abilities of the maturing child were, therefore, considered to be no more than reflections of his or her making use of newly available neuronal connections. Such a hypothesis is, I believe, reflected in the widely held assumption that drives are inborn and that the developmental process only affects the mode of expression of already present primordial drive structures.

The demonstration in recent years (cf. Globus, 1971; Hubel, 1979) that both dendritic arborization and the structure of the neuron are significantly affected by the environmental conditions under which they are maturing calls this hypothesis into question. To the extent that the ultimate form of these anatomic structures reflects a developmental process, it is not possible to consider their behavioral and psychological correlates to be manifestations of inborn instinctual drives as defined by Freud's four criteria.

The vignettes that follow are intended to support this thesis. In each instance, when maturation occurred in the absence of an environment adequate to facilitate devel-

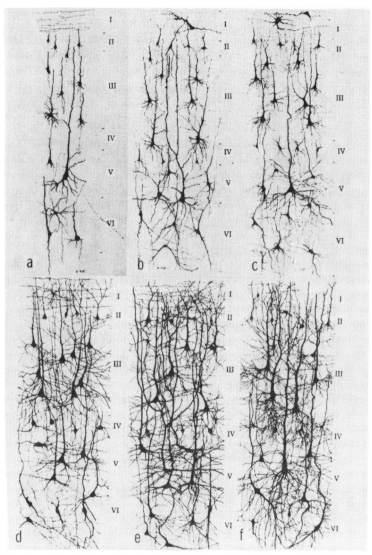

FIGURE 3. Postnatal development of human cerebral cortex around Broca's Area (FCBm); camera lucida drawings from GolgiCox preparations. a: Newborn; b: 1 month; c: 3 months; d: 6 months; e: 15 months; f: 24 months. (From Conel, 1939–1959. Reprinted by permission of the publishers, Harvard University Press, © 1939 by the President and Fellows of Harvard College; © renewed 1966 by Jesse LeRoy Conel.)

opment, identifiable drives did not emerge. I begin with
an excerpt from Itard's (1802-1806) description of the
emergence of puberty in his ward Victor the Wild Boy of
Aveyron. It will be apparent from the account that Victor
matured to the point where he experienced considerable
excitement and arousal in association with the maturational changes of puberty. He satisfied, in other words,
two of Freud's defining criteria (source and impetus) for
an instinctual drive. At the same time, it is equally clear
that his arousal occurred in a vacuum. In the absence of
adequate self-object differentiation and internalized object representations his arousal came to naught. The account that follows merits repeating both for the vivid
picture of Victor's plight and for Itard's speculations concerning its origins. The latter can, I believe, readily be
translated into the terms I have used in this essay. Seven
years after Victor came into his care, Itard reported:

> LIII. In speaking of the intellectual faculties of our
> savage, I have not concealed the obstacles which ar-
> rested the development of certain of them, and I have
> made it my duty to describe exactly the gaps in his
> intelligence. Following the same plan in my account of
> this young man's emotions, I will disclose the animal
> side of his nature with the same fidelity as I have de-
> scribed the civilized side. I will suppress nothing. Al-
> though he appears to feel keenly the pleasure of
> usefulness, Victor remains essentially selfish. Full of
> alacrity and cordiality when the services required of
> him are found to be not opposed to his desires, he is a
> stranger to that courtesy which measures neither pri-
> vation nor sacrifice; and the sweet sentiment of pity is
> yet to be born within him. If in his relations with his
> governess he has sometimes been seen to share her sad-
> ness, this is only an act of imitation, analogous to that
> which draws tears from a young child who sees his
> mother or nurse weep. *In order to commiserate with*

*other peoples' troubles, it is necessary to have known
them or at least to be able to imagine them. This cannot
be expected from a young child or from such a creature
as Victor, foreign as all those pains and privations which
are the basis of our emotional suffering are to him.*

LIV. But what appears still more astonishing in the
emotional system of this young man, and beyond all
explanation, is his indifference to women in the midst
of the violent physical changes attendant upon a very
pronounced puberty. Looking forward to this period as
a source of new sensations for my pupil and of interesting observations for myself, watching carefully all
phenomena that were forerunners of this mental crisis,
I waited each day until some breath of that universal
sentiment which moves all creatures and causes them
to multiply should come and animate Victor and en-
large his mental life. *I have seen this eagerly awaited
puberty arrive or rather burst forth, and our young savage consumed by desire of an extreme violence and of a
startling constancy and this without any presentment of
its purpose or the slightest feeling of preference for any
woman.* Instead of that expansive impulse which precipitates one sex towards the other, I have observed in
him only a sort of blind and slightly pronounced instinct
which, as a matter of fact, does make him prefer the
society of women to that of men without in any way
involving his heart. Thus, I have seen him in a company
of women attempting to relieve his uneasiness by sitting beside one of them and gently taking hold of her
hand, her arms and her knees until, feeling his restless
desires increased instead of calmed by these odd caresses, and seeing no relief from his painful emotions
in sight, he suddenly changed his attitude and petu-
lantly pushed away the woman whom he had sought
with a kind of eagerness. Then he addressed himself
without interruption to another woman with whom he
behaved in the same way. One day, nevertheless, he
became a little more enterprising. After first employing

the same caresses, he took the lady by her hands and drew her, without violence, however, into the depths of an alcove. There, very much out of countenance, and showing in his manners and in his extraordinary facial expression an indescribable mixture of gaity and sadness, of boldness and uncertainty, he several times solicited the lady's caresses by offering her his cheeks and walked slowly around her with a meditative air, finally flinging his arms about her shoulders and holding her closely by the neck. This was all, and these amorous demonstrations ended, as did all the others, with a movement of annoyance which made him repulse the object of his transitory inclinations [emphasis mine].

After describing the measures—e.g., baths, purgings, and bleedings—which he undertook to alleviate Victor's plight, Itard goes on to say:

LVI. Such has been the critical period which promised so much and which would without doubt, have fulfilled all the hopes which we had entertained for it, if instead of concentrating all its activity upon the senses it had also animated the moral system with the same fire and carried the torch of love into this benumbed heart. *Nevertheless, on serious reflection, I will not conceal the fact that when I counted on this mode of development of the phenomena of puberty, I was not justified in comparing my pupil mentally to an ordinary adolescent in whom the love of women very often precedes, or at least always accompanies, the excitement of the reproductive organs.* This agreement between need and inclination could not occur in a creature whose education had not taught him to distinguish between a man and a woman, and was indebted solely to the prompting of instinct for his glimpse of this difference without being able to apply it to his present situation. Also, I did not doubt that if I had dared to reveal to this young man the secret of his restlessness and the aims of his desires, an incalculable benefit would have accrued. But, on the other hand, suppose I had been permitted to try such an experiment, would I not have been afraid to make known to our savage a need which he would have sought to satisfy as publically as his other wants and which would have led him to acts of revolting indecency? Intimidated by the possibility of such a result, I was obliged to restrain myself and once more to see with resignation these hopes, like so many others, vanish before an unforeseen obstacle [emphasis mine].

The following account of Mrs. Fraiberg's encounter with Peter, our autistic congenitally blind subject (Fraiberg and Freedman, 1964) reflects an analogous set of circumstances:

> After a while he came close to me and fingered me. Then, without any change of facial expression and without any show of feeling, he began to dig his fingernails into the skin of my arm, very hard, and causing me to wince with pain. From this point on it was nearly impossible to divert Peter from digging his nails into me or alternately pinching me with great intensity. It is impossible to describe this experience, I cannot call it sadistic. It was as if he did not know this was painful to me and I really felt that on the primitive undifferentiated level on which Peter operated he was not able to identify with the feelings of another person. This digging into me had the quality of trying to get into me, to burrow himself into me, and the pinching had the quality of just holding onto me for dear life.
>
> I observed that when Peter lost an *object* he was mouthing, he showed no reaction to loss and did not search for it. Repeated observation in this session and in others confirmed this point. Very clearly this child had no concept of an object that existed independent of his perception of it.
>
> While his mother was with us I observed that his reaction to her was in no discernible way different from

his reaction to me, to the nurse, or to the dog. At no time, then and for many weeks after I began to work with him, did he ask a direct question, express a need through gesture or language, or answer a question put to him. His mother told me that until very recently he did not call her "Mama" but referred to her as "Too-hoo." She explained that this word derived from her own greeting to him when she entered the house.

Peter always referred to himself in the third person. The word "I," his mother told me, had entered his vocabulary before he had gone to the institution last year, but when I was able to observe him directly I felt that "I" was not employed for self-reference and was mechanically interpolated into speech as if he had been given lessons in "I" and "you."

There were no toys to which Peter had any attachment. When he showed transitory interest in *objects* he brought them to his mouth, sucked on them, chewed them. He did not explore them with his hands, he did not manipulate them. Prehension was poor and the fingers were rigidly extended. The only well-coordinated movements observed were those employed in bringing an *object* to the mouth.

It would appear that neither Victor nor Peter had established introjects which could serve as the basis for the development of a sense of self and the differentiating of self from non-self. In the absence of these developments the somatic arousals to which they were subjected remained inchoate and without aim or object. Their deficiency was twofold. In the first place, they did not have the capacity to conceptualize a consummatory act that would relieve the somatic pressure under which they were laboring. Secondly, they also lacked a matrix of internalized object representations which would enable them to cathect a contemporaneous external object with which to gratify their aims.

Of the two, the latter deficiency would seem to be the more problematic. As Itard (1802-1806) observed, it would have been possible to have acquainted Victor with "the secret of his restlessness and the aim of his desires." However, to have done so in the absence of a matrix of object representations and relationships would, he feared, have led to "acts of revolting indecency" in that Victor "would have sought to satisfy" (his needs) "as publically as his other wants." Some aspects of the process by which such a matrix of internalized representations gets organized are indicated by the two vignettes which follow. In each instance a youngster was maintained under conditions of massive environmental deprivation through at least the first five years.

Marie Mason (1942), who at the time of her report was director of the speech and hearing program of the University of Ohio, reported on her experience with a six-year-old girl born illegitimately to an aphasic mother. The mother was totally uneducated; she could neither read nor write and communicated with her family through gestures. From the time the pregnancy was discovered she, and subsequently her child, were kept in a locked room behind drawn shades. Six and one-half years later, carrying her child who could not walk, the mother made her escape. Mason saw the child when she was admitted to a children's hospital.

The child spent the first two days in tears. Mason's overtures were greeted by gestures of repulsion from "the wan looking distraught child whose face bore marks of grief and fear" (p. 296). She had no language. Sensing that no direct approach was possible, Mason attempted to involve the child by playing dolls with another little girl while ostensibly ignoring the patient. She was successful. Within a year and a half the child had acquired a vocabulary of between fifteen hundred and two thousand words, could count to one hundred, identify coins, and perform arithmetic computations to ten. Mason describes her at eight and one-half as having an excellent sense of humor, and as being an inveterate tease and an imaginative, affectionate, and loving child. In less than two years, this child made the transition from a world of silence, fear, and isolation to an excellent adjustment in the average expectable social world of childhood.

Contrast Mason's report with Kingsley Davis's accounts (1940, 1946) of a girl of "more than five years" who was found "tied to an old chair in a storage room on the second floor" (1940, p. 554) of a farm home in Pennsylvania. Isolation was instituted by her mother when the infant was between six and ten months old. The nurse, who kept the child for most of the period prior to her isolation, described her as entirely normal. A note made two years after her discovery reads as follows:

> Anna walks about aimlessly, makes periodic rhythmic motions of her hands, and, at intervals, makes gutteral and sucking noises. She regards her hands as if she had seen them for the first time. It was impossible to hold her attention for more than a few seconds at a time—not because of distraction due to external stimuli but because of her inability to concentrate. She ignored the task in hand to gaze vacantly about the room. Speech is entirely lacking. Numerous unsuccessful attempts have been made with her in the hope of developing initial sounds. I do not believe that her failure is due to negativism or deafness but that she is not sufficiently developed to accept speech at this time . . . [Mason, 1946, p. 433].

In the ensuing two years, up to the time of her death at approximately eight years of age, this deprived child established adequate toilet habits, was able to feed herself with a spoon, would partially dress herself, and began to talk. Her speech, however, was estimated to be at the two-year level. By this time she was regarded as congenitally feebleminded.

The, perhaps not so subtle, distinction to be made between these two cases is that Mason's child was isolated with her mother. Despite the absence of speech and the extremely limited access to a broader environment, she was able to make those basic internalizations which allow for a differentiation of self and non-self and the making of internal representations of both self and a parenting figure. Obviously, she had made attachments to her mother and was able to experience her separation from mother as a loss.

Time does not permit a more exhaustive review of the numerous reports of youngsters who have been subjected to extended periods of isolation during their early developmental years. Suffice it to say that marked retardation in the development of both somatic structures and cognitive abilities, disturbances in affective expression, inability to enter into object relations, and a state of apathy and disinterest are described in all such individuals when they are found. In some instances, however (e.g., von Feuerbach, 1832; Mason, 1942; Skeels, 1966; Kagan and Klein, 1973; Dennis, 1973), the syndrome appears to be reversible. In others (e.g., Itard, 1802-1806; Davis, 1940, 1946; Singh and Zingg, 1942; Freedman and Brown, 1968) the effects are apparently immutable. Three variables appear to be relevant to the outcome in these cases.

1. Apparently, the nervous system retains sufficient plasticity so that the effects of massive deprivation from the neonatal period can be reversed if correction of the environment is achieved by the time the child is three.

2. Also reversible are those cases in which the deprivation begins after a period of adequate mothering. Helen Keller (Dahl, 1965) had eighteen months of normal

infancy before she was struck down. The legendary Kaspar Hauser (von Feuerbach) was over three before he was incarcerated. Evidently, sufficient immutable organization of neural structures had developed in these individuals so that there was a basis on which they could begin again to organize experience once appropriate stimulation was available from the environment.

3. Finally, the circumstances under which deprivation is imposed are critical. This is, perhaps, most eloquently illustrated by the case reports of Mason and Davis which I have already summarized.

III

Kubie (1948) proposed a hierarchy of instincts for which he used as the differentiating criterion the length of the interval which the individual could tolerate between the emergence of the *impetus* and the achievement of the *aim*. Thus the need (*impetus*) to breathe, which, if the organism is to survive, must be satisfied within minutes by the replenishment of oxygen (*aim*), stands at one extreme. At the opposite pole is the sexual drive. There are no reliable comparable data which tell us how long one can tolerate sexual tension (impetus) without orgastic discharge (*aim*). This is the case because the *object* upon which the instinct can operate is so highly variable (Freud, 1915). We have, for instance, no knowledge of the relative frequency with which internalized representations make possible orgastic discharge (*aim*) in the form of erotic dreams and nocturnal emissions. We do know, however, that for sexuality—in contrast again to breathing—the *object* need never be "biologically appropriate"; there is no doubt that individual survival is possible without the organism ever having had contact with a partner with whom procreation can occur. The multitude of variations on the theme of sexual expression would, of course, be impossible were this tolerance not present. Otherwise stated, one does not put off breathing, nor does one make decisions as to when to breathe or whether to breathe oxygen or some other gas. Both delay and variation are, however, characteristic of the sexual drive. At the same time the *aim* of adult genital sexuality (orgasm) is, like the *aim* of breathing (maintenance of oxygenation) fixed and immutable.[2] Where along such a continuum of instinctual behaviors one would begin to use the designation instinctual drive may involve a somewhat arbitrary decision. Clearly, however, the criterion would involve the ability to delay gratification of the aim and the flexibility to use alternative objects in the pursuit of its gratification.

Kubie's analysis is, however, cross-sectional and focused primarily on the economic aspects of instinct and instinctual drive phenomena. Notably absent is any discussion of genetic considerations. He does not, for example, consider the implications of such facts as (a) that in addition to the very limited permissible hiatus between

---

[2] Despite the obvious adaptive importance of the ability to be aggressive the aim of aggression is much less readily defined. Thus Hartmann, Kris, and Loewenstein (1949) state, "Active aggression refers to the wish to harm, master or to destroy an *object*; passivity refers to the wish to be mastered, harmed or destroyed" (p. 17). While such a postulation is certainly compatible with the reports of many adult analysands, to assign such highly sophisticated goals and clarity of self-*object* differentiation to infants or even very young children requires a leap of faith which I find difficult to accomplish. Ives Hendrick (1943), on the basis of what seem to me to be very similar considerations to those I am putting forward, proposed an "instinct to master." Anticipating Fraiberg's observations, he also proposed that the concept of sadism be confined to aggression toward a sexually cathected *object*. He further proposed that the term "aggression" be reserved for those forces motivated by the desire to destroy either the rival of a sexual *object* or the antagonist of a narcissistic need.

the emergence of the impetus and achievement of the *aim* in regard to the "breathing instinct" respiration is present in essentially adult form literally from minutes after birth; and (b) that the sexual instinct appears to go through a much more complicated developmental process so that genital primacy only becomes a consideration after many years of development during which the *aim* of the pregenital sexual drive is defined in terms of the whole body pleasures associated with the interaction with the caretaker (*object*). Lichtenstein (1961) has pointed out that the process of nurturing which this situation implies must be crucial in the establishment of the beginnings of identity. Sexuality or, more specifically, that congeries of sensory and motor experiences which we epitomize as pregenital sexuality provides the matrix in which the process of self *object* differentiation and the establishment of identity as well as adult sexuality can occur. The two, it should be underscored, develop *pari passu*. For each individual, those idiosyncratic characteristics that epitomize his or her personality are laid down in the same complex exchanges with the caretaker which determine the specific characteristics of his or her adult sexual style. The *object* of the sexual drive as it is defined in any given individual is, therefore, a product of the developmental process which is idiosyncratically that person's.

Taken together, the cross-sectional economic analysis provided by Kubie and the longitudinal genetic discussion of Lichtenstein underscore the borderland position of the instinctual drive with respect to soma and psyche. A complete definition of any given drive—by Freud's criteria—obviously involves both the rigorously defined anatomic structures—e.g., endocrine glands and specific neural structures and pathways—and those more elusive anatomic changes that are the tissue correlates of the psyche. As these latter come to be defined, the gap between soma and psyche will progressively diminish. At the same time the relevance of idiosyncratic experience of the complete definition of drive will be underscored. To the extent that a complete definition of any given drive includes both *aim* and *object*, it must await its appearance until both the maturational and developmental processes that make such sophisticated psychological structures possible emerge. This, of necessity, is the result of a long developmental process that insures that drives will be unique expressions of the psychological history of the individual.

REFERENCES

Call, J. (1980), Some prelinguistic aspects of language development. *J. Amer. Psychoanal. Assn.*, 18:259-290.

Conel, J. L. (1939-1959), *The Post Natal Development of the Human Cerebral Cortex*, vols. 1-7. Cambridge, Mass.: Harvard University Press.

Dahl, H. (1965), Observations on a "natural experiment": Helen Keller. *J. Amer. Psychoanal. Assn.*, 13:533-550.

Davis, K. (1940), Extreme isolation of a child. *Amer. J. Sociol.*, 45:554-565.

——— (1946), Final note on a case of extreme isolation. *Amer. J. Sociol.*, 52:432-437.

Dennis, W. (1973), *Children of the Creche*. New York: Appleton-Century-Crofts.

Fraiberg, S., & Freedman, D. A. (1964), Studies in the ego development of the congenitally blind. *The Psychoanalytic Study of the Child*, 19:113-169. New York: International Universities Press.

Freedman, D. A., & Brown, S. L. (1968), On the role of coenesthetic stimulation in the development of psychic structure. *Psychoanal. Quart.*, 37:418-438.

Freud, S. (1915), Instincts and their vicissitudes. *Standard Edition*, 14:105-195. London: Hogarth Press, 1957.

Globus, A. (1971), Neural ontogeny: its use in tracing connectivity. In: *Brain Development and Behavior*, ed. M. B. Sterman, D. J. McGinty, & A. M. Adinolfi. New York: Academic Press, pp. 253-264.

Hartmann, H., Kris, E., & Loewenstein, R. M. (1949), Notes on the theory of aggression. *The Psychoanalytic Study of the Child*, 3/4:9-36. New York: International Universities Press.

Harvey, W. (1651), Excercitationes de generatione animalium. Quibus accedunt quaedum de partu, de membranis ac humoribus uteri & de conceptione. *New Engl. J. Med.*, 300:733, 1979.

Hendrick, I. (1943), The discussion of the "Instinct to Master." *Psychoanal Quart.*, 12:561-565.

Hubel, D. (1979), The visual cortex of normal and deprived monkeys. *Amer. Scien.*, 67:532-542.

Itard, J. M. B. (1802-1806), *The Wild Boy of Aveyron*, trans. G. Humphrey & M. Humphrey. New York: Century, 1932.

Kagan, J., & Klein, R. E. (1973), Cross-cultural perspectives on early development. *Amer. Psychol.*, 28:947-961.

Kubie, L. (1948), Instincts and homeostasis. *Psychosom. Med.*, 10:15-30.

Lichtenstein, H. (1961), Identity and sexuality. *J. Amer. Psychoanal. Assn.*, 9:179-260.

Mason, M. (1942), Learning to speak after 6½ years of silence. *J. Speech & Hearing Disor.*, 7:295-304.

Moore, B. E., & Fine, B. D. (1967), *A Glossary of Psychoanalytic Terms and Concepts*. New York: American Psychoanalytic Association.

Perry, J. H., & Freedman, D. A. (1973), Massive neonatal environmental deprivation: A clinical and neuroanatomical study. *Res. Pub. Assn. Nerv. & Ment. Dis.*, 51:244-268.

Singh, J. A. L., & Zingg, R. M. (1942), *Wolf Children and Feral Man*. New York: Harper.

Skeels, H. M. (1966), Adult status of children with contrasting life. *Monogr. Soc. Res. Child Devel.*, 31:1-65.

von Feuerbach, A. (1832), *Kaspar Hauser*, trans. H. G. Longer. Boston: Allen & Ticknor.

von Senden, M. (1931), *Space and Sight*, trans. P. Heath, vol. 3. Glencoe, Il.: Free Press, 1960.

Yakovlev, P. I., & LeCours, A. (1965), The myelogenetic cycles of regional maturation of the brain. *Regional Development of the Brain in Early Life*, ed. A. Minkowski. Oxford: Blackwell Scientific Publications, pp. 3-70.

2

Response to Dr. Freedman

MICHAEL FRANZ BASCH, M.D.

What is the nature of human motivation? Freud answered the question by saying that only a wish can move the mental apparatus, but left it to us to fill in the prosaic details that might enable us to cash in that metaphor for hard currency at the bank of human development. Freud, as we know, hypothesized that hunger and thirst forced the infant out of the preferred somnolent, nirvanalike state to seek gratification. Unable to meet his own basic needs the infant cries, is nourished by his mother, and from that attachment comes, as a matter of course, the psychological evolution that leads to human behavior. You recall that Freud postulated that the primary motivation for development was fear—fear of the loss of the source of lifesaving nourishment, fear of the loss of the mothering object, then fear of loss of the love of the object, and finally fear of the loss of the love of the internalized

---

Portions of this discussion have been taken from: (1) "The Concept of Self: An Operational Definition," in *Developmental Approaches to the Self*, ed. Benjamin Lee (New York: Plenum Prss, 1983), pp. 7-58; (2) "Selfobjects and Selfobject Transference: Theoretical Implications," in *Psychoanalytic Crossroads*, ed. Arnold Goldberg and Paul Stepansky (New York: Analytic Press, in press).

parental dicta, i.e., fear of the loss of the love of the superego.

Freud was always fond of Charcot's maxim to the effect that theories are fine but they do not prevent the facts from existing. It applies here. You are familiar with Spitz's (1946) work that showed that the path to maturation is not so simple or direct as Freud believed it was. Infants who are tended appropriately in terms of hygiene and nutrition but receive no mothering do not automatically develop a sense of security, do not become attached to the person who cares for them, do not show normal psychological development, do not thrive in spite of the physical care they are receiving, and may very well die.

Everyone knows now that good parenting is as vital as physical care for an infant, perhaps more so. But what is involved in that? What have we gained when we say, paraphrasing Freud, that only good mothering will move the infant's mental apparatus? Well, we all know what good mothering is, don't we? And where does it come from? It is instinctual, of course, a product of the hormonal shifts that occur in pregnancy and with lactation—motherliness is a natural phenomenon, a by-product of bearing a child. Or is it?

Dr. Freedman's research on the development of sensorily handicapped children has long had an admirer in me because it answers many important questions that potentially help us to bridge the gulf that so often seems to separate psychoanalytic reconstructions of development from the direct observation of infants and children by experimental and academic psychologists. What Dr. Freedman has documented is that it is not fear, but the communication between infant and mother that creates a system in which both infant and mother develop; that is, the biological mother becomes a psychological mother to her baby, and the baby realizes its potential for psychological growth. As Freedman has shown so clearly in his past papers (1979, 1981, 1982) and reviews in the present one, a blind child does not get the signals his mother is sending and therefore cannot respond to them. The mother, getting no feedback from her child, tends to withdraw; the result is a child that has a much better chance of becoming autistic than, as Freedman has shown, either a nonhandicapped or a sensorily handicapped deaf child whose deficit does not interfere with early mother-infant communication. In other words, the blind child does not become autistic because he is blind; he becomes autistic because he cannot serve as a selfobject for his mother until such a time as the parent is secure in her mothering function. On the other hand, as Dr. Freedman has taught us, if the diagnosis of blindness is made early enough, and if the mother is taught how to stimulate her baby in ways meaningful to him, then the blind infant will, in turn, respond to her, the dialogue will be restored, and the danger of autism will be avoided.

Dr. Freedman's examples of so-called feral or wolf children, i.e., children deprived of human communication, buttress his observation of the sensorily handicapped. The story of Victor as told by his physician demonstrates clearly, a point also made by Harlow and Harlow (1962, 1972) in their primate studies, that instinct and the drive or impetus it provides for action are not sufficient in higher animals to generate anything approaching appropriate adaptive behavior.

Where I find myself in disagreement with Dr. Freedman is when, having demonstrated that human goal-directed behavior cannot be the result of inherited instinctual patterns, he attributes such behavior to instinctual drives, an assertion for which no proof is forthcoming, the quotation from the glossary published by the American Psychoanalytic Association notwithstanding. I would like to advance a different explanation.

The behavior that insures the preservation of the individual and the species in animals higher on the evolutionary scale is learned, not inherited behavior. Learning to survive in our complex society begins in the cradle; as analysts we know that infants lay down impressions about the world as represented by the parents which shape their character and style of adaptation in the years to come. The question then is, how do nonverbal infants learn from and communicate with their parents?

Here instinct does come in, but not in the form envisioned by psychoanalysis, that of drives or psychic energies, but in the form of an inherited subcortical system of responses that transforms quantitative stimuli into qualitative memory traces that we call affects. Engrams of affective reactions associated with the memory of the event permanently record the infant's response to stimulation. This process engraves the nature of its transactions with the environment on the infant's brain, thereby providing the psychological bedrock for learning on which all later mental development is built, and to which all later experiences are ultimately referred for their meaning.

When it comes to the affective reactions of infancy nothing is hidden. The facial expressions of babies are exactly the same ones associated in adulthood with such emotions as joy, interest, anger, fear, surprise, disgust, distress, and shame, but, though open to inspection, the significance and implications of these reaction patterns of early infancy have, for the most part, been neglected by psychology. No one really took seriously such obvious questions as the following: Does a baby know he is happy when he smiles? If he knows, how can he picture it to himself without being able to reflect through words upon his state? If he doesn't know he is happy, why is he smiling? Speculation aside for the moment, parents have always used the affective expressions and sounds of babies as reliable indicators of an infant's needs and have responded accordingly, implicitly acknowledging thereby that the baby is not just a receiver but also a sender of messages.

Neurological evidence now available indicates that affective expressions are under subcortical control. Tomkins (1962-1963, 1970, 1980) suggests that initially the various affective responses are related to stimulus intensity and to intensity gradients and are probably mediated by the autonomic nervous system. In other words, affective behavior patterns are, like the infant's perceptual capacity, inherited programs with which the infant meets the world. Each pattern has its mild and its extreme form and a range between the two.

Although the affective response, being mediated by the autonomic nervous system, is a total bodily response, involving body temperature, the skin, hair, glands, muscles, and viscera, in humans it is the face that has become the prime communicator of affective states. Let me just briefly list the main, objective—that is, recordable and reproducible—signs used by researchers (and by parents) to identify the eight ranges of affective response in infants that form the basis for our emotional life. There is a continuum from surprise to startle, depending on the suddenness and intensity of stimulus onset, in which we see the infant's eyebrows go up and his eyes blink. The range from interest through excitement is shown on the face when the eyebrows go down, the eyes track the stimulus, and there is an attitude of looking and listening. The scale of mild enjoyment to joy is signaled by a smile, the lips are widened and out, and there is slow, deep breathing. On the negative side there is the range from distress to anguish as indicated by crying, arched eyebrows, corners of the mouth turned down, tears, and rhythmic sobbing. Even more dramatic is the behavioral series beginning with anger and culminating in rage. Here the face is in a frown, the jaws are clenched, and the face is red. Contempt or disgust is shown by lifting the upper lip into a sneer. The range from fear through terror is manifested by a cold, sweaty face, with eyes frozen open, facial trembling, and hair erect. And shame through humiliation is demonstrated when both the head and eyes are cast down (Tomkins, 1962, vol. 1, p. 337).

Just as the mere 26 letters in our alphabet can be combined to generate the wealth and nuance of our verbal language, so the even richer variations to be found in the respective ranges of each of the eight basic affects will, in time, blend and mix, with not only face and body but the variations of the voice communicating our feelings at any given time. Affect is a nonverbal language, sometimes accompanying the spoken word, as the Greek playwrights of old used the chorus to underscore the lines of the principal actors, but more often, as Freud taught us, acting as a counterpoint that, for those alert to it, reveals the consciously or unconsciously concealed truth behind the spoken words. No drive is involved here. The brain, whose function it is to order stimuli and generate and transmit messages, does not need to be driven to perform its function any more than the heart needs to be driven to beat or the gut to metabolize food. Structure guarantees function; no more is needed.

How, to return to the question I asked at the beginning of this section on affect, does the baby know how to react when he is as yet in no position to reflect on the nature of the stimuli to which he is exposed? Tomkins (1980) suggests that initially and essentially the basic, primary affect responses are related only to stimulus density, that is, to the number of nerve impulses transmitted per unit of time, and to the gradient of that stimulation. Traced on a graph, surprise, interest, and fear, and their extensions are all the result of a continuous rise in stimulus intensity above a particular infant's nonreactive, resting level; which of these three reactions—surprise, interest, or fear—will be elicited is determined by the rate, height, and duration of the stimulus vector. Distress or anger reactions are manifested when stimulus intensity is maintained steadily at a higher than optimal rate for a length of time. Joy and its variant results whenever there is a sudden, sharp, drop in the stimulus pattern, no matter what the nature of that stimulus may be. (Having playfully tossed the baby in the air, we catch it, and the baby laughs—not because he knows he is safe after having been in danger, but because there has been a sudden decrease in the stimulus input that the act of tossing him up and letting him fall had produced.) Shame is the result of an inadequate stimulus reduction, a tension produced by less than satisfactory resolution of a stimulus gradient that had begun but was not carried to completion.

In the study of affect we find the biological foundation that explains motivation, i.e., the intensity of ideas, that Freud sought in vain in the nineteenth-century conceptualization of instinct, psychic energy, and drive. How body becomes mind, how tension becomes recognized as need, the "mysterious leap" as Freud termed it, all appear to be much less puzzling given the transformation of quantitative stimulus gradients into the experience of quality that we associate with our affective/emotional life. Affective transformation seems to involve the same sort of process that our brains are able to carry out when they take other purely quantitative stimulation generated by electrons in varying wave lengths that impinge on our sense organs and transform them into the imagery of sight, hearing, and so on.

We can now re-examine the question of what it is the infant experiences when he signals his affective state. Certainly no reflection is involved. It is the baby's way of adapting to stimuli in the only way he can, given his inability to move closer to what attracts him or to escape what hurts or frightens him. His only option is to engage his caretaker and induce her to do for him what he cannot do for himself. The highly developed facial musculature of the infant and the automatism of the affective reaction are ideally suited to setting up an error-correcting feedback system in the mother-child unit in which the child provides the indicator by which the mother can judge whether her efforts on his behalf have been successful. We can now answer in the negative the question of whether a baby knows he is happy when he is smiling. No, the baby does not know he is happy, but his mother attributes that emotion to him and that's what is important. "Happy" is a concept that has no meaning as yet for an infant, nor is there a concept of self that could serve as a reference for such a subjective judgment. Eventually, the affective state, like other experiences, can become symbolically conceptualized and labeled verbally; only then, in my opinion, should it be called an "emotion."

The picture of communication in the first eighteen months of life that I am drawing here has further implications for psychological theory. The wide range of autonomic, inherited experiential patterns described by Tomkins which become the basis for an explanation of man's emotional life are in keeping with everyday observation and with clinical experience. As a result we are no longer limited, as we have been in psychoanalysis, to trying to account for the quality of experience by categorizing it as being either love or hate, i.e., the outcome of the discharge of either sexual or aggressive instincts. Neither do we need to explain emotional life as being due to either the damming up of a postulated psychic energy with resulting unpleasure or its discharge accompanied by pleasure. I have dealt more extensively with the issue of affect theory and its significance for psychoanalysis in two earlier publications (1975, 1976a). But I hope that, though necessarily brief, my review has demonstrated how the variety and quantification of affect replace the metaphor of a psychic energy or drive by giving us a better, and, more important, a scientific explanation for what we experience as the intensity of our thoughts and the force of our wishes.

But what about Freud's instinct theory and the drives? What happens to them in the light of developmental research of the sort done so ably by Dr. Freedman?

Freud himself made it explicitly clear that his theories about drives and instincts were *biological* speculations that he adduced to explain his clinical findings. As he said, these ideas were imposed upon rather than derived from psychoanalytic observations (Freud, 1915). He acknowledged that these hypotheses were vague and unsatisfactory at best, and, as you know, he referred to the instinct theory as the "mythology" of psychoanalysis.

Science has made significant advances since Freud first lamented the paucity of reliable information regarding man's instinctual life. Not only biology, but ethology and control theory, neither of which had formal existence in Freud's day, have to a great degree clarified the biological issues involved and permit us to re-evaluate Freud's speculations in this area.

A number of Freud's assumptions about development and motivation have been radically altered since cybernetics and control theory replaced mechanistic discharge theories as explanations for the vicissitudes of the behavior of living systems. The notion that the motives for or the meaning of thought and behavior depend upon an energic force of libidinal or aggressive nature, in neutral or unneutralized form, has been repeatedly and tellingly rejected by biologists, neurophysiologists, and physicists, as documented in the psychoanalytic literature by Kubie (1963), Holt (1965, 1976), Rosenblatt and Thickstun (1970), Peterfreund (1971), and others (Basch, 1976b). The brain, similar to the thermostat that controls the activity of a furnace, governs or steers the organism through a hierarchy of error-correcting feedback cycles that compare a particular perceptual set with the conditions that prevail, and, if the two do not match, puts in motion that behavior that will be most likely to achieve the desired congruence of set and reality.

"Instinct" is the term we apply to those feedback patterns or portions of feedback patterns that are inherited. The more primitive the organism, the more its behavior is tightly controlled by instinct. As one goes up in the hierarchy of the animal kingdom, instinctual behavior becomes more and more a *general* blueprint, rather than a specific, predetermined routine. By thinking of affect as only the conscious manifestation of instinctual drive, Freud telescoped two different levels of biological organization: the instinctual blueprint for survival that underlies all behavior, and the affects, an advanced control mechanism that serves as an inner releaser for inherited and learned behavior patterns. It should be understood that instinct encompasses a great number of control mechanisms that seek to insure self-preservation, affect being only one of these. What analysts mean by "drive" is "motivation," and motivation is not an energic matter, as Freud thought it was. In the more primitive phyla, like insects and fish, the motivation for behavior comes from the external releaser, the sensory feature to which the animal is programmed to respond. In higher animals, including man, the immediate motivation for behavior is the inner releaser, the affective reaction recruited by a particular event (Tomkins, 1962-1963, 1970, 1980). The sense of "drivenness" that we experience is a manifestation of the degree of affect aroused.

However, we are not yet finished with the biological, for, as we know, Freud proposed a second dual-instinct theory based on his analysis of adults suffering from psychoneuroses. In this latter instinct theory self-preservation is replaced by the instinct of aggression, and the instinct for the propagation of the species is replaced by the sexual instinct.

About the only significant ethologist to subscribe to an aggressive instinct was, or is, Konrad Lorenz (1966), but his view has been overwhelmingly rejected on the basis of the evidence showing that aggression, unlike hunger, is not an independent motivational force. No predictable periodicity for aggression has been reported, no metabolic changes accompany the absence of aggression, as would occur with the absence of food, water, or air; and, though one needs to eat, drink, and breathe, there is no need to attack if there is no provocative stimulus (Scott, 1958). Within family groups of primates, shortages of food or water, or the absence of a sexual outlet, do not routinely lead to aggression; indeed they may result in cooperative sharing. Aggression is most reliably produced by bringing a stranger, an intruder, into a particular group. Aggression is a defensive behavior, a response to disorganization; aggression is affectively triggered and is in the interest of self-preservation. Therefore, aggression is a tool and not a basic instinctual need as Freud believed it was. Furthermore, the practice in psychoanalysis of lumping assertion, competitiveness, and mastery under the rubric of aggression and tension reduction is an unwarranted use of metaphor based on the terminology of physics (Arnold, 1960).

Apparently some of the same arguments that are raised in objection to the notion of an aggressive drive hold true in the case of sexuality. Holt (1976) cites the work of Frank Beach, whom he calls the most distinguished authority on the sexual behavior of animals, to the effect that the male of the species in the mating season is not driven by an accumulation of sexual excitation that needs to be discharged. Rather, it is the presence of a suitable partner that stimulates the affect of excitement and amplifies the sexual urge. For instance, it has been shown in animal experiments that the male, having been given unrestricted opportunity to copulate with the female, comes to a point where he ceases to have sexual intercourse. The tension-reduction theory would attribute this to discharge of accumulated libido. Yet when a new receptive female is introduced to the male, at that point, though supposedly drained of sexual tension, he is immediately moved to have sexual relations again, showing that sexuality is a matter of interest. The presence or absence of affect, not of sexual energy, is at stake here. This and other findings indicate that genital sexuality is better thought of as an appetite, and is stimulus-bound, rather than as a tension-accumulating drive seeking discharge. The feeling of genital drivenness that may be experienced by the human male or female in the absence of a suitable partner is accounted for by the human capacity for symbolic representation which can serve as a perpetual stimulus to the affect of interest and excitement regardless of external circumstances.

Drive theory as advanced by psychoanalysis is not in keeping with the facts now known about motivation in other animals and in humans. The direct observations made by Dr. Freedman and the conclusions drawn from that data about development, with which I am in full agreement, like the clinical data of psychoanalysis, can be better explained by a theory that replaces Freud's hypotheses about the working of the brain with what has been learned about the functioning of that organ in the last fifty years.

REFERENCES

Arnold, M. B. (1960), *Emotion and Personality*, Vols. 1 & 2. New York: Columbia University Press.

Basch, M. F. (1975), Toward a theory that encompasses depression: a revision of existing causal hypotheses in psychoanalysis. In: *Depression and Human Existence*, ed. E. J. Anthony & T. Benedek. Boston: Little, Brown & Co., pp. 483-534.

—— (1976a), The concept of affect: a re-examination. *J. Amer. Psychoanal. Assn.*, 24:759-777.

—— (1976b), Theory formation in Chapter VII: A critique. *J. Amer. Psychoanal. Assn.*, 24:61-100.

Freedman, D. A. (1979), The sensory deprivations. *Bull. Menninger Clin.*, 43:29-68.

—— (1981), The effect of sensory and other deficits in children on their experience of people. *J. Amer. Psychoanal. Assn.*, 29:831-867.

—— (1982), Of instincts and instinctual drives: Some developmental considerations. *Psychoanal. Inquiry*, 2:153-167.

Freud, S. (1915), Instincts and their vicissitudes. *Standard Edition*, 14:117-140. London: Hogarth Press, 1957.

Harlow, M. F., & Harlow, M. K. (1962), Social deprivation in monkeys. *Sci. Amer.*, 207:136-146.

—— (1972), The language of love. In: *Communication and Affect*, ed. T. Alloway, L. Kramer, & P. Pliner. New York: Academic Press, pp. 1-18.

Holt, R. R. (1965), A review of some of Freud's biological assumptions and their influence on his theories. In: *Psychoanalysis and Current Biological Thought*, ed. N. S. Greenfield & W. C. Lewis. Madison: University of Wisconsin Press, pp. 93-124.

—— (1976), Drive or wish? A reconsideration of the psychoanalytic theory of motivation. In: *Psychology versus Metapsychology: Psychoanalytic Essays in Memory of George S. Klein*, ed. M. M. Gill & P. S. Holzman [*Psychological Issues*, Monogr. 36]. New York: International Universities Press, pp. 158-197.

Kubie, L. S. (1963), The concept of psychic energy. *J. Amer. Psychoanal. Assn.*, 11:605-611.

Lorenz, K. (1966), *On Aggression.* New York: Harcourt, Brace & World.

Peterfreund, E. (1971), *Information, Systems and Psychoanalysis* [*Psychological Issues*, Monogr. 25/26]. New York: International Universities Press.

Rosenblatt, A. D., & Thickstun, J. T. (1970), A study of the concept of psychic energy. *Internat. J. Psycho-Anal.*, 51:265-278.

Scott, J. P. (1958), *Aggression.* Chicago: University of Chicago Press.

Spitz, R. A, (1946), Hospitalism: A follow-up report on investigation described in Volume 1, 1945. *The Psychoanalytic Study of the Child*, 2:113-118. New York: International Universities Press.

Tomkins, S. S. (1962-1963), *Affect, Imagery, Consciousness*, Vols. 1 & 2. New York: Springer.

————— (1970), Affects as the primary motivational system. In: *Feelings and Emotions*, ed. M. B. Arnold. New York: Academic Press, pp. 101-110.

————— (1980), Affects as amplification: Some modification in theory. In: *Emotions: Theory, Research, and Experience*, ed. R. Plutchik & H. Kellerman. New York: Academic Press, pp. 141-164.

Reply to Dr. Basch's Response

DAVID A. FREEDMAN, M.D.

I do not believe it is accurate to say that "behavior that insures the preservation of the individual and the species . . ." is learned not inherited. By the same token, neither is it accurate to consider such behavior simply inherited. I suggest that what is inherited is a range of possible behaviors which reflect the organism's anatomic and physiological potentialities. Which of these will become elements in the repertoire of actual behaviors is, indeed, a function of the ambience in which maturation is occurring, and to this extent they are learned. Here is the crux of Dr. Basch's and my apparent difference. I say apparent because I feel we are trying to state the same idea albeit in different words. We agree that the infant is born endowed both with a repetoire of patterns of re-action and the potentiality for yet others to emerge. These are in all probability gene determined. Given average expectable circumstances, they ultimately become asso-ciated with the specific psychological experiences which we both would call affective. The question remains whether it is more useful to designate these behaviors as affect from the beginning as Dr. Basch would have it, or to consider them proto-affective as I contend.

In support of my position, I cite the following:

1. In addition to Freud and the glossary of psychoanalytic terms, all the dictionaries I have consulted include a subjectively felt experiential element in their definitions of affect. I believe my usage is, therefore, less likely to confuse than is his. At the same time, I am not prepared to ascribe the ability to have such experiences to the neonate. In my unwillingness to do so, I am in agreement with Dr. Basch who also points out that subcortically determined modes of expression are not accompanied by the felt subjective experiences which the authorities I cite consider to be affect. I have chosen to call these reactions proto-affective. In defense of this position I, like Dr. Basch, will use a nonpsychological metaphor. Rather than the beat of the heart or the metabolic function of the gut I will invoke locomotion. I suggest that the random leg-kicking movements of the neonate have the same relation to the toddler's and child's later abilities to walk, to run, and to kick a football that proto-affective behavior (by which I think I mean pretty much the same thing as Dr. Basch does by affective expression) has to affect. Without such movements in infancy, the later abilities will be seriously compromised if, indeed, they will appear at all. What forms they will take when they are allowed free and appropriate expression in the neonate will be influenced by later internalizations, and by the ambience in which ongoing maturation and development occur. The question arises: at what point do you dignify the movement of the legs with the designation locomotion and, by the same token, when do you consider the smile of a neonate an expression of affect? Admittedly, the second differentiation is more difficult than the first, but the principle involved is the same. Certainly, one would be

hard put to consider the REM-associated smile of Emde et al.'s microcephalic neonate affective.

2. While I concede my inability to draw this fine line, I believe the problems associated with lumping neonatal affective behavior together with affect far exceed the advantages. How, for example, is one to account for dissociations of affective expression and subjective feeling as one witnesses these in individuals with certain neurological diseases, in good actors, and in psychopaths and hypocrites? I remind you, too, that it has been pointed out repeatedly that seriously depressed patients who rather suddenly appear to be calm and at peace with themselves are at particularly high risk for suicide. Dissociation of the behavioral phenomenon affective expression from the psychological phenomenon felt affect is a fact of observation which a viable theory of affect must be able to explain.

I also have a problem with the tension-reduction characterization of joy. At least it seems to me that infants can be extremely joyous because of the play—I would say the mutuality of the play—if you will, a state of self/selfobject fusion—whatever the levels of emotional tension which obtain when the pair is being joyous.

Finally, I agree with Dr. Basch's intent when he says the baby has "no option but to . . .". However, I would prefer to use sparer language and say the affective responses or proto-affective responses of the baby serve to induce the caretaker to move closer. The baby's limitations in this regard were beautifully illustrated by Massie's (1978) study of eye behavior. Observers, blind to the ultimate outcome, studied home movies of mothers and their infants. The most striking finding was the difference between the eye behavior of the mothers whose babies became psychotic and that of those whose youngsters developed normally. Failure to make eye contact by the former group was noted regularly, and the difference between the two was significant to the .01 level. The infants' eye behavior did not differentiate.

REFERENCE

Massie, H. N. (1978). Blind ratings of mother-infant interactions in home movies of pre-psychotic and normal infants. *Amer. J. Psychiat.*, 135:1371-1374.

3

Infancy and the Psychoanalytic Situation

JOSEPH D. LICHTENBERG, M.D.

HISTORICAL SURVEY

The late 1950s marked something of a turning point in psychoanalysis. In the flush of a great wave of popularity and the confidence born of twenty years of experience with ego psychology, that is, with the second phase of psychoanalytic technique, analysts were emboldened to widen their scope of therapeutic endeavor. The debate over the advisability of widening led to a reappraisal of what constituted the essential elements of psychoanalysis. A work that stands out in this multifaceted attempt to place the techniques of classical analysis on a more firm conceptual footing was Stone's (1961) *The Psychoanalytic Situation.* To quote Janet Malcolm (1981): "Stone's plea for humaneness and flexibility and common sense is encased in the most subtly reasoned, profoundly erudite, and awesomely 'difficult' of meditations on a complex subject" (p. 44). Stone (1961) makes two central points: first, that it is an essential requirement for analytic success that the analyst convey a sense of his physicianly commitment since "the intrinsic formal stringencies of the [analytic] situation . . . contraindicate superfluous deprivations in the analyst's personal attitude" (p. 22); second, that the primary unconscious meaning of the psychoanalytic situation lies in the reverberations it stirs of tensions that exist for the young child. Stone singles out as especially significant "that period of life where all the modalities of bodily intimacy and direct dependence on the mother are being relinquished or attenuated" (p. 86). I shall not detail Stone's rich argument but merely note that these two central issues form the basis for debates that persist to this day: (1) How best does the analyst convey his humanity and his physicianly intention, while establishing and preserving a therapeutic regimen aimed at increased self-awareness and understanding? (2) What is the anlage from critical early (preoedipal) periods of development that constitute the underpinnings for all transference relationships?

Stone notes that most writings on technique, as it applies to the psychoanalytic situation itself, contain more warnings of what *not* to do than positive indication of what to do. Stone's own main point occupies a middle position. Humanness is described against the background of what Stone believes to be a major deterrent to analytic success: "arbitrary authoritarianism" (p. 52) in refusal to answer questions, and mechanization of the analyst's functioning by "superfluously remote and depriving attitudes" (p. 54). But Stone's own "positive" recommendations refer mostly to attitude—and, while that is, I believe, a powerful statement in itself, it has a somewhat nebulous quality in practice. (See Lichtenberg and Slap, 1977.) One of his most positive directive statements refers to interpretation having value beyond insight. "The interpretive function, I believe . . . , has a tremendous primary transference valence, but only when linked by compelling unconscious associations, via recognition of the impulse to help, to relieve suffering, with the primary caretaking attitudes which give all early teaching its affirmative infantile significance" (p. 63). Stone's emphasis throughout his book is on explicating the "primary transference valence"—the ways in which all the elements of the psychoanalytic situation, the use of speech, normal and excessive deprivations, the recumbent position, etc., link in with infantile experience. Interpretation as such he takes essentially as a given—the communicating to the patient of intrapsychic conflicts of a sexual and aggressive nature construed within an id-ego-superego conception of the mind. Stone's point, then, is not to question what is interpreted, but to give greater depth to an understanding of how and why it works. To do so he gives greater weight to the dyadic relationship between mother and child. In his account of the child's early life, Stone relies on traditional views plus some of the infant observations of Spitz. His book can be seen as pointing toward two groupings of conceptual developments in which much was to happen—what is interpreted and what residuals from infancy remain in the grown-up. Conceptually, Stone's book broke little new ground in each. His reassessment of the relative value of insight as such, in comparison with all of the other elements of the psychoanalytic situation, provides, I believe, a most elegant statement of a reconceptualization of elements in the curative process.

The first effect, then, of the reappraisal of classical analysis consequent to the widening scope was to refocus analytic attention temporally and structurally backward from the oedipal phase into the early life of the developing infant and toddler. Stone astutely links "the states of relative physical and emotional 'deprivation-in-intimacy' " (p. 105) of the psychoanalytic situation with a crucial point in infancy, the series of basic separation experiences in the child's relation to his mother (p. 105), the point Mahler was later to call the phase of separation-individuation. Stone states: The "psychoanalytic setting in its general and primary transference impact tends to reproduce, from the outset, the repetitive phases of the state of relative *separation* from early objects, and most crucially . . . that period of life where all the modalities of bodily intimacy and direct dependence on the mother are being relinquished or attentuated, pari passu with the rapid development of the great vehicle of communication by speech" (p. 86). For Stone, the transference represents at its base a dialectic between "the insistent irredentist craving for union with the original object" and "the craving for understanding, instruction, and facilitation of the displacement of interest to the environment" (p. 94), Stone is describing a way to formulate transference as it occurs in the ordinary psychoanalytic experience. He is not proposing a program for interpretation itself—nor even, as Kohut was later to do, an investigation of the precise dynamic interplay of the craving for union with the craving for understanding as they appear in the analysis.

I shall stop here and indicate what I mean by "a program for interpretation." All analysts would concur that what is interpreted derives from the data of the patient's communications (verbal and nonverbal). But as we all agree when we pay homage to Freud and his discoveries, we do not approach each encounter with the unconscious as *terra incognita*: Although we suspend prejudgments, we are guided by the knowledge of prior analytic discoveries. This and this association cue us to the possibility of a primal-scene experience. This and this to a fear of anal penetration, etc. These sets of cues constitute, I suggest, a program or schema that aids us to recognize conscious, preconscious, and unconscious configurations regardless of the disguises (defense mechanisms) that hide them, while simultaneously restricting us to the continuous rediscovery of the, by now, familiar. Thus the daily work of analysis consists of applying a learned, and deeply appreciated, schema as the communications of the analysand point to an appropriate match. New discoveries can then be made within the general context of the schema—or new discoveries can be made on a scale large enough to challenge the value of the existing schema, thus leading to the proposal of a new one.

Freud's own discovery of ego psychology and the signal theory of anxiety is an example of a proposal so broad in scale that it called for the development of a new schema to replace that of id psychology. A new program for interpretation was gradually developed, based on knowing what to look for by virtue of the schema—a drive derivative, a defense against it, a compromise formation, a conflict involving a prohibition, and a quantity of affect signaling the effectiveness or ineffectiveness of the ego's response to the demands made on it. This was essentially the program of psychoanalytic interpretation that Stone took for granted.[1] What he felt required explanation was what made interpretations based on this schema effective or ineffective. Effectiveness lay in the dynamism of the analytic situation as it resonated with the analysand's early life experiences. As I have indicated, Stone's pointing to infancy was not at all to demand a new program for interpretation. Nonetheless new schemata for listening, conceptualizing, and interpreting did result from the

[1] Stone's (1961) statement of the beneficial effects of insight gained from interpretation are "the neutralizing of instinctual energies, the conversion of primary-process elements into directed thought, the extension of the integrating scope of the ego" (pp. 100-101).

widening scope. These new schemata have in common new, albeit very different, reinterpretations of the preoedipal phases.

The Kleinian was the first such program, one that antedated Stone's work. Klein's approach articulated a fully developed schema for interpretation that was focused on preoedipal phases. American analysts tend to underestimate the powerful hold in terms of number of direct adherents and indirect effects on theory making of this Kleinian program. The Kleinian schema was derived from analytic work with fairly disturbed children and in that sense is related to the widening scope. It was not developed to deal with a special group of patients with preoedipal problems, but since it regards all patients as developing their basic structure from the outcome of these conflicts, its program of interpretations covers the whole spectrum of cases. The Kleinian analyst is enabled to engage a patient of whatever type problem in a discourse that translates relatively inchoate awareness of unrest into symbolically coded statements for the unrest. Good breasts and poisonous milk, the loving self and the hateful other, and its reverse, the envy that would destroy the good, the reparation that would restore the harmed, the gratitude that would repay the effort to help, are all highly evocative images with which to transact business between a troubled person in a state of regression and a conscientious, intelligent, physicianly oriented psychoanalyst. And while most of the Kleinian conceptions of infantile life are not confirmed by the recent explosion of information about the first two years of life, impressive fragments of it are.

For example, the mother-infant interaction does begin at birth; and it is a highly dynamic interplay, mother and infant constituting a two-way exchange. However, the principal dynamic of this exchange is to lay down a matrix of regulatory transactions about schedules of active alertness, feeding, crying, and sleep. It is normally characterized by a great deal of pleasurable exchange, and, except in highly pathological situations, there is no observational support for Kleinian "star wars" imagery of destruction being projected onto breasts and introjected via poisoned milk. Nor is there any evidence for a primal form of envy, or even the capacity to conceptualize or experience the earliest exchange with the mother in such cognitively organized terms. While direct observation can't provide decisive evidence to disprove a premise about the inner life of the psyche, the findings of infant research and clinical premises demand some degree of confirmatory integration to support convincingly a conception about the very young infant.

A second program for interpretation that was specifically related to the widening scope was Kernberg's schema for the treatment of borderline personality disorders. Kernberg observed that many of the formulations of Klein and of the object-relations school of the middle group of English analysts fit the observable discourse and behavior of the patients at the Menninger Foundation. Previously, therapists had been baffled by the manner in which these patients conveyed obviously dependent neediness mixed with inexplicable states of antagonism. Whatever tack the therapist took might seem to work for a while, but then would paradoxically lead to negativism—often in extreme forms. Kernberg reasoned that these patients had internalized a state of seesawing modes of relating based on essentially negative experiences. They had built their characters around, and erected defenses against, the expression of these aggression-dominated infantile relationships.

This enabled Kernberg to develop a theory that would weld more or less effectively the conflict theory of ego psychology, the theory of internalized representations of self and object of Jacobson, and the aggression-dominated motifs of infancy from the Kleinian schema. The program for interpretation that he evolved enabled a therapist or analyst, for the first time, to "read" the text of his patient's puzzling inclinations to pull to and push away, to praise and denounce, to worship and hate, to envy and appreciate. What the therapist could read, he could confront, and what he could confront, he could care about, and what he cared about he could treat and be perceived by the patient as treating. What of Kernberg's premises about infancy? Kernberg's theory conforms nicely with the concept of a matrix of mother-infant interaction out of which develops the shape of the infant's inclinations. At the actual neurophysiological level what happens experientially is regarded by some researchers as affecting such basic organic phenomena as the rate of myelinization and the formation and strength of inhibiting and feedback loops. At the behavioral level of organization, regulation of hunger, alertness, sleep, and elimination derives from patterning in the interactional exchange; thus those manifestations that psychoanalysis labels drive derivatives can be conceptualized as developing secondarily to object relations.

But there are, I believe, many differences between the nature of the interactions as observed and as construed by Kernberg. The most important of these deals with splitting. While Kernberg does not hold with the Kleinian developmental timetable or the death-instinct concept, he leans heavily on oral envy and other primary manifestations of aggressive drive as explanatory concepts. Key to his conception is "splitting" which he regards as the basic means of organizing experience in infancy. In this formulation, the infant is primed biologically to organize all experience into good = pleasurable or bad =

painful groupings. The task is thus to integrate these divergent groupings, a task presumably made difficult or impossible by an excess of unpleasure experiences resulting from or connected with primary aggression. Here again the evidence from infant observation lends little support. Most researchers take a holistic view of the infant's organization. I, too, believe (as I have argued elsewhere, Lichtenberg, 1981d, 1982, 1983b) that in normal development the self as director once formed as a psychic entity is an essentially unified structure. What could be called splitting as an observable phenomenon (the toddler's psychological designation of a pairing of self and caretaker as "bad" while designating another pairing as "good") takes place beginning in the second year under the severe stress of a failure of adequate empathic support—sometimes, of course, of an unavoidable nature.

Two of the most intriguing schemata available to the psychoanalyst today come at the problem from opposite directions. Mahler begins with infant observation and provides a schema rich in new perspective. She offers no specific program for interpretation as such. Kohut (1971) begins with clinical data and provides a radically different program for interpretation. He expresses skepticism about reliance on direct observation, on what he stated as belonging to "the conceptual realm of a psychoanalytic interactionalism" (p. 219 n). Mahler's schema has been used by others to develop a program for interpretation—one that comes close in certain ways to that of Kernberg, whereas Kohut's program for interpretation and the theory it is based on have been used by others to provide a basis for viewing infantile experience. Metaphorically speaking, Marian Tolpin created "Kohut's baby"—a smiling joyful infant giving and receiving eye contact, coos, and giggles. Indeed this hypothetical creature conforms to the baby of observation, replacing the cocoon neonate of the theory of primary narcissism. But by confining the source of his data to empathic reconstructions in adult analysis, Kohut overlooked the opportunity provided by infant researchers, especially those who seek adaptive rather than pathological principles for guides to development.[2] Without being tied in to a detailed developmental schema based both on observation and reconstruction, self psychology's core concept of self cohesion lends itself to concretization and/or murkiness as to its level of abstraction. Alternatively, Kohut's assertion of the primacy of assertiveness, with aggression seen as a consequence of frustration, provides a clear postulate for direct observation and for comparison with the Klein, Kernberg, and Mahler postulate of primary aggression. As I read the evidence (Lichtenberg, 1982), it points to assertiveness with its regulatory effects of functional and efficacy pleasure as primary. In fact it is commonly interference with the gratification of the functional and efficacy pleasure that provides the stimulus for reactive aggression.

These two ways of viewing events in the infant's and toddler's sequencing of reaching, crawling, climbing, pushing, tearing, dropping, hitting, biting, tantrums, crying, etc., lead to different programs for interpretation. A theory of a primary aggressive drive, with derivatives becoming defended against and tamed, points to one interpretive approach: a theory of primary assertiveness that with support leads to functional and efficacy pleasure, and with frustration leads to reactive anger, points to a different interpretive conception. The other difference centers on the formulation of separateness and in-

---

[2] Kohut's (1980) parenthetical statement "(I should like to mention here that Sander's work in particular . . . promises to enrich self psychology, and, in turn, to be enriched by it)" (p. 475) points in this direction.

dividuation as partial goals—Kohut's view—or end points of a developmental sequence—Mahler's view. As a partial goal, separateness means the taking over of functions from the caretaking mother, such as responding internally to anxiety, while retaining a need for the general support of others—the mature forms of mirroring and idealization. As an end point of preoedipal development, separation and individuation (object constancy) means that the seeking of the older child and the adult for various forms of mirroring or alter-ego experiences or for idealization is defensive. How this issue is viewed will make a considerable difference in what is interpreted as pathological in analysis and what criteria for termination are followed.

The universe of concepts that is opening up to us from infant research is indeed so complex that it is understandable that analysts might wish to remain distant and skeptical. Moreover, skepticism is inevitable when so many formulations of what are cornerstones of our theories have come up for questioning. For example, a stage of primary narcissism is contradicted by the infant-mother and infant-father relatedness at birth. The theory of symbiosis is challenged by the active role of the infant as behavioral initiator of interaction. But most of all the core question of the psychoanalytic theory of symbiosis centers on how the experiences of the infant from three to ten or eleven months old are registered. Although psychoanalysis has a variety of theories of internalized representations, infant researchers give us an account of what I have termed (Lichtenberg, 1981a, 1981c, 1983b) a biological-neurophysiological-behavioral level of organization. Then in time (during the second year) there is a level of organization in which communication is based on a sign-signal interchange in which a discrete sense of self and the other is increasingly established. Shortly thereafter a full level of symbolic representation is reached and sealed forever as the human's unique affecto-cognitive experience through the use of language. This is, I believe, somewhat mind-boggling, and it requires a great deal of rethinking. But undoubtedly it does mean something to our clinical approach. Gedo (1979) has addressed these problems as they affect a program of interpretation. He asks: if behavior receives its first regulation in a presymbolic form, do some of these behaviors—especially maladaptive ones—persist? If so, then must we not encounter them in analysis? Since these would be without mental representation in the usual sense of symbolic registry, do we not need to broaden our means of observing and interpreting, to bring about change in behaviors as basic as these?

I believe questions such as these are indeed mind twisters, and I shall attempt to give some clinical examples to make them easier to comprehend. But at the outset a contradiction must be struggled with. The tool at hand for comprehension of the very proposal I am making about an absence of symbolic representation in the infant or adult is symbolic representation and symbolic logic. How to imagine not having what each of us manifestly has and uses all the time is no easy matter—and particularly when I suggest that fairly complicated problem solving can and does take place without symbolic representation (see also Basch, 1975). A simple explanation may give the flavor of my meaning. I throw you a ball—what do you do? You raise your arm to catch it, observe its flight, make a judgment about its speed, and place your hand accordingly. Of course you do no such thing! Your hand goes up and gets the ball. A reflex, you might say. No, I argue. A reflex is an innate automatic response. Its lack of variance prohibits bodily problem solving. Mislabeling it a reflex fails to deal with the issue, which is: do you need a conceptual representation of a ball and a thrower to perform bodily problem solving? I suggest that the infant in the first year who learns to roll the ball back and forth with his mother needs only the perceptual actuality of the situation—no permanent representation of a ball, of mother or of self. I can't prove he doesn't have one—but it can be argued effectively that he doesn't need one, whereas for operations he will perform in the second year, he does need symbolic representations.

CLINICAL ILLUSTRATIONS

I shall present three clinical vignettes from completed analyses of adults. The first illustrates the persistence of a basic regulatory deficit; the second, the residua from an early experience in the form of a bodily symptom, and the third, problems of a primary cognitive deficiency. The findings in the first two cases are suggestive of pathology that develops prior to and independent of memory coding via symbolic representation. The findings in the third are indicative of problems that lie outside the realm of trauma or interpersonal conflict and in turn contribute as independent sources to disturbances in symbolic representation and to intrapsychic and relational problems.

EXAMPLE 1

Mr. K. entered analysis at a point of great indecision in his life involving his career choices, his recent marriage, and his relationship to his family. I shall deal here with only one facet of his long and, for the most part, successful treatment. During the analysis, he gained a lot of weight. This occurred in plateaus that roughly paralleled stages of intense resistance as one or another problem area was worked with. One of his fears—stated initially as a threat and a prediction—was that he would become like his obese mother. The meanings of his body image and his fear of identification with his mother were a major concern of the analysis. Being identified with his mother meant not being identified with his ethically disappointing father, and thus not being a psychopathic philanderer. But not being identified with father meant giving up a form of food-intake regulation—since father, who had been an overweight child, had developed a way to remain thin by bouts of sudden engorging followed by extreme food restriction. During his abstinent periods, the father tyrannized everyone else about his or her eating. Being identified with mother was also an idiosyncratic source of fantasied strength since Mr. K conceptualized bulk as a form of armor that would allow him to resist penetration or enclose or encase the penetrator's phallus in his fat. Being identified with mother was alternatively a source of weakness, in that it meant that he would be a depressed martyr whose general insensitivity to the feelings of children made him unloved but easily exploited—a form of parenting Mr. K feared he was following with his own child.

My point in giving these examples is to illustrate the rich "find" of symbolic representations that surrounded a nuclear symptom. Analytic progress resulted from these discoveries—technically achieved through a complex tapestry of transference experiences centering on my presumed and often actual failure to perceive empathically the seesawing waves of his sexual desire and his vocational ambition. As a positive result, career decisions were made, parenting improved, gender-identity confusion disappeared, the marriage was consolidated, and his depressive tendencies were markedly reduced. But his moderately severe obesity persisted.

Throughout the analysis whenever possible I tried to inquire about the details of his eating. This met with the greatest resistance—his pattern was similar to his mother's habit of being a concealed gorger, that is, one who ate a salad in public and bags full of cookies in private. What emerged in time was another possibility assumed by me from the smallest of nuances. A question I asked about hunger led to anger and denial. Somehow on that particular occasion I sensed so positive a feeling about my helpfulness that the resistance struck me as repetitive pro forma, and I detected a slight indication of a wistful wish to give an answer. I suggested this and to the relief of both of us Mr. K agreed and said he really couldn't give an answer about hunger. Mr. K was a man full of answers—a bright student to whom not knowing something was a source of embarrassment. His flat statement puzzled me, but it occurred to me to take it at its face value. With this as a starting point, we were able to construct (not reconstruct) a notion of his infancy that suggested a major deficit in the regulation of food intake.

Mr. K literally did not know when he was hungry. Hunger was a word he had used without meaningful connection to a perceived physiological state. Only during the late stages of the analysis, if he restricted his food intake, did he begin to experience a body sensation that from his description seemed to both of us to be hunger. He also did not experience satiety. He would eat foods he labeled as desirable as long as he could, to the point of nausea. Taste as a discrimination seemed very underdeveloped—the reason for the desirability of a particular food was usually external—father hated it or his best friend in adolescence loved it. Our further construction, based on known interactions later, was that mother and father, rather than being attentive to their baby in a usual manner, were preoccupied with their fights over eating, and caught up in their fears about their son's food intake. Thus both failed in the sensitive mirroring of the child's basic inner state that permits the pattern of hunger and satiety to achieve consensual validation in the infant-caretaker exchange. Consequently, the regulation of hunger and satiety through responsiveness to internal physiological cues could never be taken over from the caretaker-infant exchange, internalized, and given later appropriate symbolic representation. The highest level this reached for Mr. K was the internalization of sign-signal communication of *eat = don't eat* as a part of a dominance-submission-rebellion interchange. Subsequently, the multiple symbolic representations connected to body form and anxiety regulation that eating received overlay the basic regulatory deficit.

Mr. K left the analysis hopeful that, freer of the stresses of all the conflicts and other self-destructiveness that overlay the basic regulatory problems, he could, by careful attentiveness of a self-educative nature, handle his eating more adaptively and pleasurably.[3]

Discussion

Besides examples of deficient regulation of vegetative activities, regulatory deficits may affect other functions. Psychoanalytic theory has long included concepts about the regulation of stimulation, but this subject has largely been subsumed under the issue of sexual overstimulation. Freud wondered to what degree this problem was con-

---

[3] I have previously reported the analysis of a 27-year-old man who had had a milk allergy and a coeliac-like syndrome in infancy. "He would sometimes gorge himself, other times neglect eating; he would retain feces and urine until painfully distended before he became aware of his need; he would sleep irregularly and would be fatigued without any awareness of cause, or would play tennis to the point of exhaustion without recognition of limit" (Lichtenberg, 1978, p. 374).

stitutional. Infant research indicates that regulation of stimulation in general is a significant feature of care-taker-neonate interaction from birth on. The pattern of the neonate's responsiveness to stimuli ranges from highly active, through average, to quietly active, and in the abnormal, from infants who fall apart in the effort to process ordinary stimuli to underreactive infants who make attachment and engagement extremely difficult. A look at the normal range strongly suggests that an infant's "basic core" (Weil, 1970) with respect to stimulus processing may be a precondition to the way the developing child will respond to the ranges of sensual excitation that he is confronted with. Infant researchers have even pinpointed a stage in development at about eighteen months when there is an upsurge of genital sensation and exploration (Roiphe, 1968; Kleeman, 1975). Amsterdam and Levitt (1980) suggest that the nature of the response to this upsurge has consequences for embarrassment, shame, and anxiety responses. These findings for the eighteen month old stand at the interface between the earlier mode of organization and the level of symbolic representation. This is the point where symptom formation involving intrapsychic conflictual tendencies can first be recognized. (See Lichtenberg, 1983b, for a detailed discussion.)

Infant research focuses principally on normal rather than pathological functioning. Infant researchers have attempted an increasingly sophisticated discrimination of the infant's response to specific classes of stimuli—animate and inanimate, mother and father, etc. Most noteworthy for the deprivation-in-intimacy that Stone suggests is the base of the analytic interaction are Sander's studies (1980a, b) of the brief moments of "open space" in which the infant plays actively in the social presence of his mother but without engagement desired

or pressed on him. The subtle refinements of the transference interactions in the analytic situation and the regulation of engagement and impingement and the capacity
to be alone in the presence of another, are suggested by
these findings derived from the patterns of exchange between caretaker and the young infant.

EXAMPLE 2

Mrs. G's analysis centered on her phobic symptoms,
depression, and a hypersensitivity to anxiety. Early in
her analysis she described a symptom that was unique
in my experience. Her mouth would be held open in a
gesture that was similar to a yawn but unlike a yawn
since she would not inspire air. Instead she would try to
get her mouth to close. We spoke of this as a yawn for
lack of a better designation and related it to a response
to mounting anxiety. Yet this characterization struck me
as unsatisfactory because, even if accurate, I couldn't determine why this response would occur rather than any
of the other responses she made to becoming anxious.
During the long working through of the middle phase of
her analysis she became generally more able to associate
to and master anxiety. Her "yawn" symptom disappeared—or more accurately did not occur—neither of us
being aware of its absence.

Then during the final months of her analysis, Mrs. G
was telling me an anecdote about her new baby and her
five-year-old daughter. She seemed rather comfortable
about it, and I was listening with my attention easily
placed within her state of mind. She described feeding
the baby her bottle and her daughter looking on and
asking if she could help. Somewhat reluctantly, she answered yes and gave her the baby and the bottle. Turning
away for a moment, she looked back to see the baby hav-

ing a bit of distress because the five-year-old feeder had let the bottle press too deeply into her mouth. She proceeded to describe her reason for bringing up this anecdote—that she had been initially ready to react with a panicky yell, but was able to get control of herself and simply help the child feeder reposition the bottle properly. As she talked, I basked somewhat in her pride in her mastery of her inclination to panic and her implied appreciation of me as the parent-analyst who had helped her to do so. Involuntarily and without conscious thought, I found myself opening my mouth and feeling the sensation of a nipple thrust into it too far to suck in or push out. I repeated to her this aspect of her description preparatory to asking her about my conjecture that the so-called yawning symptom was a somatic memory of a nipple thrust too far into her mouth. Before I could verbalize my questions, she reproduced the symptom for the first time in several years.

The construction we made was based on a great deal of information about her early life. A premature baby, she had spent two months in an incubator before coming home. This gap probably interfered with the attachment between mother and infant, and was aggravated by the mother's being generally anxious and preoccupied with her own mother's chronic physical illness. We postulated that her mother, pulled on the one side by this concern, had at times turned over aspects of Mrs. G's care to Mrs. G's older sister. Whatever difficulties arose, especially with regard to the mechanical nature of the too intrusive nipple, may have been aggravated by the mouth sensitivity of this premature child plus a degree of weakness in counterthrusting the bottle away. What seemed most fascinating to me was that dream material that seemed related to this experience appeared *after* the analytic work. Work with this material led to associative links to conflicts over impingement. Dreams prior to this construction, viewed retrospectively, did not reveal that the bodily registry had received a symbolic representation that I could discern.

Discussion

Examples of this type of physical or body residue of early experiences are part of the folklore of analysis. Keiser (1977) described a strange manifestation of an analytic patient holding her hands in a particularly rigid manner. Keiser deduced that during infancy the patient had had her hands tied. The patient was unable to recall this event but was able to confirm it by direct investigation. The knowledge played a useful role in her analysis. The larger question these somewhat esoteric findings raise has to do with the nature of memory from the presymbolic stage. In two instances reactions from this period have had pathological consequences. Engel (1979) reported that Monica, the little girl with esophageal atresia whom he had followed, had recovered very nicely from the consequences of the total deprivation state well recognized from the absence of mouth feeding and all interrelations that go with it. Monica managed to marry and to handle her pregnancy well. To the surprise of the investigators she fed her baby in the same distant cramped way that she had been fed in the stomach opening. I have reported (Lichtenberg, 1981d) another case in which an otherwise warm and caring mother automatically fed her babies at arm's length—the strange practice of her own mother. One of her children had a brief psychotic episode, the other a distinctly schizoid personality and difficulty in establishing eye contact.

Infant researchers have identified a number of behavioral manifestations that warrant consideration as indications of early residues of the normal or abnormal caretaker-infant interaction. Eye contact as engagement and gaze avoidance as aversion responses are an example. In addition the relationship between physiognomic expression and affect has been studied in depth. The neonate's capacity to mimic the facial expressions of his caretaker has been demonstrated. Such examples open questions about the nature of infant-mother empathy as well as the modes of picking up disturbed affect states of depression, hatred, etc. If these exchanges of affect states as physiognomic "behavior" carry a strong coding of the early experience—say for the first year—interesting questions about the recumbent position in analysis are raised. As a general rule, do we force analysands to communicate via symbolic representation of speech and thus lift the level of the discourse? If so, does this restrict the messages that some patients could and need to give about their earlier experiences? Do these come out in different behaviors outside or possibly often inside the consulting room? Is it advantageous for the analyst to keep the patient's face in view and use this information or not? (see Jacobs, 1973).

EXAMPLE 3

I have described the central problems of Mr. N's analysis elsewhere (Lichtenberg, 1983a). He was able to establish a strong working relationship and, despite considerable transference resistance, to accept interpretations and participate in a working-through process. The one aspect of his analysis that I want to describe now is a limitation in his use of metaphor and analogy. For a long time I regarded this as a manifestation of his obsessional "style" and assumed that dynamically it served as a form of character resistance against primary-process material. Thus I expected that as Mr. N became less anxious and more able to be introspective, his compulsive adherence to secondary-process cognition would relax, and he would be more able to work with metaphor and analogy. However, as the analysis progressed, I revised this assessment. First, when he was less anxious, he was freer to report dreams, and more importantly, spontaneous fantasies, thus indicating a freeing up of primary-process cognition. But this freeing up occurred without any change in his being able to process the material of these fantasies and dreams through the active use of analogy and metaphor. Second, when I worked with him actively, using analogy mixed with a more detailed explanation, he readily and appreciatively utilized the information. This indicated to me that he did not fail to employ analogy and metaphor as a pseudo-deficit for the purpose of resistance. Third, he gave examples of conversations with other people in which he could recognize this lack. From these we could recognize similarities in the analysis that explained painful feelings of embarrassment and humiliation when he could not "catch on" to suggestions I made based on metaphoric bridging.

Looking backward, I could see that his sensitivity to this impairment played a part in his reluctance to work "analytically" (symbolically) with transference material—a problem that had produced a puzzling barrier to progress. His frustration could be seen retrospectively as one of the meanings of his frequent appeals to me for help; that is, he wished me as an empathic caregiver to sense his cognitive constriction and the deleterious effect it had on his self-confidence. His wish was that I come to his aid to bridge his difficulty—to "uncramp" his mind, rather than ask him ordinary analytic questions. The ordinary questions designed to guide him to form linkages exposed him to feeling inadequate without helping him to identify the source of the problem. As his limitation in appreciating and working with analogy and metaphor was recognized and his sense of failure understood, he became more adventurous in his attempts to associate symbolically.

Discussion

Mr. N's limitation in the use of metaphor and analogy is a specific but minor example of a class of cognitive deficiencies that include a wide variety of learning disturbances of which dyslexia is probably the best known.[4] This whole area of cognitive-processing disturbances is becoming increasingly appreciated in educational circles and in the field of child psychiatry (Weil, 1977). The number of individuals with such difficulties is not inconsiderable. (Statistics vary anywhere from 2 to 10 percent [A. Lichtenberg, personal communication, 1981]). Thus the likelihood is high that an analyst will encounter a certain number of analysands with these difficulties. The problem of recognition is made difficult because the learning disability will interact with intrapsychic and interpersonal problems that then overshadow the primary deficit.

APPLICATIONS TO THE PSYCHOANALYTIC SITUATION

I predict that the new knowledge from infant research will have a profound but subtle effect on psychoanalytic

---

[4] An example from my current practice is a professional man with a very high I.Q. who can amass incredible numbers of facts but is very deficient in the ability to appreciate hierarchical arrangements. His academic career was to him and to his teachers inexplicably checkered because of the unrecognized disparity in his abilities—fact assembly leading him to be a whiz in some courses and the need for hierarchical structuring causing him to be borderline in others.

practice. The most significant feature of its findings lies in its focus on normal development. It starts with the question: how does the unexpectedly complex level of organization of the neonate, operating in an interactional matrix with a caregiver, undergo transformations into the further levels of organization of later stages? It does not move backward from the neuroses or psychoses to ask how these disturbances recapitulate in distorted form a hypothetical "normal" early stage. Thus the current infant research does not tilt toward a "demonic" imagery of infancy. But it does tilt away from an appreciation of psychic awareness, of fantasy and of the unconscious, that is, from the vicissitudes of the conflictual nature of the human experience (what Sander, 1980a, calls the inevitable polarities). Psychoanalysis will not and should not surrender its ground on many of these points; therefore changes will be slow and subtle. Nonetheless I believe that when infant research is seen as leading toward a new but useful conception of normal infant organization, and a new and useful conception of problem areas such as I have described in my clinical vignettes, analysis will gain from the new conception of normality and abnormality without losing any of its capacity to penetrate the depths of man's unconscious.

How can we apply what is known now about infancy to the psychoanalytic situation? Stone described both a framework that permits analysis to take place and the formal operations that represent its main task. The framework is the relationship between the adult physician of goodwill and reliability and the mature, responsible patient reverberating with the relationship of the mother both gratifying and separating and the infant experiencing deprivation-in-intimacy. The formal operations are the interpretations that take place within that context. Stone referred to analysts who seemed to want to manipulate the framework, and this argument persists to this day. Is the medium the message? Is the psychoanalytic situation itself—the physicianly concern and care, the empathic ambience—the curative agent? Certainly some analysts perceive a focus on deficits in early development, whether regulatory, relational, or cognitive, as implying a cure by replacement, a second version of child rearing. In fact because of the transformations between infancy and adulthood, this is both impossible and unnecessary. It is impossible because the experiential world of the infant of the first year is so different—and unnecessary because the adult has achieved the level of symbolic representation and can bring the problem-solving mode of this level of organization to bear on his problems through the regular means of interpretation.

The question then resolves itself to the interpretation of what? The answer I would give is the interpretation of whatever the analysand communicates that he has responded to and reverberated with in the analytic situation. This might be to the analyst as a discrete separate person toward whom the analysand has a sexual wish, or a wish to relieve his loneliness, or a wish to assert his superiority over, etc. Or it may be to the analytic situation which the analysand feels is helping him or is failing to help him in some general or, it is hoped, in a more and more discrete way. Thus the medium is not the message; the medium is a person—the analyst—and a milieu—the analytic situation—which serves as a wonderfully ambiguous stimulus for reverberations of specific desires and regulatory needs, past and present. The message is the communication back to the analysand of interpretations that facilitate his introspective understanding of the meaning of what he has communicated.

I have suggested that the analyst forms his constructions by having his perception shift between what the analysand is experiencing in what I term the "foreground" and the "background." In the foreground is the immediate context and meaning of the associations the patient is relating. This might be that the analyst is the recipient of well-organized wishes or that he is needed to serve some suspended, unavailable, or underdeveloped function. In the background is a general sense of the receptivity that the analysand presumes he will receive from the analyst as a transference person, persons, or milieu. At any given moment the patient may or may not have a conscious or even preconscious awareness of the psychic reality he perceives as coloring his background. For example, a patient may have come habitually to experience his masculinity or his competence as under question; as a result he may be unaware he lives his life and even the analysis as though in a state of siege. By and large the transferences that characterize the background communication in analysis tend to be centered on the broadened sense of "support systems" that succeed or fail to form and sustain self cohesion and basic trust, optimism, and a capacity for joy. The analyst's listening focus and interpretation must shift back and forth between foreground and background, gradually assisting the analysand to increase his awareness of both. This should include as much as possible a systematic exploration of both successes and failures in present and past "support systems."

Conceptualizing the analytic situation in terms of the patient's communications as responses to foreground and background stimuli provides another key analogy to infantile experience. Sander (1980b) has stated: "We traditionally rely on a linear cause-effect model—one thing leading to another. . . . This we need to replace with . . . a model . . . where there can be a background and a foreground" (p. 195). Foreground events, such as making eye contact in infancy and providing associations in analysis, are given meaning in the framework of the background of a shared organization of expectancies constructed from the infant-mother regulatory efforts in development and from the operational consistencies of the psychoanalytic situation. In infancy and in analysis foreground and background should be thought of as experiential rather than concrete entities. Each of these aspects of psychic reality develops because an individual who has achieved the level of symbolic representation shifts in his experiencing of himself and others between a tendency to generalize and a tendency to particularize (Lichtenberg, 1979). The tendency to generalize builds up the background. The tendency to particularize leads to a foreground focus. The tendency to shift back and forth between the two constitutes perceptual and conceptual roots for the associative sequencing in analysis.

Finally, I should like to comment about empathy. If the medium is not the message, what about empathy? If generalized empathic failures in caretaking have created a disturbance in shared expectancies giving rise to distrust in the background, or if particular empathic failures have created traumatic overloads around which pathological fantasy systems have formed giving rise to affective-cognitive disturbances in the foreground, then is empathy the means to repair the damage? I believe empathy is the means to the means to repair the damage. First, empathy as a general ambience is an ingredient of the "physicianly" warmth and commitment of an analyst—it is thus, as Stone indicates, the means to create the analytic situation. But empathy in a technical sense is a specific mode of analytic listening (Schwaber, 1981) and perceiving (Lichtenberg, 1981b). Thus it is the means to apprehend and comprehend the affective and cognitive experiential sense of the analysand's state of mind, providing thereby the data on which interpretation is based. The empathic mode of perception in analysis is a form of attunement that is for the most part the apprehending by the analyst through the symbolic level of representation of information communicated by the analysand also through symbolic representation. Thus the empathic attunement of infant and mother of the first year is not the usual mode of communicative interchange in analysis. Indeed this unconscious communication may exist, and many analysts including Freud have placed great significance on it—penetrating to the navel of the unknown (Major and Miller, 1981). As indicated in my second vignette, the analyst can use his bodily responses to reverberate with unconscious communications of the patient, and this may be "related to the use of the body as a prime conveyor of affect between mother and child" (Jacobs, 1973, p. 87).

Nonetheless, in the ordinary conduct of analysis the empathic mode of listening is commonly based on perceiving at a symbolic level of communication, and, if derived from a bodily level, it is then apprehended symbolically. Thus an effort to understand at the symbolic level should be exhausted before the analyst concludes that residua from before its formation have remained outside its mode of coding. I conjecture—with a readiness to be convinced otherwise—that with the exception of rare instances of bodily listening, what we perceive outside the empathic mode of listening via symbolic representation, we achieve through exclusion, deduction, and a grasp of intuitive inference within a background of considerable empathic attunement. Rather than whether the level of empathy used in empathic listening is the rare presymbolic or the usual symbolic, the key issue is the experiential terrain being explored and how it is coded. The conclusion I draw from my knowledge of infant research and the psychoanalytic situation is that a new enriched schema of the inner world of infancy sensitizes the analyst listener to a richer attunement to all possible levels of the experiential world of the analysand's transferences.

REFERENCES

Amsterdam, B., & Levitt, M. (1980), Consciousness of self and painful self-consciousness. *The Psychoanalytic Study of the Child*, 35:67-84. New Haven: Yale University Press.

Basch, M. (1975), Toward a theory that encompasses depression: a revision of existing causal hypotheses in psychoanalysis. In: *Depression and Human Existence*, ed. E. Anthony & T. Benedek. Boston: Little, Brown, pp. 485-534.

Engel, G. (1979), Monica: a twenty-five-year longitudinal study of the consequences of trauma in infancy. Presented to the American Psychoanalytic Association.

Gedo, J. (1979), *Beyond Interpretation*. New York: International Universities Press.

Jacobs, T. (1973), Posture, gesture and movement in the analyst: Cues to interpretation and countertransference. *J. Amer. Psychoanal. Assn.*, 21:77-92.

Keiser, S. (1977), Report of discussion group on: Reconstruction and unconscious fantasy in psychoanalytic treatment.

Kleeman, J. (1975), Genital self-stimulation in infant and toddler girls. In: *Masturbation from Infancy to Senescence*, ed. I. Marcus & J. Francis. New York: International Universities Press, pp. 77-106.

Kohut, H. (1971), *The Analysis of the Self*. New York: International Universities Press.

—— (1980), Summarizing reflections. In: *Advances in Self Psychology*, ed. A. Goldberg. New York: International Universities Press, pp. 473-554.

Lichtenberg, J. (1978), The testing of reality from the standpoint of the body self. *J. Amer. Psychoanal. Assn.*, 26:357-385.

—— (1979), Factors in the development of the sense of the object. *J. Amer. Psychoanal. Assn.*, 27:375-386.

—— (1981a), Implications for psychoanalytic theory of research on the neonate. *Internat. Rev. Psychoanal.*, 8:35-52.

—— (1981b), The empathic mode of perception and alternative vantage points for psychoanalytic work. *Psychoanal. Inquiry*, 3:329-356.

——— (1981c), Reflections on the first year of life. *Psychoanal. Inquiry*, 1:695-730.

——— (1981d), Continuities and transformations between infancy and adolescence. In: *Adolescent Psychiatry*, vol. 10, ed. S. Feinstein & P. Giovacchini. Chicago: University of Chicago Press, 1983, pp. 182-198.

——— (1982), Categories of aggression and frames of reference within which to view them. *Psychoanal. Inquiry*, 2:213-231.

——— (1983a), The application of the self-psychological viewpoint to psychoanalytic technique. In: *Reflections on Self Psychology*, ed. J. Lichtenberg & S. Kaplan. Hillsdale, N.J.: Analytic Press, pp. 163-185.

——— (1983b), *Psychoanalysis and Infant Research*. Hillsdale, N.J.: Analytic Press.

——— & Slap, J. (1977), Comments on the general functioning of the analyst in the psychoanalytic situation. *The Annual of Psychoanalysis*, 5:295-312. New York: International Universities Press.

Major, J., & Miller, P. (1981), Empathy, antipathy and telepathy in the analytic process. *Psychoanal. Inquiry*, 1:449-470.

Malcolm, J. (1981), *The Impossible Profession*. New York: Knopf.

Roiphe, H. (1968), On an early genital phase. *The Psychoanalytic Study of the Child*, 23:348-365. New York: International Universities Press.

Sander, L. (1980), Polarity, paradox, and the organizing process in development. Presented to the First World Congress of Infant Psychiatry, Portugal, March.

——— (1980b), New knowledge about the infant from current research: implications for psychoanalysis. *J. Amer. Psychoanal. Assn.*, 28:181-198.

——— (1983), To begin with—reflections on ontogeny. In: *Reflections on Self Psychology*, ed. J. Lichtenberg & S. Kaplan. Hillsdale, N.J.: Analytic Press, pp. 85-104.

Schwaber, E. (1981), Empathy: A mode of psychoanalytic listening. *Psychoanal. Inquiry*, 1:357-392.

Stone, L. (1961), *The Psychoanalytic Situation*. New York: International Universities Press.

Weil, A. (1970), The basic core. *The Psychoanalytic Study of the Child*, 25:442-460. New York: International Universities Press.

——— (1977), Learning disturbances with special consideration of dyslexia. *Issues in Child Mental Health*, 5:52-66.

4

Toward a Reformulation of the Theory of Aggression and Its Implications for Primary Prevention

HENRI PARENS, M.D.

INTRODUCTION

Many analysts believe that our psychoanalytic theory of aggression is neither sufficiently nor cohesively formulated. One major factor contributing to this state of affairs is that, although many of us reject the concept of a death instinct, the basic formulations of aggression we employ in our work are nonetheless based on Freud's second instinctual drive theory, the central postulate of which is that rejected death instinct. I have to presume that had I found the death-instinct-based theory of aggression clinically convincing and useful, I would not have responded so keenly to the findings I will present very briefly here—on which I reported extensively in 1979.

My colleagues and I did not expect to study the vicissitudes of aggression when, in 1969, we[1] launched our

---

[1] Robert C. Prall, M.D., Elizabeth Scattergood, M.A., and I.

Early Child Development Program, MCP-EPPI.[2] Our study of aggression was instigated by findings that caused me to question some of our basic concepts about it. The hypotheses these findings generated evolved gradually as observations accumulated; and they continue to be tested by us.

And I am eager to confess that I have presented this study and have welcomed its perhaps premature publication (Parens, 1979a) in large part because I agree with Aring (1973) that we must move with greater speed toward trying to solve the enormous problems caused by human hostility, and I believe that we analysts can and must help develop strategies for its prevention and early treatment. This view has a long history in psychoanalysis. Surveying the capabilities of psychoanalysis, Freud said in 1933, as he did on other occasions, that the contributions of psychoanalysis would include its "application to education, to the upbringing of the next generation." He believed this contribution to be "so exceedingly important, so rich in hopes for the future" (p. 146).

In these pages I want to put forward some of the hypotheses generated by our findings, briefly suggest some of their implications, and say just a few words about our current effort to develop a strategy for preventing the development of excessive hostility in children.

In 1973 and 1979 (in *The Development of Aggression in Early Childhood*) I reported that the stimulus for my studies in aggression came from an unexpected finding: while observing infants less than six months old, we found behavior which could serve as a paradigm for *neutralized* aggression. This finding created a problem for

[2] Children's Unit of the Eastern Pennsylvania Psychiatric Institute (EPPI) at the Medical College of Pennsylvania (MCP). Project C: The Development of Aggression in Early Childhood.

me of such magnitude that I pushed aside the hypothesis we initially set out to study and elected to explore this puzzling finding. Before I tell you why this finding was so puzzling, though, let me first tell you how we came upon it.

We made these path-changing observations in our Early Child Development Program at MCP/EPPI. The frame of reference we have used is classical psychoanalytic theory. The investigative method we employed is *longitudinal direct child observation* as reasoned and proposed initially by Ernst Kris (1950) and Hartmann (1950, 1958) and furthered by Spitz (1946, 1965), Anna Freud (1958, 1965), Lustman (1963), and Mahler (1965, 1968, and Mahler, Pine and Bergman, 1975).

METHODOLOGY AND FINDINGS

Our approach has been observational. Since the beginning of the study in September 1970, fifteen children and their mothers have been the focus of this work. Our original research group met twice weekly for two hours in a living room in the Children's Unit at MCP/EPPI. The mothers brought all their children who were not in school, but it was those children whom we had seen since birth who were our primary research subjects. The infants were cared for by their mothers, the project staff observing. Participation by all families was, of course, completely voluntary. (For further details on the method we used, see Parens, 1979a, chap. 4.)

I elected to approach this study of aggression not from the vantage point of the psychoanalysis of young children but from that of psychoanalytic longitudinal direct observation because I wanted to explore evidence of psychic activity from the beginning of extrauterine life. We have not only relied on the directly observed phenomenology of the infant's and the mother's activities but have viewed this phenomenology as the manifestations of intrapsychic functioning. This approach, of course, derives from the posture and methodology employed by the psychoanalyst in the clinical psychoanalysis of children.

DEVELOPMENTAL FRAME OF REFERENCE USED FOR DATA COLLECTION

Perhaps because psychoanalysts have tended to view aggression as following a path of development coincident with and dependent upon the libido, aggression theory has not been as well formulated as libido theory. In order to avoid the bias imposed by psychosexual theory on the theory of aggression (A. Freud, 1972; Solnit, 1972), I elected to employ the sequential-developmental phases proposed by Mahler's theory of *symbiosis and separation-individuation* as our developmental frame of reference. An added bonus to this selection is that Mahler's theory easily absorbs Spitz's formulations (1950, 1965) on the development of the libidinal object, a development that plays a central part in the vicissitudes of aggression in the child.

THE NATURE AND CATALOGING OF THE DATA

Now I am ready to relate the problem I unexpectedly found. While observing our children when they were under four to six months of age, we found manifestations of aggression in their behavior which challenged the classical psychoanalytic view that all aggression is, in origin, inherently destructive. Hypothetically based on the death instinct, the aggressive drive of Freud's second instinctual drive theory had until recently been the virtually unchallenged foundation of the psychoanalytic theory of aggression. It is postulated to be in origin a purely self-destructive drive. According to this postulate, during infancy, only by virtue of primary narcissism is destructiveness turned toward the outside, away from the self. Later in development, with the additional growing influence of the ego, destructiveness can be both fused with libido and neutralized. In this way, according to our existing structural and drive theories, the ego achieves protection against self-destructiveness as well as mastery over the destructive drive.

The qualitative aspects of aggressive drive manifestations in our work are determined by clinical judgment; the assumption that a drive discharge—whether in action or fantasy—is motivated by neutralized or unneutralized aggression depends on various manifest characteristics of the discharge. We assume, for example, that much unneutralized aggression exists in the psyche, where impulsiveness, undue intensity and large pressure to discharge, and lack of control over pain-inducing or destructive action are characteristic of such discharges, as is found in harsh temper tantrums or rampaging cannibalistic fantasies. By contrast, where an aggressive discharge is characterized by the ability of the self to modulate it, to control it sufficiently, to discharge it in graduated doses and in a socially acceptable manner, those of us who hold to the great heuristic value of structural and drive theories speak, then, of the ego's having to a greater *rather than* a lesser degree neutralized aggression. And we have assumed that much constructive activity, including, for example, driving a truck, doing schoolwork, and all forms of sublimations (artistic and scientific) implements neutralized aggressive energies.

Following especially from Hartmann's work, psychoanalysts assume that the *neutralization of aggression* is carried out by the ego, that it *is an ego function* which becomes operative only when the ego begins to function as an agency—that is, when the ego begins to function at an organizational level capable of experiencing *anxiety* (Freud, 1926), of experiencing a *wish* (Schur, 1966), and capable of *intentionality* of action (Hartmann, 1952). This occurs from about the latter half of the first year of life. At this time, the infantile psyche has structured, i.e., invested emotionally in, a libidinal object (in Spitz's sense), and this attachment to the object is specific and quite stable. In line with this thinking, then, one might expect to find neutralization of aggression to begin at the earliest from about six to eight months of age.

Let me string together a set of assumptions:

1. Let us assume, as I did for years, that aggression is derived from the death instinct and, therefore, is *inherently destructive*. Indeed, it is *self*-destructive and in the early months is turned outwardly by the action of primary narcissism.

2. It can be neutralized only by an ego which is already, or sufficiently on the way to becoming, an agency.

3. The ego *begins* to be structured as an agency during the last half of the first year of life, say from the age of six to eight months.

4. Indeed, we find evidence that neutralization of aggression is given its principal impetus *by the child's transient wish to destroy his occasionally too frustrating libidinal object*. We found this not to occur prior to the sufficient structuring of the libidinal object which occurs around six to eight months.

Therefore, according to Freud's second instinctual drive theory, prior to six months of age, all aggression is inherently destructive, and the ego is not yet structured as an agency and therefore cannot neutralize aggression. Bearing this in mind, consider the following activity in behavior which we had not expected to find.

FINDINGS

What follows is a slightly altered narration of the film (Parens and Prall, 1974) which we presented to illustrate the theory-challenging observational data we found.

As Jane 0-3-19 [age stated in terms of years-months-days], is being fed by her mother, she makes her first attempts to control the spoon that mother is putting into her mouth. One can see the effort invested in self-feeding, the early motor effort to control the feeding process. The mother integrates her feeding efforts with those of her daughter. Jane then sleeps for twenty-five minutes lying on a cover spread on the floor. During the next thirty-minute period [after waking], much occurs worthy of our attention.

Within minutes of waking Jane begins to look at objects—her mother and observers. She smiles broadly, already (at this age) focusing on her mother, and then looks around at articles on the floor, looking at several quite intently as she briefly fixes her attention on them in passing. She now turns her attention to a set of plastic rings on a string, which she begins to explore. She begins by pulling them apart, mouthing them. The sensorimotor effort is visible on her face, and one soon hears vocal concomitants of that effort. She moves the rings back and forth while she looks at them, a serious expression on her face, and a good deal of pressure can be inferred from the way she seems to be working. She waves her arms as she attempts to reach the rings which she has inadvertently just pushed out of reach. When mother (cooperating with us) then advances the rings so that Jane can reach them again, she does so promptly, her attention continuing to be focused on those rings. The affect which bespeaks the effort she makes to bring the rings to her mouth, the effort with which she pushes and pulls them, [eventually] suggests [to us] that this pressure is in the service of assimilating the rings.

The activity is of course interrupted by physiological needs, as well as by socialization. She looks around and smiles at her mother. She then returns to the rings. Notable is the intense, worklike affect—the constancy of the effort she invests in exploring the rings and the inner-drivenness of that activity. Much energy seems to be invested in the exploratory mouthing, pulling, and pushing of the rings. While she explores these rings, there is no thumbsucking activity. Repeatedly she mouths the rings, sometimes with simultaneous pulling movements of her arms and lifting her torso, and her legs are activated as well; indeed, her entire body is involved in her effort. Her facial expression and entire body posture indicate the tension of, and the large effort invested in, that protracted activity.

After eighteen minutes of nearly continuous effort, she pauses, lying down on the mat. One [can infer that] she is tiring. She pauses for about fifteen seconds, looks up at her mother, smiles softly, and returns to the rings, at once very busy. Soon she pauses again, and one begins to see signs of unpleasure on her face. She cries and stops her exploratory activity, rings in hand. Now, for the first time in a twenty-minute period, she puts her thumb in her mouth and lies quietly. (Has her oral exploratory activity aroused her oral mucosa? Has this arousal, together with tiredness and frustration, led to the need for libidinal gratification, at least to the use of her thumb?) She returns to the rings. The effort continues to be strong, but one now senses unpleasure as she seems to experience some frustration, presumably arising from her activity in relation to the rings.

From here on she alternates between exploration of the rings and thumbsucking. While she sucks her thumb she lies rather quietly on the mat, giving the impression that she is recovering from her tiredness and unexplained frustration. Her body curls up again, her legs kick up, and she sucks rather vigorously, experiencing some frustration in that too. She stops the thumbsucking, cries momentarily, and looks up at her mother. She pushes the rings away from her. The noise of the rings being pushed away seems to make her turn her attention, again momentarily, to those rings. She spits up a bit, and her mother picks her up to comfort her. Jane has now been awake for about twenty-five minutes and has been continually busy.

This type of pressured, driven, exploratory activity was observed in our infants from the ages of eight to sixteen weeks on during periods of wakefulness and physiologic and psychic comfort. In some infants it was of greater intensity than in others; with some these activity periods were of greater duration than with others. In Jane, the strong pressure and duration of this exploratory activity, from the time she was nine weeks old, were impressive. When she was awake and her physiologic needs were relatively quiescent, she looked constantly—at her mother's face, at observers, at a bell, at the lighted window, at the source of a noise. The persistence of this looking, exploring activity was compelling. Jane, like our other children, did not elect to look; she seemed driven from within to look (Parens, 1979a, pp. 23-25).

Because this type of datum generated questions and theory-modifying hypotheses which I will soon state, I must take a moment here to address briefly a question I have often been asked in one form or another in the course of scientific presentations. "Why do you call this activity aggression?" "What element in this activity do you mean?" Or, "Can't this behavior be better explained in terms of primary autonomous ego apparatuses, functions, and undifferentiated or neutral ego energies?" "Isn't this a motility drive, and if so what does it have to do with aggression?" And, "Is this behavior not ascribable to 'pleasure in function'?"

In our work, we often try to tease out the red thread

of certain elements in the complex fabric of manifest behavior and inferrable psychodynamics. Over decades of
work, child analysts have developed a notable degree of
competence and reliability in inferring the meaning
of certain everyday behaviors in children (A. Freud,
1965). Although we are on more precarious and uncertain
grounds in drawing inferences from the behavior of very
young children, even from the first months of life on we
can infer the interplay of primitive, little differentiated
drive and primary autonomous ego activity. I am trying
to tease out the motivational force which seems to compel
the three-month-old infant to the type of activity detailed
above. What I see in and infer from Jane's behavior is
this: primary autonomous ego apparatuses are set in
motion by internal pressures. External stimuli *evoke* an
inner pressured reactivity, they do not create the reactivity; the stimulus, so to speak, channels the pressure
in its direction; thus, external stimuli become the "object"
of the internal pressure. Even the primary autonomous
ego apparatus, which is capable of a specific function,
requires a motivating force that will make it function as
it does. It is that internal force to which I draw attention
here. And, of course, to tease that out is no simple matter.

There is an interplay within the child of ego apparatuses and their emerging functions, the pressure of
motivating forces, and the experiencing of events, to mention those elements of most concern here. Already very
early, the quality of an erotic inner pressure in sucking
activity with its exciting and soothing behavioral manifestations can be distinguished from the inner drivenness of getting a hold of, asserting oneself upon, an
apparent pressure to have control of. Of course narcissism
(libido) and ego functions play a part in the activity detailed; and from early on, in this type of activity, ego,
narcissism, and pressured assertiveness operate synton-

ically, hand in hand, a point I discussed extensively in my monologue with Hartmann (Parens, 1979a, chap. 2). I wish to explain the inner drivenness I tried to highlight in the behavior detailed above in terms of psychic energy,[3] the qualitative aim of which differs from that of libido. In 1973, I detailed the reasons why I find this not to be a physiological form of energy; in 1973 and 1979a, I detailed the reasons why I reject the concept of noninstinctual, neutral ego energies and why I consider this activity the best representative of a current of the aggressive drive that is inherently nondestructive.

In sum, then, in describing this behavioral datum I infer a part played by primitive functioning of primary autonomous ego apparatuses, by pleasure in function, by narcissism, by libido (especially in the sucking activity and the libidinization of ego apparatuses set in motion), but I ask you to consider the part played only by the motivational force within Jane, that inner drivenness to explore, hold, seemingly assert, or act upon the rings as she pulled, pushed, and mouthed them. It is this inner force, I suggest, that instigates and fuels the behavior described. It is my hope that the reader will be able to envision—without necessarily agreeing with my inference—that this vignette illustrates activity fueled, motivated by an inner force. What is the nature of that inner-drivenness?

I remind you, according to our until recently existing

---

[3] Despite the difficulties caused by the concept of psychic energy, I still find its explanatory value to be large and not taken over satisfactorily by that of other explanatory models of intrapsychic motivations. Any motivation concept eventually has to account for its inherent force. There is no motivation without an inherent unit of force. What is the nature of motivational forces? I think that, although I find it often useful to speak of motivations per se, the concept motivation cannot be the lowest common denominator of the energic factor in psychic activity.

theory of aggression, that prior to six months of age the ego cannot yet neutralize aggression, and all aggression is inherently destructive. What, then, are we to say of this *seemingly neutralized* aggression manifest in the behavior of this four-month-old child? Finding this activity in infants under six months of age, then, presented us with a dilemma, with a disharmony between observable data and our existing theory.

To investigate that dilemma, as we carried out our longitudinal naturalistic observations of the children, we looked in their behavior for the *manifestations of instinctual drive activity* (Loewenstein, 1940). I found, after months of struggle, that the enormous difficulties we encountered in sorting out and cataloguing behavioral observations were alleviated by our categorizing *manifestations of aggressive drive activity* into the following four groups: (1) unpleasure-related discharges of destructiveness; (2) nonaffective discharges of destructiveness; (3) discharges of nondestructive aggression; and (4) pleasure-related discharges of destructiveness.

These categories of manifestations of aggression are now briefly described.

The unpleasure-related discharge of destructiveness

The interrelation of two features distinguishes this category from the others. First, one can infer *inherent destructiveness* in the child's behavior. By inherent I mean that this type of discharge is not learned; it is an innate disposition ready to function at birth. By *destructiveness* is meant the tendency to tear down structure (an operative system, animate or inanimate); this is done *against resistance* since all structures (systems) have a greater or lesser degree of stability. Second, these discharges are invariably accompanied by, associated with, a *manifest affective state of unpleasure.*

In this work the rage reaction of infancy is taken as the paradigm for this category of aggression discharge. Although opinions on this matter vary, the rage reaction in infancy seems to have discharge qualities clinically characteristic of destructiveness. Of course, the human neonate can neither conceptualize nor destroy an object; but an unmitigated discharge of this type at a later age would readily be identified by the clinician as destructive. Repeated observation leads me to hold that the rage reaction of infancy is a somatopsychic—not only a physiologic (Spock, 1965)—discharge pattern in which destructiveness seems manifestly aroused by sufficient unpleasure in the infant.

The nonaffective discharge of destructiveness

This category is distinguished from the others by two coexisting features. First, as with the category described above, there is an inferrable tendency to *destroy,* i.e., to tear down structure which is unavoidably done against resistance. Second, this discharge appears essentially devoid of, and seems *not associated with, an affective concomitant.* Although an unpleasure affect may be present due to the pain of hunger, for example, the destruction of structure itself is essentially devoid of affect; hence it is *nonaffective.*

Following a line of thought suggested by Eissler (1971), I consider this category of destructive discharge to be represented in early psychic life by *feeding activity.* Eissler equated the intake and assimilation of food not only with the gratification of needs for libidinal and physiological supplies, but also with making the object disappear by destroying it. *Note, however*, that such destructiveness serves *self-preservation*.

The discharge of nondestructive aggression

This category is distinguishable from the others by virtue of its *not having an inherent destructive* character though it is recognizable by its characteristics to pertain to *aggression*. I mean activity as: pressured manipulation and exploration, determination to get hold of, to assert oneself upon, to control, and to thrust toward mastery of self and environment, including its animate and inanimate objects. The earliest form of this type of aggressive discharge appears during the third month or so in pressured motoric activity. The compellingness, inner-drivenness inferrable in the activity, and its constant appearance during states of alert wakefulness at this age give me the impression of drive activity and of aggression. At a manifest level beyond the first year of life, this category of discharge can become troublesome to distinguish from *neutralized hostile destructive* discharges; the distinction of an *inherently nondestructive* from a *neutralized hostile destructive* discharge is best assured when such a discharge emerges prior to the ego's capability to neutralize destructiveness.

The pleasure-related discharge of destructiveness

This category, the last we found to emerge ontogenetically, is distinguishable from the others by the interrelation of two features: *destructiveness* and *a manifest pleasurable affect*. We found pleasure-related destructive discharges of a convincing kind only from the end of the first year of life on. At that time, after the structuring of the libidinal object, *teasing* and *taunting* by the child seem to exemplify best the category in question. As development proceeds, pleasurable and intentional causing of pain in others ("sadism" in the broad sense of the word) emerges quite more convincingly. Its intentionality (Hartmann, 1952) presupposes that the ego begins to be structured as an agency before such destructive discharges occur.

I want to underline that though it is useful to categorize the manifestations of aggressive drive discharges according to their phenomenology and discernible psychodynamics, such categorization is not easy nor is it always satisfactory. Its greatest assets, which make its weaknesses tolerable, have been (1) the order it lent to an otherwise bewildering amorphous mass of data; (2) the fact that such categorization led to the hypothesis that there are various trends in the aggressive drive; and (3) the provision of one more approach to the difficult problem of discerning clinically and formulating theoretically the nature of aggression, its epigenetic evolving, the conditions for its discharges, and the character of its contributions to conflict, to adaptation, and to psychic development.

FORMULATION OF HYPOTHESES

By means of a large leap that is not only the prerogative of the clinician-investigator but in fact his responsibility, I drew from these manifestations of aggression in behavior the following set of hypotheses. Lest you throw up your hands in despair, allow me to borrow from Lustman (1963) and remind us of Einstein's 1934 admonition as he spoke of just this, the thorny path from empirical data to postulation: "The way is so difficult that no methods whatever must be barred; no source of meaning whatever, imaginative, theoretical, or whatever kind, are [sic] to be excluded." Or as Professor H. H. Price said, regarding the leap from observation to inference to hypothesis, "One should not be too strongly deterred by the fear of talking nonsense. . . . If the Logical Positivists had been alive in the early part of the seventeenth century, physics would never have got itself started" (quoted in Lustman, 1963, pp. 68-69).

After I categorized the data as described above, I found that this classification facilitated recognizing and sorting out types of aggressive behavior and I also found persistence and continuity in these types of aggressive behavior. Sufficiently encouraged to go on, these categories eventually led me to hypothesize that the aggressive drive consists of varying trends, or currents, as Freud said of the libido. Although the behavior was classified in four categories, the leap from empirical data to formulation led me to hypothesize only three trends in aggression.

1. *Nondestructive aggression*: We set out to solve the problem created by evidence of nondestructive aggression manifest from the first months of life.

This finding became the initiator of a set of hypotheses: (a.) There is an inherent nondestructive trend in the aggressive drive evident within months from birth, *well before neutralization* of aggression by the ego is possible; (b.) Aggression, therefore, *is not inherently only destructive*, contrary to the basic tenet of our existing psychoanalytic theory of aggression; (c.) Freud's (1920) second theory of aggression holds that aggression derives from the death instinct, and that under the influence of the libido (by fusion) and the ego (by neutralization) destructiveness is changed to serve self-preservation, mastery, adaptation. But observation of normal children shows that the death-instinct basis of aggression is not convincing. It is important to note, though, that without the death-instinct postulate, some basic aspects of psychoanalytic aggressive drive theory are without theoretical underpinnings.

2. *Nonaffective destructiveness*: Observation also shows that there is aggression that is inherently destructive without being hostile which derives phylogenetically from prey aggression. This is destruction of animate structure for the sake of alimentation, of *self-preservation*.

3. *Hostile destructiveness* (in the generic sense): Observation also shows evidence of *hostile destructiveness* that is observable from neonatal life. This aggression does *not* appear or arise *spontaneously*. However, the mechanism and capacity for its experience and expression are built into the somatopsychic continuum and are ready to function at birth.

Most important for us is that the mechanism requires a precondition for its activation which is: *sufficient or excessive unpleasure*.[4] Recognizing this precondition clarifies several things: (a) the discharge of hostile destructiveness is not compulsory; it often suffices that the condition of excessive unpleasure be removed; (b) it gives to aggression an *affective* quality which the other destructive trend—prey or nonaffective destructiveness—lacks, namely, *an unpleasure-derived quality best exemplified in rage, hostility, and hate*; (c) this trend in aggression has an *aim* which unlike the other trends in aggression seems to be destructiveness for its own sake. In chapter

---

[4] We distinguish this hypothesis from the frustration-aggression hypothesis of Dollard for a number of reasons I cannot detail here. Let me just say that we found multiple experiential causes of rage: in addition to frustration, there are physical pain, narcissistic injury as insults, teasing and taunting, and others. Therefore, we propose (Parens, 1979a) that *excessive unpleasure* is a lower common denominator than frustration in the production of hostility in humans.

3 of my book (Parens, 1979a) I hypothesize and detail how the precondition of *excessive unpleasure changes the basic aim of the aggressive impulse* by giving it a unique negative affective valence.

4. *Pleasure-related destructiveness*: This last trend to emerge epigenetically, from the beginning of the second year of life on, is distinguished by three features: *destructiveness* discharged in association with *pleasure* affects, and it often seems to appear *spontaneously*.

When 13-month-old Jane sat on 7-month-old Renee's head; when at 15 months she playfully pretended to bite her mother; when 19-month-old Candy smilingly pushed her head hard into her mother's face, did these discharges arise *spontaneously*? We were led by the children's behavior to infer a *pre-existing condition* which determined this type of destructive discharge. It was similar to the time when 14-month-old Candy seemed to just walk up to 2½-year-old Donny and strike him one rather solid blow on the arm. It appeared to be spontaneous. We say it was not. Three days before Donny had struck Candy harshly, she had cried, but we then saw no manifest discharge of destructiveness against Donny; rather she displaced her destructiveness onto her sibling Cindy and onto toys. Now, three days later, with the ego in control, Candy seemed to calculatedly unleash destructive feelings toward Donny. Many a time from the beginning of the second year of life on, such delayed destructive discharges were encountered in all the children, and it could be determined in many instances that these discharges were *not* spontaneous, but indeed had *an intrapsychically registered antecedent*.

Similarly, we found the *pleasurable affect* associated with such discharges often to be suspect. Teasing and taunting—and by extension, in the future, bullying, scapegoating, and ultimately, persecuting—which seem to begin at the turn into the second year of life, appeared in many instances to be determined by an antecedent experience of psychic pain, of excessive unpleasure. I came to understand the dynamics of such "pleasure-related discharge of destructiveness" to be the delay of an *un*pleasure-related destructive discharge, modified by the ego's emerging capabilities not only to delay and modify the component affect experienced but also to inhibit, displace, effect reaction-formations, make a game of (pre-sublimate), and discharge *under ego control*. Therefore, this type of data represents the pleasurable discharge of *hostile destructiveness and is but a variant of hostile destructiveness*. Like the direct expression of hostile destructiveness, this trend also does *not* arise spontaneously.

The term "aggression," then, as I use it (Parens, 1973, 1979a) is the general or umbrella word for the drive as one entity. It encompasses the various basic forms the aggressive drive may take. The drive has several discernible trends or currents which develop interdigitatingly over time (as I have tried to detail in 1979a, chaps. 10 through 16). I mean trends or currents as Freud meant when he spoke of *affectional* and *sensual* currents of the sexual drive, as distinguished from oral, anal, genital modes of libidinal expression (see Parens and Saul, 1971). The basic trends of the aggressive drive, I suggest, are *nondestructive aggression, nonaffective destructiveness*, and *hostile destructiveness*. Those most important to our work (and society) are nondestructive aggression and hostile destructiveness. The first is extremely important to self-assertiveness and self-determination, is intimately tied up with narcissistic aims, adaptation (including ego functioning), and creativity. It operates much as Hartmann suggested for noninstinctual neutral ego energies and neutralized destructiveness. So far as the pool of psychic energy goes—regretfully a much beleaguered concept nowadays—it pertains to that energy available to the ego, being syntonic to its functioning.

The hostile destructive trend is, of course, that which we think of in terms of hate and rage, and makes for ambivalence (see Abraham, 1924; Parens, 1979b). It is best known to us in the part it plays in intrapsychic conflicts, in conflicted object relations; it influences the character of id derivatives, of the superego; it often creates havoc in ego functions, in the development and stabilization of the self, and in object relations, which does not exhaust the list of its influences.

In chapter 3 of *The Development of Aggression in Early Childhood* I develop the position that the three basic trends in aggression can be shown to meet the criteria set down by Freud in 1915 for the definition of an instinctual drive.

AUTOMATIZATION OF HOSTILE DESTRUCTIVENESS

These hypotheses on hostile destructiveness lead me to postulate further that the human child is *not born with* an ever-replenishing load of hostility that he/she must discharge. Rather, the child is born with a ready-to-function mechanism that will *transform aggression into hostile destructiveness.*

In chapter 3 of my book, I have proposed how hostile destructiveness becomes *mobilized* in the child, how it attaches first and foremost to the child's libidinal objects, and how as a result it becomes invested in the child's earliest object and self representations. I elaborate how, *because of their indelibility and omnipresent influence, the hostile destructiveness invested in the earliest object and self representations becomes the fountainhead of hos-*

tility in the psyche. And (following on some comments made to me by Dr. Joseph Slap [personal communication, 1975]) I propose that this is how hostile destructiveness becomes *automatized* in the psyche and gives the clinical impression of being an instinctual drive.

These hypotheses lead me to the conviction that we can influence the mobilization and automatization of hostile destructiveness in humans. While the potential mobilization of hostile destructiveness is part of every child's psychic apparatus and constitutional endowment, its actual mobilization and accumulation in the psyche derive from the child's experiences. Although excessive unpleasure experiences may derive from varied physical and congenital sources—as in children who have allergies or as we found in minimally brain-disordered Cindy—its most common and largest source seems to be, as Freud (1930) observed, the vicissitudes of libidinal object relations. We ought, therefore, to look at how parents rear their children and to explore ways by which their children and, in consequence, society can be better protected against the development of excessive hostility.

IMPLICATIONS FOR PRIMARY PREVENTION

In *The Development of Aggression in Early Childhood*, concurring with Aring (1973), I wrote that we must expend more energy on developing interventional and preventive measures against the development of untoward hostility and destructiveness. At that time, I put forward a number of such recommendations, which I will only mention here.

1. We can help parents, caregivers, teachers, and other child tenders learn and recognize that *excessive unpleasure experiences* mobilize hostile destructiveness in the child. The key phrase is "excessive unpleasure."

Unpleasure is unavoidable; let me also remind the reader that benign experiences of unpleasure lead to adaptation, to learning and growth. As I have emphasized, it is when unpleasure is felt as excessive that it may wreak havoc in the psyche.

2. Children ought to be protected against *too frequent and too prolonged* excessive unpleasure experiences. Because of the long period of childhood psychic immaturity, for a number of years the child's parenting objects serve as his/her auxiliary ego. Variation in the child's psychic adaptive capabilities makes for a complementary variation in necessary adaptive reactivity on the part of the parents.

Indeed, children vary widely in the way in which they tolerate unpleasure. But in all instances during the earliest years, a sufficiently identifiable basic phenomenon occurs which it behooves every parent to learn: *each particular child's ways—behavioral, vocal, and/or affective—of expressing the experience of excessive unpleasure.* Of course, we are speaking of the need for empathy in parenting.

3. We must learn how and teach parents how to *enhance the intrapsychic modification of hostile destructiveness* in the child.

The nurturing environment can create conditions in the child's life whereby the mobilization of hostile destructiveness can be markedly reduced. Even in optimal circumstances, however, it is not possible to prevent totally the mobilization of hostile destructiveness in the human child. Fortunately, there is within the child a far-reaching potential capability to lessen the amount and to mitigate the intensity of hostile destructiveness mobilized within him/her. This gradually developing capability in the child's own psyche to detoxify hostile destructiveness is carried out by two intertwining intrapsychic processes: the *fusion* of libido with aggression, and the *neutralization* of hostile destructiveness. The key factor we observed which propels the development of these intrapsychic functions seems to be the child's wish to protect the love-object from the child's own hostile destructiveness mobilized against that object.

4. Since the evolving of both fusion and neutralization of aggression in the child depends on *a sufficiently positive attachment to the object*, it is imperative that the child is helped to secure such a sufficiently positive attachment.

I concluded these recommendations with a *plea for education for parenting*.

We have found that too often parents do not optimally foster their child's attachment to them, and they often do not know how to minimize or help the child cope with benign or excessive unpleasure.

Our work informs us that parental love alone does not secure a sufficiently positive relationship on the part of the child toward the caregiving parent. Securing a positive relationship also requires some understanding and acceptance of the child's developmental psychodynamic functioning; and it requires skill in child-rearing based on sufficient understanding of psychic development, on the ability to recognize what is growth promoting and growth inhibiting. We can go beyond intuition and empathy to ensure improved understanding and skills in parenting.

Therefore, I have added two further recommendations: For the present generation of parents who have had no formal education in parenting, professionals trained in child development (based especially, I believe, on psychoanalytic-psychodynamic child-development theory) should provide a parent-education service, *not in the context of psychotherapy, but in the context of education*; and for our children who will otherwise also achieve parenthood without formal preparation for it, we mental-health professionals must help provide schools with appropriate education-for-parenting curricula from the earliest grade levels on. We are speaking of a curriculum that will give children an opportunity to learn, in a formal school setting, about *parenting functions, human development*, and *child-rearing issues and methods*, all based on psychodynamic understanding. Our experiences with such curricula with students from kindergarden through grade twelve, to date, have met with more success than anticipated.

TOWARD PREVENTING THE DEVELOPMENT OF EXCESSIVE HOSTILITY IN CHILDREN

Having so urged in 1979, our Early Child Development Program staff is currently developing a new research project about which I will say only a few words. This proposed project is a direct outgrowth of over a decade's work in the development of aggression and in education for parenting. Challenged by our own position, Dr. Linda Giacomo, Dr. Susan V. McLeer, and I have now begun to put these recommendations into effect by further developing and testing a set of educational interventions to be carried out by us with parents in the course of their rearing their children from birth to three years of age. The principal aim of these interventions is to teach parents means of preventing the development of excessive hostility in their children.

Although we proceed with uncertainty, we are propelled especially by our own work and the plea so eloquently and impatiently stated in 1973 by Charles Aring that we put more of our energies toward developing methods to prevent excessive hostility and intervene early in its development in humans. Although many analysts will have misgivings about this effort, I believe that the time has come for some of us to try to open avenues for the application of some of our findings and knowledge in the service of *preventing* numerous individual and collective emotional problems. We cannot wait for the unlikely day when psychoanalysis has unchallengeable theories before we analysts venture in this direction. It may indeed be one of the best testing grounds for our hypotheses and our science.

SUMMARY

This is an updating summary paper of specific aspects of our work on aggression. Many analysts agree that our psychoanalytic formulations of aggression are neither sufficiently nor cohesively formulated, in large part because they are based on Freud's 1920 death-instinct postulate which many analysts reject. In the course of psychoanalytic longitudinal direct observation of children, we developed a strategy for cataloging behavioral manifestations of aggression into four categories. These categorized findings then generated hypotheses which continue to be tested to date. The methodology, categories of manifestations of aggression, and basic hypotheses they generated are briefly presented in this paper.

The hypotheses are then organized into three major trends in aggression which I propose are trends of an instinctual drive. These are *nondestructive aggression, nonaffective (prey) destructiveness*, and *hostile destructiveness*; the last includes sadism (in the broad sense). By virtue of their having essentially the same aim pattern, I propose that these trends constitute components of a single instinctual drive, aggression.

Critical in these formulations are the findings which lead to the hypothesis that hostile destructiveness is *not* an *inborn* drive component. Rather, it is a transmutation of aggression into its specific form of hostile destructiveness, a transmutation which requires an experiential precondition: that of excessive unpleasure (pain). Because hostile destructiveness can be mobilized from birth on and can become automatized quite early by frequent experiences of excessive unpleasure, this trend can give the impression of being inborn.

I propose, furthermore, that this finding generates hypotheses and strategies for preventing the development of excessive hostility in children. The hypotheses underlying such strategies are: (1) Too frequent and too many experiences of excessive unpleasure from birth on lead to the mobilization and potentially the development of excessive hostility in children. (2) Therefore, children need to be protected against such excessive unpleasure experiences, but not against benign unpleasure experiences, since these motivate growth-promoting adaptation. (3) Under specific nurturing conditions, children develop two basic mechanisms to mitigate the unavoidable mobilization of hostility that results even in the best of expectable nurturing environments. These mechanisms are the *fusion* of hostility with libido and its *neutralization* by the ego. (4) The specific nurturing condition referred to in hypothesis (3) is a sufficiently positive mother (parent)-child relationship which yields sufficiently positive self and object cathexes. And (5) As our experience shows, psychodynamically oriented education-for-parenting programs are a fruitful method toward not only preventing the development of excessive hostility, but also preventing or mitigating many common emotional disorders in children.

We concluded with a few words about our study which aims at developing a strategy "Toward Preventing the Development of Excessive Hostility in Children."

REFERENCES

Abraham, L. (1924), A short study of the development of the libido. In: *Selected Papers of Karl Abraham*. New York: Basic Books, 1953, pp. 418-501.

Aring, C. (1973), Aggression and social synergy. *Amer. J. Psychiat.*, 130:297-298.

Eissler, K. R. (1971), Death drive, ambivalence, and narcissism. *The Psychoanalytic Study of the Child*, 26:25-78. New York: Quadrangle Press.

Freud, A. (1958), Child observation and prediction of development: A memorial lecture in honor of Ernst Kris. *The Psychoanalytic Study of the Child*, 13:92-124. New York: International Universities Press.

—— (1965), *Normality and Pathology in Childhood: Assessments of Development*. New York: International Universities Press.

—— (1972), Comments on aggression. *Internat. J. Psycho-Anal.*, 53:163-171.

Freud, S. (1915), Instincts and their vicissitudes. *Standard Edition*, 14:111-140. London: Hogarth Press, 1957.

—— (1920), Beyond the pleasure principle. *Standard Edition*, 18:1-64. London: Hogarth Press, 1955.

—— (1926), Inhibitions, symptoms and anxiety. *Standard Edition*, 20:77-174. London: Hogarth Press, 1959.

—— (1933), New introductory lectures on psycho-analysis. Lecture 34: Explanations and applications. *Standard Edition*, 22:136-157. London: Hogarth Press, 1964.

—— (1930), Civilization and its discontents. *Standard Edition*, 21:59-145. London: Hogarth Press, 1961.

Hartmann, H. (1950), Psychoanalysis and developmental psychology. *The Psychoanalytic Study of the Child*, 5:5-17. New York: International Universities Press.

—— (1952), The mutual influences in the development of the ego and the id. In: *Essays on Ego Psychology*. New York: International Universities Press, 1964, pp. 155-181.

—— (1958), Discussion of Anna Freud's "Child observation and prediction of development: A memorial lecture in honor of Ernst Kris." *The Psychoanalytic Study of the Child*, 5:7-17. New York: International Universities Press.

Kris, E. (1950), Notes on the development and on some current problems of psychoanalytic child psychology. *The Psychoanalytic Study of the Child*, 5:24-46. New York: International Universities Press, 5:24-46. New York:

Loewenstein, R. M. (1940), The vital and somatic instincts. *Internat. J. Psycho-Anal.*, 21:377-400.

Lustman, S. L. (1963), Some issues in contemporary psychoanalytic research. *The Psychoanalytic Study of the Child*, 18:51-74. New York: International Universities Press.

Mahler, M. S. (1965), On the significance of the normal separation-individuation phase. In: *Drives, Affects, Behavior*, vol. 2, ed. M. Schur. New York: International Universities Press, pp. 161-169.

―――― (in collaboration with M. Furer) (1968), *On Human Symbiosis and the Vicissitudes of Individuation*. New York: International Universities Press.

―――― Pine, F., & Bergman, A. (1975), *The Psychological Birth of the Human Infant*. New York: Basic Books.

Parens, H. (1973), Aggression: A reconsideration. *J. Amer. Psychoanal. Assn.*, 21:34-60.

―――― (1979a), *The Development of Aggression in Early Childhood*. New York: Jason Aronson.

―――― (1979b), Developmental considerations of ambivalence. *The Psychoanalytic Study of the Child*, 34:385-420. New York: International Universities Press.

―――― (1980), Toward promoting healthy emotional development: Education for parenting. Unpublished manuscript.

―――― Pollock, L., & Prall, R. C. (1974), Film #3: *Prevention—Early Intervention Mother-Child Groups*. Audio-Visual Medial Section, Eastern Pennsylvania Psychiatric Institute, Philadelphia.

―――― & Prall, R. C. (1974), Film #2: *Toward an Epigenesis of Aggression in Early Childhood*. Audio-Visual Medial Section, Eastern Pennsylvania Psychiatric Institute, Philadelphia, Pa.

―――― & Saul, L. J. (1971), *Dependence in Man: A Psychoanalytic Study*. New York: International Universities Press.

Schur, M. (1966), *The Id and the Regulatory Principles of Mental Functioning*. New York: International Universities Press.

Solnit, A. J. (1972), Aggression: a view of theory building in psychoanalysis. *J. Amer. Psychoanal. Assn.*, 20:435-450.

Spitz, R. (1946), Anaclitic depression: an inquiry into the genesis of psychiatric conditions in early childhood. *The Psychoanalytic Study of the Child*, 2:313-342. New York: International Universities Press.

―――― (1950), Anxiety in infancy: a study of its manifestations in the first year of life. *Internat. J. Psycho-Anal.*, 31:138-143.

―――― (in collaboration with W. G. Cobliner) (1965), *The First Year of Life*. New York: International Universities Press.

Spock, V. (1965), Innate inhibition of aggressiveness in infancy. *The Psychoanalytic Study of the Child*, 20:340-343. New York: International Universities Press.

Part II

Interdisciplinary Problems

Introduction: Psychoanalysis and the Promise of Interdisciplinary Research

GEORGE MORAITIS, M.D.

Interdisciplinary studies in psychoanalysis are as old as the science of psychoanalysis itself. Freud often turned to the social sciences and the humanities in search of evidence that could validate the universality of his theories. In doing so he raised issues and posed questions that aroused powerful reactions from the professionals of other disciplines. Some of the questions generated are still being debated in our times. Professor Spiro's paper, "Psychoanalysis and Cultural Relativism: The Trobriand Case," and Dr. Weiss's response to it is an example of such a debate.

Dialogues among psychoanalysts and the scholars of the humanities and the social sciences have often led to an impasse or premature closure, and psychoanalytic interpretation of the scholar's work frequently creates the impression of having reduced it to relatively few and, to an extent, predictable propositions. By and large the psychoanalyst has been generous in providing the scholar with ideas and themes derived from his clinical theories and experiences, but has done very little in developing an instrument or method with the help of which these ideas can be tested and their validity assessed.

The term "applied psychoanalysis," which has been widely used to describe these enterprises, indicates that the interdisciplinary activity is perceived as taking place in one direction only, that is, psychoanalysis lends its acquired knowledge to other disciplines with no acknowledgment that it receives anything in return.

Some time ago, Gedo and Wolf (1976) pointed out that "it has been fashionable among psychoanalysts to look upon Freud's discipline as something sui generis, created from the void" (p. 12). The origin of such a myth can probably be traced to Freud's reluctance to acknowledge that humanistic studies and philosophical issues influenced the shaping of psychoanalytic theories along with clinical data and the physical sciences. The belief of creation from the void may simply represent a romantic perception of the history of psychoanalysis, based on the psychoanalyst's passionate need to establish the new science as an autonomous and independent entity in the intellectual community. Such views, however, inevitably affect not only the analyst's perception of the history of psychoanalysis, but also the perceptions of the future position and development of psychoanalysis in the intellectual community and the culture at large.

Freud's effort to emphasize the uniqueness of psychoanalysis and define it as a discipline distinctly different from others is by no means surprising. All sciences select and maintain an area of endeavor that becomes the limited "universe" within which they operate. By establishing such boundaries, the investigator attempts to obtain some control over the variables that affect his observations and limit his work to manageable proportions. The human mind does not have the capacity to master the universe in its entirety. In view of these limitations, the investigator demarcates a part of it which he defines as the area of his investigation and which becomes "the limited universe" within which he operates and to which he dedicates all his professional activities.

A discipline can be maintained only by establishing boundaries that are clear and, to an extent at least, acceptable to all disciplines operating in a given scientific and scholarly community.

Understandably, Freud attempted to draw these boundaries as clearly as he could and place psychoanalysis apart from the domain of the other disciplines. He achieved this by defining (1) the territory within which psychoanalysis operates and (2) the observational post that the psychoanalyst must maintain as he explores this territory. He named his territory "the unconscious" and established the clinical method of psychoanalysis—and, more specifically, the analyst's stance—as the observation post of the new science.

The physical sciences have not attempted to invade Freud's territory, the unconscious. They have, however, questioned its existence and shown little interest in taking into account the psychoanalytic observation post and the data that have been accumulated from its use. Despite Freud's vigorous efforts to place psychoanalysis under the *Weltanschauung* of science, the community of sciences has treated psychoanalysis at best with benign neglect and, at times, with contempt.

More recently, even the physical sciences have come to realize the subjective nature of all human perceptions. It is reasonable to assume that such a realization has increased the scientist's awareness that the perception of reality is a psychological phenomenon that needs to be studied as such. Although this may be true, there is no evidence that the scientific community has turned to psychoanalysis for help. Investigators in the physical sciences have not as yet felt the need to investigate the input of their own humanity into their data through the utilization of the psychoanalytic method. They may have come closer to realizing the existence of the territory "unconscious" which Freud discovered, but have not as yet shown significant interest in the psychoanalytic observation post as a research tool that can facilitate their pursuits.

As opposed to the physical sciences, the humanities do not only acknowledge the existence of the unconscious but have massively invaded the field with the help of the social sciences. Perhaps more accurately it can be said that the humanities perceive psychoanalysis as a guest, and all too often an unwelcome guest, in a territory that they have always considered as theirs. "Know thyself" was not introduced to poetry and to philosophy by psychoanalysis. The art of introspection is at least as old as the ancient Greek culture and has been cultivated in the Western civilizations by a number of important thinkers, starting with Montaigne during the sixteenth century. During the last several decades scholars have again directed their attention inward with renewed enthusiasm. They have come to recognize the degree to which their observations are shaped by their own minds. In this contemporary, postpositivistic period of intellectual history, the concept of interpretation and the search for meaning have been advocated as an alternative to the pursuit of knowledge, as a result of which to "doubt" and to "wonder" are more respectable than to "know." To blur is more acceptable than to define. Ambiguity has become a more reliable indicator of wisdom and often an acceptable point of arrival.

Psychoanalysis has contributed significantly to this

intellectual climate. After eighty years of intensive efforts the recognition of the "psychic reality" has greatly increased. In all scholarly activities there is evidence of an increased sense of awareness of the existence of the internal world and a decreased sense of confidence in the accuracy of man's perceptions of the external reality. Our reliance on our own sense organs has been dramatically reduced, and we no longer can afford to use them alone as evidence of knowledge. The intricate nature of the relationship between external and internal that all disciplines have come to recognize indicates that any level of knowledge of the external world includes some elements of self-knowledge, and any level of self-knowledge must take into account perceptions of external reality.

As the boundary between internal and external is becoming blurred, so too is the territorial boundary of psychoanalysis. Psychoanalysis can no longer maintain the illusionary monopoly of the exploration of the unconscious which has openly become the field of endeavor of many disciplines.

It can be argued that the autonomy of psychoanalysis as a science and as an intellectual discipline can still be defended as long as its observation post, the psychoanalytic method, is kept intact. The method and tool pride of the psychoanalyst which Heinz Kohut identified a long time ago are the outcome of such convictions. Excessive reliance on the method, however, is a defensive position that facilitates rigidity and isolation and interferes with growth and development. This is particularly true when method is confused with procedures and rituals in a way such that the essence of it is compromised in the process.

I believe the time has come to redefine both the territorial boundaries of psychoanalysis and its observation post, the psychoanalytic method. This is a critical period in the development of psychoanalysis which demands the abandonment of old myths and the acknowledgment of certain realities. Psychoanalysis was not created from the void and neither can it survive in it. No science can establish territorial boundaries and observation posts without negotiating these with other sciences and scholarly disciplines. Psychoanalysis cannot merely "export" knowledge without accepting input from other intellectual disciplines. To survive in the intellectual community the professional psychoanalyst must become an active participant who is prepared to influence and be influenced, both to give and to take.

The papers presented in this section have been written in this spirit. They are not papers in "applied psychoanalysis." They represent pieces of interdisciplinary studies in which psychoanalysts attempt to enter into a dialogue with a historian, a sociologist, and an anthropologist. This of course is not an easy task. Engaging in a dialogue is basically different from participating in a debate. Participants of a debate do not really address each other. They address a third party, an audience visible or invisible for the benefit of which they enter into a competitive exchange with each other. A dialogue is a collaborative effort, not a competitive one. Such collaboration not only takes into account the relative accuracy of a presented thesis, but constitutes a process in the course of which a series of ideas are developed without undue pressure to arrive at closure.

My collaborative work with professionals of the social sciences and the humanities has convinced me that interdisciplinary research cannot be effectively carried out without the proper methodology that takes into account the structural consistency and organization of the disciplines involved—the history, boundaries, language, values, and aims of a given discipline must be understood if a true and productive dialogue is to emerge. Even more importantly, such methodology must take into account the humanity of the thinker and the uniqueness of his thinking. Psychoanalysts probably have very little difficulty in accepting the notion that ideas are not created from a void, but are deeply embedded in the thinker's personality. It seems, however, that the reverse is also true. Ideas have a powerful influence on personality and, to a significant extent, determine its development.

After years of experience it has become evident that the clinical psychoanalytic method is in essence a form of dialogue. Some practitioners may see it as more of a dialogue than others, but by and large analysts no longer see themselves as a blank screen. The analyst's experience in the clinical situation must be utilized in his dialogues with professionals of other disciplines. Of course the psychoanalytic method cannot be simply transplanted from the clinical situation to the interdisciplinary field. Modifications are needed to meet the demands of the new situation, and they must be carefully thought through. As I have indicated elsewhere, I have experimented with such collaborations and with considerable success. Although I am sure there are other approaches to such an enterprise, it seems to me that the essence of such a collaboration for the psychoanalyst rests with his capacity to acknowledge, tolerate, and, it is hoped, utilize the input these dialogues generate for the advancement of the science of psychoanalysis. Interdisciplinary studies should not become another form of psychoanalytic practice. They constitute a truly academic activity designed to promote crossfertilization of the participating disciplines.

Psychoanalysis may not be very popular among the social scientists and the humanists. Sometimes the objections are loud and the hostility evident. It seems to me, however, that a good deal of this negative position is a form of rhetoric that should not be taken at face value. In my dialogues with the professionals of these disciplines I have detected a strong desire for a meaningful exchange with the psychoanalyst when it is offered under circumstances that are not experienced as demeaning. The situation is very different as far as the physical and applied sciences are concerned. Despite eighty years of intensive efforts we have not yet proved our case. From the time of its discovery psychoanalysis has strongly claimed and defended its scientific status. The other sciences, however, continue to be oblivious to our claim and disinterested in our findings. There are, of course, exceptions. Cognitive studies and, more recently, infant research offer an opportunity for a dialogue between the psychoanalyst and other scientists. It seems, however, that most of these enterprises are primarily one-sided. The psychoanalyst is attempting to collect from others data not collectible by the use of the formal psychoanalytic method. Some of these data are easily integrated into the existing psychoanalytic theory, but some are not. In such a case, what is the proper course of action? Should the psychoanalyst revise his theories or ask his collaborator to take another look at his experimental findings? In the absence of a true dialogue based on a methodological structure there is no way to answer such questions.

Psychoanalysis has often been described as the bridge between the sciences and the humanities. By placing his discipline between the two ends of the intellectual spectrum the psychoanalyst has attempted to maintain a precarious and, to an extent, unattainable balance. Caught between the competition and antagonism of the humanist and the "benign neglect" of the scientific community, the psychoanalyst imagines having two homes when in actuality he has neither. He is reluctant to accept the limited hospitality the world of the humanities has offered him, and despite all the psychoanalytic rhetoric there are no signs of recognition of psychoanalytic contributions to the field of knowledge by the scientific world.

The psychoanalyst cannot find a home for his discipline by submitting his credentials to epistemology. It is not sufficient to "prove" his case through a series of intellectual syllogisms. He must demonstrate his usefulness through his work, so that other scholars and scientists will feel motivated to enter into a dialogue with him. In the clinical situation we never demand recognition from our patients for what we have done for them. After a successful analysis, however, the patient "knows" of the analyst's contribution and is grateful for it. Interdisciplinary exchanges should produce a similar sense of satisfaction and discovery to both sides. It is this sense of discovery that constitutes the basis of the psychoanalytic "home" in the clinical and interdisciplinary field. In order to achieve that, the psychoanalyst must address the vital issues of the intellectual community and demonstrate the usefulness of his discipline on the frontiers of scholarly and scientific activities.

In this section we present four papers and some of the responses they generated, as a small sample of the type of interdisciplinary exchange that can facilitate the much-needed dialectic between psychoanalysis and the scholars of other disciplines. Professor Spiro's paper addresses an old issue in psychoanalysis and anthropology, and places it under the light of new ideas. Dr. Gehrie and Professor Kracke, both anthropologists with extensive knowledge of psychoanalysis, as well as Dr. Weiss, a psychoanalyst, respond to the paper.

Professor Levine, a sociologist, makes a comparison between the ideas and lives of Freud and Weber and proceeds to develop a specific thesis about the effects of these ideas on our culture. In my response to him I point out the differences between scientific principles and moral values which correlate with the difference between the "limited universe" of the investigator and the larger universe of a given culture.

The two papers pertaining to *The Education of Henry Adams*, one written by Professor Schwehn and the other by myself, are designed to illustrate to the reader how a true interdisciplinary dialogue can facilitate the scholarly pursuit of each collaborator.

We realize this is too brief a presentation to do justice to the fundamental issues this introduction has touched upon. A lot more needs to be said. In this publication our effort is limited to identifying some of the vital issues in interdisciplinary research, the recognition of which can facilitate the opening of new horizons not only to psychoanalysis but to other scholarly disciplines as well.

REFERENCE

Gedo, J., & Wolf, E. (1976), From the history of introspective psychology: The humanist strain. In: *Freud: The Fusion of Science and Humanism*, ed. J. E. Gedo and G. H. Pollock [*Psychological Issues*, Monogr. 34/35]. New York: International universities Press.

5

Freud, Weber, and Modern Rationales of Conscience

DONALD N. LEVINE, Ph.D.

> "As the rationalized mythology of our culture, modern science has played a larger role in reformulating our moral sense than its defenders often care to admit."—Philip Rieff (1978)

Sigmund Freud and Max Weber belong to that elite of historical personalities whom Benjamin Nelson (1965b) described as "men of extraordinary range, intellectual and spiritual titans, far removed from the general run of those who win mention in the annals of politics, science, scholarship, or learned pretense" (p. 149). They deserve to be understood, he added, not as mere disciplinary specialists, but as makers of ideas, movers of men, and re-

This paper was written at the Center for Advanced Study in the Behavioral Sciences. I am grateful for financial support provided by the Center, the Guggenheim Foundation, and the National Science Foundation #BNS 76 22943. For helpful comments on an earlier version of this paper, I am much indebted to Horace Judson, John Perry, and Guenther Roth.

spondents to questions of ultimate significance.[1] Indeed, there is scarcely an aspect of the human condition Freud and Weber did not touch. And yet, despite their extraordinary range, the struggle to create a very distinctive discipline is central to the story of each of their lives. We can learn much about the ambiguous connection between the sciences of man and modern moral sensibilities by reflecting on the broadly similar contours and repercussions of those struggles.

I

We hesitate to compare them, these originative individuals, not least because they founded disciplines often thought of as antitheses: psychoanalysis examines conflict and integration within the individual psyche, and requires investigators to use their own inner responses to subjects as tools of observation; sociology looks at processes of conflict and integration among pluralities of actors, and typically demands that observers exclude their personal responses to subjects. And we recall the condescension with which each of these discipline-builders regarded the other's specialty. For Freud, after all, sociology was merely "applied psychology" (1921, p. 71); for Weber, psychoanalysis, though potentially promising, was marred by inflated pretensions and misguided disciples (Marianne Weber, 1975, pp. 375-380), while in any case he thought it was grossly erroneous to regard any kind of psychology as a foundation for sociology (1968, p. 19).

Differences of this order have tended to obscure some

[1] This passage appears in an essay in which Nelson compares Weber to Luther, Hegel, and Marx. That he consistently thought of Freud in the same company is clear from many other writings (1954, 1957, 1965a).

striking similarities between the two disciplines—in particular, their parallels in historical development.[2] Note, for example, that both disciplines took shape in the same years. Although earlier writers had anticipated their key ideas, both psychoanalysis and sociology assumed their modern institutionalized form between 1895 and 1915. During this period, the first professional journals of the two fields were founded and their first professional associations established. The half-decade in which Freud published "The Interpretation of Dreams" and "Three Essays on the Theory of Sexuality" was flanked by the publication of what are arguably the four decisively germinal works of modern sociology—Durkheim's *Le Suicide* (1897), Weber's essays on the Protestant Ethic (1905, 1906), Simmel's *Soziologie* (1908), and Cooley's *Social Organization* (1909).

The emergence of both fields, moreover, aroused storms of opposition.[3] In their embattled beginnings, they were nourished by devoted proponents whose activities have been described in the suggestive language of collective behavior as the "psychoanalytic movement" and the "sociological movement." Although the intellectual heartland of both disciplines was Continental Europe, they developed extensively as stable professions only in the more open society of the United States, just as both were suppressed by the totalitarian regimes of Bolshevik Russia and Nazi Germany.

Such similarities in the historical setting of these dis-

---

[2] This is not to mention the many ways in which the two disciplines have been viewed or used as providing complementary contributions to the analysis of comparable problems. On the latter topic, see Wallerstein and Smelser (1969) and Levine (1978).

[3] This is not to gainsay Sulloway's strong argument (1979) that the extent to which Freud's ideas were opposed by his contemporaries, especially in the early years of the psychoanalytic movement, has been greatly exaggerated by Freud and his followers.

ciplines suggest that we might fruitfully look for points of comparison between their pre-eminent originative thinkers.[4] Superficial resemblances appear at once. Both Freud and Weber were born in Central Europe just after the middle of the nineteenth century—Freud in Moravia in 1856, Weber in Thuringia in 1864. Both were highly successful university students in conventional fields and served tours of military duty in their twenties. Each lived at his parents' house through young adulthood (Freud until 27, Weber until 29), a practice common at the time for aspiring professionals. At 30, each achieved his first independent professional status—Freud opening his medical practice in Vienna in 1886, Weber acceding to a chair at Freiburg in 1894. Each was married within months of his thirtieth birthday, Freud to Martha Bernays, Weber to Marianne Schnitger. Both marriages were stable though not always happy; both women were devoted wives and outlived their husbands by several years.[5] In

[4] Although sociology did not, like psychoanalysis, take shape under the aegis of a central presiding genius, most sociologists today would probably agree that Max Weber was our single most impressive founding father. Although, moreover, in contrast to the talmudic thoroughness with which Freud's writings have been continually studied within the psychoanalytic community, Weber's works only began to receive much scholarly attention from sociologists after the middle of this century; today they remain texts with which sociologists of many specialties actively contend and which contain research programs and ideas still judged by many to be at the frontier of the field (see, e.g., Schluchter, 1979, pp. 11-13; Collins, 1980). Weber's *current* stature within sociology can thus be taken to qualify him to stand alongside Freud as the pre-eminent founding genius of his discipline (a fortiori of that conception of it which he baptized as "interpretive sociology.") Even so, it should be noted that this honor must be shared with Emile Durkheim and Georg Simmel, a point which Ben Nelson alluded to in the 1965a paper mentioned above.

[5] The contrasting roles played by these women in the two marriages should be noted. Martha Freud was the more conventional housewife and mother. She gave birth to and raised six children. She shared little of Freud's professional interests. Marianne Weber remained childless, but was much more of an intellectual companion to Max. She co-hosted his famous intellectual salons, and it is to her editing of Weber's posthumous publications and rich biography of her husband that we owe much of the recovery of Weber's lifework.

the first decade of this century both men made visits to the United States, visits associated with significant developments in their careers. In contrast with these and other biographical parallels, one major difference must be noted: Weber died, suddenly and prematurely, in 1920 at the age of 56, from pneumonia, part of the influenza pandemic following World War I, whereas Freud, although losing his daughter Sophie to that same epidemic, survived to the age of 83.

Freud and Weber resembled each other temperamentally as well—startlingly so. Of serious, often stern demeanor,yet they were men of lively humor; masters of irony, both in self-deriding wit and in polemic; possessed of a demanding sense of honor, and prickly in pride; distant in personal relations, and marginal to the institutional establishments of their time; harsh in judging others, yet capable of empathy and help for an enormous diversity of other human types; impatient with sentimentality of any sort; scornful of modern apologists for religion, yet powerfully attracted to the interpretation of religion as a historical phenomenon; animated by a lust for understanding and a capacity for intellectual work of gigantic proportions, and devoted above all to an ethic of intellectual integrity.

Of all the parallels between the lives of Freud and Weber perhaps the most dramatic is the fact that in the very same year, 1897, both men entered a period of emotional turmoil triggered by the recent deaths of their fathers, periods which biographers of each have identified as turning points in the development of their mature intellectual orientations. The death of Freud's father made him "feel quite uprooted," and intensified a malaise, extending from 1894 through 1900, in which he suffered moods of depression, moments of intellectual paralysis, and various somatic disturbances (Jones, 1953, pp. 324-325; Sulloway, 1979, p. 215). Freud's response to this turbulence included his rigorous self-analysis, in the course of which he uncovered early erotic feelings toward his mother and hostile wishes against his father, discoveries that provided insights and confirmations for his prodigious work on the interpretation of dreams and on the Oedipus complex.

Weber's experience was more traumatic. In June 1897, on or just after his parents' wedding anniversary, Weber had an angry confrontation with his father, in which he "ordered his father out of his house to permit his mother and himself the undisturbed enjoyment of one another's company. It was the first time that Weber had ever revealed to his father the full depths of his bitterness" (Mitzman, 1970, p. 152). Seven weeks later, without the two men meeting again, his father died. The aftermath was a spell of nervous exhaustion that began five years of intense suffering, including chronic insomnia, depression, and intermittent paralysis of his mental functions (far worse than Freud's). Describing the onset of this affliction, Marianne Weber (1975) wrote that "an evil thing from the unconscious underground of life stretched out its claws toward him," but she records Weber's own view that the illness was "perhaps only a long-gathering cloud, whose final discharge would almost be like a liberation from a mysteriously threatening, hostile power," a liberation which "might prepare the way for a greater *harmony* of his vital powers in the future" (pp. 234, 236). When Weber recovered, he embarked on one of the most momentous periods of intellectual creativity ever achieved, and in directions—Mitzman has shown—that reflect the working through of materials reflecting a long suppressed closeness to the values of his mother.

II

Although further details of the dynamics of these acute episodes of what Ellenberger (1970) has termed "creative illness" are fascinating to compare, what I want to stress here is that those periods marked watersheds in the transition from one kind of disciplinary orientation to another. Freud, in his thirties, considered himself a neurologist and neuroanatomist. He analyzed human phenomena in terms of neuronal connections, and utilized the impersonal imagery of mechanical equilibria, electric circuits, and circulatory systems. He sought, as he wrote in 1895 in the words of his unpublished "Project for a Scientific Psychology," "to represent psychical processes as quantitatively determinate states of specifiable material particles" (p. 295).

By his late forties, Freud had adopted a new professional self-image. Abandoning the biophysical approach, he viewed himself now as a revolutionary in the field of *psychology*. Although, as Sulloway (1979) has shown in his masterly intellectual biography, Freud retained a strong though transformed identification with biology, his discipline building, based on his earlier discovery that the somatic symptoms of hysterical patients had a psychological meaning, was couched in terms of the interpretations of meanings and motives. The new discipline of psychoanalysis did not, he argued, deny the importance of biological or constitutional factors; but its distinctive mission and expertise were to disclose the hidden and forgotten motives underlying human behavior. Freud (1927a) would go on to insist that "psycho-analysis is not a specialized branch of medicine," but only a "part of psychology" (p. 252).

Weber's professional orientation also changed in mid-career. Trained in legal and economic history, Weber started his career with appointments in economics at the Universities of Freiburg and Heidelberg. His scholarly writings analyzed historical phenomena in terms of such impersonal categories as forms of property, size of rural estates, forms of trading association, and conflict between economic classes. Following the period of his breakdown, Weber turned away from a career as a professor of economics. Like Freud, Weber came to prefer to work outside the constraints of a university environment. What is more, he could no longer stand being tied down to the discipline of economics. And in the first major scholarly production following his recovery, Weber shifted his analytic interest to emphasize the ideas and motives that organize different kinds of economic activity, an emphasis reflecting insights he had gained during the 1890s: the significance of subjectively held ideals in inducing farm workers to emigrate from the estates of East Prussia, and the role of religious ideas in developing the spirit of modern capitalism.

In his late forties, moreover, Weber began to identify himself with the discipline of sociology, a field he had previously referred to with a certain disdain.[6] He did not,

---

[6] Weber's shift to sociology was prompted by a number of considerations, including his interest in promoting the *empirical* examination of certain subjects, notably law and the state, which had largely been studied from a normative perspective; his wish to undertake the *comparative* examination of questions that previously were studied chiefly in a particularized, historical manner; and his hope (to some extent shattered by his experience with the German Sociological Association) to find colleagues similarly disposed to investigate social phenomena in a "value-free" scientific manner. Weber's disdain for much of what was produced in his adopted field never faded. "Most of what goes under the name of sociology is humbug [*Schwindel*]," he declared in his farewell address at Heidelberg in 1919. It was to rescue sociology from its collectivistic and organicist concepts, he once remarked, that he had come to label himself a sociologist, and this concern underlay his repeated stress, in programmatic statements, on its mandate to interpret the actions of individuals.

however, embrace the prevailing sociologies of the day but rather a new version, which he designated *Verstehende* (interpretive) *Soziologie*—a sociology oriented to understanding the subjective meanings and motives of individuals. Although Weber never neglected the importance of such variables as geographic settings, demographic factors, property arrangements, and technological levels, he came to argue for his kind of sociology that what was "decisive for its status as a science" was its capacity to provide interpretations of meaningul action, a task which "it alone can do" (Weber, 1968, pp. 24, 17).

Thus, Freud and Weber began their intellectual careers in disciplines that disposed them to analyze human phenomena in impersonal terms through the language of material causation. As they became increasingly sensitive to the significance of subjective meanings and motives in accounting for action, they became dualists, holding and never relinquishing the view that both material conditions and purposive ideas are important determinants of conduct. Yet, despite the continuing prominence of biological notions in Freud's thought and Weber's lifelong preoccupation with institutional structures and economic imperatives, each man moved beyond his earlier disciplinary commitments to create a new discipline whose mission he held to be a distinctive capacity to provide ways of understanding the vicissitudes of human intentionality.

Beyond a shift in disciplinary self-image, Freud and Weber developed in two other ways that were remarkably similar, following their periods of depression and emo-

tional crisis. Both emerged as critics of modern civilization. In the first decade of this century, both issued generalized critiques of modern conditions as a source of
pernicious constraints on human freedom. Weber began
in 1905 with scattered shots against the stifling effects
of mechanized industrial production and capitalist commerce, and went on to attack the no less repressive "animated machine" of state bureaucracy.[7] Freud, with his
1908 paper on "civilized" sexual morality and modern
nervous illness, prefigured his later critique of the powerfully repressive price of modern civilization.

Neither man was disposed to mobilize constituencies
to take arms against the repressive forces which he diagnosed so cuttingly. Instead, each found a way to sublimate in his professional work his desire to enhance
freedom under the conditions of modern life. Thus, another parallel change in their orientations was the disposition to stress the emancipatory potential of the new
disciplines they were shaping. The aesthetic, therapeutic,
and political functions of the new sciences seemed less
important than the capacity to help people become more
aware of the unconscious premises of their thoughts and
deeds and thereby reach heightened levels of self-conscious free choice. Freud was consistently cautious about
the therapeutic potential of psychoanalysis, a caution
that increased with age, but he never lost faith that the
interpretation of dreams was the road to the unconscious,
and that the arduous work of psychoanalytic collaboration was justified because it helped the analysand "to
acquire the extra piece of mental freedom which distinguishes conscious mental activity . . . from unconscious"
(Freud, 1915, p. 170).

---

[7] For more extended discussion of Weber's views on the repressiveness of modern economic and political institutions, see Beetham
(1974) and Levine (1981).

Weber (1948) rejected as illusions the older justifications of scientific endeavor—science as the way to "true being," "true art," "true nature," "true God," or "true happiness" (pp. 140-143)—as well as the attempts of his contemporaries to make social science a vehicle for political action. Rather, he saw sociology valuable chiefly as a means to enhance subjective freedom. It does this by disclosing the empirical and normative implications of alternative values and goals, thereby enabling actors to transcend the "inarticulate half-consciousness or actual unconsciousness" of the meanings of their action which characterizes the "shallowness of our routinized daily existence," so that activities are not "permitted to run on as an event in nature but are instead to be consciously guided." This reflected his conviction that when we are conscious of performing actions rationally—in the absence of physical and psychic compulsions, vehement affects, disturbed judgment, and encrusted custom—we then experience the "highest measure of an empirical feeling of freedom" (Weber, 1968, p. 21; 1949, pp. 18, 124-125).

III

Protracted emotional crises drove Freud and Weber toward the creation of the new disciplines of psychoanalysis and interpretive sociology—disciplines whose programs were to investigate human motives and whose declared missions were to help combat the repressive features of modern society by fortifying actors with additional reserves of mental freedom. But what were those emotional crises?

Whatever else was involved—and, of course, much was—it is clear that Freud and Weber alike experienced a deep conflict between the commitment to the professional norms of scientific work and an urge to play some kind of prophetic role. Much as they sought to abide by—indeed, to institute—rigorous procedures for the analysis of human phenomena, they struggled no less to find a way to shape the conscience of their times. In adulthood, each expressed discomfort with the pedantic requirements of a career in science. Something of the romantic tenor of Freud's boyhood dreams to become a great military or political leader never left him. "I am not really a man of science, not an observer, not an experimenter, and not a thinker," Freud confessed at the age of 44. "I am nothing but by temperament a *conquistador* ... with the curiosity, the boldness, and the tenacity that belongs to that type of being" (Jones, 1953, p. 348). Weber's strong political aspirations are well-known, and they pursued him all his life.[8] It seemed that as a young man he had little calling indeed for what he would later describe as the true life of a scientist, one who eschews the quest for active experience, who can readily put on blinders, and who is disposed to make tens of thousands of quite trivial computations in his head for months at a time. "Nothing is more abominable to me than the arrogance of the 'intellectual' and learned professions," he declared in his mid-twenties (Mitzman, 1970, p. 66).

With the doors to political activism closed to them—Freud because of his Jewish background and his expedient adjustment to a career in medical practice, Weber because of his disdain for the quality of German politicians and the inffectualness of the Wilhelmine par-

[8] "All his life Weber was passionate in following political events, relating to them, and speaking of them. ... Max Weber did not become a leading statesman; he remained a political writer. But although he did not come to engage in political action, he lived as in a state of perpetual readiness to do so" (Jaspers, 1946, pp. 7, 9).

liament—each seems to have transformed his ambition to be a leader of men into a wish to become some kind of moral prophet. Although they shared a deep antagonism to organized religion, and were convinced that for educated moderns to resort to religion betrayed a weakness of character and intellect, Freud and Weber had the strongest admiration for the religiously inspired leader Oliver Cromwell and, like Cromwell, maintained strong identifications with prophetic figures from the Old Testament. At fifteen, Weber (not a Jew) had studied Hebrew in order to read the Old Testament in the original. Both men devoted their last major substantive investigations to the study of ancient Judaism, producing interpretations that were revolutionary, in different ways, for emphasizing the world-historical impact of the moralizing work of the biblical Jews. As is well known, Freud attributed his capacity to tolerate a position of heroic nonconformity to having a character specifically Jewish. It was Moses (albeit Egyptianized) whom he credited with laying the basis for that character, and Freud more than once intimated that he likened himself to the figure of Moses (Freud, 1939, pp. 107-111; Fromm, 1959, pp. 76-80). Weber similarly seems to have maintained a strong identification with the haranguing prophets of Judea, and with Jeremiah in particular (Weber, 1948, pp. 26-27; Marianne Weber, 1975, pp. 593-594).

If Freud and Weber did not hold Nietzsche's view that the Jews had introduced a debilitating moral force into European culture, they did have a keen post-Nietzschean sense that their time was one in which the old gods were dead or dying, that people were searching for new ones, and that a heroic response was in order. Both felt some impulse to provide prophetic answers for their contemporaries and aroused in their followers and readers some expectation that they had the capacity to provide those answers. On the other hand, both felt constrained to tell themselves and others time and again that the wish for new prophets represented an immature desire and that in any case they held no warrant from their strictly observed professional code to minister to such a wish.

Close observers of the two men have left us comparable accounts of what seems to have been a prophetic disposition, riven by conflict. Max Graf (1942, p. 471), participant in the Wednesday-evening meetings of the first psychoanalytic society, described the atmosphere of those sessions as that of a religious meeting and portrayed Freud as a kind of religious prophet, albeit the prophet of a new scientific methodology (see also Sulloway, 1979, pp. 480-481). Philip Rieff's (1978) intimate review of the Freudian canon concludes: "Freud did not have a religious temperament. He looked forward to no salvations. . . . Freud is a prophet nonetheless. . . . He could not avoid drawing morals from his diagnoses and influencing attitudes by his interpretations. In psychoanalysis, Freud found a way of being the philosopher that he desired to be" (pp. x, 3). Erich Fromm (1959) has made the point less circumspectly: "[Freud's] wish to have founded a new philosophical-scientific religion was repressed and thus unconscious" (p. 93).

Heinrich Rickert (1926, p. 236), Weber's lifelong friend and colleague, observed that Weber struggled with a passion to pull others along with him like a mighty preacher, and that his charismatic effect as lecturer stemmed from conveying to his listeners a sense that he was suppressing an appeal that was much more powerful than his words let on. Karl Jaspers (1946), Weber's student and friend, hailed Weber as "the true philosopher of the time in which he lived," but went on to note that "Weber did not teach a philosophy; he was a philosophy. . . . As his life was a unique philosophic expression . . . so his scholarly work is a unique, fully actualized expression of his mode of concrete philosophizing. . . . Sociology is only an arm of Weber's deeper philosophical nature, a nature that he keeps concealed and that becomes visible only indirectly" (pp. 42, 8, 41).

What these descriptions suggest is that both men worked out the following compromise formation: they devised disciplines through which they could pack into the interstices of their professional work the elements of a new moral annunciation.

What was the content of that annunciation? I suggest that it consisted, in both cases, of the following five elements.

First, psychoanalysis and interpretive sociology were, in effect, each deemed by their creators to be the prime vehicle of moral enlightenment for civilized persons living in the age of modern science. They were thus to replace the authoritative agencies of church, state, and social custom.

Second, these disciplines were not to replace old beliefs with new doctrines. Both men insisted that the practitioners of their disciplines were not to be purveyors of value judgments, and they both railed against those who tried to construct and impose *Weltanschauungen* on patients or students.

Third, the moral contribution of these disciplines was seen, rather, as a matter of enhancing the rational capacities of autonomous actors. It was to free them from being bound by the inner compulsions of unconscious drives and the external compulsions of group opinion.

Fourth, this entailed the patient and dispassionate examination of all relevant facts in one's situation and of one's own unconscious assumptions about them. The effect of the passions in creating and sustaining illusions was to be counteracted through the efforts of professionals trained in the neutral analysis of human wishes: the mirroring responses and interpretations of the psychoanalyst, the value-neutral empathic understanding and explanatory hypotheses of the interpretive sociologist.

Fifth, this purely formal and technical approach to moral education presumed a commitment to certain values. Freud and Weber joined an apparently neutral procedural formula to a gospel of intellectual integrity, courage, subjective freedom, and self-responsibility. Intellectual integrity is required if investigators are to provide truthful and adequate interpretations. Courage is required if investigators and their clients are to assimilate what are inevitably painful facts about human realities. Subjective freedom from unconscious compulsions of varying sorts is the proximate goal which justifies those demanding exertions, and personal responsibility is the ultimate objective for which enhanced subjective freedom is needed. Time and again, forthrightly or by implication, Freud and Weber emerged as advocates of this complex of values.

This was no ethic for the fainthearted. It promised no garden of pleasures or universal happiness. Psychoanalysis in Freud's mature view was a long and arduous process, making great demands on analyst and analysand alike. It could provide "the inestimable service of making the patient's hidden . . . impulses immediate and manifest" (1912, p. 108), but this could at best result in transforming a person's neurotic symptoms into "common unhappiness" (1895b, p. 305). In similarly sober terms, Weber announced:

> We are not striving for a world in which more men will have greater happiness. No one who sees the prospects of things anticipates that more happiness lies ahead in the forseeable future. We strive rather to promote the distribution of those traits of personal self-responsibil-

ity . . . which our culture has taught us to hold dear. [quoted in Nelson, 1965b, p. 158].

Their ethic called above all for the abandonment of tenacious illusions about the world, illusions that reflect the persistence of childish needs for dependence and consolation.[9] Freud and Weber alike hoped that " 'the trained relentlessness of vision' for the world as it is" which their teachings instilled would help those who followed them to gain "greater strength to endure it and be equal to its everyday manifestations" (Marianne Weber, 1975, p. 684).

IV

In the last few decades critics of Freud and Weber have called attention to some of the problematic repercussions of these moral teachings. Weber has been faulted for abandoning any principled defense of liberal constitutionalism, thus making it easier for erstwhile followers like Robert Michels and Carl Schmitt to go on to embrace Fascism and Nazism. Freud has been accused of propounding ideas used by some of his followers to advance a cult of unbridled hedonism and an ideal of shamelessness. Such charges typically neglect to point out that

[9] Freud protested "against every romance and against the enthusiasms that accompany each stage of life—the id illusions of dependence, love, happiness, union; the super-ego illusions of the good society, progress, brotherhood, fatherhood, finally even of health; the ego illusion of reason, energetic, independent, and purposeful in a purposeless and meaningless universe" (Rieff, 1978, p. xii).

"Everyone who finds himself encumbered or inconvenienced by what I am tempted to call the 'Social Reality Principle' will want to polemicize against Weber. Weber is both 'stumbling block' and 'scandal' to all who ardently quest for the total and the instant regeneration of self, society and culture; all utopians and ideologists—whether of the left, right or center—who are confirmed in their irrefutable assurances by every turn of history" (Nelson, 1965a, p. 193).

totalitarianism and hedonism are positions far from what either man personally found tolerable, that those positions have been roundly attacked by most of their followers, and that no author can be held responsible for the misuse of his ideas by others. Even so, it remains important to ask whether there is anything in their teachings that does lend itself to being cast in such questionable directions. In particular, is there any basis to the repeatedly leveled charge that the teachings of Freud and Weber support a kind of nihilism—a position that rules out any firm, rationally defensible moral commitments?[10]

It must indeed be acknowledged that a purely formal ethic of maximizing subjective freedom is compatible with courses of action that most of us find morally repugnant. Recent efforts to promote the teaching of this sort of ethics in American schools, as William Bennett (1980) has now argued, have only accentuated already pervasive trends toward moral cynicism and flabbiness.[11] That people can freely elect to annihilate groups whom they detest, to devote their lives to sadistic pleasures, or to support the idea of nuclear warfare—all of these options in the name of freedom, of course—is a fact of our times.

---

[10] For discussions of the charge that nihilism is implied by their teachings, see, for Freud, LaPiere (1959, p. 53) and Rieff (1978, p. 321); for Weber, Strauss (1953, pp. 36-78) and Factor and Turner (1979).

[11] "A child starting school in America in the 1980's can now begin his education with 'instruction' in values-clarification at the elementary level, wherein he will learn 'that there is no right and wrong' and that 'life is a lovely banquet' in which he can take what he likes. Then he can go on to high school and engage in 'cognitive moral development' where he will learn to question all forms of authority, particularly that of the family, whose 'conditioning,' as this Hastings Center report calls it, he will learn to recognize for what it is. From there, he can go on to college where he will learn to question the 'permanent validity' of American cultural ideals—that is, if he has ever heard of them" (Bennett, 1980, p. 65).

Freud and Weber get into the embarrassing position of seeming to tolerate such positions because they did not distinguish sharply enough between their professional ethics as disciplined investigators and the moral orientations appropriate for human beings and citizens. As we have seen, their urge to provide a prophetic charter for modern man was reined in by a strong sense of professional propriety as well as by an aversion to efforts to promulgate illusionary moral codes for modern publics. By subordinating their moral prophecies to what could be justified for the circumscribed professional work of psychoanalysts and interpretive sociologists they undercut the possibility of grounding what might have been a more adequate moral position.

The two men responded to this dilemma in different ways. Freud continually expressed his commitment to certain substantive values, but he tended to present them as givens and did not attempt to ground them through philosophical argument. On the one hand, he took the value of psychological health as a scientific premise. He believed that the functional capacities for productive work and genital love were self-evidently pre-eminent human ideals. As a corollary of this belief, he advocated a greater degree of instinctual (erotic) satisfaction in order to reduce the extent of guilt, aggression, and neurotic suffering which he linked with excessive suppression of Eros in the modern world. On the other hand, Freud took for granted the enduring value of the monumental achievements and demanding standards of European high culture. He thought it self-evident that people would continue to cherish those achievements: "New generations . . . who have [simply] experienced the benefits of civilization at an early age . . . will feel culture as a possession of their very own and will be ready to make the sacrifices as regards work and instinctual satisfaction that are necessary for its preservation" (Freud, 1927b, p. 8).

Weber, by contrast, evinced greater philosophic clarity in these matters than Freud, but at the cost of appearing to abandon support of a moral community where any values whatsoever were assumed as fundamental. Weber heaped scorn on those followers of Freud who considered mental hygiene to be the touchstone of morality. He lampooned the values of the psychiatric profession—with their idea of "the wholly banal, healthy nerve-proud person [*Nervenprotz*]," oriented to "discredit some 'norms' by proving that their observance is not 'beneficial' to the dear nerves" (Marianne Weber, 1975, p. 377). He expressed still greater impatience with any effort to smuggle in any value judgments under the guise of science. "*No* branch of scholarship and no scientific knowledge, be they ever so important—and I certainly number the Freudian discoveries among the scientifically important ones if they stand the test in the long run—provide a *Weltanschauung*," he noted (Marianne Weber, 1975, p. 380).

If Weber did not share Freud's commitment to the value of mental hygiene, he did share his enthusiasm for the monuments and high cultural standards of European civilization. Here, too, however, he insisted that to assert such values meant to take a relatively arbitrary personal stand, one that could not be advanced as though speaking in the name of professional scholarship. He remained clear and consistent in proclaiming that "the intrusion of normative statements into scholarly questions is the work of the Devil"; in the work of scholarship, he sermonized, "there is no place for an essay that wants to be a sermon" (Weber, 1924, p. 417; Marianne Weber, 1975, p. 380).

The positions of both men are vulnerable. Freud is

vulnerable to the Weberian objection that his implicit values and world view appear as arbitrary injections, inadmissible rhetoric insofar as they were promulgated in the name of a specialized science of psychic phenomena. Weber is vulnerable to the objections of those who argue, as did Freud, that certain constraints must be acknowledged as moral givens, which is to say that life in society is unthinkable without some balance between gratifications and renunciations. Freud argued publicly, as Weber did only privately or implicitly, that renunciation of some degree of egoism, aggression, and sexuality is indispensable for civilized life.

To acknowledge these weaknesses is not to argue that an ethic of strenuous self-understanding and self-determination cannot be justified. It is to elicit, rather, certain expanded implications of that ethic which Freud and Weber did not articulate.

To begin with, to elevate subjective freedom as the ultimate value is psychologically unrealistic. To maximize the pursuit of self-analysis and glorify, above all else, the freedom to choose can numb the capacity for action. Intense and total self-consciousness invites an overload of stimuli and options which disorient and paralyze the will. The flow of conduct requires a number of sturdy constraints.

Freud and Weber could afford to neglect such considerations because they took for granted the existence of many such constraints. Weber assumed that most action would continue to be shaped by the pressures of custom and institutional regulation. Freud assumed that the agents of society would continue to instill moral directives, and that in any case individual psyches were structured in part by certain reaches of "primal repression," antecedent to all socialized morality. In our own time, however, confusion flourishes in part because positions

associated with Freud and Weber—however incor-
rectly—seem to provide no authority or legitimacy for
such sources of control. Our culture encourages that pro-
fusion of unlimited strivings which Durkheim (1897)
classically described in his portrait of anomie, which Simmel (1971, p. xlii) represented as the oppression by a vast
world of cultural commodities, and which Rieff (1978)
more recently has scored as "the absolute dominion of
desires, the mass production of endless 'needs' as the object of late modern culture . . . a prescription for filling
our common lives with panic and emptiness" (p. 371).

What this suggests, then, is that an ethic of self-
awareness and self-determination must be buttressed by
a more realistic social psychology, one that hearkens to
some older and perhaps wiser traditions running from
Durkheim back to the Greek philosophers. This entails
an emphasis on the capacity for the control of impulse
and the curtailment of egoistic strivings, on the formation
of habits of character in early childhood and their maintenance throughout life by just and effective laws and
institutions. For Freudian psychology, this must mean,
in particular, a willingness to view families as well as
isolated individuals as the units of analysis and treatment. For Weberian sociology, it must mean a willingness
to focus on the agencies of moral socialization—an area
of sociological concern rather neglected in the Weberian
corpus.

To attend to the social psychology of good character
formation is not to abandon the quest for personal autonomy; it is, I am arguing, the only realistic way to make
genuine autonomy possible. But the attainment of autonomy does not mean, I must add, that persons are
thereby supposed to be free to carry out any actions they
choose. At this point another line of revision must be

inserted, one deriving from the tradition of moral philosophy.

This tradition asserts that the free use of reason necessarily imposes substantial restraints upon what one considers acceptable lines of conduct. For Freud, the psychic agent of moral inhibition, the superego, was essentially an irrational formation. It was a body of injunctions and ideals expressive of authority, originally located in the parents, and animated by aggressive impulses turned against the self. The work of psychoanalysis was to use the voice of reason to reduce the constricting effect of all noxious unconscious activities, including the unconscious sense of guilt. For Weber, reason could be associated with the creation of strict normative codes, an alliance that produced what he called value-rational types of action. But Weber regarded such orientations as doctrinaire, closing off degrees of rationality and freedom made possible by a more fully developed rational orientation, which he called *Zweckrationalität*—best translated as means/end-rationality. This kind of rationality Weber held to be morally relevant to the highest degree, inasmuch as it requires actors to take into account the costs and consequences of their practical goals, and to scrutinize the logic of their moral premises for clarity and consistency. Nonetheless, beyond this, Weber assumed that actors have complete freedom, and that there is no way to establish consensus or impel assent to moral notions through the use of rational argument.

This Weberian assumption has been thrown into question by recent developments in moral philosophy. Approaching the matter in a variety of ways, several philosophers have sought to revive the project of demonstrating that substantive moral implications follow from a formal ethic of intellectual integrity—for example, by adhering to what R. M. Hare (1965) depicts as the

notions of universalizability and prescriptiveness entailed in the very usage of the term "ought," what Alan
Donagan (1977) has formulated as the principle of respect
for all rational creatures, or what Alan Gewirth (1978)
has codified as the "principle of generic consistency."
Although such efforts remain open to debate, it is noteworthy that the idea of founding a substantive morality
on a properly understood notion of consistency or rationality is far from dead in professional philosophy, and continues to appeal to some of the most thoughtful of
contemporary moral philosophers.

Although Weber is correct, I believe, in maintaining
that a commitment to reason is something that cannot
itself be rationally induced, his own position provides the
basis for the more expanded orientation I am suggesting
here. If the work of psychoanalysis or of interpretive sociology is to go on at all, it presumes the nonrational
grounding of an interest in rational habits of mind among
professionals and clients alike, and it presumes as well
the willingness to be bound by the "dictates of reason"
wherever they lead.[12]

V

That Freud and Weber, men of extraordinary originality,
with such diverse disciplinary backgrounds and such contrasting new disciplinary commitments, should nevertheless have undergone such comparable intellectual and

---

[12] To say this is not to invalidate Weber's claim regarding the
irreconcilability of certain ultimate values. The issue is complex and
requires extended discussion. Let me simply clarify the kind of position I am adopting here by suggesting a basic distinction—between
a rationally determinate moral domain, involving types of action
which are universally prescribed, and a morally pluralistic domain,
involving types of action where individuals seek to actualize themselves by pursuing culturally variable ideals.

spiritual journeys during the same historical period suggests that something may be gained by reviewing those journeys in broader cultural context.

Central Europe at the end of the last century can be seen as a crucible in which two revolutionary cultural forces unleashed in the sixteenth and the seventeenth centuries were brought together under extraordinary circumstances. Following Benjamin Nelson's ideas for the interpretation of this process, we can say that the medieval "court of conscience," a central tribunal which claimed the right and had the will to oversee the acts and opinions of all Christians, was successfully challenged by two discrete developments. The first was the Protestant Reformation, which opposed the idea of a human court of conscience with the notion of individual responsibility in the realms of religion, morality, and politics. The second was the scientific and philosophical revolution, which established new canons for valid knowledge and objective certainty. These developments sundered those logics of decision whose close interdependence is signified by the duality of reference of the Latin *conscientia* (and French *conscience*): the moral conscience, on the one hand, and philosophical and scientific knowledge, on the other. Those two revolutions, constitutive of the makings of early modern cultures, thus involved, in Nelson's terms, fundamental "reshapings of the rationales of conscience." As Nelson (1968) observed, "from the late 19th century forward, first mainly in Germany . . . then in the United States and elsewhere, the by-products and the off-shoots of these makings were fused at great heats" (p. 166).

Freud and Weber were in the vanguard of those who struggled to rejoin those two dimensions of modern *conscience*, scientific rationality and ethical autonomy. They sought, in effect, to link the tradition that proceeded from Galileo, Descartes, and Hobbes through Ricardo, Helmholtz, and Darwin with a tradition that proceeded from Luther, Calvin, and Kant through Fichte, Kierkegaard, and Nietzsche. They began with superb training and performance in the impersonal modes of scientific rationality, so highly developed in German and Austrian universities in the latter half of the nineteenth century. Their indomitable individuality led them to struggle against the suppression of subjectivity that this entailed. Finding in their work in the early 1890s that the subjective orientations of actors seemed highly significant for explaining some of the phenomena which their professional disciplines could not otherwise fully account for, they proceeded, through a process involving intense inner turmoil, to fashion disciplines that focused on the internal motivations of individual actors, and whose value, furthermore, they could justify as leading to a historically unprecedented level of moral autonomy. The result was a rationale of conscience which maintained, first, the cognitive supremacy of modern scientific modes of observation and analysis, and yet, second, an ethic based on maximizing the autonomy of actors through enhanced rational understanding.

To achieve that synthesis, it should be noted, scientific rationality and moral autonomy had to be qualified in certain ways. The scientific values they most prized and encouraged were not the impersonal norms of parsimony, logical closure, operational reliability, and axiomatization, but the trained capacity to accept personally distasteful and painful realities. The notion of subjective freedom they most prized and encouraged was not that given to sentimental enthusiasms, utopian fantasies, and impulsive spontaneity, but one nourished by openness to information, intellectual integrity, thoughtfulness, and a sense of responsibility.

Of powerful appeal in their time and ours, the modern

rationale of conscience forged by Freud and Weber has two serious shortcomings, as I have suggested. Writing at a time when old-style patriarchal authority and Victorian prudery seemed insufferable (Weinstein and Platt, 1969) and when newer modes of industrial and political organization seemed irremediably coercive, Freud and Weber tended to exaggerate the extent of repressiveness in modern culture (Rieff, 1978, p. 338; Levine, 1981). They neglected the other side of the critique of modern culture which thinkers like Durkheim and Simmel found no less problematic, the dissolution of standards and of stable points for moral orientaton. Sticking, moreover, to a strict construction of their mission as disciplinary specialists, they neglected to examine and to advocate both the social requisites of moral autonomy[13] and the possibilities for creating rational grounds of constraint on arbitrary freedom.

To sustain a rationale of conscience that is adequate for our time therefore requires, I believe, that those who have internalized the ideals of Freud and Weber must perform the work of transmuting those ideals. It requires that a policy of analysis, terminable and interminable, and an ethic of honesty and self-conscious choice be supplemented by a forthright endorsement of the constraints that can be built into socialized character and engendered by the expanded use of reason in ethics.

REFERENCES

Beetham, D. (1974), *Max Weber and the Theory of Modern Politics*. London: Allen & Unwin.

---

[13] For an exception to this general neglect, one might cite the emphasis in some of Weber's political writings on the significance of parliament as a school for developing the moral autonomy of political leaders.

Bennett, W. J. (1980), Getting ethics. *Commentary*, 70:62-65.

Collins, R. (1980), Weber's last theory of capitalism: A systematiza-
tion. *Amer. Soc. Rev.*, 45:925-942.

Cooley, C. H. (1909), *Social Organization*. New York: Scribner's.

Donagan, A. (1977), *The Theory of Morality*. Chicago: University of
Chicago Press.

Durkheim, E. (1897), *Suicide*, trans. G. Simpson. New York: Free
Press, 1951.

Ellenberger, H. F. (1970), *The Discovery of the Unconscious*. New
York: Basic Books.

Factor, R., & Turner, S. (1979), The limits of reason and some limitations of Weber's morality. *Human Studies*, 2:301-334.

Freud, S. (1895a), Project for a scientific psychology. *Standard Edition*, 1:283-397. London: Hogarth Press, 1966.

———(1895b), Studies on hysteria. *Standard Edition*, 2. London: Hogarth Press, 1955.

——— (1908), "Civilized" sexual morality and modern nervous illness.
Standard Edition, 9:177-204. London: Hogarth Press, 1959.

——— (1912), The dynamics of transference. *Standard Edition*, 12:97-
108. London: Hogarth Press, 1958.

——— (1915), Observations on transference-love. *Standard Edition*,
12:157-174. London: Hogarth Press, 1958.

——— (1921), Group psychology and the analysis of the ego. *Standard
Edition*, 18:67-145. London: Hogarth Press, 1955.

——— (1927a), "Postscript" to the question of lay analysis. *Standard
Edition*, 20:251-260. London: Hogarth Press, 1959.

——— (1927b), The future of an illusion. *Standard Edition*, 21:3-58.
London: Hogarth Press, 1961.

——— (1939), Moses and monotheism. *Standard Edition*, 23:3-140.
London: Hogarth Press, 1964.

Fromm, E. (1959), *Sigmund Freud's Mission*. New York: Harper.

Gewirth, A. (1978), *Reason and Morality*. Chicago: University of Chicago Press.

Graf, M. (1942), Reminiscences of Professor Sigmund Freud. *Psychoanal. Quart.*, 11:465-476.

Hare, R. M. (1965), *Freedom and Reason*. New York: Oxford University Press.

Jaspers, K. (1946), *Max Weber: Politiker, Forscher, Philosoph*. Bremen:
J. Storm Verlag.

Jones, E. (1953), *The Life and Work of Sigmund Freud*, vol. 1. New
York: Basic Books.

LaPiere, R. (1959), *The Freudian Ethic*. New York: Duell, Sloan &
Pierce.

Levine, D. N. (1978), Psychoanalysis and sociology. *Ethos*, 6:175-185.

——— (1981), Rationality and freedom: Weber and beyond. *Sociol.
Inq.*, 51:5-25.

Mitzman, A. (1970), *The Iron Cage: An Historical Interpretation of Max Weber*. New York: Knopf.

Nelson, B. (1954), The future of illusions. *Psychoanal.*, 2:16-37.

―――― (1957), *Freud and the Twentieth Century*. New York: Meridian.

―――― (1965a), Comments. In: *Max Weber und die Soziologie heute*, ed. O. Stammer. Tübingen: Mohr, pp. 192-201.

―――― (1965b), Dialogs across the centuries: Weber, Marx, Hegel, Luther. In: *The Origins of Modern Consciousness*, ed. J. Weiss. Detroit: Wayne State Press, pp. 149-165.

―――― (1968), Scholastic rationales of "conscience": Early modern crises of credibility and the scientific-technocultural revolutions of the 17th and 20th centuries. *J. Scien. Study of Relig.*, 7:157-177.

Rickert, H. (1926), Max Weber und seine Stellung zur Wissenschaft. *Logos*, 15:222-237.

Rieff, P. (1978), *Freud: The Mind of a Moralist*. 3d ed. Chicago: University of Chicago Press.

Schluchter, W. (1979), The paradox of rationalization. In: *Max Weber's Vision of History*, ed. G. Roth & W. Schluchter. Berkeley: University of California Press, pp. 11-64.

Simmel, G. (1908), *Soziologie*. Leipzig: Duncker & Humblot.

―――― (1971), *On Individuality and Social Forms*, ed. D. N. Levine. Chicago: University of Chicago Press.

Strauss, L. (1953), *Natural Right and History*. Chicago: University of Chicago Press.

Sulloway, F. J. (1979), *Freud: Biologist of the Mind*. New York: Basic Books.

Wallerstein, R. S., & Smelser, N. J. (1969), Psychoanalysis and sociology. *Internat. J. Psycho-Anal.*, 50:693-710.

Weber, Marianne (1975), *Max Weber: A Biography*, trans H. Zohn. New York: Wiley.

Weber, Max (1905), *The Protestant Ethic and the Spirit of Capitalism*, trans. T. Parsons. New York: Scribner's, 1958.

―――― (1906), The Protestant sects and the spirit of capitalism. In: *From Max Weber: Essays in Sociology*, trans. H. H. Gerth & C. W. Mills. London: Routledge & Kegan Paul, 1948, pp. 302-322.

―――― (1924), *Gessamelte Aufsatze sur Soziologie und Sozialpolitik*. Tubingen: Mohr.

―――― (1948), *From Max Weber: Essays in Sociology*, trans. E. A. Shils & H. A. Finch. Glencoe, Ill.: Free Press.

―――― (1949), *The Methodology of the Social Sciences*, trans. E. A. Shils & H. A. Finch: Glencoe: Free Press.

―――― (1968), *Economy and Society*, ed. G. Roth & C. Wittich. New York: Bedminster.

Weinstein, F. J., & Platt, G. (1969), *The Wish To Be Free*. Berkeley: University of California Press.

Commentary

GEORGE MORAITIS, M.D.

The comparative historical review of Freud's and Weber's efforts to create and establish a new discipline points to some striking similarities in the personal experiences and temperaments of the two men, as well as to some parallels in the timing and stages of development of their ideas. Each experienced a "creative illness" which occurred at the early stage of his professional career, eventually led to changes in professional orientation during the mid-career period, and gave birth to his respective new disciplines, psychoanalysis for Freud and interpretive sociology for Weber. What is even more striking is the commonality in the value system under which these two intellectual leaders organized their respective disciplines. Both emerge as critics of repressive elements in our civilization; both became proponents of "self-conscious free choice" and subjective freedom. Neither advocated violence. Freud pursued the therapeutic orientation that would lead to freedom from neurotic suffering, and Weber advocated the enrichment of routine and daily existence through rational action. Professor Levine criticizes them both for having neglected "to examine and advocate both the social requisites of moral autonomy and the possibility for creating rational grounds of constraint on arbitrary freedom."

At first glance Freud and Weber look like strange bedfellows. This is particularly true for the psychoanalyst who rigidly draws the boundaries of his discipline and limits his activities within what he considers "bona fide" psychoanalysis. It could be argued that Freud's perception of subjectivity is basically different from Weber's, and it would be misleading to assume that the intellectual positions of these two investigators complement each other. I am under the impression that Professor Levine deliberately de-emphasized basic differences in Freud's and Weber's perception of man's internal world in order to place the emphasis on the commonality of value systems evident in the two intellectual movements that they spawned. This value system is described as "a new moral annunciation," and the author identifies the following common elements in it.

1. Each discipline was deemed by its creator as the prime vehicle of moral education.

2. Both railed against those of their followers who tried to construct and impose *Weltanschauungen.*

3. Both aimed to enhance the rational capacities and autonomy of the individual.

4. Both facilitated the dispassionate examination of human wishes.

5. "Freud and Weber joined an apparently neutral procedural formula to a gospel of intellectual integrity, courage, subjective freedom and self responsibility."

It seems to me that the five elements under which psychoanalysis is identified are too conflictual to represent a unified position. If psychoanalysis refuses to impose a *Weltanschauung* and aims to enhance the autonomy of the individual, how can it also be the prime vehicle of moral education that is engaged in the teaching of a gospel? Is the author of this paper describing an inherent inconsistency in Freud's and Weber's intellectual position? I doubt it. More likely the inconsistency involved reflects the difference between intellectual principles when used as an investigative tool and when put to use in a broader context as an instrument of change, therapeutic or social. Psychoanalysis as a body of knowledge and as a scientific theory aims to investigate phenomena that were for the most part unrecognized before Freud's scientific journey into the unconscious began, at a time when science was under the influence of nineteenth-century positivism. In order to protect the scientific nature of his work he adopted, perhaps somewhat too eagerly, the principles of science, and made a conscious and systematic effort to dissociate the new discipline from any connection to religion and mysticism. He rejected Jung's invitation to establish a new religion and placed psychoanalysis under the *Weltanschauung* of all sciences. Perhaps he protested too much and took too much for granted. In order to do justice to his intellectual position, however, it is important to acknowledge that he designed the principles he advocated so as to bypass, to whatever extent possible, issues of moral judgment and the right-versus-wrong duality. Such a position is quite consistent with the principles of all scientific investigations, strict adherence to which facilitates the investigator's capacity to bring his subjectivity under discipline and control.

The application of these principles to psychoanalysis and especially to therapeutic psychoanalysis is, of course, a lot more complicated than in other sciences. The laboratory of the psychoanalyst involves a close and intense interaction with another human being that brings into the situation not only his professional principles but also his own more personal, moral value systems. When this occurs, and it occurs to various degrees in all therapeutic analyses, the analyst's communications are experienced as moral teachings or even as gospel by the analysand who may, because of reasons of his own, experience the need to perceive such a gospel even if it is not there. Such occurrences are by-products of an applied science that are likely to occur when sciences are utilized for the purpose of changing human behavior. They reflect the limitations of scientific knowledge as an instrument of change and remind us of the difficulties involved in maintaining scientific principles outside a well-controlled environmental situation. Professional principles can be compared to ideals that can only be approximated even by the most ethical and experienced practitioner. Becoming the prime vehicle of moral education is not consistent with the principles of psychoanalytic theory and practice. When it occurs, the principles have been compromised by imposing a *Weltanschauung* on the patient at the expense of his autonomy.

There are similarities between scientific principles and moral rules and values. Both represent ideals that aim to establish a code of acceptable behavior. Despite their similarities, however, it is erroneous to equate morality with professional principles and to ignore the fundamental differences between the two.

Morality aims to affect and direct all aspects of human behavior by establishing rules that are applicable at all times, and in all places and situations within the culture. Morality has no boundaries and as such it represents a point of arrival, a destination that is an end in itself. In contrast, professional principles are basically instruments designed to facilitate the professional's capacity to pursue knowledge and utilize it for practical purposes. They provide the professional with boundaries and structure that limit the scope of his activities to manageable proportions. All sciences, with the help of their principles, select and maintain an area of endeavor that becomes the "limited" universe within which they operate. These limitations represent the boundaries of a given discipline beyond which the investigator is no longer under the rule of the professional principles. The laboratory of the scientist correlates to the physical, tangible boundaries of his limited universe, the re-creation of which is an essential part of the scientific method. The distinction between professional psychoanalytic activities and parlor analysis is closely linked to the practitioner's capacity to maintain the boundaries of the discipline in his professional activities. The capacity to maintain these professional boundaries constitutes not morality but professional competence, and failure to do so is not immorality but an indication of incompetence and ignorance.

Professsional boundaries do not remain static; they undergo constant change and redefinition, which is usually too limited to effect significant change in the professional ethic. Freud and Weber went beyond that. They created new disciplines by arriving at a distinctly new area of scientific endeavor, a new "limited" universe, the relative autonomy of which can only be maintained by adherence to a new professional ethical code. Professor Levine persuasively emphasized the similarities between the value systems of Freud and Weber. This phenomenon probably indicates that the two investigators operated largely within the boundaries of the same "limited" universe despite the apparent differences in content and rhetoric.

I prefer to look at Freud's and Weber's work as a new discovery rather than a new morality—a discovery powerful enough to introduce a perception of human nature and culture substantially different from the previous ones. Discoveries of such magnitude have wide and far-reaching implications that cannot be contained within the "limited" universe of a given discipline and its professional ethic. Once the information is released the investigator has very little control of its effect and use by the group at large. It is unrealistic to expect scientific investigators to provide us, along with their discoveries, with the social engineering needed to make them useful for our society and culture. At best, every discovery is only a partial truth which will lead to new discoveries in the times to come. Freud's discoveries were no exception to that. He first approached moral restraints as barriers that impeded his investigations and his patients' recovery from neurotic suffering. By the time he developed the structural model he came to realize the internal nature of psychological conflicts, and he saw that morality was a necessary and important part of the internal psychic organization that he linked to superego.

Professor Levine is quite accurate in stating that Freud took for granted our culture's capacity to maintain its standards and values. His attitude toward religion is probably a good example of a rather cavalier approach to an important instrument of cultural constraint. He correctly assumed, however, that psychoanalysis contributed to culture by facilitating the personal growth and development of the individuals who were exposed to psychoanalytic therapy and became, as a result of it, more productive and with more effective internal restraints and structure. He also wrote a number of essays in group psychology and applied psychoanalysis that have contributed to the understanding of our culture. Despite all these, however, the scientific paradigm of psychoanalysis makes no provisions for a systematic study of the psychology of culture. It remains a strictly individual psychology that takes external reality and culture as a given or as a reflection of intrapsychic events. The shortcomings

Professor Levine identifies in Freud's modern rationale of conscience are neither accidental nor idiosyncratic. They are the by-products of the limitations of the psychoanalytic scientific paradigm. Like any other science, psychoanalysis restricts its activities within the boundaries of its paradigm, which provides consistency and continuity to the "limited" universe of the discipline. Extending the boundaries of science is not a simple undertaking. It involves a resassessment of all data and the method by which they were collected, in combination with a re-examination of the theoretical structure that rests upon them. Freud extended the boundaries of psychoanalysis during his lifetime. The shift from the topographic to the structural model is a good example of that. I share the expressed wish that he had gone further.

During his long and intense effort to persuade his readers about the existence of the unconscious as the true psychic reality, Freud took external reality for granted. The recognition of his discoveries contributed to the decrease in man's reliance on his sense organs and undermined man's confidence in the perception of external reality. Psychoanalysis and interpretive sociology, however, should not be credited or considered liable as the only disciplines that effected the cultural changes that affected the morality of our society during the twentieth century. I would like to refer to those changes as a new cultural paradigm that has affected all levels of creativity, social life, and, of course, morality. Despite my confidence in psychoanalysis as a powerful new intellectual force, I doubt that changes of this magnitude can be explained as the outcome of Freud's or Weber's ideas alone. It is equally likely that the intellectual positions postulated by both Freud and Weber were significantly influenced by prevailing trends in the intellectual community and culture, for which they became two of the spokesmen.

The understanding of the interaction between cultural changes and intellectual movements within a given culture is an extremely complicated process that must be studied in both directions, and in a manner that takes into account the relative autonomy and interdependence of both.

Dr. Levine's scholarly presentation provides the psychoanalyst with the kind of feedback and constructive criticism that is needed in order to re-examine the effect of his science not only on his individual patients but on the society at large. It aims to increase the psychoanalyst's sense of responsibility and accountability as a professional and extend the boundaries of his profession so as to bring his scientific microcosms into better alignment with the macrocosm of our culture.

6

Psychoanalysis and Cultural Relativism: The Trobriand Case

MELFORD E. SPIRO, Ph.D.

INTRODUCTION

Ever since the publication of Malinowski's classic, *Sex and Repression in Savage Society* (hereafter *SR*), it has been an anthropological truism that the (male) Oedipus complex—assuming that it is found anywhere—is restricted to the traditional, Western "patriarchal" family. In *SR*, as every anthropology undergraduate knows, Malinowski demonstrated that in the Trobriand Islands (an archipelago in the Western Pacific), in which descent is matrilineal and the mother's brother is the locus of jural authority, the boy's primary libidinal attachment is to his sister (rather than his mother), and his hostility is directed to his mother's brother (rather than to his father). Malinowski called this constellation the "matrilineal complex," presumably because he expected it to be found in other matrilineal societies of the Trobriand type.

The early attempt of Jones (1925) to refute Malinowski's formulation fell on deaf ears—mostly because his thesis that the sister and mother's brother are dis-placements for the mother and father, respectively, was almost entirely speculative—not only among anthropologists, but even among such classical psychoanalysts as Fenichel (1945, p. 97). If, then, even the Oedipus complex—the centerpiece of Freud's developmental theory—was culturally relative, it seemed to most anthropologists that psychoanalytic theory was a culture-bound edifice, one that could not be taken seriously by a discipline that took all of mankind as its subject matter.

In my view this was a hasty conclusion. For although it may indeed be the case that the Oedipus complex is culturally relative, a careful examination of the Trobriand data suggests that the Trobriands, at least, do not constitute evidence for that conclusion. Indeed, there is good reason to believe, as I have shown elsewhere (Spiro, 1982), that the Trobrianders have a very strong Oedipus complex. This paper, however—which is an abridged version of one chapter of that book—has a more restricted aim: it attempts to show that the evidence adduced by Malinowski does not support his argument that the Trobrianders have a matrilineal complex. First, however, we must examine his argument.

Although acknowledging that in the West the boy has an incestuous attachment to the mother, his hostility to the father, Malinowski held, is aroused not so much by his rivalry with him for the love of the wife-mother but by his (the father's) punitive authority. Hence, he argued, the father plays no role in the formation of the matrilineal complex because in matrilineal systems—at least in that of the Trobriands—he is uniformly loving and kind. He protects and plays with the children, and he helps and nurtures them, but he does not punish or exercise authority over them. This being so, the hostility dimension of the matrilineal complex is found not in the father-son relationship, but in the relationship between the boy and his mother's brother, for the latter, not the father, is the locus of jural authority. Nevertheless, since the authority of the mother's brother is principally manifested when the boy attains puberty, it is not until then that he becomes the object of the boy's hostility.

The mother is also excluded from the *dramatis personae* of the matrilineal complex, despite the fact that both "instinct" and "custom" serve to "bind" mother and infant to each other, "giving them full scope for the passionate intimacy of motherhood" (Malinowski, 1927, p. 32). The experience of weaning initiates the first important difference between mother and child in Western and Trobriand society, respectively, for weaning takes place in the Trobriands at a relatively late age—between two and three—after the child has already become relatively independent. The child's experience between the age of four and six marks the second, and crucial, developmental difference between the Trobriands and the West. Thus, whereas in the West the boy's erotic feelings must undergo repression, in the Trobriands children are permitted complete sexual freedom. At the same time, the mother "withdraws completely but gradually from his [the son's] passionate feelings." Put differently, "all of the infantile craving of the child for its mother is allowed gradually to spend itself in a natural, spontaneous manner" (p. 75).

Rather than the mother, the sister is the principal object of the boy's erotic desires in the Trobriands. His desire for her, however, is "systematically repressed from the outset" (p. 68) because of the special severity of the brother-sister incest taboo. Indeed, it is the special severity of this taboo that causes the boy's erotic desire to be singularly intense. This is so for two somewhat different reasons. First, its severity causes the thought of the sister "to be always present." Second, since the taboo is "imposed with great brutality and kept up with rigid strength" (p. 101), the inclination to violate it is commensurately strong.

That in a nutshell is Malinowski's argument for the formation of a matrilineal, rather than an Oedipus complex in the Trobriands. I now wish to examine the evidence that he adduced in its support, beginning with the mother-son relationship.

THE MOTHER-SON RELATIONSHIP IN THE TROBRIANDS

According to Malinowski, at the very age—between three and six—when the Western boy is struggling with his incestuous desire for the mother, the Trobriand boy's "passionate feeling" for her has already spent itself in a "natural" and "spontaneous" manner. This being the case, in his relationship with the mother (as well as the father) there is "nothing suppressed, nothing negative, no frustrated desire" (1927, p. 72). It is more than a little disappointing, then, that Malinowski offers no evidence in support of these contentions: there is no description of any kind regarding the boy's actions, feelings, or fantasies regarding the mother. In lieu of any evidence for the spontaneous disappearance of the boy's early "passionate feeling" for the mother, let us turn to Malinowski's argument that it is theoretically expectable.

Malinowski's first argument is that since Trobriand weaning is relatively late, the "first wrench" experienced by the Western child when separated from the mother—the wrench of abrupt independence—"is eliminated" in the case of the Trobriand child (1927, p. 35). Since, however, genitality and dependency are separate variables, it is hard to understand how the ease of the boy's "detachment" from his dependency on the mother might affect the detachment of his libidinal desire for her. Indeed, even the dependency argument is weak, for, during the two or more years in which the child is nursed, he and the mother sleep together, both being separated from the father. When, however, as Malinowski points out in *The Sexual Life of Savages* (1929, p. 235)—hereafter *SLS*—the process of weaning begins, the infant is separated from the mother, and he sleeps with the father or grandmother which means that though he may not experience the wrench of abrupt weaning, he does experience the wrench of abrupt separation from the mother at the very time that weaning also occurs.

But wrench or no wrench, genitality, not dependency, is the relevant variable so far as the oedipal question is concerned, and it is difficult to understand how the Trobriand boy's genital attachment to the mother is effected by weaning. For if he is weaned at the lower end of the age range mentioned by Malinowski—about two years—that should have little effect on the boy's *genital* desire for the mother inasmuch as he has not yet achieved genital primacy. If, on the other hand, the boy is weaned at the upper range of the weaning period—about three years—he may enter the "phallic" stage while still being nursed. If so, then whatever the effect gradual weaning might have on the boy's dependency needs, oedipal theory would expect that such prolonged nursing would, if anything, intensify his libidinal desire for the mother. And not only oedipal theory. For since, according to Malinowski, the infant "reacts sexually" to his "close bodily contact" with the mother (1927, p. 42), the prolongation of such bodily contact occasioned by protracted nursing should lead to the persistence, if not the exacerbation, of his sexual reactions.

Let us turn, then, to Malinowski's second argument. Since, so he contended, the Trobriand boy is given complete sexual freedom, "the ideas and feeling centering around sex on the one hand, and maternal tenderness on the other, are differentiated naturally and easily, without being separated by a rigid taboo. [Hence] since his normal erotic impulses find an easy outlet, tenderness towards the mother and bodily attachment to her are naturally drained of their stronger sensuous elements" (1929, p. 523).

This argument, as comparative ethnographic data indicate, is no more cogent than the first. To take but one ethnographic example, kibbutz children of the same age, who to a large degree are separated from their parents, who never experience the intense physical and emotional relationship with the mother that is found in the Trobriands, and who, like Trobriand children, enjoy a sexually permissive regime, nevertheless (according to Nagler) take the mother as the main object of their sexual impulses (Neubauer, 1965, p. 260).

But there is no need to turn to other cultures to show that Malinowski's argument is not self-evident, for it is refuted by his own data on the Trobriands. Thus, if it is the case that the Trobriand son's sexual attraction to the mother is dissipated by the sexual freedom enjoyed by children, we would expect the daughter's attraction to the father to be similarly dissipated. Yet, Malinowski reports, her attraction to him persists throughout childhood, and it is not until puberty that it is repressed. Since, then, boys and girls alike achieve an "easy outlet" for their libidinal feelings for their parents, why are the boy's feelings for his mother drained of their "stronger sensuous elements," while those of the girl for her father persist with undiminished strength? Malinowski's answer to this question is not very persuasive. The prohibition on father-daughter incest, he argues, is not only a measure of, but actually increases, their libidinal bond

(1927, p. 69). Dubious as this answer might be, if it holds for the father-daughter prohibition, why does it not apply with equal force to the mother-son prohibition? To this objection Malinowski offers no answer.

Malinowski's case for the early dissipation of the Trobriand boy's libidinal tie to his mother is finally proven, so he contends, by the total absence of conscious incestuous desires for the mother on the part of adults. Neither in dream nor in deed is incest found between a mother and her adult son. So far as the former is concerned, not only do adult males report no dreams of mother incest, but all queries concerning the existence of such dreams evoke "a calm and unshocked negation" (1927, p. 91). Similarly, there are not only no known cases of actual mother-son incest, but the latter is regarded "as almost impossible" (p. 524). To clinch his argument, Malinowski quotes his informants as saying that since the mother is an "old woman," only an "imbecile" would desire to have sexual relations with her (p. 91).

This argument—the centerpiece of Malinowski's thesis that the matrilineal complex has taken the place of the Oedipus complex in the Trobriands—is obviously misplaced. For if the existence of the male Oedipus complex is evidenced by a conscious sexual desire for the mother, it would follow that the former is absent in normal males not only in the Trobriands, but in the West as well (in which, however, Malinowski concedes it is present). Normal adult males in the West, no less than in the Trobriands, regard mother-son incest as "almost impossible," and they, too, find their mother no more desirable sexually than any other elderly woman.

Oedipal theory, it will be recalled, does not claim that a (normal) adult male has a conscious sexual desire for his mother. It claims, rather, that this desire is confined to early childhood, beginning around the age of three and ending (either by its extinction or repression) around the age of six (as a result of castration anxiety). Conscious incestuous desire for the mother beyond early childhood is expected only in cases of psychopathology. Moreover, if his desire is repressed, it is not the mother of his adult years, but the mental representation of the mother of his childhood that is normally the object of the son's desire. In short, Malinowski's finding concerning the absence of conscious incestuous desires for the mother in Trobriand adults is not only consistent with oedipal theory, but—contrary to his assumption—is required by it.

Lest I be misunderstood, I wish to stress that I am not proposing the absurd thesis that the absence of conscious incestuous wishes for the mother in the Trobriands is evidence for the presence of an Oedipus complex. Rather, I am arguing, *pace* Malinowski, that their absence does not constitute evidence for the presence of a matrilineal complex.

THE BROTHER-SISTER RELATIONSHIP IN THE TROBRIANDS

That the sister takes the place of the mother in the Trobriand matrilineal complex is especially proven, Malinowski argues, by the severity of the brother-sister incest taboo, by dreams and deeds of brother-sister incest, and by a myth of that type of incest. Let us briefly examine each in turn.

In support of the special severity of the brother-sister taboo Malinowski observes not only that from an "early age" the boy's sexual advances toward his sister are "reprimanded and punished," but that the adults react to such advances with "horror and anguish" (1929, p. 520). Moreover, brother and sister are forbidden to be present at the same time in any form of children's play, let alone in sexual play. Finally, to assure their sexual avoidance at puberty, the boy is required to leave the parental home. On the latter point, however, we are confronted with a contradiction, for in another context Malinowski claims that the reason boys must leave the parental home is that they "not hamper by their embarrassing presence the sexual life of their parents" (p. 62).

None of these arguments is convincing. Let us begin with the boy's extrusion from the home. Even if we accept the first reason for his extrusion, that would not support the hypothesis that the brother-sister incest taboo is more stringent than the son-mother taboo. In village Burma, for example, where the mother-son taboo is more stringent than the brother-sister taboo (and the father-daughter taboo more stringent than either), brother-sister (but not son-mother) avoidance is practiced, although descent is bilateral and the father's authority is 'patriarchal' (Spiro, 1977, chap. 5). Nor is Burma exceptional in this regard, for as Murdock (1949, p. 277) reports in his cross-cultural study of avoidance taboos, institutionalized brother-sister avoidance is second only to that between a man and his mother-in-law as the most frequent type of kin avoidance, a finding which holds regardless of descent system. Moreover, mother-son avoidance is absent in every society in his sample.

Malinowski's first argument for the special stringency of the brother-sister taboo fares no better. Although the boy is not permitted to be present when his sister is engaged in sexual games, he must also be absent from the "sexual games" of his parents. But the clinching refutation of the special stringency of the brother-sister taboo was provided by Malinowski himself when, in yet another passage, he wrote: "The idea of mother incest is as repugnant to the Trobrianders as sister incest, *probably even more*" (*emphasis mine*, 1927, pp. 100-101).

Malinowski's next two arguments for the primacy of the boy's incestuous attachment to the sister derive from the relative incidence of mother-son and brother-sister incest, both in dream and in deed. Although Trobriand males never report dreams of mother incest, they do report dreams of sister incest which, moreover, "haunt and disturb" them (1927, p. 91). In addition, whereas queries concerning mother incest dreams arouse no affect, those regarding dreams of sister incest produce a "strong affective reaction . . . of indignation and anger." As for actual incest, whereas there are no reported cases of mother-son incest, there are a few known cases of brother-sister incest (1927, pp. 91-95; 1929, pp. 528-529).

Although Malinowski's interpretation of these findings is plausible, other interpretations are equally plausible. Thus the emotional reaction of Trobrianders to dreams of sister incest may be simply explained by the fact that they are the only incestuous dreams that in fact occur. That they occur more frequently than dreams of mother incest is not unproblematic, but, for reasons I have detailed elsewhere (Spiro, 1982), there are good grounds for believing that in many Trobriand dreams of sister incest, the sister is an unconscious symbolic representation of the mother. Finally, that actual incest with the sister, while none with the mother, is reported is not in itself evidence for a greater incestuous attachment to the sister, because the same finding is reported for the West (Lindzey, 1967) where, Malinowski concedes, the mother is the primary incestuous object. Indeed, the relative incidence of all three forms of reported or known nuclear-family incest exhibits precisely the same pattern in the West that Malinowski reported for the Trobriands: brother-sister incest is much more frequent than that between father and daughter, whereas mother-son incest is all but nonexistent (Lindzey, 1967).

"The most telling evidence" for the thesis that the libidinal desire of the Trobriand boy is directed primarily to the sister consists, according to Malinowski, of a myth in which the origin of love magic is attributed to brother-sister incest. According to this myth (1927, pp. 114-116), a boy prepared a concoction of love magic in his hut. Later, his sister entered the hut and accidentally brushed against the vessel containing the concoction, causing some of it to fall on her. As a result she was consumed with lust for her brother and, despite his repeated attempts to elude her, she relentlessly pursued him until, finally, he capitulated to her desire, and they committed incest.

It is difficult to understand how this myth attributes the origin of love magic to brother-sister incest since, according to the text, the brother already knew of and prepared love magic prior to the incestuous act with his sister. Indeed, in a later publication (1929, pp. 545) Malinowski himself admitted that, rather than accounting for the origin of love magic, this myth merely accounts for its transfer from one island to another. Nevertheless, since this myth depicts brother-sister incest, it shows—so Malinowski claims—that unlike "patriarchal" societies, in which the prototypical incest myth consists of mother-son incest, in matrilineal societies it consists of brother-sister incest; and this demonstrates—so he argues—that in matrilineal societies, the primary incestuous object is the sister rather than the mother. Unfortunately, the comparative study of myth does not support this argument. Thus, in a survey of oedipal myths in Micronesia, Indonesia, and Melanesia, Lessa (1961, chap. 18) discovered that myths of mother-son incest are found with equal frequency in matrilineal and patrilineal societies alike.

THE MOTHER'S BROTHER-SISTER'S SON
RELATIONSHIP IN THE TROBRIANDS

Although the proposition that the boy's hostility in the Trobriands is directed to the mother's brother (rather than to the father) has long been taken as an established ethnographic fact, this proposition rests on only two pieces of inferential evidence. First, in "prophetic dreams of death" (the frequency of which we are not told), it is "usually the sister's son who will foredream his uncle's death" (1927, p. 95). Second, the first victim of disease-causing sorcerers must fall in the category of "near maternal relatives" (1927, p. 95). The latter argument is disingenuous (if not misleading) because the uncle is never singled out as one of those "near maternal relatives." Thus, in the passage just quoted, Malinowski writes that the "near maternal relative" is "very often" the mother, and in an earlier, nonpolemical book, he explicitly singles out the mother and sister as the sorcerer's victims, while the mother's brother is not even mentioned. In effect, then, an inference from a single ethnographic fact—prophetic dreams of death—must carry the entire evidential burden for the claim that the uncle, rather than the father, is the principal object of the boy's hostility.

The fact is, however, that the primary grounds for this claim are not inductive, but deductive. That is, it is based on Malinowski's theoretical assumption that in any society the boy's hostility is directed to the person who holds jural authority over him; and since the locus of jural authority in the Trobriands is the mother's brother, it can then be deduced that it is he (rather than the father) who is the object of the boy's hostility. Now, although the logic of this conclusion cannot be faulted, the theoretical assumption on which it is based is not unproblematic. For although the mother's brother is indeed the locus of jural authority in the Trobriands, the degree to which this structural fact engenders hostility in the sister's son must depend surely on the manner in which that authority is manifested in their relationship, and on this crucial question we have no information.

If, then, we are to assess Malinowski's claim we must take another tack. If the uncle's jural authority accounts for his becoming the principal target of the boy's hostility, he must presumably have an opportunity to express his authority in some kind of ongoing interaction with him. From Malinowski's description, however, their interaction would appear to be infrequent at best. Before puberty, the boy lives with his natal family (1929, p. 61), and since residence is virilocal, this means that during his childhood he and his uncle not only live in separate households, but in different villages (1927, pp. 24, 48). Since, then, the uncle's authority can only be "exercised from a distance" (p. 48), it follows—as Malinowski himself acknowledges—that his authority "cannot become oppressive in those small matters which are *most* irksome" (p. 49; emphasis added).

If, then, his authority is not "most irksome" before puberty, how oppressive is the uncle's authority after puberty? Here the evidence is contradictory. For although in one passage Malinowski (1927, p. 75) reports that puberty is the period when the boy first develops "repressed antagonisms" toward his uncle, in another passage he writes that, because it is at puberty that the uncle instructs him in tribal lore, this is the period during which the boy's "interest in his mother's brothers . . . is greatest and their relations are at their best" (p. 67). Hence, he continues, it is not during puberty, but rather somewhat "later on," that "friction with the maternal uncle makes its appearance" (p. 67). When that is, however, we are not told.

Since, then, the uncle is a punitive authority figure neither in childhood nor at puberty, it is difficult to understand how he might be the primary instigator of the boy's hostility. If, nevertheless, Malinowski is correct in claiming that the uncle is the conscious focus of that hostility, it is hard to avoid the conclusion that the latter is displaced from somewhere else.

THE FATHER-SON RELATIONSHIP IN THE TROBRIANDS

The Trobriand father is variously described by Malinowski as a "beloved, benevolent friend"; as "only loving and tender"; "a hardworking and conscientious nurse . . . always interested in the children, sometimes passionately so [who] performs all his duties eagerly and fondly" (Malinowski, 1927, p. 33); with the infant, he is "tender and loving," and with the child he plays, "carries it, and teaches it such amusing sports and occupations as takes its fancy . . . with a strong affection . . ." (p. 38); as they grow older, he "continues to befriend the children, to help them, to teach them what they like and as much as they like" (p. 48).

Now even after discounting for the hyperbole in that description, the Trobriand father still emerges from Malinowski's portrait as a warm and kindly person. Hence, having rejected on a priori grounds the notion that a son might develop hostility to his father because of his perception of him as a rival for the mother's love, it is understandable that Malinowski should have concluded that hostility is absent from the Trobriand son's relationship with his father. If, however, that a priori assumption is not accepted as self-evident, one would want some supporting evidence for that conclusion. To be sure, Malinowski *asserts* that the Trobriand boy's feelings for the father are uniformly warm and loving, and that he harbors no hostility toward him; but in the absence of evidential support that assertion is problematic because it is inconsistent with contrary evidence from the Trobriands.

In the first place that assertion is contradicted by evidence presented by another ethnographer who, on the basis of his observations of the father-child relationships in the Trobriands, reports that "the *psychological* relation between father and child is essentially the same under the Trobriand matrilineal as under a patrilineal system of kinship" (Powell, 1957, p. 142; emphasis added). That can only mean, if we restrict the generalization to our present topic, that the boy's hostility to the father in the Trobriands is little different from what it is in the West.

A second, and more troublesome contradiction, is Malinowski's own report that Trobrianders regard the "bonds of fatherhood [and marriage] . . . as artificial and untrustworthy under any strain" (1929, p. 161). That the "untrustworthy" quality of the bond of fatherhood might indicate some degree of hostility in the father-son relationship is supported by another of Malinowski's findings, and the most important contradiction of all. According to Trobriand belief, so Malinowski reports, every death—except for one caused by suicide or a visible accident—is caused by sorcery, and in the case of a man's death "the principal suspicion of sorcery attaches always to the wife and children" (1929, p. 161). In short, contrary to Malinowski's claim that the son harbors no hostility toward the father, the Trobrianders themselves believe that his hostility is so intense that it leads not only to patricidal wishes but also to (magical) patricidal deeds.

SUMMARY AND CONCLUSIONS

On the basis of the foregoing assessment, I have argued that there is little evidence to support the claims that in the Trobriands the early libidinal feelings of the son for the mother disappear gradually and spontaneously, or that the sister is the primary object of his libidinal desires, or that the mother's brother is the primary target of his hostility, or that he harbors no hostility to the father. Although this assessment does not mean that the Trobrianders have an Oedipus complex—that is an independent question which is examined elsewhere (Spiro, 1982)—it does mean that there is little warrant for the widely held belief that they have a matrilineal complex—a psychological constellation in which the boy loves his sister (rather than his mother) and hates his mother's brother (rather than his father).

If, then, the case for a Trobriand matrilineal complex is as weak as this assessment has suggested, we are left with a perplexing scientific question, one on which I should like to bring this paper to a close. Why is it that almost every anthropologist—there are notable exceptions—accepts it as an incontrovertible scientific fact that on the basis of his ethnographic investigations Malinowski proved that a matrilineal complex exists in the Trobriands; and that this proof shows that the Oedipus complex is a culture-bound syndrome? And why is it—to continue with the question—that psychoanalysts as different as Kardiner and Fenichel have joined in that conclusion?

Now, the reaction of the analysts may perhaps be explained by the waggish definition of a "classic"—and *Sex and Repression* is certainly a classic—as a "book that everyone talks about but no one reads." The reaction of the anthropologists, who may be presumed to have read the book, is then all the more puzzling. In either event, the fact that an almost universally accepted scientific proposition, with such far-reaching theoretical implications, should rest on such a vulnerable empirical foundation must surely be accounted as a most intriguing problem for the sociology of knowledge. It is one worth investigating.

REFERENCES

Fenichel, O. (1945), *The Psychoanalytic Theory of Neurosis*. New York: Norton.

Jones, E. (1925), Mother-right and the sexual ignorance of savages. *Internat. J. Psycho-Anal.*, 6:109-130.

Lessa, W. A. (1961), *Tales from Ulithi Atoll*. Berkeley: University of California Press.

Lindzey, G. (1967), Some remarks concerning incest, the incest taboo, and psychoanalytic theory. *Amer. Psychologist*, 22:1051-1059.

Malinowski, B. (1927), *Sex and Repression in Savage Society*. New York: Meridian Books, 1955.

—— (1929), *The Sexual Life of Savages in North-Western Melanesia*. New York: Eugenic Publishing Company.

Murdock, G. P. (1949), *Social Structure*. New York: Macmillan.

Neubauer, P. B. (ed.) (1965), *Children in Collectives*. Springfield, Ill.: Charles C Thomas.

Spiro, M. E. (1977), *Kinship and Marriage in Burma*. Berkeley: University of California Press.

—— (1982), *Oedipus in the Trobriands*. Chicago: University of Chicago Press.

Commentary

MARK J. GEHRIE, Ph.D.

The presence of five panels on "Interdisciplinary Studies" on the program of the Fiftieth Anniversary Celebration of Psychoanalysis in Chicago reflects our continuing interest in the role and relevance of psychoanalysis outside of its strictly clinical setting. It is beyond contention that over eighty years of clinical psychoanalysis have pushed back the limits of understanding of mental dynamics and emotional experience. We know that, properly applied, psychoanalysis can offer the analyst and analysand a vehicle for understanding and therapy that is unparalleled in its power and potential for the individual. Many other schools of psychological thought have tacitly acknowledged this through their own dependence upon fundamental, psychoanalytically derived principles of understanding. Indeed, many psychoanalytic principles have become so much a part of popular, lay psychology as to be representative of contemporary Western culture.

The power of these psychoanalytic ideas notwithstanding, we frequently lose sight of the fact that, once we step out of the delimited setting of the consulting room, many of our carefully validated *clinical* principles

183

become hypothetical. We are often so taken with the idea of being able to generalize about social and psychological patterns that it is frustrating to recall the *real* limits of our verifiable knowledge. This is not, however, a preface to giving up the effort that Freud himself characterized as having potential beyond clinical psychoanalytic treatment. It is meant as both caution and encouragement, so that the effort we do make in this direction will not be in vain.

Much has been said and hotly debated about psychoanalytic epistemology in general. Without citing specific works, it is fair to say that many contributors from philosophy and psychoanalysis have long argued the question of whether *any* of the data of psychoanalysis should be invited into the realm of twentieth-century scientific thought. There remain unsettling questions about methodology and theory, about verifiability and reliability. Regardless of the outcome of this debate, from the point of view of interdisciplinary studies it is without question that psychoanalysis remains a hermeneutic endeavor: a search for the meaning in experience and events, through the process of interpretation. Furthermore, as Devereux (1978) has maintained, the nature of this kind of endeavor necessarily becomes "pluridisciplinary" rather than interdisciplinary; each new question or piece of data requires a "double analysis" (Gehrie, 1978a) in which we strive to bring together hermeneutic frameworks that ordinarily exist on different planes.

Psychoanalysis is not a social science in the same sense as anthropology. However, when used in conjunction with anthropological or ethnographic kinds of materials, it becomes a complementary (hermeneutic) frame of reference. In such an undertaking, the principles under which it should be applied are different from those which govern the clinical situation. For example, in clinical work, psychoanalytic clinical generalizations are often appropriately used as guides in the effort to understand and categorize a patient's associations. In work with cultural materials, these same generalizations may not be used *as if* the data to which they were being applied were the same. We make, I believe, a fundamental error if we assume that our own associations to cultural materials (or, for that matter, the associations of a "native" to his own culture) are logically equivalent to a patient's associations in an analysis. True "complementarity," therefore, lies not in the effort to force one set of materials into a slot usually reserved for another. It is this kind of category error that has accounted, in my opinion, for the long-term disappointment and dissatisfaction that has plagued multidisciplinary efforts in psychoanalysis and anthropology.

True anthropological ethnography produces a kind of data that is as unique and valuable as true psychoanalytic data. Differences between the two are, of course, profound, although there is a feature relevant to both. This feature is the dependence upon a hermeneutic framework for the evocation of meaning. To put it most simply, this means that the meaning of events and/or behaviors in both fields is constantly changing; there is no certainty or absoluteness which is immutable. The history of a culture, like the history of a person, depends for its creation upon the historian. To ask "what *really* happened" in either context is to force a framework upon the data which might not apply, and which demands that the data be organized in a way that might implicitly change the quality of the data itself.

Freud wanted his psychoanalytic theories to have an applicability outside the consulting room. However, though he did so with clinical work, he did not provide us with a method for making that transition. His efforts in that direction force us to continue searching for a way to handle data from a complementary frame of reference while simultaneously maintaining our interpretive point of view. When a question such as the relevance of the concept "Oedipus complex" for people of another culture is raised, we are faced with a considerable challenge to maintain a truly complementary view. Since many of the issues stemming from the Jones/Malinowski debate have been covered elsewhere (Parsons, 1969; Gehrie, 1977, 1978b) as well as by others in this section, I will limit my comments to hermeneutic issues which I believe pertain to a multidisciplinary approach.

As long as anthropologists were content to study and categorize noncomplex, non-Western, very small-scale social groups (such as tribes), the demands upon their theories were similarly noncomplex. It was certainly true that there were divergences of theoretical and methodological perspective—such as the emic/etic debate, for example.[1] But regardless of one's preference for the insider or outsider point of view, the essential subjectivity of the native's *experience* was almost never a focus of attention. Rather, the issue was much more likely to be: who decided what categories of kinship were most relevant—the native or the ethnographer? Now that anthropology is increasingly focusing its attention beyond the boundaries of simple societies, it has been faced with establishing

[1] The terms "emic" and "etic" are derived from the linguistic concepts of "phonemic" and "phonetic," respectively denoting units of meaning or units of structure in language. Expanded beyond the purely linguistic application, these terms are used as shorthand to describe certain general approaches in anthropology: those that emphasize the meaning of cultural behaviors in contrast to those that pre-eminently emphasize the structure or organization of a social system. Most commonly, the emic view is used to denote the "native's-eye-view" of things, and the etic view the perspective of the outsider, or that of the comparison-minded ethnographer.

criteria for comparison which go beyond categorization. For example, if anthropologists are to ask questions about psychology that go beyond treating it as a simple, culture-dependent variable, then some means must be found to collect data which offer us the possibility of interpretation. The ethnographic method, though seldom used for this purpose, does in fact offer an excellent opportunity for this. Whether or not the particular focus of the ethnographer is the individual (such as in the life-history or case-history approach), or even a larger group (so long as no one in the group remains entirely anonymous to the ethnographer), there are opportunities to pursue the realm of subjective experience.

Efforts to duplicate the psychoanalytic clinical environment in the fieldwork situation are liable to be fraught with difficulty, especially since such attempts often focus on what is lost or left out in comparison with the situation in the consulting room. The context of anthropological fieldwork offers the ethnographer a unique opportunity to experience an emotional climate that reflects something essential about the culture; it is this *experience of the fieldworker* that becomes the basic data. This approach requires that the reseacher/ethnographer be emotionally available for the task. In a sense, all clinical psychoanalysts are ethnographers, and their work of understanding precedes clinical generalizations. It is, of course, impossible not to have generalizations in mind when listening to a patient, but the optimally functioning analyst continuously monitors his own reaction to the patient's associations. In the case of the ethnographer there must also be a continuous effort at self-monitoring. Although not traditionally interwoven with anthropological training as an *emotional* task, the awareness of *cultural* bias on the part of the fieldworker has always been considered essential. It is inevitable that when difficulties arise in the interface between the disciplines this essential part has somewhere been neglected. The anthropologist must allow the culture he is studying to be experienced internally, and he must use that experience as an essential source of information. In this sense, culture is an *internal* phenomenon, not merely a collection of behaviors, institutions, traditions, or rules for social organization and kinship relations.

The Jones/Malinowski debate suffers from the worst kind of errors on both sides. Malinowski sought empirical evidence to disprove an abstract theory, and Jones's refutation implied that the social organization alone was "evidence" of the existence of the Oedipus complex. In neither case was the significance of the natives' experience taken into account, nor that of the ethnographer. (Much later, after Malinowski's death, many of Malinowski's real feelings about the people he studied came to light in *A Diary in the Strict Sense of the Term* [1967]. Though even this was considerably edited, its relevance to much of his work is obvious. Unfortunately, this kind of material is often overlooked by many anthropologists whose training has not prepared them to use it. Devereux's *From Anxiety to Method in the Behavioral Sciences* [1967] belongs to this same category.) I submit, therefore, that the Jones/Malinowski debate was not really a debate in the sense that alternative views of a single phenomena were discussed with an aim toward understanding and resolution. On the contrary, it served more as a forum for each of the two disciplines to assert its primacy, and to reject the premises of the other. Psychoanalysis and anthropology will not develop an intellectual continuity or the capacity for cooperative endeavor through such an approach.

A meaningful effort to carry psychoanalytic kinds of insight outside of the consulting room will depend on the willingness of collaborators to examine *thoroughly* the relevant principles of both fields. It will also be necessary to accept variances in method and techniques of interpretation of data that may initially disturb the sense that each field is fully or fairly represented. The key, in my view, will be the mutual willingness to consider emotional experience as evidence of (internalized) cultural process.

REFERENCES

Devereux, G. (1967), *From Anxiety to Method in the Behavioral Sciences*. New York: Humanities Press.

—— (1978), *Ethnopsychoanalysis*. Berkeley: University of California Press.

Gehrie, M. (1977), Psychoanalytic anthropology: a brief review of the state of the art. *Amer. Behav. Scientist*, 20:721-732.

—— (1978a), On the dual perspective of psychoanalytic anthropology. *J. Psychol. Anthro.*, 1:165-201.

—— (1978b), The psychoanalytic study of social phenomena: a review essay. *The Annual of Psychoanalysis*, 6:143-164. New York: International Universities Press.

Malinowski, B. (1967), *A Diary in the Strict Sense of the Term*. New York: Harcourt, Brace & World.

Parsons, A. (1969), *Belief, Magic and Anomie*. New York: Free Press.

Commentary

SAMUEL WEISS, M.D.

What is disconcerting about this paper is that Spiro's criticism seems to be so obvious and Malinowski seemed to have been so naïve. Was this the emerging science of anthropology in the 1920s? And if so, why has Malinowski been so venerated until now? It would appear, from Spiro's account, that most of Malinowski's conclusions were based more on assertions than on painstaking constructions based on his observed data. What was the reaction of the anthropology community to his publication? Was he presenting new ideas? What about his method? Certainly in science we already had a substantial body of methodology. What was the reception to his ideas and methods? Is it conceivable that no one objected for fifty years until Spiro came along to sound the clarion call?

Unfortunately, Spiro's seemingly appropriate criticism takes Malinowski's work out of its historical context, and we need to know what that context was. What was the state of anthropology in the 1920s? What was Malinowski looking for in his study? What did he wish to accomplish? For example, was he reacting so strongly to Freud's ideas on the Oedipus, which were after all rev-

191

olutionary for that time, that his primary aim in the study was to disprove Freud? If that were so, then it is more explainable that he would subvert his observations or even ignore them in the service of proving his position, or—more correctly—of disproving Freud's.

I think that one's point of view and frame of reference do inevitably influence what one observes and how one will interpret one's observations. As scientists it is hoped that we enter the research arena with open minds, but we do have theories and hypotheses about what we are going to study. It probably is more than coincidence that most of us tend to prove what our theories state. We usually have significant narcissistic investment in our point of view. I have, on many occasions, listened to clinical data being presented, or to theories based on clinical data, about which I would strongly disagree with the presenter, even though I was listening to the same data that he had used in his theory formation. It has often been said that it is almost impossible to present clinical material at a conference because that material will be understood and interpreted differently by many of the listeners. Each listener is anchored by his own theoretical bias. It is a difficult problem, and there are no easy answers to this dilemma.

An additional and important problem is the time in which the study is done and its influence on the researcher. An art forgery, of a different time period, invariably gives itself away to the expert by virtue of its reflecting some aspect of its own period, be it the technique, materials, style, or whatever. The historian, by the same token, reflects his own *present* time, and so his view of a previous century, for example, will be an understanding of the past in the light of the present. From that point of view, it makes sense that an eighteenth-century history of the fourteenth century, for example, would be and should be very different from a twentieth-century history of the fourteenth century.

Viewed from such a vantage point, it becomes very difficult to study this critique of Malinowski without having available more data of his time period. Freud today is quite acceptable—perhaps not so fashionable anymore, but still quite acceptable. He has entered the mainstream of our lives in a way that the layman often isn't even aware of. Many people will talk about a Freudian slip without knowing its origin. Spock, based on Freud in a somewhat misguided way, to be sure, was the pediatric Bible of the white middle class for twenty-five years. The movies have popularized the concept of the unconscious, etc.

I'm sure that the climate for psychoanalytic ideas was very different in the 1920s. Psychoanalysis and psychoanalytic ideas were viewed with a deep suspicion. Perhaps it was most important to put down and ridicule such ideas. For the scientist, it was perhaps more important to disprove than to ridicule.

Another aspect, perhaps much more related to psychobiography, would be to know more about Malinowski and what motivated him to study the Trobriand Islanders and to take what sounds like a polemical position. But I don't have any biographical data on Malinowski, and that kind of exploration is far removed from Spiro's paper and therefore from this discussion, at least at this time.

This brings us to the issue of methodology. What seems clear from Malinowski's data, as conveyed by Spiro, is that he dealt only with manifest content and there does not appear to be any conceptualization of the idea of a latent content. For example, although he can acknowledge a triangle, such as mother-brother-son, there is no awareness of the possibility that this can represent other configurations, like mother-father-son. Nor did he even address the question: what if there is no brother, what if there is no sister? This is a question that obviously cannot be asked with regard to a mother or a father. I assume that anthropologists deal in symbols all the time. Yet at this point, Malinowski became very concrete and literal.

It is one thing to speculate about Malinowski's motives, but why did the anthropological and, according to Spiro, the psychoanalytic community accept Malinowski's assertions? Why did Spiro accept those assertions, and why does he not accept them now?

I think it is interesting that Spiro, in his seminal work, *Children of the Kibbutz*, first published in 1958 and subsequently revised, opens chapter 10 with the following statement, "The education theorists of The Federation maintain that the Oedipus Complex is precluded in the kibbutz by several of the characteristics of collective education." And further on he says, "Despite the negative evidence, however, there is other evidence that points to the existence of Oedipal feelings in these children."

Is there some hidden, latent reason why Spiro has become a defender of the Oedipus complex, why the oedipal configuration has become a magnet for his interest? Conversely, with his knowledge of anthropology and psychoanalysis, why has it taken him so long to take on Malinowski? If there are unconscious determinants in Malinowski's assertions, are there not likely to be unconscious determinants in Spiro's critique? I cannot answer the question, but the answer must lie both in Spiro and in his—our—time.

In 1981 Rudolph Binion, a historian, presented some of his methodology in history and biography at the Chicago Institute for Psychoanalysis, in which, at least in part, he has adopted and adapted a psychoanalytic model for the study of history and historical figures. What he does first is to study all the available data on a person or time period exhaustively. Then, by the use of empathy he tries to put himself into that time frame or into the mind and feelings of the figure. "If I were so-and-so, what would I feel and what would I do?" He arrives at an answer. And being a researcher, he does not stop there. He goes back to the data or explores for further data to see if his intuitive hunch can be confirmed by concrete evidence.

Spiro also uses himself as an important instrument in studying the process. One of the important pieces of data that gives him the conviction that there is indeed an oedipal conflict among the kibbutz children is his study of the children's relationship to him. And, like Binion, he tries to go further and provide additional supportive material.

But this type of approach is largely a product of our times. It may be a by-product of psychoanalysis, of the concept of transference and countertransference and empathy. Was this kind of approach available to Malinowski when he did his studies? Was the concept of transference widely understood, were ideas of ego defenses such as displacement understood? If not, what tools did he have available to him? Paralleling the development of the field of psychoanalysis, with its emphasis on the unknown and the hidden, psychology began to make us aware of the vagaries of perception and cognition. For example, a group of people observing the same happening would report it differently, as if they had not each winessed the same event.

If Malinowski was suspicious of psychoanalysis and its emphasis on the unconscious, was he less observant of the problems of perception? We still struggle against the wish to see what we want to see and to hear what we want to hear. This issue is not limited to the lay public or to our patients; it is an endless struggle in ourselves as well, and the best that we can do is to approach the problem rather than to solve it.

The problem centers on the Oedipus complex itself. Spiro points out Malinowski's failure in understanding Freud's Oedipus complex. That is, Malinowski sees the problem as involving a hostile authority figure to which the son reacts. Spiro can see past this to the issue of the son's rivalrous feelings toward the father; yet his understanding of the Oedipus seems strangely naïve as well.

It might be useful at this point to present Freud's view of the Oedipus and the aspects of it that have caught the imagination and interest of the professional public, and those areas that have remained obscure, and largely neglected, and to attempt a further elaboration of the oedipal conflict in the light of some of our current understandings.

In Little Hans, Freud delineated the most popular aspects, the most commonly accepted aspects of the oedipal conflict, some rather crucial parts of which have been misunderstood. In this version of the theory, the son has a sexual interest in his mother and wants to possess her for himself. He sees the father as standing in his way, a rival, and so he wishes him out of the way, dead. For reasons that need further elaboration, the child does not retain such hostile wishes toward the father but projects them onto the father. Projection is a defense mechanism in which the impulse, aimed outward at someone else, is now perceived as aimed by that someone else toward oneself. What was misunderstood by Malinowski was this concept; it is commonly misunderstood by most people, who perceive it as the father being harsh and threatening to the son, perhaps because he perceives the son as a rival or because he is a nasty person.

I would like to add parenthetically that where one

does in fact find a father who does threaten the son with castration, we have quite a different kind of psychological configuration, not an oedipal one.

It is not usually understood that the father's castrating wishes to the son are the son's own projections of his own hostile impulses toward the father. Why does the hostile impulse have to be projected? If we were to conceptualize the need for a defense against an impulse, then the type of defense used might be related to the phase of development. Is the child afraid of retribution, so that he has to disown responsibility for the hostile impulse? Perhaps. Freud goes on, in the Little Hans case, to emphasize instead that the son also loves the father, so that the hostile impulse immediately becomes entwined in conflict, the child's love versus his hate. The issue is neatly resolved by displacement. Little Hans can continue to love his father and enjoy the father's love as well. It is now an issue which involves the horses in the Vienna streets. The intolerable impulse has been projected, which is phase-appropriate, but still intolerable because it has been projected onto a loved object; so it is then displaced, which is also phase-appropriate, onto the horses. Little Hans no longer hates his father; the father no longer threatens Hans; it is now the horses who hate Hans and threaten to bite him. Father is now perceived as loving and protecting Hans from the horses—that is, from his own impulses—and because of his fear, Hans cannot go outside and therefore ends up staying in the house with his mother. The sexual impulse to the mother is therefore not renounced. It is the hostile impulse to the father that is.

Another, perhaps more profound aspect of the Oedipus which is largely ignored has to do with the role of the mother as the potential castrator. Freud himself didn't quite know what to do with this and seemingly did not integrate it into the main body of the theory. It surfaces again in our understanding of adolescence, when, according to Blos, the boy's castration fear is attached to the phallic mother. I think that Benedek was probably alluding to this phenomenon, at least in part, when she referred to the developmental task of adolescence as being that of overcoming the anxiety of approaching the opposite sex. For the boy this meant fear of the vagina dentata, among other things—the castrating vagina. For the girl, it was the fear of being penetrated.

As we go back to the oedipal period itself, the boy's fear of the mother is seemingly related to her rage at being deprived of a penis, her envy. How does this fit with the boy's sexual love of the mother? Are we dealing primarily with adult reconstructions of childhood rather than with the reality of children? We still have a long way to go to understand the relationship, if any, between genetic reconstructions in the adult and ongoing development in the child.

In their important research Roiphe and Galenson note the increasing comfort of the 1½-year-old boy with regard to his having a penis and an emerging masculine position, and the girl's increasing distress at discovering her lack.

Can some mothers sublimate their lack and take comfort in their having produced a male offspring, as Freud suggested? Or is that again the kind of male chauvinism that Freud was accused of? Or is it irrelevant what the mother's reaction is? Are we again dealing with the child's own impulses, projected? If so, what could be stimulating the child's hostile impulses toward the mother? Could it be related, at the oedipal level, to the fact that mother chooses father as her sexual object? Does mother's absent penis in itself produce anxiety, fear, and rage, since it introduces the idea of differences, change, possible loss? And what about the possible central importance of self-esteem issues?

Does the boy not know at some level that he could not perform and could not satisfy the mother's sexual wishes? Does he not know that his small penis cannot fill the mother's large cavity? Is his renunciation, partial and temporary, perhaps based on issues of shame, a very important affect during this developmental period? Does the hostility to the father have anything to do with envy of the father, at the dyadic level, envy of his larger, more powerful phallus? And at the triadic level, envy of his possession of the mother? But does the hostility to the father, stirred by the above issues, provide a way out of the shame dilemma, so that the boy's self-esteem is preserved? He can thus be "forced" to renounce his sexual wish and thus avoid the shame of his small member and his inability to perform.

In very recent years the self psychologists have come up with a theory that the infantile neurosis, that is, the oedipal conflict, is in a sense a by-product of some failure in development of self, and therefore not an invariable and inevitable developmental consequence.

The point I am trying to make is that there are many aspects to the concept, oedipal complex. And we have not even addressed the important issue of the girl and her oedipal development. It would have been most intriguing and useful to have studied such development, too, in a matrilineal culture. Freud was a product of his time, and thus it was his main thrust to interpret the world from the male's point of view. As our culture has changed, we see more evidence of other equally important issues, such as a boy's envy of a girl's capacity to bear children, separation-individuation issues, issues of self development, and the like.

Personally, I am no longer satisfied with the label,

phallic phase. I much prefer exhibitionistic phase of development, which thus includes the girl's development as well, which is not all penis envy. I also, parenthetically, prefer toddler phase to anal phase, since there are many important landmark events taking place in a child's life at that time that are not related to the toileting.

Although Freud was a product of his time and Malinowski a product of his, it would seem clear that Malinowski was profoundly influenced by Freud, if only in the negative sense. He could not approach the study of a matrilineal culture and see what it told us about a boy's and a girl's oedipal development, for example, but he had to prove that Freud was wrong in his theory.

With the expansion of psychoanalysis to the treatment of other than oedipal neuroses, we are becoming aware that other aspects of development may be as important or even more important than the oedipal one. From that standpoint, Spiro's dissertation, although necessary, may already be late and the thrust of his comments no longer central to our evolving interests.

Commentary: Malinowski and the Sphynx

WAUD H. KRACKE, Ph.D.

Malinowski's theory of the Trobriand Oedipus complex is an especially felicitous topic with which to mark the fiftieth anniversary of the Chicago Institute for Psychoanalysis, for it was very much in the air in the year the Institute was founded. Malinowski's definitive work on Trobriand child development—the fuller and more careful study, *The Sexual Life of Savages*, not the more contentious earlier series of articles published as *Sex and Repression in Savage Society*—came out in 1929, and its 3d edition was published in 1931. More importantly, this topic gives us an opportunity for reflection on some of the developments that have taken place in psychoanalytic thinking about oedipal issues over the fifty years since Malinowski wrote.

A good discussant should raise challenging issues and stimulate controversy. Unfortunately, I find myself in some difficulty in this regard, since I agree with everything that Professor Spiro has written in the foregoing paper. In fact, my experience has been quite similar to his. Although on first reading I did have some suspiciousness at the neatness of Malinowski's argument, it was only when I used Malinowski's book in teaching that I became fully aware how riddled his argument was with flagrant contradictions. The mother's brother, who is supposed to be the primary representative of authority for a boy, is not only (as Dr. Spiro has pointed out) geographically distant (Malinowski, 1927, p. 48), but is largely excluded from the boy's home except on formal occasions such as the delivery of *urigubu* payments, because of the stringent brother-sister avoidance rule which excludes personal contact beween a grown man and his sister (1927, p. 69; 1929, pp. 36, 521). And why would the boy's love for his sister be repressed and amplified when his love for the mother, equally prohibited under matrilineal exogamy rules (1929, pp. 55, 522-523), is supposedly satisfied, satiated, and drained off? To these basic flaws, which Dr. Spiro has brought out excellently, I might just add mention of one more: Malinowski's theory would predict that the female Oedipus complex in the West would exist only in its negative form (since a girl grows up in the same patriarchal family that a boy does, and therefore like her brother should feel tenderly toward her mother and resent her distant father). This may be one reason why Malinowski (1927) restricts his discussion to the *male* Oedipus complex in both societies: when he touches on the European girl's experience, it is to deny that the oedipal-age girl had any competitiveness in her relationship with her mother like the boy's with his father (p. 36)—although by the end of Part I (chap. 8) he seems to have forgotten this, when he says (p. 69) that the Trobriand girl's Oedipus complex is the same as that of a girl in the West.

A basic problem with Malinowski's theory is his failure to acknowledge, or make any reference to, the element of sexual rivalry that is central to the dynamic of the Oedipus complex. Anne Parsons (1964) made a valiant attempt to remedy this defect, by suggesting a revised version putting the Trobriand boy in a fantasied competition with the mother's brother for his mother's love. But this reformulation is still inadequate, for she would have the boy reacting entirely to his mother's fantasies about her brother, totally ignoring the real sexual relationship between his mother and father.

Since I cannot take issue with any of the major points that Professor Spiro makes, but can only applaud and second them, I am left with a choice of several possible directions in which to take my discussion. One might be to raise the question of why such a careful and thorough ethnographer, the same man who gave us the careful reasoning and detailed documentation of *Coral Gardens and Their Magic*—a book which establishes exacting rules for sound ethnographic evidence—felt impelled in this case to twist and strain his data to produce and defend such a fragile and patently self-contradictory theory. As has been competently done for Freud's (1914) equally fanciful reconstruction of human evolution (Freeman, 1967), one can speculate on the conflicts and anxieties that impelled Malinowski to espouse such a theory. His published diaries (Malinowski, 1967), with their repeated passionate references to "Mother" (note especially the sequence of erotic fantasies on pp. 27-28, culminating in "longing for mother"), would provide ample material for speculation on Malinowski's own psychodynamics, and why it was so important for him to depreciate the universality of the Oedipus complex. His own feelings may have been so close to consciousness that the notion of the Oedipus complex was simultaneously fascinating and profoundly threatening to him.

I will resist the temptation to engage in a psychoanalysis of Malinowski's diary, however, and instead will raise two other questions that have to do with the broader implications of what Dr. Spiro has so skillfully established. First, what does Malinowski's misconception of the Oedipus complex, and his misguided effort to develop a cross-cultural modification of oedipal theory, clarify about the change in conceptualization of oedipal issues over the past fifty years? And second: what kinds of influence *do* matrilineal institutions such as those of the Trobriand Islands have on the development and resolution of Oedipal conflicts?

Malinowski conceived of the "Oedipus complex" as a strictly sociological configuration of family roles. This conceptualization was perhaps understandable at the time, as even analysts tended to talk about the "Oedipus complex" in terms of the configuration of personnel involved in it—mother-son-father, father-daughter-mother. But his version of it was vastly oversimplified, omitting entirely the dynamic element of sexual competition[1] which Anne Parsons later tried to restore in her revision of his theory. (Also, Freud had already stressed in "The Ego and the Id" that the "negative" form of the Oedipus, son competing with mother for father's love, is as prevalent and basic as the positive; but we can forgive Malinowski for not being familiar with all of the psychoanalytic literature then available.)

---

[1] Worse, as Dr. Weiss points out in his discussion, Malinowski fails to understand the two important points that the child's fantasy of a hostile father is largely a projection of his own feelings, and that the whole complex of feelings is generally unconscious and expressed only through indirect symbolism in dreams, for example, not openly. These are but symptoms of a deeper failure of understanding on Malinowski's part: he fails to understand that the Oedipus complex (like other psychoanalytic formulations) takes place in psychic reality, rather than being overtly expressed in behavior. Similarly, he regards "repression" as being equivalent to social condemnation—a social, not an intrapsychic, phenomenon.

By now, I think, the analytic conception of oedipal issues has shifted away from this conception of "the Oedipus complex" as a configuration of roles in a family, toward a conception of "oedipal" as a level of developmental achievement. The term "Oedipus complex" is used much less in psychoanalytic discussion these days, but is replaced by the adjective "oedipal," used in several distinct but related contexts. The "oedipal stage of development" is a period from ages three to five, more or less, when a child, having (ideally) confronted the frightening and intriguing fact that others—his parents—are separate people with their own needs and wishes, now becomes interested in the relationships *between* these other people, and in where the child himself (or herself) fits into the scheme of these relationships. "Oedipal" is also used to refer to the attainment of this level of concerns, and for the resulting structure of personality functioning.

The oedipal period involves a series of important changes. Social roles of behavior take on a new kind of meaning for the child: they are no longer merely external rules to conform to, but are now internal guides for the child's social behavior. Questions of how one is like or unlike others and what one is capable of becoming (versus what one can never become), particularly in one's genital endowment, assume central prominence. It is in this context of newly dawning awareness of relationships between others that the child's passionate wish to possess one parent collides with the awareness of the love that parent holds for the other. Castration concerns are in the context of jealous retaliation and sexual identity, not (as earlier in life) in the context of concerns over bodily integrity (Roiphe, 1968). The place of the father in the Oedipus and its resolution, that of drawing the child (male or female, in different ways) out of the nexus of the ma-

ternal relationship, is another aspect that has more recently been emphasized.

This sense of what is going on in a child at the oedipal
phase of development is quite different from the rigid
sociological formula that Malinowski was working with,
and indeed from the terms in which Jones and other contemporary analysts talked about "the Oedipus complex."
Obviously, all of these oedipal issues that I have just
mentioned would be played out in the child's life and
fantasies *in terms of* the significant persons in his or her
environment, especially parents but any others in a regular caretaking role as well. Several recent articles have
described the role of grandparents or other household
figures in a child's oedipal configuration, most recently
an article last year by David Werman (1980) on "The
Effect of the Family Constellation and Dynamics on the
Form of the Oedipus Complex." Likewise, the Oedipus
complex itself is seen no longer as the isolated key to
development, but as having continuity with earlier and
later phases which present their own versions of the issues in various lines of development, and have their impact on the way the child handles oedipal conflicts.

Misguided though he was in his specific formulations,
Malinowski was probably right about one general intuition: that the structure of the family in which a child
grows up, and the beliefs about key relationships, must
influence the way in which he experiences the main developmental issues with which he is faced. Now that Dr.
Spiro has cleared away the debris of Malinowski's creaky
arguments, we can face afresh the basic question: How
might the social conditions Malinowski describes —prolonged maternal warmth, permissive attitude toward the
open expression of sexuality, and, in particular, matrilineal family institutions—affect the child's experience
of oedipal developmental issues, and his solution of them?

Sexual permissiveness is the easiest to deal with, perhaps, because it occurs in so many societies. My own experience in a society of South American Indians with very relaxed sexual standards has shown that these do have an effect on oedipal fantasy life, but it is very different from the effect that Malinowski posits. Rather than leading to totally conflict-free sexuality, the effect in Kagwahiv society is that sexual fantasies in general are more openly expressed and accessible to consciousness, *including* punitive fantasies of castration and other conflict-laden oedipal fantasies. These are expressed in dreams of adults (as well as children) with a minimum of disguise. I have presented elsewhere some dreams of Kagwahiv adults which express oedipal themes with a minimum of disguise (Kracke, 1979, 1980). In other societies with more relaxed attitudes toward sexuality, conflict-laden childhood fantasies and experiences concerning sexuality seem to be less deeply repressed than in ours.[2] A Hopi Indian like Don Talayesva could recount circumstantially a primal-scene experience that happened to him at the age of three (Simmons, 1942, pp. 37-38). I suspect that the same may be true in the Trobriands, and that the openly expressed fantasies may have caused Malinowski some discomfort—hence, perhaps, his vagueness of detail on this topic, substituting contention for observation.

The effects of matrilineal family organization are a little more difficult to parcel out, since as Dr. Spiro indicates Malinowski provides so little concrete detail, and

---

[2] This is *not* to say that repression is absent in such societies, or even necessarily less pervasive. In Kagwahiv society, for example, where competitiveness is strongly discouraged in children and cooperation encouraged, the aggressive and competitive components of childhood conflicts, including oedipal rivalry with the father, are quite often heavily disguised and displaced in dreams.

we have far fewer comparative instances to rely upon. The mother's brother would seem to me more analogous to a teacher, a parent substitute whose role is to help wean the child away from the oedipal situation and introduce him to the values of society rather than to play a central role in the oedipal drama himself. The mother's brother begins when the boy is about six, Malinowski (1927, p. 49) says, to solicit the child's help in his garden or his presence on an expedition, increasing his demands to their full level as the boy reaches adolescence (p. 67). But what effect would matrilineal ideas about descent have on the oedipal configuration itself? One can speculate that, if anything, they might intensify the conflicts, at least for a boy: for, on the one hand, prolonged nursing and postpartum sexual abstinence might tend to heighten the erotic tensions in a boy's relationship with his mother, whereas, on the other hand, the universal mother-son incest taboo in matrilineal societies is reinforced by the rule of exogamy, as Malinowski himself rather backhandedly points out (p. 232).

One could also suggest that the resolution of the Oedipus in paternal identification may be made somewhat more difficult. For identification with the father, although it would initially be encouraged by the warm father-son relationship Malinowski describes, meets a social barrier in the matrilineal definition of family relationships. These institutions would become meaningful for a child at about the oedipal period of life, just the period when social rules assume relevance for him so that paternal identification in this critical period might be inhibited. This argument is somewhat tenuous, however, since identificatory bonds do not require social sanctions in order to become strong. And, in fact, Malinowski's description of the lifelong bonds between father and son, and the length to which fathers will go to pass their inheritance on to *their* sons rather than to their sisters' sons, is a strong indication to me of the existence of an identificatory bond between fathers and sons.

This, in any case, is all highly speculative. In a very few cases, we have direct psychological evidence on the emotional development of individuals who have grown up in other matrilineal societies. I will just mention two cases. Among the strongly matrilineal Hopi Indians, Dorothy Eggan in the 1940s and 1950s collected hundreds of dreams from several individuals, with associations, and she analyzed the dreams with some consultative help from Dr. Thomas French—an important figure in Chicago psychoanalysis—and using French's approach (formulated in French and Fromm, 1964). More recently the psychoanalysts Paul Parin, Fritz Morgenthaler, and Goldie Parin-Mattey (1981) conducted a study among the Anyi, a matrilineal Akan people once part of the Ashanti state.

One of Dorothy Eggan's chief sources of dreams was Don Talayesva, whose autobiography recounted to Leo Simmons is well known under the title *Sun Chief.* I have mentioned the primal-scene memory he told to Simmons, which was in a classically oedipal mold. He was lying on a sheepskin, in their summer house, felt the floor shake, and was sure his father was beating his mother mercilessly; the next morning he was angry at his father, and also at his mother for being so nice to his father despite it all. The dynamic importance of the memory for him was confirmed by whole series of adult dreams which reproduced it, reported in an article by Dorothy Eggan (1949, pp. 186-189, 194-195), in which a woman's husband maltreats her and she leaves her husband to seduce Don. These dreams invariably were set in locales from his early life, and in one the seduction took place on a sheepskin mat. This encodes a highly competitive and jealous relationship with his father, one of his dominant modes of relating to other men.

But another childhood memory was of being rescued by his father from the snare of the Spider Woman into whose shrine he had ventured. This second way of relating to his father, showing a need for an admired and protective male figure to rescue him from being enmeshed in the world of women, seems to characterize much of his relationship to Simmons and to some other men in his life, both Hopi and white. This kind of hunger for an idealizable father is also striking in Parin and Morgenthaler's interviews with Anyi men, who grew up in families where (as among the Ashanti) husband and wife might be living in completely separate matrilineal households. Like Don, many of these men seemed unsure of their masculine identity, searching for admirable male figures with whom to identify. And Roheim (1950, pp. 156, 162) hints that paternal identification was problematic on matrilineal Normanby Island, near the Trobriands, where he conducted some psychoanalytic inteviewing. While such difficulties with paternal identification are not, of course, limited to matrilineal societies, it seems probable that they may be more intense and pervasive in matrilineal societies than in patrilineal ones or in bilateral societies like our own.

This hypothesis is certainly neither as dramatic nor as exotic as Malinowski's "matrilineal Oedipus complex." Many other more particular hypotheses could be developed on the basis of case studies such as Don Talayesva, or of analytic research such as that by the Parins and Morgenthaler. But modest hypotheses like the one I have suggested, and the particular understanding of the roles played by the members of a child's household (be they parents, uncles, grandparents, servants, or whatever) in each child's particular oedipal configuration, will bring us much closer than Malinowski's grand theorizing to answering the riddle of the interaction between man's nature, social institutions, and the child's emotional development. Malinowski must be given credit, however, for posing the question—some fifty years ago—even if his answer (as Professor Spiro has so clearly shown) was premature.

REFERENCES

Eggan, D. (1949), The significance of dreams for anthropological research. *Amer. Anthropologist*, 51:177-198.

Freeman, D. (1967), Totem and Taboo: A reappraisal. *Psychoanal. Study of Society*, 4:9-53.

French, T. M., & Fromm, Erika (1964), *Dream Interpretation: A New Approach*. New York: Basic Books.

Freud, S. (1914), Totem and taboo. *Standard Edition*, 13:1-164. London: Hogarth Press, 1955.

Kracke, W. (1978), Dreaming in Kagwahiv: Psychic uses of dreaming in an Amazonian Indian culture. *Psychoanal. Study of Society*, 8:119-172.

——— (1980), Amazonian interviews: Dreams of a bereaved father. *The Annual of Psychoanalysis*, 8:249-267. New York: International Universities Press.

Malinowski, B. (1927), *Sex and Repression in Savage Society*. New York: Meridian, 1959.

——— (1929), *The Sexual Life of Savages*. London: Routledge, 3d ed., 1931.

——— (1935), *Coral Gardens and Their Magic*. London: Allen and Unwin.

——— (1967), *A Diary in the Strict Sense of the Term*. London: Routledge and Kegan Paul.

Parin, P., Morgenthaler, F., & Parin-Matthey, G. (1981), *Fear Thy Neighbor as Thyself*. Chicago: University of Chicago Press.

Parsons, A. (1964), Is the Oedipus complex universal? *Psychoanal. Study of Society*, 3:278-328.

Roheim, G. (1950), *Psychoanalysis and Anthropology*. New York: International Universities Press.

Roiphe, H. (1968), On an early genital phase with an addendum on genesis. *The Psychoanalytic Study of the Child*, 23:348-365. New York: International Universities Press.

Simmons, L. (1942), *Sun Chief*. New Haven: Yale University Press.

Werman, D. (1980), The effect of the family constellation and dynamics on the form of the Oedipus complex. *Internat. J. Psycho-Anal.*, 61:505-512.

7

Reviewing Henry Adams

MARK R. SCHWEHN, Ph.D.

In the opening chapter of his nine-volume *History of the United States during the Administrations of Thomas Jefferson and James Madison*, Henry Adams (1889-1891) sketched the following imaginary scene as a kind of symbolic picture of his elaborate analysis of the state of American society and politics in 1800:

> A government capable of sketching a magnificent plan, and willing to give only a half-hearted pledge for its fulfilment; a people eager to advertise a vast undertaking beyond their present powers, which when completed would become an object of jealousy and fear,—this was the impression made upon the traveller who visited Washington in 1800, and mused among the unraised columns of the Capitol upon the destiny of the United States [1:31].

This passage alludes to a portion of Edward Gibbon's (1829-1830) *Autobiography*, a text that Adams knew well. In that book, Gibbon recalled the moment when the idea of writing the *Decline and Fall of the Roman Empire* had first occurred to him "at Rome on the fifteenth of October 1764, as I sat musing amidst the ruins of the Capitol while the barefooted friars were singing Vespers in the temple of Jupiter . . ." (p. 124).

The image of Gibbon on the steps of the Church of Santa Maria di Ara Coeli, musing amid crumbling columns about the meaning of the fall of Rome, obsessed Adams. He carefully prepared the imaginary scene in his *History* by noting, in a passage immediately preceding the one quoted above, that in 1800 congressmen and the chief executive clustered together "as near as possible to the Capitol, and there lived, *like a convent of* monks . . ." (1889-1891, 1:30-31; emphasis added). Their Capitol, moreover, "threatened to crumble in pieces and crush Senate and House under the ruins, long before the building was complete" (1:31). In *The Education of Henry Adams*, a book that Adams composed in 1905, fifteen years after he had finished his *History*, he revealed that, during the summer of 1860, he had more than once sat on the very spot where Gibbon had sat some hundred years before. Adams returned to this place, in fact or in imagination, several times during the course of his life (p. 91).

In the course of my own thinking and writing about Henry Adams, I have had occasion to return "more than once" to this allusive passage in his *History* and to the text of which it is a part. In re-viewing Adams's life and work again and again, I have written two different historical interpretations of his *History*. In the essay that follows, I should like to recount those two interpretations and to describe the process that led me to my current reading of that text. I should like finally to suggest some of the methodological implications that might be derived from my experience.

II

I began my study of Henry Adams almost ten years ago as a part of an effort to understand the development of modernism in Western thought. In my Ph.D. thesis, I sought to clarify the nature of modernism by focusing upon the ideas of both Henry Adams and William James and by construing the development of some of these ideas as strands of a larger cultural pattern. I interpreted Adams's *History* by placing it within the sequence of its author's intellectual life and by locating some of its major themes within the network of problems that Adams faced during the 1870s and 1880s. In addition, I tried to elucidate those aspects of Adams's cultural context that seemed directly pertinent to a historical understanding of his work (Schwehn, 1978).

The substance of my interpretation emphasized the ironic structure of the *History*. The book was, I argued, the story of the improbable but triumphant growth of American democratic nationality despite the persistent failures of American leaders, despite even the initial mental deficiencies of the Americans themselves. The *History* accordingly stressed the dissonance between consciousness and purpose, on the one hand, and unconscious nature, on the other. As a result of Adams's absorption of Lyell's developmental geology and Spencer's evolutionary positivism, he had come to believe that American democracy had "as fixed and necessary development as that of a tree; and almost as unconscious . . ." (Cater, 1951, p. 134). Since democracies progressed only by developing naturally, according to laws exactly like those that governed the physical universe, principled and idealistic political action was ineffectual at best. Indeed, American nationality emerged triumphant at the end of the period 1800-1817, even though American politics, the major preoccupation of the American people during this period, tended to retard national development (Schwehn, 1978, pp. 79-80).

The *History*'s ironic interpretation of American politics served to rationalize Adams's own political failures. During the 1870s he had been active in the Liberal Reform Movement, which sought to expose and check corruption in government, to restore political parties to a state of ideological purity, and to devise some system whereby government would rest in the control of those best equipped to deal scientifically with social and economic questions. After these efforts failed repeatedly during the 1870s, Adams abandoned politics for scholarship. That scholarship, informed as it was by the evolutionary positivism that Adams had adopted during his tenure as a Harvard history professor, fortified his will to believe that *all* political action was superfluous in a democracy. Thus, as I wrote in 1977, Adams's *History* "served to justify his own temporary occupation in writing it" (Schwehn, 1978, p. 65). It proved, to his own satisfaction at least, that scholarship and not politics was the only viable pursuit for the intellectual in a democratic society.

III

In 1978 I presented my interpretation of Adams's *History* to Dr. George Moraitis, a Chicago psychoanalyst. This presentation constituted a part of a long-term experimental collaboration between Dr. Moraitis and myself. During the course of our experiment, I selected portions of my own work on Henry Adams, such as my chapter on Adams's *History*, or portions of Adams's own writings. After Dr. Moraitis, who knew nothing about Henry Adams, read these materials, we met to discuss them. I will not recount our procedures at greater length here, because our experiment was modeled closely upon an earlier collaboration between Dr. Moraitis and another historian, Carl Pletsch. This earlier experiment has been described, from Dr. Moraitis's (1979) perspective, in his article, "A Psychoanalyst's Journey into a Historian's World: An Experiment in Collaboration." My own objectives during the experiment were clear. I sought to discover the nature and perhaps some of the roots of my own long-term involvement with the life of Henry Adams. I hoped that as I became more aware of the range and the depth of my own subjectivities, my study of Henry Adams would become more "objective," i.e., freed from the potentially distorting effects of unexamined motives upon the substance of my interpretation.

During our discussion of my Ph.D. thesis, I realized that I had strongly identified myself with Henry Adams. The sources of this identification were many and various, but it manifested itself most markedly in my initial refusal to publish any psychological or partially psychological interpretations of Adams's work. Indeed, in my Ph.D. thesis, I had sought to conceal or suppress all of my rather elaborate psychological hypotheses about Adams. I believed that psychological explanation was inherently reductionist, and I argued that any psychological interpretation of Henry Adams's life and works would invariably diminish his intellectual stature. I also invoked the historian's ultimate principle to justify my doubts about publishing my own psychological hypotheses: I denied that I had sufficient evidence to substantiate them.

I also offered other defenses of my refusal to press psychological interpretations in my projected book, objections whose logical force ought not be denied simply because some of them may have sprung from dubious motives. First, I argued that my projected book sought to emphasize the connections between Adams's works and the culture of which they were a part. Hence, psychological interpretations, however well informed, seemed irrelevant to *my* purposes. This might be called the defense of my position in formal terms. Second, I feared that, regardless of the care and restraint with which I employed psychological interpretations, my envisioned audience would seize upon *just those* aspects of my work as the crucial part of my over-all argument about the development of modernism. This might be called the defense of my position in rhetorical terms. Finally, I maintained that my efforts to understand the meaning of my materials, such as Adams's *History*, entailed recovering the intentions that governed those works, not the motives that were accidentally and contingently related to them. This might be called the defense of my position in methodological terms.

I am still somewhat persuaded by my own formal and rhetorical defenses against the use of psychological interpretations in my present book, and these reservations will doubtless shape the final form of my over-all argument. Nevertheless, I do believe that all of these defenses stemmed in part from my desire to protect Henry Adams. Furthermore, in seeking to protect Adams, I was, up to a point, seeking to protect myself, and I often resisted our collaborative investigations by finding excuses for postponing our sessions. As a result of this resistance, the timing of our meetings was highly irregular. Even so, my reading of the *History* has changed appreciably as a result of our experiment, and I no longer maintain my methodological objection to using psychological interpretations in my work.

IV

In 1980, after Dr. Moraitis and I had stopped meeting together to discuss Henry Adams, I wrote an article on Adams's *History* entitled "Making History: Henry Adams

and the Science of Democracy."[1] It presents a multicontextual interpretation of Adams's work, and I still remain
as committed as I was during the 1970s to this kind of
historical explanation. Indeed, I incorporated a great deal
of my thesis chapter into this article. I added, however,
a psychological dimension to my interpretation, a dimension that emerged directly from my collaboration with
Dr. Moraitis and yielded new and, I think, more incisive
readings of the *History*.

Unlike the thesis chapter, the 1980 article explored
the psychological relationship between Henry Adams and
the leading character in his *History*, Thomas Jefferson.
Once I had discovered how closely I had become identified
with Henry Adams, I realized how closely Adams had
identified himself with Jefferson. Most Adams scholars
have minimized Adams's positive characterizations of
Jefferson, and they have tended to explain negative ones
by the seemingly plausible argument that Adams was
settling family grievances against the man who had so
soundly defeated John Adams in 1800.[2] On the basis of
a wide range of historical evidence that is both internal
and external to the text of the *History*, I wrote in 1980

[1] This paper, not yet accepted for publication, will be made available upon request.

[2] The most recent version of this error appears in Otto Friedrich's
biography of Henry Adams's wife Marian Hooper. Friedrich claims
that "it was with a pretense of praising the vanished hero that Adams
began his infinitely malicious portrait [of Jefferson]" (1979), p. 284).
A more subtle instance of the same error appears in Ernest Samuels,
Henry Adams: The Middle Years (1958), pp. 388-392. Samuels observes that "Adams could not help but identify himself with Jefferson";
however, Samuels believes that this identification sprang principally
from Adams's appreciation for Jefferson's wit and refinement (p. 388).
Samuels then reverts to the standard thesis to explain Adams's criticisms of Jefferson. Many of them, especially those that Adams undertook in response to promptings from his brother Charles, came
from "the effect of family tradition" (pp. 391-392).

that Adams had lavished such unsparing criticism upon
Jefferson, "not in spite of his identification with him, but
because of it" (Schwehn, 1980, p. 20). This hypothesis led
me to an understanding of certain features of Adams's
characterization of Jefferson that otherwise seem mysterious or unimportant. Moreover, I now understand how
Adams's very choice of Jefferson as his leading subject
permitted him to exercise some of his own ambivalent
feelings toward his distinguished ancestors in the course
of writing about a man who was at once a bitter enemy
and a close friend of Adams's great-grandfather.

The psychological dimension of my historical interpretation of Adams's writings also deepened my understanding of numerous passages in the *History*. As an
illustration of this understanding, I should like briefly
to reconsider the passage from Adams's *History* that I
quoted at the beginning of this present essay. In my 1980
piece I did not discuss this particular passage, but I believe that its meanings become more accessible in the
light of the psychological aspects of my 1980 interpretation of the *History* as a whole. One measure of the value
of an interpretation is its capacity to illuminate portions
of a text that would otherwise remain obscure.

As I have already suggested, the scene that the imaginary traveler surveys in 1800 symbolizes Adams's preceding analysis of the state of American society at the
turn of the nineteenth century. "The city of Washington,"
Adams (1889-1891) wrote, "rising in solitude on the
banks of the Potomac, was a symbol of American nationality . . ." (1:30). By virtue of its allusion to Gibbon's decision to write the *Decline and Fall of the Roman Empire*,
the passage also suggests the grandiosity of Adams's design, and it connects the theme of Adams's *History* to
Gibbon's theme. Gibbon, musing amid ruins, decided to
trace the history of a falling action, the decline of Rome.

Adams, placing an imaginary traveler among the unraised columns of the Capitol, forecasted the rising action of his work, the history of the progressive development of American democracy. As I noted in my 1980 piece, several features of Adams's *History*, such as its erudite allusions, its sly and sometimes savage ironies, and its carefully balanced phrasings, bore the stamp of Gibbon's influence. When Adams completed the narrative portion of his work, he compared his feelings upon that occasion to Gibbon's feelings upon the completion of the *Decline and Fall*. Adams was indeed inviting the kind of comparison that has been made by at least one critic of his work. Yvor Winters (1943) has judged Adams's *History* to be "the greatest historical work in English, with the possible exception of the *Decline and Fall of the Roman Empire*" (p. 29).

Though the formal and thematic elements of this allusive passage seem clear enough, some of its phrasings seem obscure. For whom would the completion of the American experiment in democratic nationalism "become an object of jealousy and fear?" For the imaginary traveler? For other nations? For the narrator of the *History*? Adams certainly was jealous and fearful of American power. Indeed, as I have tried to show in my 1980 essay, the same democracy whose progress Adams explained in his *History* had vitiated his inherited world view, had thwarted his political ambitions, and had thereby confirmed his feelings of impotence and despair. I have also suggested in the 1980 essay that Adams's whole life was marked by a syndrome of impotence, including his deep feelings of physical inferiority, his envy and hatred of his older brother, Charles Francis Adams, Jr., precisely because of Charles's masculine strength and military valor, his childless and tragic marriage, and his repeated failure to attain any position of political power.

Since the envy of masculinity so pervaded Adams's life, I believe that the very image that he used in this passage from his *History* to symbolize American nationality provides a clue to the sources of the obscurely assigned feelings of jealousy and fear. The symbol of completely developed American democracy is, by extension so to speak, a fully erected column. Indeed, the phrase "unraised columns" seems utterly oxymoronic unless it has sexual connotations as well as architectural denotations. In any event, Adams chose to symbolize the rise of American power in indisputably masculine images. As for the central character of his *History*, the one with whom Adams had become so deeply identified, the one who was powerless to control the growth of the country that he sought to govern, "Jefferson's nature was feminine . . ." (Adams, 1889-1891, I:323).

Jefferson was not the first of Adams's "feminine" figures to be perplexed and overtaken by the uncontrollable masculine force of American democracy. Adams twice interrupted his work on the *History* to write novels, both of which featured female protagonists. The dramatic action of one of them, tellingly entitled *Democracy*, consists of the tragic romance of Madeleine Lee, a woman who sets out for Washington in order to discover the secret of American power. As early as 1871, Adams had begun to contrast impersonal, rational, and masculine forms of life with personal, emotional, and feminine ones. And long after he completed his *History*, Adams continued to contrast various forms of power—political, economic, spiritual, military, and technological—in terms of gender. The most famous chapter of his *Education*, entitled "The Dynamo and the Virgin," marks the culmination of this tendency.

By now it should be clear that the passage I have been interpreting represents a classic instance of an overdetermined verbal action. I have been arguing that, in addition to formal and thematic considerations, feelings of grandiosity and sexual inadequacy also worked to determine the passage's composition. The *History* shows how Adams managed to transfuse these feelings that were doubtless two parts of the same psychological syndrome into the tensions between the impersonal, inexorable, and masculine evolution of American democracy and the "feminine" Jefferson who was "sensitive, affectionate, and, in his own eyes, heroic" (p. 324). The passage, then, is a kind of microcosm of the *History* as a whole, for both of them represent cases of the transmutation of psychic stress into cultural expression disciplined by the requirements of the historian's art.

V

Thus far, I have tried to detail how and why my interpretation of Henry Adams's *History* changed in the course of my collaboration with a psychoanalyst. Yet these new readings of the *History* have in turn encouraged me to reexamine the intellectual merits of some of my former defenses against the use of psychological interpretations in my projected book on modernism. I should like briefly to reconsider some of those objections now, before suggesting some of the methodological implications of the experimental collaboration itself for historians, especially biographers.

I now believe that what I referred to earlier as my formal objection to psychological interpretations was misguided. A historical account of the development of modernism should at least provide some understanding of how intellectual transformations occur. In terms of my own projected study, such an understanding is best rendered through an intelligible account of how and why Henry Adams and William James changed their minds over time, developing, in the course of these changes, ideas that finally contributed to a distinctively modern style of thought. Both men came from families that were exceptionally accomplished and hence formidable; moreover, families are arguably the principal agencies of the transmission of culture from one generation to the next. Any account of the intellectual development of Adams or James would therefore be incomplete without considerable attention to their family relationships and to some of the psychic strains that these relationships engendered.

When I first voiced my formal defense, I believed that I was simply reporting a choice that I had made between a culturally oriented and a psychologically oriented interpretation. I now believe that, although it is possible to distinguish between the cultural and the psychological components of a historical interpretation, it is often fruitless and perhaps misconceived to make sharp distinctions or to assert causal relationships between the cultural and the psychological features of an individual's intellectual development. I say this, not on the basis of some theory of culture or psychological development, but on the basis of my efforts to make historical sense of the life and works of Henry Adams and William James. Take, for example, the masculine/feminine distinction that I emphasized in the course of my interpretation of the allusive passage from Adams's *History*. Understanding the meaning of this distinction for Adams and interpreting his use of it in the *History* entail, as I have suggested above, some attention to the psychic conflicts engendered within the context of his family. But historical understanding of the *History* also entails an appraisal of the significance of the fact that Adams's dichotomy between intuitive, emotional, and feminine qualities, on the one hand and scientific, rational, and masculine ones, on the other, represented, as I wrote in 1977, "a widespread cultural tendency among upper class Victorian men." In Adams's case at least, culturally defined gender distinctions doubtless shaped the way that he was reared, and the way that he was reared in turn shaped his own self-conception. That self-conception prompted him to develop a certain set of masculine/feminine distinctions, to cultivate a unique network of associations between those distinctions and, say, the relationship between American nationality and political idealism, and to articulate these associations as tensions within his *History*, a form of expression that was at once personal and cultural. Did culturally defined gender distinctions determine Adams's psyche, or did Adams's psyche, together with the minds of others, determine gender distinctions? Did cultural conflicts cause psychic distress, or did psychic distress cause cultural conflict? These latter questions manifest, I believe, a certain kind of conceptual confusion to which historians are especially prone. Asking such questions is rather like asking whether one side of a lens is convex because the other side is concave or whether the other side is concave because the one side is convex.

Alas, I fear that questions such as the ones posed above are very much like the ones that historians most commonly ask one another. The defense against psychological interpretations that I articulated in rhetorical terms stemmed from just such a fear about my envisioned audience. The most common complaint about multicontextual historical explanations is that such explanations typically fail to single out one context in terms of which all of the others can be understood. Reviewers often seek to remedy this perceived failing by seizing upon one of the contexts that a given book provides and arguing that it *really* explains or illuminates the book's subject better than all of the others combined. My fear was that my

audience would seize upon the psychological aspects of
my interpretation as the key to the whole of it, an, given
my identification with Henry Adams, I expressed this
fear in terms of a rhetorical argument for omitting psychological interpretations altogether.

Can these anticipated objections to multicontextual
interpretations be effectively countered? I believe that
they can be countered in three ways. First, the readers
of a multicontextual interpretation need to be reminded
that contextual explanations are not disguised causal
explanations. Readers who insist that a historian should
privilege one of his contexts are often really asking that
he should specify a principal cause of the process he seeks
to interpret and explain. Second, the readers of a multicontextual interpretation need to be informed that the
choice of this kind of explanation is linked to a certain
conception of the subject matter of history. I believe that
the subjects of my history are beings whose mental processes are informed, developed, transmitted, and expressed in cultural terms. A human being's culture
defines his mind and his mind defines his culture; in that
sense he is like the lens I described above. A person's
psychological side does not cause his or her cultural side
any more than his or her cultural side causes that person's psychological side. Instead, both sides "define" the
contours of the human being just as concavity and con-
vexity "define" the shape and the powers of a particular,
indeed any particular, lens. This view of the subject matter of history is certainly open to dispute. My only point
here is that multicontextual explanation, as opposed to
causal explanation, is connected, in my case at least, to
this conception of my subject.

Finally, the historian can counter the standard objections to multicontextual explanations by casting his
interpretation in a form that best realizes his own pe-

culiar purposes. This essay is not the place to mount a defense of narrative explanation, but I do believe that narration seems especially well suited to the purpose of articulating subjects within several relevant contexts without either losing sight of the subjects altogether or reducing them to mere illustrations of some oversimplified explanatory principle. I believe that much of what Clifford Geertz has written about anthropology applies to intellectual history: intellectual history is not a positivistic science in search of causal laws but a descriptive science in search of meanings. But intellectual history, like all history, aims to understand change over time. I therefore believe that the intellectual historian is well advised to cast his or her "thick description" in narrative form.

My methodological defense against psychological interpretations was more closely related to both my formal and my rhetorical defenses than I had initially believed. It is, of course, perfectly possible, and even at times useful, to distinguish theoretically between motives, defined as a complex of psychological impulses that are accidentally and contingently related to an action, and intentions, defined as characterizations of the action itself. I have, however, found this distinction much easier to maintain in theory than to exercise in the practice of historical interpretation. What, for example, am I to make of my own claim that Adams's *History* "served to justify his own temporary occupation in writing it?" Does this claim characterize Adams's *point* in writing the *History* (does it describe the work's intention?), or does it posit a psychological condition antecedent to and contingently connected with the writing of the book (does it describe a motive?). I confess that I am not sure about the answer to this question, nor am I sure about the exact point of the distinction that the question raises. It seems to me that motives and intentions shade into one another in the same way, and partially for the same reasons, that psychology and culture shade into one another. In any event, I have found motives and intentions equally pertinent to a historical understanding of the text of Adams's *History*. Thus, in my brief methodological prologue to my 1980 essay, I wrote as follows: "Interpreting Adams's classic history entails two related tasks. Adams's changing views of the nature of the historical process must be explained, and his *History* must be understood by placing it within the several different contexts which serve to clarify the motives that inspired its creation."

VI

"One sees what one brings," Henry Adams (1907) wrote during the course of his account of why he, his "idol Gibbon," his friend Augustus St. Gaudens, and his contemporary John Ruskin viewed the Gothic cathedrals of Northern France in such radically different ways (p. 387). During the course of my collaboration with Dr. Moraitis, I learned the extent to which I had seen what I had brought to my study of Henry Adams. I had, of course, brought myself to that study, and in learning more about myself and the sources of my involvement with Adams, I also learned why I had failed or refused to see some of the material of Adams's life and work that had always been, in some sense, in front of my eyes. Or, to put matters a bit differently, as I began to modify my interpretation of Adams's work during the course of our experiment, some of the evidence in support of my emerging interpretation became, for the first time, visible as evidence.

The relationship between our experiment and my most recent views of Adams's life and work is difficult to state with confident precision. During the course of this present essay, I have suggested that my 1980 reading of Adams's *History* "emerged during the course of" or "resulted from" our experiment, but these ways of stating the connection may be too strong. I do believe that my thinking about Adams's *History* did change between 1977 and 1980, and I have tried to specify and document those changes here. But of course I can never be certain about the extent to which my interpretation would have changed without the experiment.

For this reason, and for several others, I commend such collaborative experimentation to other historians, especially biographers, on humanistic rather than scientific grounds. It would be odd indeed to suggest, for example, that my 1980 interpretation of Adams's *History* should be appraised by repeating the experiment that in some sense led to it. It should be obvious that the experiment is in no sense repeatable. Furthermore, the validity of my 1980 interpretation depends upon the logical character of the arguments I have advanced on its behalf and upon the sufficiency of the evidence I have marshaled in support of them, not upon the nature of the experimental procedures I happened to follow in arriving at it. Even if I could confidently claim that my 1980 interpretation of Adams's *History* resulted directly from my collaboration with Dr. Moraitis, I would have to add that the validity of the result was in no sense contingent upon the methods that brought it about. And, of course, it is certainly conceivable that my 1980 interpretation is less valid than the one I had formulated in 1977 prior to our experiment.

Still, historians do see what they bring to their researches, and they have readily written a great deal about the effects of ideological, cultural, and temporal biases upon their work. They have been less ready until recently, however, to reflect upon the extent to which their work is shaped by unconscious or unexamined psychological processes. My collaboration with Dr. Moraitis provided one disciplined way to reflect upon this matter, and I would defend the value of our experiment on this basis alone. It was also valuable to me, however, because it enabled me to learn more about myself in the course of learning more about my subject and to learn more about my subject in the course of learning more about myself. As a result of this experience, I now believe that biographers are necessarily involved with their subjects in ways that they do not fully comprehend. If they choose to reflect upon this involvement in a disciplined manner, a collaborative experiment with a psychoanalyst might well be the best means for doing so. But though I can promise that such an experiment will yield self-knowledge, I cannot predict with any certainty that it will make a bad biographer into a good one or a good biographer into a better one.

REFERENCES

Adams, H. (1889-1891), *History of the United States during the Administrations of Thomas Jefferson and James Madison*, New York: Scribner's, 1891.

———— (1907), *The Education of Henry Adams*. Boston: Houghton, Mifflin, 1973.

Cater, D. (1951), *Henry Adams and His Friends*. Boston: Houghton Mifflin.

Friedrich, O. (1979), *Clover*. New York: Simon & Schuster.

Gibbon, E. (1829-1830), *Autobiography*. London & New York: Oxford University Press, 1950.

Moraitis, G. (1979), A psychoanalyst's journey into a historian's world: an experiment in collaboration. *The Annual of Psychoanalysis*, 7:287-320. New York: International Universities Press.

Samuels, E. (1958), *Henry Adams: The Middle Years*. Cambridge, MA: Harvard University Press.

Schwehn, M. (1978), *The Making of Modern Consciousness in America: The Works and Careers of Henry Adams and William James*. Unpublished Ph.D. thesis, Stanford University.

——— (1980), Making history. Unpublished manuscript.
Winters, Y. (1943), *The Anatomy of Nonsense*. Norfolk, Va.: New Directions.

8

The Two Readings of The Education of Henry Adams

GEORGE MORAITIS, M.D.

I became familiar with *The Education of Henry Adams* during the course of my collaborative work with Professor Schwehn which took place in 1978. A few years ago I described one of these collaborations with the biographer of Nietzsche, which was structured in a very similar way to the one I am about to discuss (Moraitis, 1979). I met with Professor Schwehn several times for a two-to-three-hour session and discussed with him selected materials that were assigned by him. In this, as in the previous collaboration, we proceeded with the understanding that the historian and I remain experts in our respective fields only. More specifically, I consider myself a visitor to the historian's laboratory and invite him to introduce me to the area of his study in whatever way he considers feasible and consistent with the limitations of available time. The objective of the collaboration is to study the development of the historian's creativity and identify the origins of the ideas and attitudes presented in his writings. I assume that all historical investigations are subject to influences from the historian's personality. These influences can be identified as transference reactions in the sense that elements of the material under investigation reverberate with perceptions generated from experiences of the investigator's past and produce emotional responses that affect the investigator's notions about his subject.

Transference reactions associated with reading biographical materials are bound to be relatively common. They occur when we read novels, view films and plays, etc., and they may be intense. In contrast to the transference reactions of the professional historian, however, they are generally transient, and lack depth. The stimulus seems to act like the day residue of a dream in precipitating the emergence of a memory and in evoking a wish. It triggers an affective release in the form of sadness, fear, or nostalgia which has pleasurable components even when painful. The reader can often make conscious connections between the stimulating material and the experiences in his own past with which it reverberates. The whole process is close to consciousness and represents a re-enactment of the past.

In depth study of an author's creative work, however, creates transference reactions of a more complex nature. This is particularly true when the reader attempts to master the work of authors who made contributions of great originality.

The realization that someone's perception of the universe is grossly different from one's own precipitates anxiety because the new ideas represent an intrusion deliberately designed by the author to challenge the reader's values and sense of self. The reader who does not put the book aside will attempt to regulate the input of novelty the reading has created, by blocking out from his conscious perception certain aspects of the author's ideas, and by accentuating the importance of others. Such selective perception of a given text, when conscious and deliberate, provides the reader with the impression that he can logically argue in defense of his own position. When unconscious, however, it represents a true transference reaction because it aims to re-create a certain perception of reality to which the reader is attached by avoiding the full impact of disagreeable new perceptions. The conscious selective perception of the input, however, cannot be maintained indefinitely, especially for the scholar whose work is under the constant influence of his sense of intellectual honesty and the over-all value system of his profession. Gradually, the less conscious input that the reading of a given text had generated will surface, and the reader will feel compelled to integrate it into his over-all perceptual system at the expense of earlier perceptions and convictions.

In order to conceptualize better the distinction between common transference reactions associated with reading material and the transference reactions of the scholarly reader, it is important to make a distinction between creative and adaptive motives within the structure of an individual's personality. True scholarly reading is in the service of the individual's creative functions. His aims are not soothing or pleasure but discovery, which can only be achieved through a strict adherence to his professional ethics and values which should supersede any adaptive aims to whatever extent possible. In order to maintain such a value system, the scholar must allow his creative functions to enjoy a certain level of autonomy from the rest of his personality. Such autonomy protects the scholar from experiencing the new ideas and input as an immediate danger to his personal sense of self and capacity to adapt. Furthermore, it provides him with the opportunity to work through these ideas gradually and systematically and without the massive intrusion of affects and urges from the rest of his personality.

Inevitably, internal conflict will ensue as a result of the new input, but not before the reader has given himself the opportunity to be persuaded unconsciously at first and consciously later by aspects of the author's communication. Internal harmony seldom if ever is experienced by the scholar who attempts to grasp ideas of great originality. His struggle is creative when he, with the help of his professional value system, allows for the registration of new input and provides the author with the opportunity to persuade him.

In this paper I will attempt to discuss my own experiences with two readings of a historical document that occurred three years apart. In describing the observations I made of myself and of my collaborator I will attempt to identify distinctly different responses to reading material that seem to correlate to two different sectors of the reader's personality. This observation has some important implications about the nature of transferences as they occur during the course of the scholar's work and about creativity in general.

My collaboration with Professor Schwehn began with his asking me to read selected portions of his dissertation which pertains to the development of modern consciousness in America and contains a good deal of biographical material about Henry Adams and William James. My collaborator's thesis had already been accepted, and he was in the process of revising it for publication. Following the first exploratory session, during which we focused primarily on Henry Adams, he suggested that I read the novel *Esther* written by Adams and published under a pseudonym so that nobody would "profane it." During the second, rather dramatic, session we discussed this novel at great length. I was impressed with the ineffectiveness of the characters in the story and the "play-acting" quality of their interactions. I had a difficult time sustaining my attention on the book and attempted to understand why the author fails to engage his reader. The main character, Esther, seems aimless, depressed probably because her father is dying. She is not an active member of the society she lives in, and no information about her background is provided. She cannot be engaged socially with the other characters in the novel or drawn into marriage, but consistently maintains her polite, proper, and pleasant attitude.

The discussion about Esther led gradually to the women with whom Henry Adams came in contact. We talked about the death of his sister from tetanus, which he had witnessed, and the death of his wife, who committed suicide after thirteen years of marriage. Gradually, we turned our attention to the male characters in the novel. My collaborator emphasized Adams's idealization of his father and the importance of his distant presence for Henry. Henry Adams was the secretary for his father as Esther in the novel seems to be for hers. Because of an error on the part of the historian I had assumed at the time that Henry Adams's father had died shortly before the novel was written, which led me to believe that the writing of the novel represented an effort to grieve for his father's death. I had concluded that he expressed his grief by identifying with a fictional woman who was also grieving her father's death. Adams's identification with Esther raised in my mind questions about the author's feminine identification and a possible negative Oedipus. Only recently did the historian realize his error as a result of his reading of this manuscript. Adams had not written the book *Esther* at the time of his father's death; instead, my collaborator had read Adams's work at the time of his own father's death.

This new revelation reinforced the initial impression about my collaborator's identification with Henry Adams. Henry Adams was a small man, frail and with a sense of ineffectiveness. He saw himself as the variation and unable to compete physically with other males of his age. With a good deal of affect my collaborator provided a good deal of information about his early identification with Henry Adams which he connected with the fact that he, too, was unusually small up to the age of nineteen and had suffered a good deal as a result of it. My collaborator's father was a minister, as were many of his ancestors, and he shared all the moral values of the Adams family.

My collaborator's associations confirmed the presence of an intense transference reaction which was barely under the surface of his consciousness. He revealed his feelings to me with candor and openness. Had this been a therapeutic situation the direction to take would have been obvious. We would have explored in more detail the investigator's past, in an effort to understand more accurately the hidden meaning of the early experiences revealed to me. This, of course, would not have added that much to our understanding of Henry Adams and his intellectual work. To be consistent with the objectives of our work we took a different direction. To begin with, we took notice of the fact that two investigators, a historian and a psychoanalyst, with very different professional backgrounds, had reached a consensus about the meaning of a given document and developed a sense of in-depth communication with each other and the subject under study. We thought that this provided a triangulation that could add to the validity of the interpretation.

It is important to note, however, that though my collaborator did not even refer to *Esther* in his dissertation, he assigned this book to me for reading at the very beginning of the collaboration. I understood his approach as an attempt to protect his work from transference reverberations in order to maintain the necessary objectivity and neutrality that enabled him to complete his dissertation. Only in the presence of a trusted collaborator did he decide to deal directly with material that aroused transference reactions of great intensity. The investigator's capacity to regulate the input of investigative material into his own work is directly related to the degree of stimulation the materials produce. When overstimulated he has to temporarily take steps to shield his creative function from overwhelming influences and contain his activities within certain protective boundaries.

It took several months before we resumed the collaboration, and when we got back together it was no surprise to either of us that my collaborator assigned for reading several chapters from *The Education of Henry Adams*. The preface, "Quincy," "Boston," "Twenty Years Later," and the "Dynamo and Virgin" were some of the chapters assigned, but my reading extended considerably beyond them, covering most of the book. I did not reread *The Education of Henry Adams* until three years later when I selected this topic for the conference on biography.

The two readings of *The Education of Henry Adams* spaced three years apart were in several respects an education for me. Each reading helped me understand something about the author and his ideas. Even more educational for me, however, was the comparison between the two readings which helped me understand something new about myself as a professional and about the psychoanalytic view to which I adhere. Having given the reader of this paper some information about how my study of *The Education of Henry Adams* began and how my first intervention provided some insight for my collaborator, I will proceed by focusing primarily on my own educational experience.

My first reaction to *The Education of Henry Adams* was negative. I was appalled by what I took as lack of psychological sophistication and assumed that, given the intellectual abilities of the author, he must have taken great efforts to maintain the unpsychological nature of his work. My collaborator emphasized the deliberate intent of Adams to create a sense of discontinuity and disorientation in the reader; if he were there, the collaborator said, he would have been pleased with my response to his book. I wondered why Adams did not feel the need to put things together. I identified the author's comfort and even pleasure in discovering ignorance in himself and in others and his distaste for continuity and "unity" and probably even education as we know it.

My collaborator saw in Henry Adams an old man filled with genuine grief and distress over the illusionary unity of the formulas proposed, who alerts the reader that these formulas have nothing to do with realities or true discoveries. In contrast, I identified the author's difficulty in describing his feelings and his avoidance in providing personal information in his book. My intent was to make clear to my collaborator how transference elements had biased the view of his subject. I wondered how Adams justified in his mind omitting from the account of his life twenty crucial and dramatic years which included the death of his parents, the marriage to and suicide of his wife, and several major publications. I did not, at that time, give sufficient credence to Adams's intent to present in his book the story of his education, not of his life, and did not take notice of how separate the two stories were in the author's mind.

Only during the second reading did I come to realize how determined I was at that time to read in *The Education of Henry Adams* a story that the author, with equal determination, did not write. I was so busy reading between the lines that I was not paying sufficient attention to the lines as written. As a matter of fact, I thought of putting all the statements Adams made about his personal life in sequence and reading them to the exclusion of the rest of the book. My fantasy was a clear indication of how selective my reading was. I was identifying the author's defensiveness in not telling us the story I wanted to hear. But in the process I had failed to recognize my defensiveness in reading what was written and dealing with the intellectual input the book produces. I approached the text with certain preconceived notions that had emerged from the previous session with my collaborator during which we had discussed the novel *Esther*. I saw Henry Adams, or more accurately the character he created in the book, as an angry, depressed, obsessive individual whose negativistic view of the world served a defensive purpose psychologically. I assumed that early in his life he developed expectations of himself and of others which were highly idealistic and largely unrealistic, and went through life suffering the inevitable disappointments. Becoming president was for him the very least he could accomplish in his life, and failure to do so probably represented an intolerable disgrace. I understood his attack against people in power as an expression of envy and narcissistic rage and his admiration of the power of women as an idealization of women based on identification with them. I sensed that he maintained a highly exaggerated perception of himself and his influence upon others despite the overt display of modesty and the continuous claims to ignorance.

Understandably, my collaborator felt deeply disturbed by my perception of Henry Adams, for whom he had maintained all along a good deal of idealization. He was willing to accept his own feelings of inferiority and envy, but refused to go along with my interpretation of Adams's

ideas as the product of these feelings. Our positions were
in direct contrast to the ones I described in my collaboration with the biographer of Nietzsche, in which the
historian was emphasizing Nietzsche's neurotic pride and
I was defending Nietzsche against the historian's negative transference. With eloquence and enthusiasm, Professor Schwehn described Henry Adams as the man who
offers himself as a symbol to illustrate what happened to
modern man. To understand him one must rely on aes-
thetics and not on any psychological or social theory. The
metaphors he applies are comparable to the metaphors
of the poet. He refers to the stupendous failure of spirituality in the nineteenth century and to the grotesque,
mindless force of the dynamo. "All the steam in the world
would not create a cathedral." All human scientific theories retreat into the horizon of a universe that escapes
human understanding. Scientific theory is a parody of
knowledge and sooner or later proves to be silly.

At the end of his long elaboration, my collaborator
realized the degree of his enthusiasm, which made him
apologize for his "passionate sermon." He was particularly disturbed by my treatment of Henry Adams's ideas
as an outgrowth of his personality conflicts. Such an approach to the text, as it became evident later, was an
attempt on my part to avoid taking conscious notice of
the intellectual input the reading of *The Education of
Henry Adams* had generated in me. In retrospect I identify this avoidance as a transference reaction that had
been precipitated by the author's ideas, that skewed my
capacity to maintain a more even approach in the analysis of this historical document. In contrast, my collaborator's transference reactions were triggered by his
knowledge of Henry Adams's personality, with whom he
identified. The intensity of this identification affected his
capacity to appreciate other aspects of Adams's person-

ality and place him more accurately into historical perspective.

My first reading of *The Education of Henry Adams* was highly selective in the literal and psychological sense of the word. I read primarily the parts my collaborator assigned and expanded my reading only in the areas that attracted my curiosity and interest. I approached the text with certain preconceived notions that had emerged from the previous session with my collaborator during which we had discussed the novel *Esther*.

I returned to *The Education of Henry Adams* upon my own initiative. Recently, as I was searching for appropriate topics for a presentation at the "Vital Issues" conference. I realized how strongly I wanted to pursue the study of this document. In contrast to the first time I had no difficulty involving myself with the book and read all of it systematically. In a personal sense the most moving moment of the second reading occurred when I came to the realization of the effect of Henry Adams's ideas upon my thinking and my work. In a recent paper of mine, "The Analyst's Response to the Limitations of His Science," I described a patient who was opposing my efforts to "know" and "understand" her and was defending her claim to "ignorance." I suggested in the paper that I should have appreciated the unique nature of my patient's experience, resisted my need to interpret, and shared with her the awareness of my own ignorance. This is precisely what Henry Adams is inviting the reader to do with himself and with the "persona Adams" as presented in the book—an invitation that I consciously was not aware of during the first reading of it. Later on in the same paper I compared the effort of some people to create a perception of themselves that resembles in clarity and consistency a seventeenth- or eighteenth-century painting to that of others who see themselves like the abstractions and distortions of images we see in contemporary paintings (p. 15). It occurred to me that I had borrowed this imagery from *The Education of Henry Adams*. It was Adams (1907) who saw himself as the "child of the 17th or 18th century" ("Quincy," p. 4) and projected his own image into the twentieth-century intellectual world.

My paper, written a few months after my first reading of *The Education of Henry Adams*, is in a sense a statement about my psychoanalytic education. I described in it my original blind adherence to the explanatory theories in psychoanalysis, the frustration and disappointment I experienced in the application of these theories, and finally the realization that "considering the stage in development and the nature of the science of psychoanalysis . . . we do not have the instrument that would explain all aspects of the patient's behavior and under certain circumstances we may better serve our science by taking notice of certain clinical data without the compelling need to classify them under one or another theoretical schema . . ." (Moraitis, 1981, p. xx).

The term "explanatory theories" directly relates to the concept of unity as used by Adams. The direction I postulate is the movement from unity to multiplicity that constitutes the core theme in *The Education of Henry Adams*.

Even if I take into account that the thesis postulated in my paper could have had its origin in a number of other sources, I still have to answer why I refused to deal with ideas so close to my thinking during the first reading and the discussion of this document with my collaborator. The second reading of *The Education of Henry Adams* made quite clear in my mind that my selectivity of the first reading was defensive in nature and not accidental. I had directed my conscious attention to the author to the exclusion of his ideas probably because of the fact that his ideas had such a profound effect on me. My psychological reaction constitutes, in my mind, an example of reading on two levels which I will attempt to analyze.

Henry Adams did not write the *Education* for his contemporaries. He addresses an audience a century ahead of his time. We represent his intended readers. He accurately anticipated the collapse of man's faith in a mechanical universe and the frustration of his efforts to reach "objective reality." For a contemporary reader, Henry Adams's ideas are not difficult to empathize with. For the contemporary psychoanalyst it may be even easier. Psychoanalysis today is disengaging itself from the mechanistic energic theories with which it was first introduced by its founder, and is re-examining its relationship to the physical sciences. The psychoanalyst constantly searches for meanings, the multiplicity of which defies previous efforts to unify them under one or another preconceived schema. Given my enthusiastic support for the new direction of psychoanalysis, I doubt that my resistance, evident in my first reading of the book, is actually connected to my objections to the author's intellectual positions per se. My interest in *The Education of Henry Adams* was not restricted to my intent to help the historian with his work. It was also motivated by the fact that this historical document deals with issues of education, a subject of particular interest to me for a number of personal and professional reasons. So far, psychoanalysis offers no systematic theory of education, and it has even been argued that it does not need one. Such views discourage the psychoanalytic study of man's pursuit of knowledge and tend to emphasize self-knowledge as if the two were unrelated.

In his preface, Henry Adams (1918) declares about his book: "The object of study is the garment, not the figure.

The tailor adapts the manikin as well as the clothes to his patron's wants. The tailor's object in this volume is to fit young men, in universities or elsewhere, to be men of the world, equipped for any emergency, and the garment offered to them is meant to show the faults of the patchwork fitted on their fathers" (p. xxx). In contrast to Adams's objective, my first reading was aiming to take the garments off and expose the manikin as well as the author hidden behind it. For strictly clinical purposes, perhaps this was a perfectly understandable aim, insofar as the garment represents a protective shield or a simple extension of what lies underneath. For scholarly purposes, however, this is a very inadequate approach. The study of education, psychoanalytic or not, cannot proceed without taking into account the subject that is being educated. Adams as an educator could not study himself without examining the figure; nor can I, as an analyst, examine the figure without taking the garment seriously into account.

Understandably, such a combined approach will address motivational issues that in *The Education of Henry Adams* are totally bypassed. The accidental nature of the educational events, as the author describes them, indicates no evidence of the selectivity that the subject of the educational process exercised upon them. The persona Adams, as he emerges from the book, remains a mechanical receptor that simply accepts or, more frequently, rejects the input provided. Persona Adams responds like an inanimate, robotlike manikin that is subjected to an interminable series of false teachings and after a long and tedious Odyssey arrives at the unshakable belief about his own ignorance and that of his masters. The degree of conviction is reflected in statements such as "Chaos is the order of nature and Order was the dream of man." As the author consistently arrives from chapter to chapter, from travel to travel, and from experience to experience, to the same familiar conclusion of man's infinite ignorance, one wonders to what extent ignorance represents the Ithaca of this new Ulysses and the point of arrival he intends to reach at the expense of great effort and long years. To know everything and to know nothing may appear as the two opposite extremes in the wide spectrum of knowledge and education. Yet, in actuality, they represent the two sides of the same "unity" hardly distinguishable the one from the other. A movement from an absolute unity to an absolute multiplicity is hardly a movement at all.

During the second reading of the book, I was conscious of the extent to which Adams carried his thesis. He described education largely as a negative process during which one unlearns false learning. Viewed as such, education compares to a systematic pursuit of ignorance, which inevitably will bring down from the pedestal the idealized images of the "masters who are responsible for the false learning." In *The Education of Henry Adams* there are no heroes, no truths, and no gods. The lonely, disillusioned persona Adams reached the height of his knowledge when he "realized" that his masters were not only ignorant but impotent as well. They were lacking both knowledge and power.

It can be argued that the persona Adams is too much of a caricature to do justice to the author's intellectual position. My eagerness to diagnose him could have been an expression of my anger against a persona who was inadvertently ridiculing an intellectual position with which I was basically in sympathy. Adams, of course, created the persona in his book not as a caricature but as a variation. There was no comic intent involved in the persona. The joke was on the teachers who never succeeded in taming the boy. The unintended ridicule of the persona Adams emerges from the imagery the document evokes in the reader, especially the reader who searches for the personification of an ideal. Freud (1905) said that a caricature tends to create "the exaggeration of traits that are not otherwise striking and it also involves the characteristics of degradation" (p. 208). I think my reaction to the persona Henry Adams was on that level. It indicated in my mind a fallacy in my perception of reality with which I was not emotionally prepared to deal. Only three years later was I ready to return to the book and deal consciously with the ideas it generated. In the meantime I had come to realize the pride and arrogance of modern man, myself included, that is hidden behind the deceptive apologies about our ignorance. In the explanations of the big unknown, the universe that surrounds us, as well as the inner depths of our own psyche, the explorer is in frequent need of shelter, way stations which provide a sense of comfort and relief for the tension that the encounter with novelty creates. Resignation to ignorance can be as effective a shelter as the illusionary sense of knowledge. They both provide experientially a sense of arrival that can play into the explorer's notions that he has reached his destination. Both the traveler who thinks he knows his point of arrival and the one who thinks he knows he cannot ever arrive share the illusion that the destination is familiar and predictable, an illusion that interferes with the true appreciation of novelty.

Adams accurately predicted that man's concern about the limitations of his knowledge will dominate the intellectual world of the twentieth century. In science as well as in all scholarly pursuits we are reminded of the limitations of our senses and our capacity to perceive accurately both external and internal reality. Psychoanalysis has been greatly influenced by these trends. For the last several years basic assumptions of psychoanalytic theory, such as metapsychology and the centrality of the oedipal complex in psychopathology, have been questioned or discarded. In the process, old heroes are de-idealized, and there seems to be reluctance to create new ones. The harder we try, the less we are sure about what we really know. Education, psychoanalytic or not, can be defined no longer as a fixed point of intended arrival but as a process in need of systematic psychological study. The pursuit of knowledge is an urge deeply rooted in the human psyche. Individuals and societies may triumphantly declare their convictions of knowledge or resign before the formidable task and confess their ignorance. Psychoanalysis cannot help the scholar establish the relative accuracy of these declarations. It can, however, approach knowledge as a problem of the human mind that can be studied through introspection and, it is hoped, through developing a systematic method of inquiry.

The psychoanalyst who ventures into the social sciences must develop a wider motivational hypothesis to explain the scholar's pursuit of knowledge and pleasure in discovery. The concept of sublimation and the duality of primary and secondary process prevalent in psychoanalysis do not suffice to explain man's compelling struggle to perceive the universe on an organized level. Lately a lot has been written in psychoanalysis about the development of the sense of self and the individual's capacity to maintain it. In contrast, man's capacity to perceive the other, the non-self, has not been dealt with in psychoanalysis. Some assume that the one is the simple outcome of the other—that once the sense of self is developed there will be enough psychic structure available for the perception of the non-self. Others may simply postulate that such inquiry is outside the realm of psychoanalysis. It seems to me, however, that to place the perception of the self into proper perspective, the perception of the "other," of the non-self, must also undergo a parallel development. To facilitate a more balanced view of himself man must direct his attention to the "other man" and to the "other" that is not a man. We should not rest assured that reality-oriented thinking is the outcome of a successful adaptational struggle. Logic and reason, the supreme functions of the human mind, can be present from the beginning of life. And the so-called secondary process may not be so secondary after all.

Psychoanalysis may not need to "rest its arms" when confronted with the task of understanding creativity. If man's desire to know, to discover, is "primary" in nature, education and the scholar's pursuit of knowledge represent an effort to satisfy a basic human need that exists along with others and does not necessarily derive from them. Such a conceptualization can open the door to the study of creativity without the limitations imposed by the present theoretical schemata. The study of autobiographical documents provides a good illustration of this point. Great thinkers offer information about themselves in order to facilitate the reader's understanding of their perceptions. The autobiographical writings of creative personalities are not excesses in self-indulgence. The psychological reader must appreciate this basic principle in order to arrive at the proper interpretation.

Henry Adams, like many other authors with great gifts, produced an important piece of autobiographical writing toward the end of his life. Writings like *The Education of Henry Adams* represent a historian's effort to go beyond the writing of history and reveal parts of himself in an attempt to make history. Henry Adams's *Education* reveals not only his ideas but also the spectacles through which the author perceived the world and developed them. The reader who takes possession of these spectacles can use them in two ways. He can examine them as clues that will facilitate the understanding of the author's personality, or he can wear the spectacles in order to see the world as close as possible to the way Henry Adams saw it. My two readings of *The Education of Henry Adams* are designed to illustrate how complementary these two approaches are. This paper represents the autobiographical account of a psychoanalyst who ventured into the world of intellectual history. At first I used Henry Adams's spectacles as an instrument to examine the subject's personality. After a period of time I came to realize that in the process I had come under the power of my subject's intellect and perceptions in a way that had affected my own perceptions of the science I serve and the larger world in which it belongs.

The revelations Henry Adams offered us about his educational garment provide enough glimpses of the humanity of the author to ascertain that Henry Adams was not just another student. He refers to himself as a variation and puts the blame for this on the scarlet fever that left him small and frail. In my first reading of this document I took his statement as a thinly disguised sense of superiority. My second reading of it, however, convinced me that a more accurate word to describe him is exception, rather than variation. It is evident that from the beginning and throughout his life Henry Adams showed unusual curiosity and eagerness to explore and master the complexities of the world. Such eagerness could be partly explained as a compelling need to prepare for the presidency, a preparation that in actuality can never be completed with the thoroughness that he had intended. His long odyssey, however, was not suspended when he realized he couldn't become the president. Instead, he pursued his journey that eventually revealed an image of the universe as too formidable to master, and an image of the self as too small and weak for the task.

The inwardly driven quality of his pursuit which disregards adaptational needs and self-serving considerations is characteristic of an exceptionally gifted individual who had achieved an early awareness of external and internal realities. As John Gedo (1972) pointed out in "On the Psychology of Genius," people with extraordinary gifts feel very special, and accurately so, because they are a variation. When the caretakers fail to recognize the extraordinary abilities of these gifted children, intrapsychic conflicts become inevitable.

It is hard to tell from this document whether Henry Adams was understood and recognized by his caretakers. His mother may have been just an "atmosphere," but in all probability his father was an "influence." We, as his readers, however, are now the caretakers of his creativity. In examining his work it is important to take into account his unusual gifts and appreciate the contribution of his gifts to our own pursuit of knowledge. The psychological study of creativity is in essence a study in introspection in which the investigator reports the experiences and educated assumptions generated by his subject's creative product.

In this interdisciplinary study the introspective work of the investigators was facilitated by the presence of a collaborator who provided the necessary feedback and element of control. First I provided Professor Schwehn with information that enabled him to recognize his intense identification with his subject and the restricting effect of this identification upon his scholarly work. Subsequently, Professor Schwehn provided the feedback that eventually helped me recognize my avoidance in dealing with Henry Adams's intellectual position. During the second reading of the document I became conscious of my identification with Henry Adams's intellectual position and my refusal to accept the persona Adams as a representative of a thesis that I had, at the time, highly idealized.

At this time it is difficult for me to evaluate the extent to which my intervention helped the historian in his scholarly work. He has addressed this issue in his article that appears in this volume. This collaborative experience, however, provided me with some new ideas about myself as a professional, about the science of psychoanalysis, and about the field of interdisciplinary research, for which I feel very appreciative.

REFERENCES

Adams, H. (1907), *The Education of Henry Adams*, ed. E. Samuels. Boston: Houghton Mifflin, 1973.

Freud, S. (1905), Jokes and their relation to the unconscious. *Standard Edition*, 8. London: Hogarth Press, 1960.

Gedo, J. (1972), On the psychology of genius. *Internat. J.Psycho-Anal.*, 53:199-203.

Moraitis, G. (1979), A psychoanalyst's journey into a historian's world: an experiment in collaboration. *The Annual of Psychoanalysis*: 7:287-320. New York: International Universities Press.

——— (1981), The analyst's response to the limitations of his science. *Psychoanal. Inquiry*, 1:57-79.

Part III

Creativity and the Life Course

Introduction: Aging and Creativity

GEORGE H. POLLOCK, M.D., Ph.D.

Among the various issues with which psychoanalysis currently is attempting to deal, the areas of aging and of creativity are being actively investigated. Aging throughout the course of life has moved into the forefront for various reasons (Pollock, 1981). Creativity continues to be an enigma, but less so than before. Applied analysis has attempted to study creativity from a particular perspective—retroactive reconstruction based on clinical theories. Newer and additional approaches are now coming into focus as we study creativity, the creative process, the creative product, and creativity during the entire course of life. Thus late-life creativity brings together two pivotal areas of interest to psychoanalysis today.

In applied analysis, too often the focus has been on the pathography of the creative individual. There has seemingly been an assumption that once the pathological life development of the subject was discerned, many is-

This work was supported, in part, by the Anne Pollock Lederer Research Fund of the Chicago Institute for Psychoanalysis.

sues of innovativeness, originality, and novel productivity could be explained. We know this is not so. Many individuals, if not all, have had "deviated" developmental progressions and regressions; yet they would not be considered "creative" in the customary usage of that term. Too often our emphasis on malfunction as an explanation is somewhat simplistic, reductionistic, and formulaic. We deal with many variables, and many possible disruptions can take place without either pathological consequences of chronic duration or creative outcomes. The more we learn about the total being in his or her changing milieu, the more we become aware of the complicated and delicate mechanisms in each of us—and the more we wonder how things worked as well as they did.

On the side, one can take the creative products, carefully dissect them into their components and, it is hoped, in this way arrive at new insights about the creative product or process. Freud pioneered in this endeavor, as he has in so many others; but here again we can raise questions about the uniqueness and singularity of this method. One can take a dream and from only its manifest content attempt interpretation of deeper meanings, but this enterprise is rarely useful in isolation. Knowing something of the creator, the circumstances of the creative endeavor, the multiple past and present events that contribute to the result, as well as the dimensions of the aging axis of the person, helps us in our understanding of the creative product. Historical parallels may be fake and misleading in their seductive presentations of analogies as homologues. Biographies that emphasize single variables that then become the bases of identical comparabilities can also lead us astray. These approaches can open up new vistas for us—new ways—but we must exercise caution lest our scientific endeavors be misconstrued and our pursuits of truth become artistic and aesthetic productions, which have great value but which are different from testable propositions.

In the three papers that follow, scholars have attempted to study the later-life literary, musical, and artistic creativity of selected individuals. They have carefully selected their subjects and their works and do consider the late-adult developmental model in their contributions. As in the analysis of dreams, however, it may be that to understand meaning and origins "fully" we need to synthesize all data, past and present, to come close to our goal. One of these data foci includes the age of the creator-dreamer. Age is a factor whose impact cannot be erased.

In an excellent earlier report on Michelangelo's last uncompleted sculpture, the *Pièta Rondanini*, Gerda Frank (1966) has related the dying Michelangelo's eforts to express many needs—some from earlier times, others reflecting the still unfulfilled ongoing wishes of the fading artist—to his artistic task and his need for completion. Mrs. Frank has also translated a heretofore unavailable portion of an essay by Thomas Mann, who, although only thirty-five years old at the time he wrote the account, showed the wisdom of an older individual. I am quoting excerpts from this Mann paper as it bears on the topic I am addressing here (Frank, personal communication, 1983):

> A new volume of letters by Theodor Fontane[1] has been published—something very attractive.... Are

---

[1] Theodor Fontane (1819-1898) was a German writer. "Although he is primarily important as a novelist, he did not begin to write prose fiction until he was almost 60.... The first master of the realist novel in Germany, he wrote perceptive novels which reveal the decay of contemporary Berlin society.... They include ... his masterpiece EFFIE BRIEST, 1895; Eng. translation, 1913-15" (*Columbia Encyclopedia,* 1950, pp. 737-738).

there more? They ought to be published! And I mean especially those, that date to the later days, letters of the old Fontane, because those from his youth and his middle years are insignificant in comparison to the late ones. Does it not seem that he had to grow old, very old, to truly come into his own? There are those who are born youths, who fulfill their promises early and who never ripen, let alone grow old without outliving themselves. On the other hand, there are obviously characters to whom old age is the only befitting one, classical old people, so to speak, who are destined to demonstrate the advantages of this stage in life—the ideal advantages of this stage in their most perfect form: kindness, benevolence, fairness, humor and sly wisdom—in short: the return, on a higher level, of childlike freedom and spontaneity. Fontane was one of these, and it looks as if he knew it and hurried to grow old, in order to be old for a long time. . . . [Mann, 1910, p. 301].

At age 58 he writes: "I now have attained everything worldly: loved, married, created posterity, got two medals and my name into *Who's Who*. Only two things are missing: professorial rank and death. The one I am sure of, the other I could do without. . . . What does one still want? Life is behind one, and most other 58 year olds are in worse shape." He feels he is in bad shape, life lies in the past, and what he still has to give are merely eighteen more volumes, up to *Effie Briest*—each one better than the last [p. 303].

"As the years passed by, I grew younger," wrote the 28 year old Fontane to a friend, "and the lust for life, which ought to be the heritage of the young, seems to grow in me, the longer the thread unwinds." That shows an early insight into his particularly vital personality. He was born in order to become the "old Fontane," who will live on; the first six decades of his life were, almost consciously realized, only the preparation for the two last ones, benevolently spent in the growing shadow of the final enigma. His life seems to teach us, that true maturity for life comes only with maturity for death. This strange and endearing man matured in ever more freedom and wisdom toward the attainment of the final answer, and among his posthumous papers was found the following beautiful verse:

> Life; he's blessed, whom it giveth
> Friends and children, daily bread,
> But the best part that it sendeth
> Is the knowledge that it endeth.
> Is deliverance, is death.

[Mann, 1910," p. 324]

Leon Edel's "Portrait of the Artist as an Old Man" (1982) has sensitively addressed the issue of late-life creativity, using Tolstoy, Henry James, and Yeats as illustrations for his many insights on the close linkage between aging and creativity. Edel notes that "in certain instances, aging is a way of crystallizing and summarizing the life of art and the achievement of art. And when—amid the new despair and infirmities that aging brings—the artist has experienced fulfillment of certain old unfulfilled needs, then there is an expanding power of mind and utterance that can lead to the supremacies of art" (p. 162). Furthermore, Edel notes, "Out of the sadness and decrepitude of aging, Yeats and James, and those who believe in art, make a hymn to life; they sing life where Tolstoy sang despair; they sing acceptance when Tolstoy sang repudiation. They acknowledge despair, they acknowledge their instincts and their feelings, and grow old without the rigidities of aging. Within the tattered coat upon the stick there is a radiance—the same radiance as in the self portraits of Rembrandt grown old" (pp. 162-163).

Let me briefly turn to the question of aging as we currently approach this area from a psychoanalytic frame of reference. "Immortality, we sometimes forget, comes in different sizes" (Mandel, 1982, p. 258). Some are remembered by all, some by a few, some for a long time if not forever, and some may pass into the common eternity of anonymity in a relatively short period of time. Our focus now is on the aging processes, which though related to immortality have a different significance—mortality and change. We can say that mortality also comes in different sizes, different durations, and different shapes. We who are interested in these aging processes must keep these individual differences in mind while we are at the same time seeking for universal principles that can be applied to all human beings. Let me illustrate this by calling your attention to the fact that

> Our earthly time allowance has rapidly shot up from an average of forty years to an average of seventy years plus within the experience of all the old people alive at present. Nothing comparable to it has been known before. Although it was accepted that the body had been programmed to last for the classic three score years and ten, until now there was an all-too-eloquent proof that very few of them ever did, and for a man to "see his time out," as they used to say, was exceptional. We counter this fact by declaring that one was old at forty in those days. Yet one was not—at least, not in the sense of cumulative time, which is what defines actual old age [Blythe, 1979, p. 3].

My own recent work has focused on the differentiation of aging from the aged and of the normal from the pathological state. Many questions arise when one addresses these issues. For example, is the pathological condition only a quantitative modification of the normal state? Is there a science of normal aging that emphasizes development as an ongoing process from conception to normally occurring death? What do we mean by normal, disease, health, cure? These queries can now be posed and even broken down into smaller units—e.g., biology, behavior, cogniton, affect states, social change, family-structure alterations—and their relationship with the aging process. When we become even more specific, we ask about the differentiation between senility and depressed states, recognizing that although we are not dealing here with an either/or situation, one condition can be treated and the other remains relatively untouched by therapy. The symptoms and signs can be deceptively similar, and yet intrapsychically we may be dealing with separate processes.

The great number of men and women who died or still die from exhaustion, malnutrition, or disease in early middle age were or are unlikely to show bodily senescent changes even though they manifest other signs of physical decomposition. Renaissance or Georgian man lived in a world "where it was the exception to go grey, to reach the menopause, to retire, to become senile and to acquire that subtle blend of voice, skin and behavioural changes which features so largely in our long-lived times" (Blythe, 1979, pp. 3-4).

Life for men and women who lived in earlier days (or who live in underdeveloped lands today) was incomplete—one died young. Life was filled with precariousness—fatal illnesses, accidents, acute infectious diseases—that could decimate a community. Our ancestors were always in death, even in the midst of life. They were not speaking metaphorically—it was a reality. "The common fate of a brief life bred apprehension, swift-moving ambition or piety . . . but because the majority of men knew no other life, it had a normality which is now outside our comprehension" (Blythe, 1979, p. 4). My paternal grandmother had sixteen children and died not long after the youngest arrived. She was in her late forties and in all probability would have been still capable of more pregnancies if pneumonia had not carried her away. Her life was not finished, and yet she and so many others who lived in small Eastern European villages suffered the same fate. It was quite common for a man to have several wives. Now the longevity scale has turned, and it is more common for a woman to have several husbands. What was the life course, when so many died so young? If one lived to middle age, one was lucky.

Now we expect everyone to have an old age. Is this an advancement, or is it a curse? In my clinical work with older or elderly adults it is not uncommon that the latter judgment crops up in patients' associations more often than the former. "The old have been made to feel that they have been sentenced to life and turned into a matter for public concern. They are the first generations of the full-timers and thus the first generations of old people for whom the state, experimentally, grudgingly and uncertainly, is having to make special supportive-conditions" (Blythe, 1979, p. 5). And what happens when the state retreats from Social Security, Medicare, Medicaid, and support for the elderly because such programs constitute a lesser priority than missiles and bombs? Have we not in paradoxical fashion elected death over life, hell over heaven, destruction over construction? Few of the elderly are anxious about death—they do not want chronic and intense pain, debilitating disease that renders them helpless, e.g., arthritis, skin deterioration, isolation, the absence of human contact that is warm and personal, a world where values and ideals still matter, impoverishment—spiritually and materially— disillusionment and disappointment. "Constantly, as one talked to the aged, one felt . . . [the] struggle to say who they *are*, and not just who and what they have been" (Blythe, 1979, p. 7).

And yet there are other categories of older adults, the ones who welcome solitude and quiet, the ones who want new friends even if the relationships are not close, the ones who continue with as much of life as they had before and are capable of having still more. When they reach eighty or whatever age, the realization that the future is tentative, that laws and conventions prevent them from doing some things that they are still adept at doing, that their children and social group act as preventives and not as facilitators—brings the deep depressions that tax our therapeutic ability. A colleague recently told me of an excellent surgeon, still vigorous and competent, who when he reached seventy—a young seventy—found his operating-room privileges removed, was heralded one day by a sudden round of applause at grand rounds, where he found himself being thanked for forty-five years of excellent service, teaching, and patient care, and when he left the auditorium somewhat bewildered, was asked by the departmental secretary to turn in the key to his locker and was given a change-of-address card for his mail. Wow! He walked about in a daze and visited the wards where a short time before he had been seen as a man of skill, dignity, and respect. Now he felt like the picture on the wall of the library.

When one's life ended in the forties and fifties, re-tirement was not an issue. Now it is—retirement from work, from social relationships, from an activity time-table that allowed one's rhythms to blend inner and outer worlds in harmonious fashion inevitably bring a dimin-ished sense of esteem and worth. Again we can ask, is this the benefit of longevity? What can we do? As hu-manists, as caregivers, as professionals, as members of society? Can we, through our work, help society overcome its negative feelings about the elderly? Perhaps the rea-son why old age was venerated in the past was that it was extraordinary—it was not the social, economic, or psychological problem that it is today. Could it be that some of our therapeutic pessimism regarding the treatment of older adults has been affected by our own biases of the past and of our leaders? Are we threatened by the "slow-motion departure" that characterizes some of our elderly? Do we avoid them with general statements about "poor prognosis," "nontreatability"? Do we wish only to see young, attractive Dorian Gray in order to avoid seeing one "whose last fate it is to be toyed with by time, to be mutilated and mocked by it" (Blythe, 1979, p. 10). But we are talking of the elderly old—the sixties and seventies are often healthy years, and their inhabitants still think of themselves as being in middle age. It is at eighty that the change occurs; more on this later.

Here again we tend to think of the ideal—the retiree has ample money, is in good health, has an intact family, has a circle of friends and caring relatives. Does the forty-year-old, unemployed man with a wife and three young children, apprehensive about getting enough money together for food and shelter—does this underworked, premature retiree resemble the older-adult retiree that I just mentioned? No. Is age the sole factor? No. What is it, then? A combination of various factors—one that has been little stressed thus far deals with the inner life, the degree of inner stability, the defensive operations that facilitate adaptation, even in the face of external obstacles and challenges. This is where psychoanalysis the science can contribute much to the understanding of aging from the perspective of inner mental processes. Let people talk; they will tell you much. Sometimes allowing them to do so, in fact, is therapeutically sufficient. Attentive listening is a way of showing love, involvement, investment, and caring.

The purpose of narration is not only to communicate

what the elderly feel would make them more appealing to the listener but to give them a way of integrating their lives in a fashion that shows their competency. "I can do it. See. I am not so far gone that you will think me unworthy of your time and efforts."

Let me now shift and briefly discuss new frontiers in the applications of psychoanalysis.

I. Infant psychiatry is at one end of the life-course spectrum. Studies indicate that pathological relationships can be detected, identified, and treated very early in life.

II. At the other end of the spectrum is the application of psychoanalytic principles to understanding the inner life of older adults. This involves understanding the unique features of the normal aging process as it relates to this portion of the life course and the specific features of the psychopathology and pathogenesis of disorders seen in this age group. Questions relating to the impact of earlier traumatic and psychostructural deformations on later malfunctioning as well as those relating to the pathology associated with the older years require active investigation. The basic differentiation here is what might be called "Aging or Aged: Development or Pathology" (Pollock, 1981). Aging, in its healthy sense, is viewed as development—a normal progression in life from the beginning of life until it comes to its natural end, death. The life-course developmental perspective can allow us to differentiate normal development, pathological development, deviant development, arrested and/or fixated development, and regressions to earlier fixated positions when stress induces strain which can only be dealt with through such retreat.

III. The notion of developmental fields in which we find different components combined in unique ways is suggested. This allows us to identify and study the various components in the developmental field—e.g., inner emotional, biological, sociocultural, economic, religious—at any one time, *and* to chart their progress throughout the life course.

IV. What is required is a map of development— aging—which records the unique configurations of each man's individual terrain. For example, are key kinship relationships the same throughout the life course (key kinship relationships include mother, father, children, siblings, spouses, grandparents)? The meanings and functions of each of these significant "others" change throughout the life course. Some of these meanings and functions change and are regulated by internal processes, some by external events, still others by defined sociocultural roles.

V. When we apply these concepts to older adults we find that emotional, mental, societal, and biological issues emerge as we try to understand what is normal in each phase (as indicated, differentiating these normal considerations from pathology is not an easy task). For example, are older people who have had multiple losses that have occurred as a result of aging depressed? Yes. Features of depression—anxiety, related helplessness, moderate hopelessness, isolation, waning physical strength—are found in most older or elderly adults. When do these become pathological? How should we treat them? Can we introduce concepts of prevention to reduce later pathology? What if any special skills, knowledge, attitudes are required of one who treats the normal elderly and the pathological elderly? What can society do to reduce the hurts, anguish, and concerns not only of the elderly but of their families? Jack Weinberg wrote a paper on "What Do I Say to My Mother When I Have Nothing to Say?" (1974). A meaningful subject. These and many other questions do and will confront us with increasing frequency. What can psychoanalysis offer in the way of understanding, assessment, and treatment (with a small "t") to this ever-increasing segment of our population? Money may not be enough!

VI. T. S. Eliot (1935) has noted that

> We do not know very much of the future
> Except that from generation to generation
> The same things happen again and again.
> Many learn little from others' experience.
> But in the life of one man, never
> The same time returns [p. 25][2]

I both agree with Eliot and disagree with him. We can learn from the experience of others if we are willing and able to do so. But we cannot be recycled, and that is why I do not accept the concept of the life-cycle for the individual. To return to Eliot again,

> The fool, fixed in his folly, may think
> He can turn the wheel on which he turns [p. 25].

Time past is not time forgotten—the past leaves its mark, the present its strains. Is it true, as Eliot further observes, that

> Man's life is a cheat and a disappointment;
> All things are unreal,
> Unreal or disappointing:
> The Catherine wheel, the pantomime cat,
> The prizes given at the children's party,
> The prize awarded for the English Essay,
> The scholar's degree, the statesman's decoration.
> All things become less real, man passes
> From unreality to unreality [p. 41].

And yet what is the perception of the elderly as it relates to reality? Even at the end,

---

[2] Lines from Eliot's *Murder in the Cathedral* are quoted with the kind permission of the publisher, Harcourt Brace Jovanovich.

However certain our expectation
The moment foreseen may be unexpected
When it arrives. It comes when we are
Engrossed with matters of other urgency [pp. 58-59].

We who are the observers, the treaters, the understand-
ers, try as we may to draw the fateful consequences from
causes, remote or obvious. For,

Every horror had its definition,
Every sorrow had a kind of end:
In life there is not time to grieve long [p. 77].

I do not wish to stop with the pessimism of Eliot—but we
cannot ignore what he says so poetically and perhaps so
wisely.

VII. I wish to now turn to Malcolm Cowley's latest
book *The View from 80* (1980).[3] Cowley was an editor of
The New Republic from 1929 to 1944. His has been an
illustrious life filled with honors, awards, and many literary accomplishments. Seven of his thirteen books have
been published since he was seventy years old. He notes
that he has published more books since he was seventy
than he did in his first seventy years! His latest work,
The View from 80, deals with what it feels like to grow
old. Drawing upon his own experience and that of his
peers who are in their eighties, he observes that there is
a sort of wisdom, an individual way of adjusting to circumstances, and a courage that one can observe in his
octogenarian friends. But after eighty there is not enough
time to do what one might wish to do.

I have culled from his volume some particularly significant observations that can help us see what an eighty
year old is like. Cowley states it more eloquently than I,

[3] The quotations from Cowley (1980) are reprinted with the kind
permission of Viking Press.

but perhaps I can use what he writes to sketch a profile as the basis for our studies. He remarks that he believes in big parties for special occasions, such as an eightieth birthday. It is a sort of bar mitzvah, since the eighty year old, like the Jewish adolescent, is entering a new stage of life. He undergoes a rite of passage, and is thus entitled to toasts, a cantor, and, I would add, presents and public acclaim. Seventy-year-olds have the illusion of being middle-aged, but the eighty-year-old looks at his double dumpling figure and admits that he is old. The last act has begun. The Census Bureau estimates for 1977 indicate that almost five million persons are in their eighties. They have survived the dangerous years from seventy-five to seventy-nine, when half of those who have lived till then are lost, mainly from hypertension and its complications and from cancer.

Cowley (1980) writes,

> To enter the country of age is a new experience, different from what you supposed it to be. Nobody, man or woman, knows the country until he has lived in it and has taken out his citizenship papers [pp. 2-3].

Even before eighty, the aging person may have undergone identity crises like that of adolescence.

> Perhaps there had also been a middle-aged crisis, the male or the female menopause, but for the rest of adult life he had taken himself for granted, with his capabilities and failings. Now, when he looks in the mirror, he asks himself, "Is this really me?"—or he avoids the mirror out of distress at what it reveals, those bags and wrinkles. In his new makeup he is called upon to play a new role in a play that must be improvised. . . . In his new role the old person will find that he is tempted by new vices, that he receives new compensations (not so widely known), and that he may possibly achieve new virtues. Chief among these is the heroic or merely ob-

stinate refusal to surrender in the face of time [pp. 7-8].

Cowley writes about the phenomena that tell the octogenarian he is old. "The body and its surroundings have their messages for him, or only one message: 'You are old' " (p. 3). Some of the occasions on which he receives the message are:

—when it becomes an achievement to do thoughtfully, step by step, what he once did instinctively
—when his bones ache
—when there are more and more little bottles in the medicine cabinet, with instructions for taking four times a day
—when he fumbles and drops his toothbrush (butterfingers)
—when his face has bumps and wrinkles, so that he cuts himself while shaving (blood on the towel)
—when year by year his feet seem farther from his hands
—when he can't stand on one leg and has trouble pulling on his pants
—when he hesitates on the landing before walking down a flight of stairs
—when he spends more time looking for things misplaced than he spends using them after he (or more often his wife) has found them
—when he falls asleep in the afternoon
—when it becomes harder to bear in mind two things at once
—when a pretty girl passes him in the street and he doesn't turn his head
—when he forgets names, even of people he saw last month ("Now I'm beginning to forget nouns," the poet Conrad Aiken said at 80)
—when he listens hard to jokes and catches everything but the snapper

—when he decides not to drive at night anymore
—when everything takes longer to do—bathing, shaving, getting dressed or undressed—but when time passes quickly, as if he were gathering speed while coasting downhill. The year from 79 to 80 is like a week when he was a boy.

Those are some of the intimate messages. "Put cotton in your ears and pebbles in your shoes," said a gerontologist, a member of that new profession dedicated to alleviating all maladies of old people except the passage of years. "Pull on rubber gloves. Smear Vaseline over your glasses, and there you have it: instant aging." Not quite. His formula omits the messages from the social world, which are louder, in most cases, than those from within. We start by growing older in other people's eyes, then slowly we come to share their judgment [pp. 3-5].

Let me close by returning to my initial topic: aging and creativity. The life of Cowley, among others, is exemplary in illustrating the thesis that, for some, aging enhances creativity, albeit at times in a changed form, style, or content. Cowley observes that Emerson wrote one of his best poems, "Terminus," when he was 63, although he lived to the age of 79. Renoir continued painting for years after he was crippled with arthritis. Goya, at 72, retired as an official painter of the Spanish court and then in his later years produced his famous "black paintings" and used a new technique—lithography. At 80, Goya "drew an ancient man propped on two sticks, with a mass of white hair and beard hiding his face and with the inscription 'I am still learning'" (Cowley, 1980, p. 17). Cowley notes that when Sophocles was 89, his oldest son claimed that Sophocles could no longer manage his estate and wished the law to intervene. In his defense, Sophocles read aloud to the court a draft of the tragedy about age on which he was then working—*Oedipus at*

Colonus. The judges instantly dismissed the suit. More currently, some poets have lived as long as Sophocles and have continued working to the end, e.g., Hardy, Frost, Sandburg. Some painters and sculptors have also been very productive in their later years, e.g., Michelangelo, Goya, Titian, Monet, Matisse, Chagall, Grandma Moses, Picasso, Georgia O'Keefe. Cowley also lists writers who have been productive and creative in their later years, e.g., E. M. Forster, Somerset Maugham, P. G. Wodehouse, Rebecca West, Tolstoy, Henry Miller, Archibald Mac-Leish, Lewis Mumford, E. B. White. Eubie Blake recently died at 100, giving concerts until the end of his life. Toscanini, Casals, Arthur Rubenstein, Vladimir Horowitz are but a few of the older, continually active musicians. I will not continue the list as I hope to address this area more fully in future studies, comparing scientists, artists of all varieties, and productive older individuals from different disciplines.

We know that older adults are among our most underutilized resources. Biases and prejudices die slowly, but they deserve to be examined carefully. Cicero's essay "De Senectute," written when he was 62, tells us that "The mightiest states have been overthrown by the young and supported and restored by the old" (quoted in Cowley, 1980, p. 47). This phenomenon has been repeatedly demonstrated throughout history. The creative life of the older adult, for the talented and those of genius, can be expanded and elaborated, can be fulfilling and comforting, but for the less talented as well, many dimensions of creative living are still possible. Psychoanalysis can contribute to our understanding of this developmental period as it has contributed to our knowledge of earlier life-course eras.

REFERENCES

Blythe, R. (1979), *The View in Winter: Reflections on Old Age*. New York: Penguin Books.

Columbia Encyclopedia (1950), Theodor Fontane. New York: Columbia University Press, pp. 737-738.

Cowley, M. (1980), *The View from 80*. New York: Viking Press.

Edel, L. (1982), *Stuff of Sleep and Dreams: Experiments in Literary Psychology*. New York: Harper & Row.

Eliot, T. S. (1935), *Murder in the Cathedral*. New York: Harcourt Brace Jovanovich, 1963.

Frank, G. (1966), The enigma of Michelangelo's Pieta Rondanini: A study of mother-loss in childhood. *Amer. Imago*, 23:287-315.

Mandel, O. (1982), Who's Diphilus? *Amer. Scholar*, 51:258-263.

Mann, T. (1910), *Leiden und Groesse der Meister*. Frankfurt a/M & Hamburg: Fischer Verlag, 1959.

Pollock, G. H. (1981), Aging or aged: Development or pathology? In: *The Course of Life: Psychoanalytic Contributions toward Understanding Personality Development*, ed. S. I. Greenspan & G. H. Pollock. Vol. 3: *Adulthood and the Aging Process*. Washington, D.C.: U.S. Government Printing Office, pp. 549-585.

Weinberg, J. (1974), What do I say to my mother when I have nothing to say? *Geriatrics*, 29:155-159.

9

Shakespeare's Development: Measure for Measure *and* Othello

DAVID BEVINGTON, Ph.D.

My purpose here is to analyze some recent achievements in psychoanalytic criticism of Shakespeare, and to look particularly at theories of Shakespeare's development as seen in his art. This is a subject on which psychoanalysis has a particularly useful contribution to make. In several recent and ongoing studies, we see the emergence of new and important ideas concerning Shakespeare's artistic development. His early interest in festive or romantic comedy and in the English history play, his turning from these genres to a focus on tragedy beginning at about the time he wrote *Hamlet*, and finally his fascination with tragicomedy and romance in the so-called late romances, all can be seen in terms of a coherent theory of psychological development. I shall concentrate, because of limits of space, on two book-length studies that have appeared recently: Richard Wheeler's (1981) *Shakespeare's Development and the Problem Comedies: Turn and Counter-*

Turn and Arthur Kirsch's (1981) *Shakespeare and the Experience of Love.*[1]

From the point of view of a literary critic, psychoanalytic criticism needs to avoid four main dangers. It should illumine without excessive recourse to baffling terminology, though of course the critic should be fully acquainted with Freudian and contemporary psychoanalytic theory. It should steer away from diagnostic analyses of dramatic characters that have the appearance of reducing those characters to medical case histories. An unfortunate perception that many literary critics have of Ernest Jones's (1949) otherwise brilliant analysis of *Hamlet and Oedipus*, for example, is that it presents us with a Hamlet who is ill to the point of emotional paralysis and is therefore unaccountable for his acts. Great tragedy demands that a protagonist assume responsibility for his fate. I realize that the differences between literary critics and psychoanalytic critics can be those of perception; literary critics are perhaps too apt to see as reductive what psychoanalytic critics see as explaining the tragic circumstances of everyday life. At any rate, any attempt to explain emotional illness in great tragedy should avoid the implication that a character is too ill to be responsible for his acts.

Third, psychoanalytic criticism should be wary of claims that the psychological portrait presented in the author's works necessarily resembles the actual man who did the writing. Last, psychoanalytic criticism needs to

---

[1] Also deserving of particular mention among recent psychological studies of Shakespeare are Murray M. Schwartz and Coppélia Kahn, eds. (1980), *Representing Shakespeare: New Psychoanalytic Essays*; Carolyn Ruth Swift Lenz, Gayle Greene, and Carol Thomas Neely, eds. (1980), *The Women's Part: Feminist Criticisms of Shakespeare*; Meredith Skura (1981), *The Literary Use of the Psychoanalytic Process*; and Coppélia Kahn (1981), *Man's Estate: Masculine Identity in Shakespeare*.

remind itself that the questions it asks inevitably circumscribe the kinds of answers it will receive, and that if the questions are postulated on certain orthodox or unorthodox assumptions about human behavior, the answers will come back in the same terms. It should find ways of accommodating other methods—theatrical, historical, biblical, and the like. I have chosen Wheeler and Kirsch as critics largely because they are especially sensitive to these issues. Both are members of English departments. Wheeler teaches at the University of Illinois, Urbana, and Kirsch at the University of Virginia, Charlottesville. Wheeler trained at Buffalo with Norman Holland and Murray Schwartz.

What can we hope to learn about the author's development from his works, especially when, as in the case of Shakespeare, we have so little objective biographical material to go on? Wheeler, in a section of his book entitled "What Is Shakespeare?," fruitfully addresses this problem. He reviews first of all earlier biographical theories about Shakespeare's creative genius. When Germanic scholarship of the nineteenth century first began to establish through philological means a fairly reliable chronology of Shakespeare's plays and poems, criticism had the means for the first time to consider the shape of his career. The result was Edward Dowden's (1875) classification of Shakespeare's work, set down in *Shakspere: A Critical Study of His Mind and Art*, into four phases: (1) in the workshop, (2) in the world, (3) in the depths, and (4) on the heights. That is, Dowden saw a phase of experimentation and imitation of earlier models in plays like *The Comedy of Errors* and the *Henry VI* series, followed by a period in the late 1590s of bright success culminating in the mature festive comedies, *Much Ado about Nothing, As You Like It*, and *Twelfth Night*, and in the mature history plays from *Richard II* and *Henry IV* through *Henry V*. The emphasis in these plays on happy resolutions—on marriage, or on the accession to kingship of Henry V, the laughter, the vivacity in the characterization of Falstaff or Benedick or Portia—all might seem to accord with Shakespeare's presumed success as a playwright. He was, during this period, established as the premier dramatist for the premier acting company on the London public stage.

However, Dowden perceived, this happy and productive period seemed to give way during the period 1601-1608, whether personal or external in origin, to a period of intense concentration on tragedy—*Hamlet, Othello, King Lear, Macbeth, Coriolanus, Antony and Cleopatra*—along with a few "problem plays"—*Measure for Measure, All's Well That Ends Well*, and *Troilus and Cressida*—that are either dark comedies of sexual conflict or, in the case of *Troilus*, a satirical portrayal of love and war that nearly defies generic classification. (The term "problem play," provided by F. S. Boas (1896), postdates Dowden, but is a part of the over-all effort to discover a pattern in Shakespeare's development.) Could the cause of this tragic preoccupation be found in the death of Shakespeare's son Hamnet in 1596, though that is possibly a little early to explain the tragedies beginning some four years later; or perhaps more generally in the anxieties of Queen Elizabeth's late years, including the disastrous career of the Earl of Essex, a darling of the theatergoing public whose attempt in 1601 to lead an uprising against the queen's ministers led to his downfall and execution; or in the confrontations that followed the accession to the throne in 1603 of James I? At any rate, Dowden argued, Shakespeare worked his way out of the depths and onto the heights perhaps around 1608-1609, as reflected partly in *Antony and Cleopatra* and more decisively in *Pericles, Cymbeline, The Winter's Tale*, and

The Tempest. Shakespeare returns to comic form with an added interest in the older generation and in renewal of family ties. The muted tones of melancholy and resignation seem appropriate to an author who has gained his comic vision only after traversing the abyss of tragic failure, and who stands on the verge of retirement from his art and life.

This famous theory has had its detractors and advocates ever since the 1880s, and in a real sense it is still before us today as the central issue. E. K. Chambers (1925) and J. Dover Wilson (1932) are among those, as Wheeler shows, who have seconded Dowden by advancing "confident reconstructions of Shakespeare's spiritual crises." Both are convinced that Shakespeare must have experienced profound dejection during the period 1601-1608, whether personal or external in origin. The opposite impulse, to insist that we can know nothing of Shakespeare from his writings, and that the works must be read solely on their own terms, owes its impetus to the New Critical movement, with its rejection of historical and extrinsic considerations. Wheeler cites Northrop Frye (1965) as one who argues that the "foolish procedure" of fictional biography is "now happily discredited," and that "there is no passage in Shakespeare's plays, certainly written by Shakespeare, which cannot be explained in terms of its dramatic function and context" (pp. 35, 37; cited by Wheeler, 1981, p. 22). Frye thus gives us the "Olympian" Shakespeare of superhuman detachment who may or may not have shared the anxieties dramatized in his plays; we have no evidence one way or the other. For all Frye's impatient dismissal of fictional biography, however, the pattern observed by Dowden of happy comedies and histories succeeded by dark tragedies and problem plays succeeded in turn by tragicomic romances is still there; and the question remains, what are we to make of this pattern? Frye would answer perhaps that Shakespeare was exploring the artistic limits of one genre and then another, as he undoubtedly was, moving on in search of universalization of experience. Shakespeare was also responding to other dramatists and to tastes of audiences; when he wrote history plays, that genre was generally popular on the London stage.

Wheeler, on the other hand, believes that we must also attempt to account for psychological development in Shakespeare without succumbing to easy biographical theories that oversimplify. He does so by asking how we conceptualize an author called "Shakespeare" while we study and view his plays. This conceptualized "Shakespeare" may have little to do with the man born in 1564 who came to London and wrote plays. Shakespeare's own direct experience as a child, or as a husband, certainly need not have included violent episodes of jealousy or ingratitude like those shown in his tragedies, any more than I as viewer or reader need to have experienced breakdown in my marriage in order to respond to Othello's terrible chimera of jealous suffering. All children feel jealousies; all of us are involved in fantasized experiences that would be tragic if real. Shakespeare's genius is his ability to be in strong contact with these feelings and to dramatize them so powerfully. Shakespeare need not have confronted the remarriage of his mother (and in fact he did not) to write *Hamlet*. The probability is, argues Wheeler (1981), that Shakespeare believed in marriage as a necessary and socially valid institution. Marriage is important in his drama, however, "not as an indicator of the dramatist's belief, but as a source, and a resource, of comfort and tension, strength and vulnerability, concord and violence, life and death, as the relation that at once perpetuates the family and exists in ineradicable tension with familial bonds" (p. 31).

Our sense of the author is thus integral to our quest for understanding; even if the "Shakespeare" we conceptualize exists, in the words of Michel Foucault (1977), only "at the contours of texts," (cited by Wheeler, 1981, p. 31), we do nonetheless keep coming back to and extending our idea of this "Shakespeare" as we read his works. The purpose of criticism, Wheeler offers, is to acknowledge and clarify "that endlessly circular process in which my reading of Shakespeare's plays leads toward a conception of Shakespeare that in turn influences how I read Shakespeare's plays" (p. 29). Wheeler's way to clarify this process begins with the assumption that Shakespeare "was once a child," and that his childhood, "in itself irrecoverable, had a formative impact on later experience, including the writing of poems and plays." Shakespeare "responded to the world around him and to conflict within him," and these responses "produced characteristic attitudes toward experience that shaped the writing of his texts" (p. 31). The attitudes were not static, but subject to change.

If we return now to the movements in Shakespeare's career from festive comedy and history to tragedy and romance, as observed by Edward Dowden, what pattern of development can we discover that is not narrowly reliant on fictional biography? Let us begin with the festive comedies. C. L. Barber (1969), to whom Wheeler owes a considerable debt, has shown how in these plays "holiday liberty frees passion from inhibition and the control of the older generation." "The festive comedies move out to the creation of new families," and free sexuality "from the ties of family" (p. 61; cited by Wheeler, pp. 79-80). Many festive comedies are presided over by strong, wise, loving women like Rosalind in *As You Like It* or Portia in *The Merchant of Venice*, who provide a secure world. Such women preside over the play "as an ideal image of

the beloved, an ideal grounded in relations to the mother"
(Wheeler, p. 31). In *The Merchant of Venice*, as Norman
Holland (1964) has observed, the dramatic conflict pits
not only Christian against Jew but a feminine world of
nighttime, mystery, bounty, and giving against a masculine world of daytime, vengeance, commerce, and competition. Psychologically, says Holland, *The Merchant* is
inhabited chiefly by helpless, dependent children whose
fate turns on the contest "between a loving mother, Portia, and a castrating father, Shylock" (pp. 235-236). The
feminine triumph over Shylock protects the play from the
threat of "the vengeful, possessive father." Rosalind, in
As You Like It, is a wise magician who works things out
harmoniously for all.

In order for this comic pattern to succeed in Shakespeare, however, Wheeler argues, "love relations must be
protected from directly experienced passion and from explicit interference from family bonds." The comic hero's
love for the heroine "implicitly includes aspects of the
relationship never explicitly dramatized in these plays,
a boy's relation to a mother." Comic heroes like Orlando
in *As You Like It* often have dead or esteemed fathers,
whereas no comic hero or heroine has a mother whose
presence is of central importance. The young men are not
sexually importunate; instead, the relations of Orlando
to Rosalind, or of Orsino to Viola in *Twelfth Night*, are
presented as friendships through the device of disguising
the heroine as a man. Sexual desire in men is deflected
into the language or actions of secondary figures, especially clowns or fools. The action of these plays is thus
presented to us "through truncated and disguised oedipal
situations in which the heroine provides maternal tenderness and control and in which competition among men
for the love of a woman, which could evoke the threat of
oedipal rivalry with the father, is minimized, displaced

into the subplot, or excluded altogether" (Wheeler, 1981, pp. 175-176). Shakespeare's festive comedies avoid certain conflicts as a means of achieving harmonious resolution. When these conflicts are confronted, in the early tragedy of *Romeo and Juliet*—that is, when male sexuality is allowed to be more importunate and when family conflicts are intensified—the result is catastrophe.

The history plays of this same period, the late 1590s, also achieve happy resolution in the triumph of Prince Hal, who becomes king of England and victor over France in *Henry V*. Once again, however, argues Wheeler (1981), basing his analysis on the work of Ernst Kris (1948), Shakespeare "immerses his prince in a range of conflict less deep and more narrowly circumscribed than that of the later tragedies" (p. 161). Although the earlier history plays from *Henry VI* through *Richard III* repeatedly show us domineering females like Joan of Arc and Margaret of Anjou, the second tetralogy from *Richard II* through *Henry V* banishes women to a peripheral status. Falstaff, perhaps, is a kind of nurturing, sensual matrix presiding over Hal's youth, but he too must be banished. The success that Hal achieves in maturing, in learning to give up infantile gratification by coming to terms with the constraints of the external world, is very real, and Hal is at last even provided with a wife very much on his own terms; but the autonomy arrived at concedes little to a mutual and flexible relationship with womanhood.

The Sonnets (or some of them) are also of this period of the late 1590s, and here, in the absence of the constraints of comic form obliging Shakespeare to resolve matters in a series of marriages or worldly triumphs, conflict is more open. The troubled and humiliating relationship of the persona-poet to his aristocratic friend produces in the persona-poet an "ominously unstable acceptance of shameful self-regard" (Wheeler, 1981, p. 69).

The Sonnets move away from professions of belief in marriage and procreation to dwell "on kinds of relationships subordinated to or deflected from the claims of matrimony in the comedies: the binding power of friendship and the contamination of sexual relations by promiscuity or degradation" (p. 179). The persona-poet's feverish love for the treacherous Dark Lady anticipates the mistrust of female power and sexuality that turns up so plentifully in the tragedies. Between his degraded love for a faithless, wanton woman and his chaste, idealized, all-consuming love for the friend who is socially above him, the persona-poet has moved far away from the hero's trusting love for the motherly young woman of the festive comedies.

When these sexual problems are fully explored, in the period of the tragedies, the results are catastrophic for men as for women. Deep mistrust of feminine sexuality characterizes Hamlet's relationship to his mother and to Ophelia. A failure to integrate sexual desire and tender regard in a single relationship is at the heart of Othello's mistrust of Desdemona. The specter of a woman who "seduces, betrays, usurps, castrates," and "ultimately demands death" (Wheeler, 1981, p. 150), often overwhelms the image of idealized woman as a source of life and trust; it is this spectral woman whom Othello believes he can kill by murdering Desdemona.

Measure for Measure, in the view of both Wheeler and Arthur Kirsch, occupies a pivotal position in Shakespeare's development. Because it is comic in form, and yet was written during the period of the greatest tragedies (ca. 1604, perhaps between *Othello* and *King Lear*), when Shakespeare was so deeply preoccupied with the conflicts here described, its antagonisms seem oddly at variance with the reassurances of the final scene. Even a cursory examination of the plot suggests that Shakespeare deliberately chose for this seeming comedy a tale of intractable sexual conflict and degradation. Isabella, the heroine, is a young Viennese woman who is about to become a nun when her brother Claudio is arrested for fornication by Lord Angelo, a strict and precise man who has been put in charge of Vienna to crack down on rampant vice during the mysterious absence of the Duke of the city. Isabella and Angelo are alike in that both of them are turning away from sexuality, including their own. When, however, Isabella goes to Lord Angelo to beg mercy for her brother, Angelo falls in love with her lustfully and bargains for her body to save Claudio's life. When Claudio breaks down and asks Isabella to agree to Angelo's terms, her furious and hysterical response is to wish for Claudio's swift death. Counseled by the supposedly absent Duke, who is really in disguise as a friar watching over Angelo and the rest, Isabella agrees to an assignation. Her place is taken by a woman Lord Angelo has previously courted and then deserted, the unfortunate Mariana. Angelo attempts to cover up his guilt by ordering the execution of Claudio and denying any knowledge of what has happened to the returning Duke, but the Duke in his alter ego as friar is unhooded, discovers all, forgives Angelo, and marries Isabella.

Vienna is thus, in this account and in the seamy demimonde of pimps and prostitutes that peoples the underworld of the subplot, a place of sexual degradation. Angelo, deputized by Duke Vincentio to rule Vienna during the Duke's absence, is a repressed man who attempts to repudiate all sexual desire in himself and others; his puritanism suggests, in Wheeler's eyes, "an unstable over-identification with paternal authority stabilized by his service to lofty ideals and authority outside himself." Once the Duke's departure has put him in power, "his precarious inner restraint is stripped of its external sanc-

tion" (p. 94). Just as his self-proclaimed purity "drama-
tizes a son's effort to repudiate sexual longings extended
into an entire style of life, his acknowledgment of Isabella's sacred virtue builds on a complementary tendency
to deny the mother's sexuality because it represents an
intolerable provocation." His "ideal of feminine purity
and his equation of sexuality with evil originate together;
they are polarized derivatives of the preoedipal union of
infantile sexual desire and tender regard" (p. 96). The
terrible pleasure he finds in assaulting Isabella expresses
both the "sexualized rage accumulated in his service to
a tyrannous conscience and his rage against Isabella for
undermining its power" (p. 100).

Isabella, too, in her self-imposed chastity, seeks a solution to carnality by avoidance, and shares Angelo's deep
distrust of women. The play thus expresses "a deep mistrust of impulses within the self that are provoked in men
through relations to women" (p. 116). The most radical
form taken by this fear of sexual desire is a repudiation
of life itself. The Duke, experiencing conflict vicariously
in his deputy, is kept admirable only by scapegoating
onto others the qualities of human frailty that cannot be
acknowledged in such an authority figure. This strategy
on Shakespeare's part preserves Duke Vincentio's autonomy, Wheeler believes, but at the expense of rendering
improbable the marriages with which the play ends, especially that between the "ghostly father" Vincentio and
the "aspiring nun" Isabella.

Arthur Kirsch sees in Angelo's final exposure and
humbling a curative process akin to psychoanalysis, by
means of which Angelo comes to understand the nature
of his repressions and hence to master them. Kirsch
points to a similarity of thought between Christian and
Freudian teaching: both find in Angelo an unrelieved
sense of guilt that is archetypally human, and both insist

that Angelo (and all men) must come to terms with this guilt by accepting carnality as human. Isabella is subjected to a similar process of purgation. Her idealism, not unlike Angelo's, "is inexperienced and based on an ignorance of her own human composition" (Kirsch, 1981, p. 85). She must learn to accept the sexuality she so mistrusts. Her response to her brother's plea for life is one of panic; her inexcusable rejection of him stems from her inability to "accept the reality of human instincts." She "is afraid not only of Angelo's desires, but of her own" (p. 87). What the Duke's beneficent trick in Act V does is to oblige her to plead not only for the life of her would-be seducer, but for a husband for Mariana. Her "recognition of her own femininity has taught her the human need for mercy" (p. 89). Claudio, too, must learn through testing; his healthful discovery is that a proper appreciation of the reality of death is salutary because it leads to a deeper and richer understanding of life.

Above all, argues Kirsch, the Duke wishes to enable those he manipulates to "recognize the mortal conditions of their own lives and hearts," and to "find a redeeming and fruitful expression of their humanity" in marriage and procreation. Marriage is "the deepest and most creative model and expression of human community" (p. 98). Kirsch is thus more inclined to accept the marriages at the end than is Wheeler, and sees less deviousness in the Duke; for Kirsch, the marriages work as "heavenly comforts of despair" and as images of *felix culpa* that animate "the psychic as well as spiritual movement of the play" (p. 106). There is healthy room for a difference of opinion here that helps to define what is so problematic about this play. Both critics agree, however, that *Measure for Measure* centers on conflict that is integral to the vision of Shakespeare's great tragedies.

Let us now look at *Othello*, a play on which both

Wheeler and Kirsch have written eloquently, to see illustrated the male fears of feminine sexuality and other
conflicts that we have already seen explored in *Measure
for Measure*. *Othello* is also a good play to discuss here
because, as Kirsch says, it has too often been badly served
by psychoanalytic criticism with the sort of reductive and
diagnostic analyses I have cautioned against.[2] Kirsch
(1981) puts the case well when he protests that "Othello's
energies and conflicts are not diseases to be cured or re-
deemed" (p. 11).[3] Nevertheless, the play's preoccupations
are unremittingly sexual; no other Shakespearean play
explores so relentlessly the sexual relationship between
a man and woman in marriage. The play is a severe test
for critics: many have found Desdemona daunting, or apt
to take a lover in due course, or conversely too good to
be true. The poet W. H. Auden gives a wonderfully perv-
erse reading of *Othello*; Desdemona is far too much a
woman for Auden, and he is sure, given enough time,
that Desdemona will be faithless to her husband. In other
words, Auden (1948) falls into Iago's trap and thinks of
Desdemona what the villain wishes us all to think (pp.
268-269). Kirsch argues, and I entirely agree, that she
is both morally good and very much a woman, that her
choice of Othello is both passionate and spiritual, that
she integrates sensuality and affection in a way that illustrates the biblical injunction: "For this cause shall a
man leave father and mother, and shall be joined unto
his wife, and they two shall be one flesh" (Kirsch, 1981,
p. 14).[4] Her pleading for Cassio is not flirtation with him,

---

[2] See, for example. Martin Wangh (1950); Abraham Bronson Feldman (1952); and Gordon Ross Smith (1959).

[3] The chapter on *Othello* is reprinted with minor changes from
Kirsch's earlier article (1978).

[4] Here Kirsch is quoting *The Book of Common Prayer 1559* (edited
by Booty, 1976). Kirsch notes that the biblical text from Paul's Epistle
to the Ephesians 5:28-32 varies slightly in the Geneva translation.

though she is unafraid to be fond of men other than her husband; her pleading is a part of her engrossing concern for her husband's happiness.

Othello responds warmly at first to this numinous concept of marriage; husband and wife are well tuned in their first appearances together. Even Othello's blackness does not make him an unsuited mate for her; to Elizabethans, argues Kirsch, blackness could evoke the notion that all men were once black in their sinfulness but become white in the knowledge of God. The Scriptures give sanction to the view that man can be "black, but beautiful." Othello's "sense of command, of public decorum and courtesy, his dignity, and above all his remarkable devotion to Desdemona" are evidences of the greatness of his mind and character. His age similarly betokens not impotency but wisdom, moderation, gravity (p. 21). At the same time, too, there is a sweet childishness about him in his relationship to Desdemona that suggests a child's intense feelings of affection and desire toward his mother. Othello has obviously learned to transfer his erotic feelings from himself and his real mother to another woman, Desdemona, but his image of that earlier symbiotic union remains a model for his present happiness. Desdemona's love for him is unconditional, and his intense estimation of her is in part an estimation of himself. He becomes in Freud's terms his "own ideal once more" as he was in childhood, recapturing some of the "primary narcissism of childhood."[5]

Iago is the agent of undoing of this perfect union of heroic warrior and divine feminine radiance. He represents a wellspring as deep in Othello's soul as does Desdemona; and, argues Kirsch, the conflict they represent

[5] Kirsch, 1981, p. 26, cites Freud (1912) and (1914), especially pp. 88 and 100.

is resonant in both a psychological and religious sense. Religiously, Othello loses his faith and despairs; psychologically, we realize that he is deeply convinced that he is unlovable. He succumbs to Iago's vicious insinuations about his color and age, and about the unlikelihood of Desdemona's long loving such a man as he, because, finally, "he fails to love his own body, to love himself, and it is this despairing self-hatred which spawns the enormous savagery and degradation, and destructiveness of his jealousy" (pp. 32-33). Here Othello re-enacts the painful separation from the mother, and indeed speaks of Desdemona as one "Where either I must live or bear no life,/The fountain from which my current runs/Or else dries up—to be discarded thence!" (*Othello*, 4.2.57-60) Othello's fall into jealousy shows us "the tragic vulnerability of a love so absolutely rooted in, and dependent upon, the exaltation of symbiotic union" (Kirsch, 1981, p. 33). The handkerchief, with which Othello's mother subdued his father, becomes to him an emblem of a lost primitive past and of a lost merger with his mother. His jealous rage against Cassio "is ultimately a rage against himself that reaches back to the elemental and destructive triadic fantasies that at one stage in childhood govern the mind of every human being" (p. 34). Desdemona is as much a part of Othello's soul as is Iago, and that Iago-like part is a part of the unconscious life of all men. The dissociation of affection and sensuality is, in Freud's view, a condition of human life generally, and we see it in the other love relationships of *Othello*; Cassio, for instance, idealizes Desdemona but can have a sexual relationship only with a whore. Othello's conflict is therefore representative; it is moving as a tragic story because "he enacts for us, with beautiful and terrifying nakedness, the primitive energies that are the substance of our own erotic lives" (p. 39).

Wheeler enlarges this tragic portrait to view *Othello* in the context of other Shakespearean tragedies. Othello's "hideous evocations of sexual disgust" are akin to Hamlet's brooding over his mother's incest and to Lear's raging "against the 'sulphurous pit' in the 'centaur' half of the female anatomy" (Wheeler, 1981, p. 19). Othello's denunciations of female sexuality follow when Desdemona "seeks to be fully a wife rather than the reservoir of absolute content Othello has sought" (p. 18). When Iago urges Othello to "be a man," by destroying the unsettling sexual presence of Desdemona, he gives voice to a mistrust of women also present in *Hamlet* and *Macbeth*. The polarized attitudes toward Desdemona of idealization and degradation are like those inflicted upon Isabella in *Measure for Measure*. Men in other tragedies resemble Othello, as Carol Thomas Neely (1977) has said, in that they "see the women as whores and then refuse to tolerate their own projections" (p. 228). When Othello kills Desdemona, he seeks to preserve the beauty of her body, as though, like other tragic heroes, he would purge her "of her dreaded sexuality in order to love a purified image of her" (Wheeler, 1981, p. 129). The spectral woman who seduces, betrays, castrates, and ultimately demands death is the chimera Othello thinks he can kill by murdering his wife; she is most nearly represented in actuality, perhaps, by Goneril, Regan, and Lady Macbeth, but she is most often a product of man's diseased imagination toward such women as Gertrude and Ophelia. "In *Othello*," writes Wheeler, "as in *King Lear*, the value of the woman who is a source of life and trust can only be fully realized after she is confused with, and sacrificed to, this spectral woman." Desdemona's murder on stage reminds us that "no tragedy closes upon a stage that supports a living woman" (pp. 150-151).

Wheeler groups *Othello* among the tragedies with

Hamlet, King Lear, and *Antony and Cleopatra*, identifying these as plays in which "The fear of and the longing
for merger with another provide the primary driving
force." In a separate group of tragedies, comprising *Troilus and Cressida, Macbeth, Timon of Athens*, and *Coriolanus*, "a comparably ambivalent relation to the prospect
of omnipotent autonomy provides the psychic context in
which the protagonists seek self-definition" (p. 201). In
the first group, longing for merger shapes the action and
is culminated in Othello's joining Desdemona on her
deathbed or Lear's entering with the dead Cordelia in his
arms or Antony dying in the arms of Cleopatra. In the
second group, tragic protagonists "move away from relations of unqualified trust that ultimately prove to be
destructive" (p. 202) as in Troilus's renouncing of the
faithless Cressida or Macbeth's estrangement from his
wife. Shakespeare oscillates, Wheeler argues, between
plays of one group and the other, from *Hamlet* to *Troilus*
and from *Othello* and *King Lear* to *Macbeth*, and thereby
continues a basic polarity to be found earlier in his career;
the tragic protagonists of the trust/merger group search
without success to reinhabit "the world of love grounded
in trust, often presided over by benign female presences,
dramatized in the festive comedies," whereas "the desperate recoil into movements toward travestied autonomy in Troilus, Macbeth, Timon, and Coriolanus recall
the simpler world of masculine authority, uncomplicated
by the presence of captivating women, that Prince Hal
negotiates in the *Henriad*" (p. 206). Moving forward in
Shakespeare's career beyond the period of tragedies,
Wheeler finds this same polarity reflected in the late
romances, especially between *The Winter's Tale*, with its
"longing for merger and the violent recoil from it" that
are "ultimately subordinated to achieved trust and mutuality," and *The Tempest* (p. 218). In *The Tempest*

Wheeler finds at last a resolution of these polarities, above all in the autonomy of Prospero that avoids a tragic drive toward omnipotence and inevitable collapse into failure. The late romances move, as C. L. Barber (1969) tells us, "through experiences of loss back to the recovery of family relations in and through the next generation," freeing family ties from "the threat of sexual degradation" (p. 61).

It seems to me, then, that considerable recent analysis of Shakespeare's development, highlighted here in the work of Wheeler and Kirsch, can be synthesized into a coherent theory of development that posits no biographical connection with the outward events of Shakespeare's life and yet gives us a "Shakespeare" to whom we can turn for a better understanding of how one genre evolves into another. This theory deals responsibly with what is undeniably there in Shakespeare's text, the concern with family ties and with sexuality, and it explores artistic ways in which a developing attitude toward conflict might be expressed. If explained in terms clear to all readers, and related to Renaissance thought along the lines proposed by Kirsch, it also points out a universality that can bind us to this "Shakespeare" despite the lapse of nearly four centuries.

REFERENCES

Auden, W. H. (1948), *The Dyer's Hand, and Other Essays.* New York: Random House, 1956.

Barber, C. L. (1969), "Thou that beget'st him that did thee beget": Transformation in *Pericles* and *The Winter's Tale. Shakespeare Survey*, 22:59-67.

Boas, F. S. (1896), The problem plays. In: *Shakspere and His Predecessors.* New York: Haskell House, 1968.

Booty, J. (1976), *The Book of Common Prayer 1559.* Charlottesville, Va.: Folger Books.

Chambers, E. K. (1929), *Shakespeare: A Survey.* London: Sidgwick & Jackson, 1925.

Dowden, E. (1875), *Shakspere: A Critical Study of His Mind and Art.* London: Routledge & Kegan Paul, 1905.

Feldman, A. B. (1952), Othello's obsessions. *Amer. Imago*, 9:147-154.

Foucault, M. (1977), What Is an Author? In: *Language, Counter-Memory, Practice: Selected Essays and Interviews*, ed. & trans. D. F. Bouchard. Ithaca, N.Y.: Cornell University Press.

Freud, S. (1912), Contributions to the psychology of love: The most prevalent form of degradation in erotic life. *Collected Papers*, 4:203-216. London: Hogarth Press and the Institute for Psychoanalysis, 1948-1950.

———— (1914), On narcissism. *Standard Edition*, 14:73-102. London: Hogarth Press, 1957.

Frye, N. (1965), *A Natural Perspective: The Development of Shakespearean Comedy and Romance.* New York: Columbia University Press.

Holland, N. (1964), *Psychoanalysis and Shakespeare.* New York: McGraw-Hill.

Jones, E. (1954), *Hamlet and Oedipus.* New York: Doubleday.

Kahn, C. (1981), *Man's Estate: Masculine Identity in Shakespeare.* Berkeley: University of California Press.

Kirsch, A. (1978), The polarization of erotic love in *Othello. Modern Language Review*, 73:721-740.

———— (1981), *Shakespeare and the Language of Love.* New York: Cambridge University Press.

Kris, E. (1948), Prince Hal's conflict. *Psychoanal. Quart.*, 17:487-506.

Lenz, C. R., Greene, G., & Neely, C. T. (eds.) (1980), *The Woman's Part: Feminist Criticism of Shakespeare.* Urbana: University of Illinois Press.

Neely, C. T. (1980), Women and men in *Othello*: "What should such a fool / Do with so good a woman?" In: *The Woman's Part: Feminist Criticism of Shakespeare*, ed. C. R. Lenz, G. Greene, & C. T. Neely. Urbana: University of Illinois Press, pp. 211-239.

Schwartz, M. M., & C. Kahn (eds.) (1980), *Representing Shakespeare: New Psychoanalytic Essays.* Baltimore: Johns Hopkins Press.

Skura, M. (1981), *The Literary Use of the Psychoanalytic Process.* New Haven, Conn.: Yale University Press.

Smith, G. R. (1959), Iago the paranoiac. *Amer. Imago*, 16:155-167.

Wangh, M. (1950), *Othello*: The tragedy of Iago. *Psychoanal. Quart.*, 19:202-212.

Wheeler, R. (1981), *Shakespeare's Development and the Problem Comedies: Turn and Counterturn.* Berkeley: University of California Press.

Wilson, J. D. (1932), *The Essential Shakespeare.* Cambridge: Cambridge University Press.

10

The Late Works and Styles of Eugene O'Neill, Henry James, and Ludwig van Beethoven

JOSEPH D. LICHTENBERG, M.D.

In choosing to discuss the late works of Eugene O'Neill, Henry James, and Ludwig van Beethoven, I have selected plays, novels, and compositions that, more than being simply later or last works, represent stylistic and aesthetic reorganizations. The life pattern of each of these creative artists follows somewhat similar paths. As adolescents, each showed no great promise as a significantly creative person—Beethoven alone being something of a heavily pushed and pressured prodigy, but as a pianist performer, not as a composer. Each ended up in a field related to his father's activities—James O'Neill was a prominent actor, Henry James, Sr., a writer of numerous books on religious-philosophic subjects, and Johann Beethoven, as well as his father Ludwig, were professional musicians. When O'Neill, James, and Beethoven completed their apprenticeships, they each scored striking successes—received sponsorship in intellectual circles and moved steadily toward the highest level of accomplishment of any of their contemporaries in their respective fields. Then, at a point of considerable success, each suffered a trauma that interrupted the flow of this progressive development of their art. The sources of the traumas were varied, but their reactions were similar—a period of paralysis, both personal and creative—followed by an altered organization in both their lives and their works. Each took the very elements out of which he had built his successful works and subjected them to re-examination. Then, using other elements drawn from his personal past and the aesthetic traditions of his art, he reorganized his creative output into a new style—his so-called late works. It is the interplay between life experience, past and present, and creative change that interests a psychoanalyst, and it is to this that I shall largely refer.

EUGENE O'NEILL

In his last period as a productive playwright, Eugene O'Neill wrote *The Iceman Cometh, Long Day's Journey into Night*, a one-act play, *Hughie*, and *Moon for the Misbegotten*. These plays were written between 1939 and 1942, when O'Neill was in his early fifties, though he appeared much older and was recurrently ill. Until his death in 1953, his congenital tremor worsened progressively to the point where he could no longer hold a pencil. Accordingly, he worked intermittently on revisions and on one new play but essentially wrote nothing more.

In 1936, O'Neill seemed to be at the acme of his profession. Practically alone, he had taken the American theater of his father's day from its preoccupation with trivial comedies and melodramas and the declaiming of segments of Shakespearean plays to a preoccupation with serious drama. As a young man, he had written dramas of men at sea and people on farms and in cities that were revolutionary in that they portrayed the characters as caught in psychologically tormenting circumstances. He then experimented with theatrical form, using masks, long soliloquies, and machines as symbols. He wrote dramas of such length that a long intermission had to be planned so that the audience could leave for dinner and then return. *Strange Interlude* and *Mourning Becomes Electra* were acknowledged masterpieces, and in 1936 he received the Nobel Prize for literature. Yet this was a period of strange disquiet for him. All his life, he had suffered from periods of physical illness and "nervous exhaustion," complicated in his early years by very heavy drinking. Despite the protective efforts of his third wife Carlotta, he was thin, nervous, and labile in mood. He was also frustrated by the failure of *Days Without End*, a play he had labored over for more than two years (Lichtenberg and Lichtenberg, 1972). It was the most recent of a series of failures in which O'Neill had tried to have his protagonist struggle with some important abstract issue such as science, religion, or marital love in an idealized form.

From very early on, he had wanted to portray the evils of greed; and he now became completely preoccupied with a multiplay series entitled *A Tale of Possessors Self-Dispossessed*. The plays were originally planned as five dramas to cover the lives of an Irish immigrant family and an aristocratic New England clan between 1828 and the 1930s. O'Neill's conception quickly expanded to seven, and later to nine, and finally eleven plays, some double length, going back earlier and earlier in American history. O'Neill explained the theory of the cycle as indicating "that the United States, instead of being the most successful country in the world, is the greatest failure . . . because it was given everything. . . . Its main idea is that everlasting game of trying to possess your own soul by the possession of something outside of it" (Sheaffer, 1973, p. 442). Carlotta's telling comment on Eugene's project was "his next will be a history of the human race" (p. 443).

Despite occasional interspersed illnesses including an appendectomy, O'Neill worked seven days a week on his cycle over several years. He completed scenarios of them all, wrote drafts of three (two he later destroyed entirely), and finished one play, *A Touch of the Poet*. He wrote multiple outlines, thousands of notes, and stated, "Often I start a work-day writing dialogue for the play I'm on and wind up writing suggested notes on a scene in the eighth or ninth play!" (p. 477).

From even so brief a description, I believe it should be clear that O'Neill had placed himself in an impossible position. Given his state of health, his project would have more than filled all the years he was likely to live. But more important is the fact that he had once again chosen to attempt a subject for which he was simply ill-suited, and moreover for which the drama is a difficult vehicle at best. The American drama O'Neill almost singlehandedly created is about character. Therefore, while it is possible to depict a lust for wealth and power set against guilt-proneness in individuals with a poetic strain, the portrayal of a moralizing religious preachment against materialism becomes false profundity and abstruse mysticism. O'Neill never truly made it work, and the cycle was his last and most grandiose effort to do so—an ambition he had carried from early adolescence. It was man's raw, sensitive skin O'Neill knew about—his being hurt, hurting others, and being guilty and hurting himself.

Thus what came out of this tremendous effort was essentially that, at some level of his being, O'Neill realized that, for the writing years left him, he had to tell the story he knew best—the psychological cycle of man's bouts with his personal devils—not the cycle of history and social materialism. And he had to do it without poetry—a terribly painful loss for him—but again a positive circumstance, in the final analysis. Lacking the nobility of language to do otherwise, he had to say things plainly in the words of a salesman, a bartender, his parents, or himself. I hold it to be on the basis of these factors that something wonderful happened in O'Neill's unconscious and preconscious as he labored on his cycle—he became aware that a play set in a barroom, *The Iceman Cometh*, which for years he had been turning over in his mind, had begun to crystallize. "Although one of his outsized dramas and among his most complex, *The Iceman* was so well formed in his mind, after years of incubation, that it developed smoothly on paper" (Sheaffer, 1973, p. 485).

The Iceman is indeed a play about big matters—man's personal struggle with guilt and the meaning of death: is it liberation or deprivation? It is about the horrors in the soul that lurk behind the ribald. It presents a microcosm of cultures, races, and philosophies and shows the human in each. But most of all it treats the subject of man's need for illusion. As long as even the most beaten down of God's creatures retains his personal "pipe dream," the whiskey has a kick. What O'Neill comes to is that an unreality is needed in reality and a reality is needed in unreality—or man commits deeds he cannot live with. Matricide is a horror men can't live with—whatever the rationale, real or illusory.

What made it possible for O'Neill to have this remarkable play incubating in his mind as he labored on his cycle—or, put another way, as he lived out *his* pipe dream of morally edifying and purifying the world? The answer can be deduced from the issues in two of the cycle plays. In *A Touch of the Poet*, he created a wonderful character, Con Melody, a larger-than-life poseur—around whose pretenses the whole family revolves. Through Con, O'Neill, I suggest, came to terms with his father's dominance—it did the family much harm, but it also furnished the source of pride. Thus, though pretense (unresolved infantile grandiosity) may create a painful burden on others, the creative myth it sometimes spurs gives a tragic meaning to life, rather than the meaningless tragedy of "pure" reality. This O'Neill needed to say, and he did it brilliantly in this one completed achievement of these years of labor.

But the crucial personal statement he was to make evolved in an unfinished work, *More Stately Mansions*. In this drama of complex triangular interactions between a man, his wife, and his mother, each pulls on the other to enter a state of narcissistic merger. The most dangerous threat is posed by the mother's pull on her son to enter, as he had in childhood, into a fantasy world of her illusions—delusions. This is symbolized by her invitation to him to enter with her into the secret interior of a small, templelike, octagonal Chinese summer house in an enclosed garden. Here the entry into illusion spells the loss of reality altogether into madness—with the loss of self and identity as penalty. This was, I suggest, a memory to O'Neill of his childhood attachment to his mother—the loss of self implicit in the shared world of her morphine-addictive state. O'Neill faced this catastrophically attractive state of bonding in this displaced and adequately defended-against manner. He could separate the regressive state of alcoholism—the coping mechanism of his father and of the denizens of Harry Hope's saloon—from the madness of a deluded believer—Hickey in *The Iceman* and the mother in *More Stately Mansions*.

His late period, then, comprised the fully preconsciously articulated play *The Iceman Cometh* and the worked-out, direct statement of the myths and facts of the O'Neills themselves in their *Long Day's Journey into Night*. These are plays about life and death—mythic and real. Hickey, the "Iceman," gives death to his wife and, in effect, to himself; but Eugene (Edmund) in *Journey* goes off to the tuberculosis sanitorium where he is to be reborn a playwright. But the adolescent Eugene never truly died. He was rebellious and supersensitive to the end. Nonetheless, in the final period of his work, a transformation took place, a transformation in which he became "Possessor, Self-Dispossessed" of excess intellectual baggage. Greek and Shakespearean drama were not mimicked; their lessons were incorporated in unities of form and the strength of personal statements. The impinging of abstract factors on man was no longer artificially symbolized, it was incorporated in the myths—racial, familial, and personal—that pressed each character from within outward rather than the other way around. And with these two masterworks, it was as though O'Neill was ready to say goodbye.

After the loss of his beloved dog from old age, he wrote a summing-up obituary much of which could have applied to himself. Shortly thereafter, he planned another play cycle called *By Way of Obits*. Two followed—the fictionalized story of his brother James's alcoholic suicide, tenderly and forgivingly told in *Moon for the Misbegotten*, and the unique one-act play, *Hughie*. This tale of a small-time loner who has lost his audience—through the death of the night clerk in the run-down hotel in which he lives—tells of existence, the way one man's illusions give hopeless hope to another, while each waits out his time as best he can. Here I believe the master of the complex in the drama had in his maturity pulled together so much of the theater, from the drama of classical Greece to the drama of classical O'Neill, that he was able to build a bridge unwittingly to the next phase of drama, that of the existential dilemma—his own personal Waiting for Godot.

HENRY JAMES

It is a twist of irony worthy of the Master that, subsequent to Henry James's death, his works have been dramatized with great success, considering that, during his lifetime, his most painful creative failure resulted from his attempt to write for the theater. This failure constituted a point of departure for James, since after it, in his fifties, he developed his later style. James's foray into the theater resulted from his dissatisfaction with the extent of his public acceptance, especially as it translated into financial security for his advancing years. Not that he was unsuccessful. Early in his career his works had made an unexpected splash, and he had always received critical acclaim and a positive response from a small but discriminating following. He was a purist about the novel, a student of its structure, and the innovator of a new disciplined approach in which a psychological plot overtook and at times almost replaced storytelling. But James told stories, and people wanted to know what happened in both the minds and the lives of his characters. But not *enough* people—certainly in comparison to authors with infinitely less skill and polish, whose potboilers made them rich.

James decided on the theater as a way to reach a wider audience instantly in a "commercial" setting, but he did so as would a man who desperately wants a fish but can't stand the smell of the market—he held his nose and went to work. And he worked hard, so that his failure was all the more puzzling and ignominious. At the same time, James was a realist who was prepared to abandon his effort, and he might have done so with less personal dismay had it not been for the traumatic form the ending took. After the opening-night final curtain, James was pushed out on the stage and publicly booed by a group of ruffians in the audience. This would be a narcissistic assault for any author, but for James it was a catastrophe. Henry was, from childhood on, shy and withdrawn —somewhat by inclination, largely as protection—but most importantly the shyness was a camouflage for his major activity—the all-absorbing looking and listening that provided the sources for his creativity. In intellectual and socially genteel circles, he was gregarious—but only when and where and with whom he felt accepted and appreciated. While he might tolerate failure with a degree of philosophic resignation about the limitations of the public, he was extremely reactive to boorishness and the sudden affront to his expectations.

This reaction of fragility had been present from early childhood in response to his father's instability, his mother's sweet controlling, and his older brother William's nagging. Henry's theatrical failure had followed another trauma—the unexpected death by suicide of Constance Fenimore Woolson. She had been his friend, fellow writer, and possibly a model for one of his characters about whom he said "There was never a word he had said to her that she had not beautifully understood" (James, 1895, p. 267). He responded to the news of her suicide first with paralysis, then with a personal recovery, and then months later, as was his wont, with an aesthetic recovery (Lichtenberg, 1981). He then wrote the emotional catastrophe into a story. His hero would be smitten in the face, drop into a seat, and remain in a state of shock. The story, *The Altar of the Dead*, would deal from beginning to end with all the emotions related to mourning and death and dying—with the mysterious and ghostly, almost ghoulish, relationship of the dead to the living. It is this exercise of Henry's imagination —ranging near to the macabre—that was characteristic of one way in which he handled aggression and destructiveness and the affective state of disequilibrium and terror to which he was sensitive.

Henry had not long fully recovered from Fenimore's death when his disaster in the theater occurred. It was, to quote Leon Edel, (1969), "as if some remote little being within James himself had been killed by the audience during that crucial night . . . and he had been left open to the world's indifference" (p. 168). He tried for a time to hide with a good face the effect of this major narcissistic hurt. For some time, he went about his schedule. He began to formulate plans. Mostly they were for novels and stories he would write. Some were even for plays. He wrote in his notebook: "I have my head, thank God, full of visions" (p. 109). The protective self-expansiveness of these items indicates that he was reassuring himself of the indestructibility of functioning—the cornerstone of his self-esteem. What these words omitted were his emotions. He was months away from beginning to cope with his mood of despair.

As a young adult, he had made a critical study of the novel, creating for himself a confidence built on a mixture of pretentiousness and solid intellectual mastery. This had enabled him to emerge from a prolonged unfocused adolescence. Now in middle age, struggling to restore his confidence, he resumed his intellectual attack on the meaning, the structure, and the form of the novel. He would reorganize his life's work. His artistic self would be restored through the resolution of the disappointment over his "wasted passion and squandered time" (Edel, 1969, p. 111) into a new creative self who had discovered the "key that . . . fits the complicated chambers of both the dramatic and narrative lock" (p. 111). Although he could formulate these plans to restructure his method, he could not write. For a time, a measure of grandiosity served as a protective armor. He set down elaborate outlines and demanded of himself levels of originality that paralyzed his effort. Finally, he began to write a group of four tales about the responses of a series of little girls and young female adults who exist in a world of confusion ranging from perplexity to the horror and death found in *The Turn of the Screw*.

At the end of this period, James entered his most productive phase. Edel states that "In his deep well of unconscious cerebration," James "had opened himself up—life aiding—to feeling and to love. He had taught himself to accept middle age, and to have great loneliness, and had turned again and again for solace to the discipline and difficulty of his craft. . . . In this indirect soothing of his soul, the frigid wall of his egotism had been breached to an enlarged vision of the world, and a feeling at last of the world's human warmth" (pp. 354-355).

Through what Edel calls James's backward steps into "the black abyss in order to discover his power of self-recreation" (p. 354), Henry emerged by the dual process of externalizing his disappointments into the themes and styles of his creative work and internalizing the renewed self-affirmation of his unique gift as a writer through a further enriched creative effort. The transformations in his work bear out this double process.

Representative of his late style are his novels *The Ambassadors,The Wings of the Dove*, and *The Golden Bowl*, and stories such as "The Beast in the Jungle" and "The Jolly Corner."

(1) He incorporated into the novel major stylistic elements from the drama—the unities of setting, time interval, character, and action. He now planned his novels

as a series of scenarios, similar to scenes and acts of a play, increasing the dramatic tension in each.

(2) He included more sensual and emotive touching in the interaction between people. The psychological emphasis was retained, but the range was expanded to include sexual intercourse, physical holding, and more mature elements of love.

(3) At the same time as he treated sensuality and emotion more freely, his sentence structure and the use of metaphor became more idiosyncratic. He now made revision after revision, building up images by accretion. The effect was one of controlling and manipulating the reader into the closest possible attention. James's method gave expression through the sentence structure itself, to James's intrapsychic struggles and his defense of distancing himself through intellectualization. By his interruption in the flow of the sentence and his unusual placement of verbs, he appears to be saying, I assert "this" but it cannot be unqalified; I know the vernacular people use but I cannot say it straight out any more than I can refer to the unadorned bathroom function; and the sensual and emotional are never straight out to me—they are complex, analytic, and multifaceted.

(4) In this major revision of style, James, for the first time, opened his mind to the significance of symbolism as a unifying device. His dove in *Wings of the Dove* can be compared to Ibsen's wild duck in its evocation of a set of related but rich and shifting metaphoric usages.

(5) He explored values through the careful analysis of their effect on characters, each of whom makes judgments while the author suspends his. He employed irony as the principal buffer against excessive personal involvement or sentiment on the part of any of his main adult characters.

(6) By combining the suspense of the ghost story with

the tension of the psychological interaction between subjective and objective reality, he perfected the new climax
of the psychological novel. The climax does not occur
when something happens in the form of action, although
that may incidentally be true. Rather, it occurs when
something is discovered—when insight is obtained by the
confluence of psychic recognition by two or more of the
characters who want to "know," in spite of the consequences of knowledge. When successful, James created
an experience in which the characters, the reader, and
even the author suddenly share awareness. Whereas, before, awareness almost always made the characters withdraw, now, in *The Golden Bowl* and in "The Jolly Corner,"
the shared vision cements the intimacy.

James had come to terms with that special amalgam
of mind and body that allowed the narcissistic intellectual
people about whom he wrote to want not only mental
omnipotence, but also the warmth, invigoration, and pain
of caring deeply. Life in his late novels, then, includes
loving and disappointment, even death with mourning
and grief—not the narcissistic manipulation of people in
one's own private theater of the mind.

LUDWIG VAN BEETHOVEN

Like a thunderclap of pent-up rage, the Hammerclavier
Sonata, begun in 1817, when the composer was 46, heralded the unprecedented masterworks of Beethoven's late
style. These compositions reveal the most remarkable
capacity to reorganize and revitalize an already legendary talent into a transcendent power and beauty, at the
same time as Beethoven himself was undering states of
mental disorganization and physical devitalization leading to his death in 1827 from alcoholic cirrhosis. Thus it
is possible to say of Beethoven that he had two late

styles—a musical one and a personal one. The tempo of his compositional output in his late style built up slowly, beginning primarily with his last five piano sonatas between 1816 and 1822, advancing through the monumental Ninth Symphony, the *Missa Solemnis*, and the imaginative Diabelli variations, and ending with a crescendo of five unexcelled string quartets written between February 1825 and November 1826. His personal late style has led to his being caricatured as the irascible deaf titan—or the mad genius, ranting and raving. Like most caricatures of famous people there is more than a grain of truth in this portrayal. Whereas before he had taken part in the court life of the grand nobility of Vienna, now Beethoven was frequently slovenly in dress and highly eccentric in manner. He made public rows about trivia involving money, was engaged in lawsuits about which he was often paranoid, and continued to drink sizable quantities of wine despite warnings. But the great stylistic revisions of these late works were not conceived of by an isolate or a madman. Despite his deafness, Beethoven was in touch with people, many of whom looked after him affectionately; his music was played, at least in private concerts; and he continued to receive the political protection of influential nobles.

I suggest that both revisions, Beethoven's musical leap forward and his personal slipping backward, resulted from a re-exploration of the past—conscious with his music, and unconscious with his human relations.

Beethoven, in bringing the classical style of Mozart and Haydn to full fruition, had achieved complete mastery of the dramatic principle of contrast to convey musically a sense of dynamic tension, struggle, and defeat or triumph. Now Beethoven took a serious interest in the music of Bach and Handel. From this study he evolved various combinations of the sonata form with the fugue, thereby adding rich counterpoint and polyphonic textures to the heroic classical style. He went back to Baroque church music, and combined its spirituality and splendor with classical expressiveness in the *Missa Solemnis*. Especially in the final movement of the Ninth Symphony, he used vocal intonations in both the singing and the instrumentation to achieve an intimacy of communication that push musician, singer, and listener into a totally affirmative mood state. Here the main structure from the "past" that Beethoven built on was his own construction, especially that of his Third, Fifth, and Seventh symphonies. But he added to his earlier approach a new freedom that only evolved in the late style, and is best exemplified in the variation form used in the Ninth Symphony finale, the quartets, and especially in the *33 Variations on a Waltz by Diabelli*. To quote Solomon (1977), Beethoven's biographer,

> Variation is the form of shifting moods, alternations of feeling, shades of meaning, dislocations of perspective. It shatters appearance into splinters of previously unperceived reality and, by an act of will, reassembles the fragments at the close. The sense of time is effaced—expanded, contracted—by changes in tempo; space and mass dissolve into the barest outline of the harmonic progressions and build up once again into baroque structures laden with richly ornamented patterns. The theme remains throughout as an anchor to prevent fantasy from losing contact with the outer world, but it too dissolves into the memories, images, and feelings which underlie its simple reality [p. 303].

What Beethoven achieved in his late style was a flexibility that allowed him (1) to use forms to continue to convey the dramatic principle of contrast, heroism, and struggle of the classical period; (2) to use the preclassic forms of fugue, counterpoint, variation, and Baroque ornamentation; and (3) to invent new combinations of the old and new. In any given work he might emphasize the old or the new. In the Ninth Symphony he restores the basic four-movement dialectic of struggle that he had abandoned a decade before; but he now includes within this form fugal and variational techniques. The five quartets of this period begin and end with more classically constructed works with the more experimental ones between. The total effect is one of opening up an infinity of possibilities—so that one can trace to Beethoven's final works Berlioz's and Mahler's unprecedented spaciousness and grandeur, Liszt's and Chopin's piano improvisations, and even I believe certain harmonic, rhythmical, and variational styles in jazz.

Thus in the creative field, when a great genius shatters the existing form and reconstructs it in flexible ways, he may open the way to new developments for generations ahead. The cycle is that of mastering the present, reabsorbing the past, and providing the keys to the future. But when we examine the shattering of the existing form with respect to Beethoven's characterological adjustment we see another, less salutary outcome. Owing to the biographic detective work of Solomon (1977) and the Sterbas (1971) we can piece together the source of this personal fragmentation and its pathologic outcome.

In 1812, Beethoven visited Antonie Brentano, a wealthy, attractive, married woman ten years his junior. For years Beethoven had paid court to a series of such women, flirting with them and receiving varied responses ranging from the encouragement of platonic affairs through maternal protectiveness to aversion and rejection. But with Antonie, the temperature of this passion-at-a-distance heated up with a devastating effect. Antonie clearly inclined toward hysteric responses and, faced with the prospect of leaving Vienna after her father's death and going off with her husband and children, "fled to Beethoven seeking salvation from that prospect—to one who represented for her a higher order of existence, to one who embodied in his music the spiritual essence of her native city" and her belated "right to choose her own beloved" (Solomon, 1977, p. 180). The effect of her presumed onslaught of love and willingness to run off with him sent Beethoven into panicked fright, and he was never the same again. Heroism and the rescue of lovers in distress had been emotionally, sensually, and idealistically satisfying to Beethoven—the ever-faithful Fidelio—when a distance from consummation could be maintained. It was a game of playing with fire in which danger was courted, but narrowly avoided, to begin the game once again.

But small flames that turn into major conflagrations can burn the house down, and Beethoven's awkward, even childish, playing of the gallant ended with Antonie's hot pursuit. And as we see so often clinically, when an oedipal edifice collapses, a preoedipal regression to polymorphous impulse-ridden tendencies may replace it. By the end of 1812, after completing the Seventh and Eighth Symphonies, Beethoven's creativity came to a full stop. In 1813, for the first time since his adolescence, he had no new projects under consideration; and he made what may have been a suicide attempt to starve himself. He also at this time began openly to pursue prostitutes. An observer described him sitting at an inn "in a distant corner at a table which, though large, was avoided by the other guests owing to the very uninviting habits into which he had fallen . . . Not infrequently he departed without paying his bill . . . He had grown so negligent of his person as to appear there sometimes positively 'schmutzig' " (Solomon, 1977, p. 221). I believe the identification with his father's descent into alcoholic deterioration is strongly suggested by this response. Beethoven's behavioral change marked the collapse of the shaky personality edifice Beethoven had built through his idealized identification with his upright grandfather, Kapellmeister Ludwig, who had died when his namesake was three.

Then, in 1814 and 1815, fate intervened twice in Beethoven's life. He had been asked to write a composition to celebrate Wellington's victory, and this bit of bombast won him more popular acclaim and financial reward than he was otherwise to experience. He primped himself for the crown heads of Europe who were attending the Congress of Vienna, and he took advantage of the opportunity to write some of his least memorable works. These seem in retrospect to be almost mockeries of his own heroic classic style. Then, just as suddenly as it came, his popularity faded and a Job's portion of blows fell on him. By 1815, his deafness was complete and he could no longer perform at all as a pianist, the source of his initial fame, and only rarely could he work as a conductor. Many of his principal patrons were lost to him in rapid succession because of death or the changing times. The spirit of an aristocracy-supported Enlightenment which had nurtured his imagination and given his music its programmatic raison d'être was giving way to a petit-bourgeois hedonistic Romanticism. But the main blow fate dealt him, at least in terms of his reaction to it, was the death of his brother Caspar Carl, who left behind a widow and a nine-year-old son, Karl. This set off an entangling interaction in which every facet of Beethoven's latent infantile conflicts and regulatory deficits was re-enacted. Each of the characters in this fantasy-based re-enactment appeared in changing roles: the widow—most commonly the bad mother, often the Queen of the Night; the nephew—the needy child or the ingrate; and Beethoven—the rescuer-protector or the totally controlling cruel sadist. In the composer's fevered imagination each character underwent such fluid fluctuations, with such massive projections and grandiose claims, that each of the three might play any of the roles of the other. All of this alternated with periods of relative calm sanity, but it was not until the poor besieged Karl, in 1826, made a serious suicide attempt—a message his uncle knew the meaning of—that a fragile peace was restored. The main elements of this tragic melodrama were that in Beethoven's distorted view the mother exerted a corrupting seductive overstimulation of her son, failed to provide him adequate protection, and was about to steal his inheritance (as his father had in fact stolen his mother's). Ludwig as the father would in the guise of the idealized grandfather protect and purify Karl against women and sexual contamination. But when this strangling custodianship was rejected, in the guise of his own father's sadism, Ludwig would attack Karl physically and mentally with every weapon at his disposal.

All in all, the custody fight over the nephew was a terribly sad affair. Nonetheless, the Beethoven of these years, despite his passions and torments, should not be thought of a sad person. I say this despite the fact that he was progressively succumbing to alcoholism, the illness of his father and maternal grandmother. The details of his life were not that bad. He was frequently in good spirits, and a series of protectors, male and female, looked after him. Moreover, he worked and worked and worked with such supreme success during this last period that he derived an appropriate sense of mastery—of "omnipotence" achieved. Near the end of his life, Beethoven himself explained the context in which I believe he should be viewed. When he insisted on selling a ring reputed to contain a diamond but instead a cheap stone, only to be told, " 'Keep the ring, it is from a King,' Beethoven rose

up . . . and with indescribable dignity and self-consciousness . . . called out 'I too am a King!' " (Solomon, 1977,
pp. 288-289). He was saying, I believe, that he knew that
he was the king of the composers of his day, and he knew
that through his late style, more than other monarchs
and their diamonds true or false, he would remain a king
for a long time past his physical end.

CONCLUSIONS

O'Neill, James, and Beethoven were each creative individuals, who, by mid-life, had brought their craft to a
new level of expression. Each then responded to a trauma
that shattered his prior pattern of adjustment. Out of the
distress of their regressive responses, the pathological
underpinnings of their prior adaption could be discerned—but also the remarkable potentiality for a reintegration at a higher level of creative expression. Each
had built his life around a messianic urge that he had
directed toward the perfection of his creative field. To do
so, each had set himself up—even as a very young
man—as one of those who in Freud's (1910) words "dared
to utter the bold assertion which contains within itself
the justification for all independent research: *'He who
appeals to authority when there is a difference of opinion
works with his memory rather than with his reason.'* " (p.
122). Such an individual, Freud asserts, probes secrets
"while relying solely on observation and his own judge-
ment." But the repudiation of authority and the besting
of the "father" carries with it its own risk—the vulnerability to narcissistic trauma in response to failure (or
success) on the one hand, (Lichtenberg, 1978) and the
resort to a paralyzing pursuit of infantile omnipotent
grandiosity on the other. O'Neill, James, and Beethoven
each succumbed to an experience that was not truly a

"big" trauma by ordinary circumstances (O'Neill—the failure of one series of plays in the midst of general success; James—the failure to add success as a commercial dramatist to his success as novelist; Beethoven—the onslaught of a hysterical woman and the ups and downs of surface popularity).

Each then revealed tendencies to project plans of an impossible grandiose nature—but emerged with accomplishments that were indeed remarkable. Each built out of the wreckage of his adjustment a new style through a process of cannibalization of knowledge, its digestion, and reconstruction. Each revisited the past for his sources—both the aesthetic past and the personal past. Each re-evaluated the authority of others—borrowing from them for his own purposes—but most of all each came to a full appreciation of his own work as the central structure on which to rebuild. Thus what each did was to mirror effectively his own contribution; and, by using his own prior productions as his central guide, each was able to integrate other elements into it. The additional elements strengthened the basic structure and permitted a new organization toward a more multipotential, "open" expressive form. This established directions that enabled future artists to proceed further in a variety of directions now opened up by the late style.

The personal toll for each varied. O'Neill's period of productivity in his late style lasted about four years (1939-1943). After that he found it impossible to write because of his tremor, and the remaining ten years of his life until his death at 65 were marred by terrible periods of distress with Carlotta, complicated by drug misuse and bromide intoxication on the part of each. In this sense O'Neill turned full circle into the addictive disturbances of all his family members. James, after eight years of wonderfully successful work in his late style, began an-

318

JOSEPH D. LICHTENBERG

other project that he hoped would be a commercial success—the collected edition of his novels and tales. He rewrote his early works to bring them up to the level of his late works and wrote eighteen prefaces exploring in detail the craft of the novelist and the form of the novel. Again catastrophe struck. The monetary returns for this four years of intense work were painfully disappointing, and James again collapsed. Only this time he recovered, no longer to write, but to live out his life as a diffident, somewhat homosexually oriented, literary figure of the "Master" until his death at 72 (Edel, 1972). Beethoven's late style ended with his death at 56. The remarkable creative spurt of these eight or more years brought him into a full, rich contact with the past glories of the musical tradition. Regrettably, with the shattering of his idealized identification with his grandfather, these years also brought him into the physical debilitation of his father's alcoholism.

In each the creative spark to achieve the greatest, superimposed on the great, burned bright, and then went out.

REFERENCES

Edel, L. (1969), *Henry James: The Treacherous Years (1895-1901)*. New York: Lippincott.
——— (1972), *Henry James: The Master (1901-1916)*. New York: Lippincott.
Freud, S. (1910), Leonardo da Vinci and a memory of his childhood. *Standard Edition*, 2;57-137. London: Hogarth Press, 1955.
James, H. (1895), *The Altar of the Dead*. In: *The Turn of the Screw and Other Short Novels*. New York: Signet Classics, 1962, pp. 252-290.
Lichtenberg, J. (1978), Freud's Leonardo: psychobiography and autobiography of genius. *J. Amer. Psychoanal. Assn.*, 26:863-880.
——— (1981), Sweet are the uses of adversity: Regression and style in the life and works of Henry James. *Psychoanal. Inquiry*, 1:107-131.

———— & Lichtenberg, C. (1972), Eugene O'Neill and falling in love. *Psychoanal. Quart.*, 41:63-89.

Sheaffer, L. (1973), *O'Neill: Son and Artist*. Boston: Little, Brown.

Solomon, M. (1977), *Beethoven*. New York: Schirmer Books.

Sterba, E., & Sterba, R. (1971), *Beethoven and His Nephew*. New York: Schocken Books.

11

The Twilight of the Gods

MARY M. GEDO, Ph.D.

Many of the greatest artists of the Italian Renaissance and Baroque periods enjoyed life-spans of legendary length. Donatello, Giovanni Bellini, Titian, Michelangelo, and Gianlorenzo Bernini—to name only the most illustrious examples—all lived on until at least the beginning of their ninth decade, and in several cases well beyond. Each continued to create magnificent art until virtually the day of his death. The three modern masters under consideration, Claude Monet, Henri Matisse, and Pablo Picasso, demonstrated equal longevity, Monet dying at 86, Matisse at 85, and Picasso at 92. Like their Renaissance counterparts, these artists also continued to be productive until their last few months or days on earth. (Monet, consumed by cancer, grew too weak to paint during the last months of his life.) But these modern masters worked without several support systems which helped to sustain the earlier octogenarian artists. This situation had à particularly deleterious effect on Picasso, whose late production by no means demonstrated the same brilliant originality as his earlier work. Unlike Monet and Matisse, he proved unable to invent or discover private

sources of inspiration which could serve as adequate re-
placements for the vanished institutions on which the
Renaissance geniuses had relied.

Their religious convictions certainly formed the primary support system for the Renaissance artists cited
above. These men, practicing Catholics throughout their
lives, all experienced a heightened religious fervor during
their final phase. Belief in God and in their eternal salvation sustained them, enabling them to continue creating for God even after several of them had outlived
their nearest and dearest relatives and friends. Donatello's final project consists of two large bronze pulpits in
San Lorenzo, Florence, with reliefs depicting details from
Christ's Passion and Resurrection. The elderly artist's
identification with his Savior is reflected in the similarly
aged, exhausted quality with which he endows his Jesus.
Although Titian had not been an especially devout Cath-
olic in his earlier life, the painting he designed for his
own tomb expresses the most profound piety. It portrays
the dead Savior in His mother's arms with the artist
himself kneeling in adoration and supplication before
this vision. Bellini, Bernini, and Michelangelo created
late works indicative of similar religious fervor. Indeed,
Michelangelo spent his final years completing the designs
for the grandest place of worship in Christendom, St.
Peter's in Rome, a commission for which he accepted no
salary. His private drawings and final sculpture, the *Rondanini Pièta*, reflect an ecstatic fusion with the martyred
Christ which parallels that of Donatello (Hibbard, 1974).

Not only did these artists enjoy the comfort of participating in Christ's death and Resurrection—they also
functioned in the midst of a supportive group of younger
and subordinate artists who formed their ateliers. The
studios of the greatest Renaissance and Baroque artists
operated almost like piecework factories, with each man

assigned duties according to his level of skill, from the little apprentice who ground the master's colors, to the skilled landscapist who painted such details in the master's canvases, to the second-in-command, entrusted with executing authorized copies of the master's greatest and most popular compositions. (Michelangelo, much more isolated than the other Renaissance artists cited above, evidently never functioned as the head of such an atelier, although he did employ assistants for all his more complex sculptural projects. This aspect of his career has not been adequately investigated; the ongoing restoration of his paintings in the Sistine Chapel may shed further light on this question. See *Art News*, 1981 and *Connoisseur*, 1982, for preliminary reports on the chapel work.)

Because all five of these artists were so progressive and far-sighted, the last style of each of them anticipates future developments in the history of art. Needless to say, few of their assistants could grasp these avant-garde ideas. In the case of Titian, this noncomprehension may actually have led to acts of sabotage on the part of his underlings. At least, a possibly apocryphal tale contends that his helpers diluted the old man's pigments with olive oil so that they would not dry, then eradicated by night what the aged master accomplished during the day. The vast number of miraculous late Titian paintings which survive, paintings which anticipate not only the art of the Baroque period but even certain technical innovations of the nineteenth century, suggest that this practice must have been limited to a few isolated incidents if, indeed, it ever occurred. In most cases, the assistants apparently faithfully, if noncomprehendingly, carried out Titian's wishes (Tietze-Conrat, 1946; Fisher, 1959).

Donatello's four major assistants in the pulpit project could not possibly have understood the terrible grandeur of his conceptions for San Lorenzo, for his wild final style

contrasts dramatically with the sweet, slightly sentimental manner in vogue among younger Florentine
sculptors during his old age. However, his studio helpers
evidently finished the bronze pulpits, within the limits
of their abilities, in exact accord with the instructions,
sketches, and clay models which Donatello left them. The
unresolved disputes among art historians concerning
which reliefs are fully autograph, which studio works,
demonstrate how faithful his helpers were to the spirit
and letter of the master's instructions (Janson, 1963).

One of the happiest examples of the mutually supportive interrelationship between the master and his
atelier concerns Giovanni Bellini. During his last years,
he had the good fortune to train two of the greatest painters in the history of Western art: Giorgione and Titian.
The presence of these future luminaries undoubtedly
stimulated the creativity of the aged Bellini, helping him
to achieve the magical transformation in style and subject
matter apparent in his last works.

All five of these Renaissance masters also enjoyed
another support system no longer available: a type of
enlightened, consistent patronage unparalleled in our
modern era. Popes, emperors, and the rulers of the powerful Italian city states supplied these men not only with
financial security, but with challenging commissions
which helped to stimulate their continuing enthusiasm
and creativity.

Monet, Matisse, and Picasso all enjoyed fame and financial security during their lifetimes at least comparable to that achieved by these Renaissance masters, but
they certainly lacked comparable support systems. Although all three men were presumably born Catholics,
none of them was in the least religious. Picasso considered
himself an atheist (albeit one who often drew Crucifixion
scenes during periods of particular stress), whereas Ma-

tisse called himself a deist and once avowed that he could believe in God only while working. Monet did not make public pronouncements about his beliefs, but he appears to have been quite uninterested in formal religion and religious practices.

Nor did any of these men duplicate the atelier system of the earlier artists. True, Picasso and Matisse both enjoyed close relationships with artisans during their final years, and both employed assistants to enable them to carry out projects they could no longer execute unaided. Monet's stepdaughter, Blanche Hoschedé-Monet, the widow of his son Jean, also fulfilled something of this role with him. However, none of them trained students (although Matisse did run a school briefly from 1908-1911) or experienced the stimulation which exchanges with gifted disciples can provide.

Nor did any of them experience the kind of stimulation which the enduring patronage of the Spanish monarchs, Charles V and his son, Philip II, offered to Titian or the Popes Julius II and Paul III to Michelangelo. But Monet and Matisse both substituted their own efforts to fill this gap. Each generated his own last great commission, a magnificent project executed, like Michelangelo's architectural work at St. Peter's, without payment. These commissions, that of Monet to paint the *Nymphéas* murals now installed in the Orangerie and of Matisse to realize the little jewel-box chapel of St. Paul de Vence, transformed the final phases of both men, providing them with a focus and a motivation to continue living and creating. Picasso, by contrast, did not generate any such commission or conceive of one grand scheme to which he could give himself with the unstinting enthusiasm of Monet for his murals or Matisse for his chapel. One might say that he remained more ambitious than Matisse or Monet, less willing to immerse himself in a single project. Alternatively, one could characterize Picasso's final phase as diffuse and fragmented in its emphasis.

The final period in the careers of all three artists began quite late in their long lives, triggered in all three cases by severe trauma, purely emotional in the case of Picasso, both physical and emotional in the cases of Monet and Matisse.

THE MIRROR OF HEAVEN

Claude Monet embarked on his last great project, the creation of the *Nymphéas* cycle which now adorns the Orangerie museum in Paris, following a prolonged period of lowered artistic activity, years when he lacked the drive to paint the large number of canvases which he had customarily completed during comparable periods earlier in his career. The depression caused by the death of his wife, Alice Hoschedé, in May 1911, followed in February 1914 by that of his elder son, Jean, after a long psychotic illness, undoubtedly triggered this decline. The double trauma of these two losses was reinforced by another threatened loss: that of the artist's visual acuity. He first began to experience visual difficulties ca. 1908 or 1909. In July 1912, he finally consulted an eye specialist, who diagnosed a beginning cataract and prescribed medicine which would allegedly retard its growth. This decline in vision gradually became more severe—with periods of slight remission—until 1922, when the artist resigned himself to the necessity for cataract surgery, performed in 1923.

The *Nymphéas* cycle represents the culmination of Monet's interest in serial painting, specifically his interest in recording subtle nuances of the changing appearance of the water garden he had created at Giverny in Normandy, changes wrought in the surface of his watery world by varying conditions of light, time, and weather. In painting the water-lily pond, Monet depicted a world entirely of his own making. He had created the pond between 1893 and 1903 on a strip of land right across from his Giverny estate. This plot lay between the railroad line and the Ru River, a tributary of the Seine. The Ru, diverted, filled and cleaned the pond, which Monet altered and enlarged several times during this ten-year period.

Monet's growing preoccupation with serial painting began around 1891 and represented the third and last important phase of his mature career. His first major style, which coincides with the so-called classic phase of Impressionism, characterized his work from ca. 1872-1880. During the seventies, Impressionism gained recognition as a new artistic movement, Monet as its leading practitioner. Impressionism involved a new approach to painting. Its artists characteristically worked out-of-doors, before the motif, painting for a very limited time until changing light-and-shadow conditions rendered further work on the canvas impossible that day. Typically, one returned to the same spot and viewpoint again and again whenever the weather conditions duplicated those depicted in the painting in process. The Impressionists worked on white (rather than pre-toned) canvases and eschewed earth colors and blacks in favor of bright tones. They created their pictorial structures through brushwork—their short, broken brushstrokes followed the contours and characteristics of their motifs—and color application. The classical Renaissance perspective system diminished in importance in Impressionist painting, which might be compared to the Naturalist movement in literature.

Most of Monet's paintings from the 1870s, particularly the oils created at Argenteuil, depict the artist's personal

world, dealing with subjects and settings he knew intimately. He concentrated on representing scenes of daily
life and pleasure, ignoring the grand themes of history
and religious painting which had preoccupied earlier artists and continued to preoccupy his more conservative
peers. Instead, he painted his house, his garden, his wife,
his child, his studio boat in its mooring, the bend of the
Seine near his home—in short, his intimate world. His
insistence on working outdoors before the motif resulted
in the creation of an oeuvre primarily composed of small,
sketchlike paintings.

   This period came to a precipitous close with the death
of the first Mme Monet in 1879, from chronic illness,
aggravated by the wearing effects of her second pregnancy, with Michel Monet, born in 1878. Although the
artist quite literally had a replacement for Mme Monet
already installed in his household, the comforting presence of Alice Hoschedé and her children did not assuage
his grief. He responded to the death of his beautiful wife
with a drastic change in his style and subject matter.
That winter, he painted a series of canvases depicting the
Seine looking as icy and forbidding as his own mood must
have been, as well as several still-life paintings featuring
dead birds, a theme he had seldom essayed before, and
which never interested him again.

   When he had recovered a bit from the first, acute
phase of his mourning, Monet began to travel, moving
restlessly from spot to spot, seeking wild and exotic new
motifs for his brush.

   He settled in the village of Giverny in 1883, occupying
the house which would become his permanent home, a
comfortable dwelling presided over by Mme Hoschedé,
who would become the second Mme Monet in 1892. However, the artist spent relatively little time in his home
until 1890 and after. Instead, he traveled to Brittany, the

Riviera, and other spots where he could find wild, picturesque scenery and spots remote from man. He painted isolated places, often employing a high, disorienting viewpoint which robs the spectator of all sense of continuity between his own space and that revealed in the painting and which sometimes even seems to threaten the viewer, who feels trapped in the wild settings Monet depicts. During these same years, he also tended to favor motifs and weather conditions which created exaggerated color effects, such as the scenes depicting the red earth and blue sea of the Riviera in full sunlight.

Monet's working methods also changed during the eighties. Like his fellow Impressionists, Pissarro and Renoir, he experienced a crisis in his procedures; what had seemed so easy ten years earlier now seemed to him very difficult, as he realized more and more acutely the problems inherent in attempting to portray outdoor scenes in plein air. He began to work on many canvases simultaneously in order to conserve time; gradually, he began to finish them from memory in his studio, rather than from observation before the motif. He also began, periodically, to destroy large numbers of canvases during fits of black depression. These *autos-da-fé* seemingly cheered him, and he emerged renewed like the phoenix, from the ashes of his murdered children.

Toward the end of the 1880s, Monet's style softened somewhat, and his interest in harsh motifs, strange viewpoints, and high colors declined. At the time, he noted in a letter to a friend that he was trying hard in his art to overcome the brutality to which his nature inclined him.

Around 1890-1891, Monet's growing interest in serial painting began to assert itself. He concentrated on creating successive views of the same subject under different weather and light conditions. His earliest series depicted haystacks in the fields around Giverny; he insisted on exhibiting these and subsequent series as an entity, rather than as individual canvases. His changed interests resulted in corresponding changes in style. Textures and colors of objects were no longer differentiated with the same emphasis as in the seventies. Nor did his brush-strokes define the character of the scene as they once had. Instead, Monet began to favor thick, layered paint surfaces, a growing tendency already visible in his works from the eighties. He built up these mosaiclike surfaces by repeated applications of pigment purged of much of its oil by being spread on absorbent blotters before use. These changes resulted in dense, mutlilayered surfaces which Monet's biographer, C. Mount (1966), aptly compares to the appearance of coral reefs.

At the same time, Monet deliberately limited his sights. His compositions began to concentrate on primary shapes, assuming a more two-dimensional quality. These new methods went hand in hand with work done in the studio. To the end of his life, Monet continued to maintain the subterfuge that he worked only outdoors on each canvas from beginning to end. It would probably be more accurate to state that working outdoors from start to finish remained his ideal, but no longer his practice. It seems likely that he painted the twenty-two enormous murals constituting the *Nymphéas* cycle in his studio from beginning to end, enlarging upon smaller sketches executed at the lily pond. Because of his secrecy about his methods, we cannot be certain about the facts of Monet's final practices, and art historians provide varying accounts of the methods utilized to create these great murals.

By the late 1890s, Monet showed himself increasingly preoccupied with subtle effects of light and atmosphere, scene and reflection. The exquisite series of canvases depicting dawn on the River Epte, the heavens reflected in the water's still surface, prefigures the final great series of water-lily paintings which form the *Nymphéas* cycle and related canvases.

Monet had painted water and its reflections throughout his career, but in his final phase the depiction of the watery world comprising his lily ponds became his magnificent obsession. After the second Mme Monet's death, he no longer traveled far from his house and gardens at Giverny. Instead, he gave himself over increasingly to the depiction of his flower beds, footpaths, bridges, and—above all—his water-lily ponds in all their changing climates and moods. In its final form, the water-lily garden was surrounded by poplars and willows as well as by an abundance of gladioli, irises, rhododendrons, and rare species of lilies. The Japanese footbridge at the mouth of the pond, equipped with a trellis laden with wisteria vines, formed yet another decorative element which Monet could record on canvas.

As Monet devoted himself increasingly to painting his water garden, several distinct series of *Nymphéas* oils evolved. Grace Seiberling, a specialist in Monet's serial paintings, notes that the earliest series, from 1899 and 1900, shows the pond in context, dealing with real space and concrete objects. The precise fall of light and shadow marks the time of day, information the artist would later provide by more subtle nuances.

In his later Water Lily series from 1902-1908, Monet began to look down,

> progressively eliminating all references to solid landscape, he showed only the surface of the pond with its clusters of water lilies floating amidst reflections of sky and trees. In so doing . . . he was creating the image of a horizontal surface on a vertical one. . . . The reality of the painting becomes one of intangibles, of the ambiguous depth of reflections, of light, of the instability of the water surface and cloud movements, of changing

colors and the artist's perception [Seiberling, 1975, p. 37].

As early as 1898, Monet had begun to dream of creating a large-scale water-lily project which he termed a "decoration." A visitor with whom the artist shared this fantasy later wrote:

> Imagine a circular room whose walls above the wainscoting would be entirely occupied by an expanse of water, the surface dappled with this vegetation, surfaces of a transparency here green, there mauve, the calm and still water reflecting the scattered clusters of flowers with the delicacy of a dream [Guillemot, 1898].

During the late nineteenth century, many leading French artists became interested in decorative painting, which did not have the pejorative connotation the term now bears. Rather, it implied a certain type of large-scale painting usually destined for a specific architectural setting, one which addressed itself particularly to "the interaction of forms in an abstract and two dimensional way on the canvas" (Seiberling, 1975, pp. 37-38).

In 1914, fighting back against the three hammer blows which fate had dealt him, Monet decided to have a special studio built which would be large enough to accommodate the gigantic project he had in mind. Perhaps the artist took courage from the fact that his stepdaughter, Blanche Hoschedé-Monet, Jean's widow, joined him at Giverny following her husband's death. An amateur painter herself, she assumed the multiple roles of companion, assistant, and housekeeper (as well as the chief recipient of Monet's titanic temper outbursts). The fact that she increasingly resembled her mother, Alice Hoschedé-Monet, undoubtedly helped to endear her to her stepfather, who became quite dependent on her. As the studio went up, Monet shared his dream of presenting a series of decorative murals to the French state with his close friend, the premier, Georges Clemenceau; the latter encouraged and aided the artist throughout. In some ways, Clemenceau fulfilled a role akin to that of the great patrons of the Renaissance and Baroque periods vis-à-vis such artists as Titian and Bernini. Clemenceau's support and friendship encouraged Monet to continue working despite the ever-increasing visual problems he was experiencing, and despite the vexations he encountered in getting the French government to agree to an appropriate building which could be suitably adapted to house the grand decorative scheme the artist had in mind. (When Clemenceau fell from power in 1920, the new government changed the site agreed upon for the murals from the Hotel Biron, which eventually became the Musée Rodin, to the Orangerie. The dimensions of the latter required Monet to discard many panels painted to the specifications of the Hotel Biron, a task rendered incomparably more difficult by the artist's ever-failing eyesight (see Stuckey, 1979; Stuckey and Gordon, 1979).

The twenty-two enormous canvases which comprise the *Nymphéas* cycle encircle two rooms in the Orangerie. The murals in room I depict *Le Matin* and *Les Nuages*; in other words, one emphasizes the appearance of the pond during the early morning hours, the other the play of reflected clouds on its mirroring surface. In the second room, another variation on the *Le Matin* theme and a cycle now called *Les deux saules, (The Two Willows)*, all feature the willows at the lily pond in early-morning light. These canvases emphasize surface pattern, abstract arabesques, and delicate nuances of color change. Before he selected the twenty-two finalists from among a large field of candidates, Monet moved the enormous canvases—equipped with wheels for portability—to various spots in his studio so he could try out various combina-

tions and effects. The last-minute change in their intended site forced the artist to discard many canvases
and adapt others to the new location. In the fits of rage
and frustration which accompanied all these last-minute
changes, the artist again destroyed many panels. An
eyewitness who visited the studio in 1922 describes
seeing a slashed canvas which seemed to him to bleed
like a wound, still hanging in tatters from its stretcher,
while beneath a table, Monet pointed to a huge pile of
canvases destined for the fire. (Whether his faithful assistant, Blanche Hoschedé-Monet, and the servants actually carried out these instructions seems open to
question; at any rate, a vast opus survived Monet's knife
and match during these years. See Stuckey, 1979, p. 116.)

The large-scale brushwork and sweep of Monet's
strokes in these late canvases match the gigantic scale
on which he worked. He now favored big bristle brushes
whose every individual component leaves its mark on the
painting. Working in the studio and more than ever ad-
dicted to building up thick, dry, scumbled layers of paint,
Monet imbued the surfaces of his paintings with depth,
one color showing through another and contributing to
an effect of tinted depth. This technique marks the culmination of procedures begun during the 1880s, when the
artist first became enamored of such encrusted surfaces
(Herbert, 1979). Undoubtedly, the scale of Monet's late
work refects his failing vision, his inability any longer
to perceive the subtle nuances and details of his chosen
setting. But his changing ability evidently coincided with
his changing interests, for he had begun to eliminate such
features before his vision troubled him. The broad, free
character of Monet's late work characterizes that of other
artists as well, from Titian to Picasso. Undoubtedly, this
characteristic old-age style measures the assurance and

freedom of these elderly artists, all more concerned with total effect than specific details.

During 1922, Monet's cataract condition had become so severe that he had to give up painting altogether, and he was not able to return to his beloved cycle until late in 1923. From that time until a few months before his death, he labored unceasingly on the paintings; the enormity of the task he had set himself began to haunt him, and he experienced bouts of insomnia. Clemenceau and other friends, worried that he might destroy the glorious effects he had created through obsessive repainting or by actually defacing his canvases in rages, begged him to stop and rest content. This he was unable to do until cancer of the lungs, the legacy of a lifelong habit of chain smoking, so robbed him of energy that he could no longer work.

Many years earlier, Monet had remarked that, had he not become a painter, he would have been a gardener. During his last months, he reverted to this second vocation, occupying himself chiefly with ordering newer, still more exotic lily plants to adorn his beloved ponds, the mirror of heaven in which he recorded the fugitive effects of a universe in miniature. Sadly, he did not live to see his *Nymphéas* installed *in situ*; he died on December 5, 1926. The "Claude Monet Museum" opened on May 16, 1927, revealing to the world the artist's final vision of his watery garden of paradise.

THE MIRROR OF DARKNESS

The loss of his mistress, Françoise Gilot, plunged Pablo Picasso into the final artistic phase of his long career. She departed in July 1953, taking their two children, Claude, age six, and Paloma, age four, with her. This forcible separation from his mistress—the only woman

who ever rejected him—devastated Picasso, always so
dependent on partnerships to sustain his creativity. During the following year, his productivity waxed and waned
with Françoise's reappearances—to bring the children for
vacation visits—and departures. During the first six
months he spent alone, he produced nothing; then he
began the series of 180 drawings known as *The Human
Comedy* series; these works reflect the artist's altered
perception of himself as a foolish old man who could not
hope to maintain the romantic interest of his beautiful
model unless he disguised himself with various youthful
masks.

After more than a year punctuated by repeated creative paralyses, periods often spent in frantic socialization and partying—a most unusual activity for Picasso—he
suddenly settled down once more at Vallauris with Jacqueline Roque, a beautiful young divorcee. Although she
had offered herself to him almost as soon as Françoise
left, Picasso had treated her with rude disdain, an attitude which ended with her apparent threat to commit
suicide if he rejected her (O'Brian, 1976, pp. 423-425). To
this artist, always so guilty over the deaths of friends,
deaths he mistakenly attributed to his magical powers,
the mention of suicide constituted a highly effective
threat. For the rest of his life, Jacqueline provided a comfortable, serene atmosphere which permitted him to return to nonstop productivity. As her price for these
services, she exerted increasing control over every aspect
of his existence, a control which became quite complete
following their marriage in 1961. Probably at her behest,
he eventually cut himself off from his surviving ex-mis-
tresses and illegitimate children; finally, even his legit-
imate grandchildren, the offspring of his eldest child,
Paulo, were denied access to the artist. Surrounded by
fawning sycophants who heaped praises on his every ef-

fort, Picasso increasingly played the role of the precious geriatric prodigy.

Unlike Monet and Matisse, Picasso did not develop any radically new style or method during these last years. Rather, both the style and the content of his work featured reprises of his many previous styles and original masterpieces, now recycled by a hand which retained much of its cunning until the very last years of his life.

Because he worked in so many different manners and media during his long career, one cannot easily summarize Picasso's earlier career in the same tidy manner possible with Monet and Matisse. To a much more obvious extent than with either of these men, Picasso's creativity always depended quite directly upon the nature and intensity of his concurrent partnerships. His great contributions to art reflect not only his reactions to past and present art history, but his intimate responses to his own history and current experiences. Quite perceptively, he compared each of his paintings to a private entry made by a diarist in his journal. Thus, his Blue Period reflects not only his response to *fin-de-siècle* sensations of malaise and the search for a symbolic expression of these feelings via the dramatic-narrative undercurrents present in his art. On a more personal level, this style also reveals the artist's private *angst*, his difficulty in making the separation from his family and achieving an independent status in the world. Similarly, his classicizing Rose Period canvases illustrate his triumph over these dependent feelings, the exultation he felt in acquiring a beautiful mistress and a worthy fellow-genius as his new psychological partner. For in Guillaume Apollinaire Picasso discovered not only an ideal replacement for his tender, supportive father, who had led him out of the darkness of his childhood crises, but a partner who demonstrated a depth and breadth of talent denied his father, an academic painter of modest abilities.

Picasso began the experiments which led to his great *Cubist* invention on an equally personalized note; initially, he planned the *Demoiselles d'Avignon*, the great proto-Cubist painting, as a vehicle starring himself and revealing his deep ambivalence toward women, an ambivalence born of his relationship with his overwhelming, mad mother. He removed most of this evidence from the definitive version of the painting; only its incoherence serves as a reminder of its creator's underlying rage toward women (Gedo, 1980b). He achieved his full-fledged Cubist inventions only after he had forged an extra-intense partnership with his fellow painter, Georges Braque. Picasso's high Cubist canvases, with their fragmentation and dissolution of classical Renaissance perspective, reflect the characteristic psychological state of his childhood, the sensations of disintegration he so often experienced. During this period, the style of Picasso's art truly became one with its content (Gedo, 1980a, pp. 81-104).

During the next decades, the twenties and thirties, Picasso alternated among his Neo-Cubist, Neo-Classical, and Expressionist styles; in developing the latter, he allied himself with the burgeoning Surrealist movement which swept French art during the mid 1920s. After the mid-1930s, his paintings more and more reflect an amalgamation or alternation among these styles; minor new developments, such as the initiation of his so-called basketry style, do not constitute the same kind of sudden, decisive change in manner which had characterized his production during the first part of his career. Thus *Guernica*, for all its magnificence, represents a fusion between his late Cubist and Expressionist styles, wedded to a pictorial format which recalls the pyramidal structure and symmetry of High Renaissance altarpieces.

During the latter half of his career, Picasso became quite active as a sculptor, an interest he had earlier pursued only intermittently. The true impact of his wrought-iron sculptures, works he forged with the assistance of Julio Gonzalez (who enacted the role of helpful genie), is only beginning to be appreciated. These sculptures constitute another of his great inventions, second only to Cubism in importance. (One might add that his much earlier Cubist reliefs and sculptures, composed of all sorts of odds and ends, show him at an equally creative moment.) Throughout his career, he took a lively interest in printmaking, another area in which he made numerous technical breakthroughs in the course of creating thousands of etchings, lithographs, and other graphics, many of them commissioned to serve as book illustrations.

Like Monet, Picasso became quite fascinated with serial painting in his old age. Unlike the Impressionist master, Picasso did not concern himself with recording fugitive effects of light and air. Rather, his series constituted a long set of commentaries on selected great masterpieces of the past. The loss of his friend, Henri Matisse, an artist with whom he had enjoyed a kind of attenuated partnership limited by the French master's failing health, stimulated Picasso to begin the earliest of his serial paintings. Declaring that the dying Matisse had willed him his Odalisques, Picasso began fifteen variations after Delacroix's *Women of Algiers*, depicting three inhabitants of a seraglio with their black servant maid. He followed this series with several depictions of Jacqueline in harem dress, then executed a charming series representing his own studio in his Cannes villa. This subject had never before been of special interest to

Picasso; in these canvases, his identification with Matisse reached its zenith. The formal elements of his art took on the characteristics of Matisse's; the lyrical rhythms, bright colors, and bold patterns of these works, all executed with careful control, testify to the potency of his identification with Matisse.

Picasso's next major serial effort—45 variations on Diego Velazquez's *Las Meniñas*, involved another of the aged master's double mergers. Just as he had magically fused both with Delacroix and with Matisse in creating the *Women of Algiers*, in painting his *Las Meniñas* group Picasso simultaneously allied himself with Velazquez, the most renowned painter in Spanish history, and with his own father, who had so admired this painting and had introduced his son to it for the first time when they toured the Prado together in 1895. The potency of Picasso's association to his father during the creation of this series is reflected in the fact that the artist constructed a special studio for the creation of these pictures next to the pigeon loft of his Cannes villa. Moreover, he interrupted work on the sequence to create a mini-series of eight canvases depicting the dove cote and its inhabitants. His father, Don José, had devoted most of his career to painting sentimentalized depictions of pigeons, and the first major work Picasso had been allowed to carry out during childhood had been that of painting the feet of the pigeons portrayed in one of his father's canvases.

Between 1959-1961, Picasso executed his most extensive serial project: a series of about 200 variations after Edouard Manet's *Picnic on the Grass*, variations created in many media and techniques. Despite the energy with which the master churned out these transliterations of the masters, they were not received with great critical acclaim, a reaction which may have helped dissuade him from continuing this type of serial work. Whatever the reason, the almost endless sets of variations on the Manet canvas marked the last of Picasso's lengthy re-explorations of past art.

During the final years of his life, the artist concentrated, instead, on developing serial motifs of his own invention. Although these themes often alluded to the history of art, they seldom depended on a specific, concrete source. A favorite theme involved the portrayal of seventeenth-century musketeers and cavaliers; the ruffs and meerschaum pipes favored by the latter recall the canvases of the Baroque Dutch masters, especially Rembrandt, always an idol of Picasso's. Another favorite scheme reveals embracing lovers who seem to fuse together more from primitive confusion about self-other than from excesses of sexual passion. Of course, depictions of his wife, Jacqueline, and of female nudes loosely based on her form, remained one of Picasso's prize interests; throughout his entire artistic career, he had typically devoted much of his output to representations of the female form and face derived from his current love. Sometimes he portrayed a mother and child—often as Venus and Cupid—but more often he depicted lolling or reclining nudes exhibiting themselves in an explicit and self-congratulatory manner.

In 1965, two major traumatic events touched Picasso in his seeming invulnerability: Françoise Gilot published her memoirs, *Life with Picasso*, and, later that same year, the artist underwent major surgery. His rage over Gilot's disclosures about the details of their everyday life once again stopped the artist's hand; for months, he produced virtually nothing, distracted by fury and by the demands of a fruitless lawsuit he launched to stop publication of the book. His surgery—perhaps for gall-bladder trouble, perhaps for prostate problems, perhaps for both—went much better than his lawsuit. Within a few months, he

seemed fully recovered and was back in high gear, turning out nudes and musketeers by the score.

Picasso's health remained amazingly good during the
last seven years of his life, although biographers report
that he suffered a gradual loss of auditory and visual
acuity, scarcely surprising developments in a man on the
verge of his tenth decade. As in the case of Monet, one
should perhaps attribute the broad, even slapdash style
and paint application evident in many of Picasso's late
canvases to his waning visual powers.

As already noted, Picasso neither obtained nor invented any grand commission which would occupy his old
age as the creation of the *Nymphéas* cycle did Monet or
the design and execution of the St. Paul de Vence chapel
did Matisse. However, Picasso did carry out several discrete public works of considerable importance. In the late
1950s, he received the commission to paint a giant-scale
mural for the UNESCO headquarters in Paris. The vast
scale this project required daunted the aged artist, unable
to climb scaffolding any longer, until he hit upon the idea
of dividing the mural into forty panels, which he painted
in small groups. Assistants assembled the canvases *in
situ* after their completion. As J. S. Boggs (1973) notes,
the motif Picasso chose for this commission, *The Fall of
Icarus*—the latter represented as a dessicated skeletal
figure—seems a particularly cynical choice to represent
an organization with the hopes UNESCO held during the
1950s (p. 214). This motif may have had a more personal
connotation as well; this quintessential story of the boy
too big for his britches suggests Picasso's own realization
that his aim had exceeded his grasp when he undertook
this ambitious project, which was not well received by
either the critics or the public. Like his Icarus, Picasso
began to seem burned out, a ghostly remnant of his once
robust genius.

His experience in his other major public undertaking, the design of the so-called *Chicago Picasso*, proved a good deal happier, perhaps because this commission represented the realization of a dream he had entertained long years before. During the late 1920s, he had painted a series of canvases showing major public sculptures of female heads poised before modernistic buildings which bear an uncanny resemblance to the as-yet-unbuilt Daley center destined to serve as the background for the *Chicago Picasso*. In this commission, Picasso drew upon another favorite motif of many years' standing, to portray a hybrid creature, part Afghan hound, part ideal woman. From the frontal position, the piece resembles the artist's pet Afghan of the period, Kaboul. From the side and rear, she reveals Jacqueline's beautiful profile and head. The ratio, scale, and proportion of solid-to-void parts of this sculpture make it the perfect foil for its setting; its unity with the building is further underlined by the fact that both are constructed from the same corten steel.

During succeeding years, Picasso provided maquettes for a number of other large-scale sculptures, but none of them seems as impressive as the Chicago monument. In all these cases, Picasso executed drawings and a cardboard model for the metal maquette; he also supplied the surface painting which characterizes several of these maquettes. At least in the case of the *Chicago Picasso*, the artist also maintained close contact with the artisans who developed the full-scale sculpture under the supervision of William Hartmann, an architect associated with Skidmore, Owings & Merrill (Spies, 1971, pp. 221-226).

In 1968, Picasso sustained yet another loss: his old amanuensis and friend since adolescence, Jaime Sabartés, died. As a memorial to his friend, Picasso donated his entire *Las Meniñas* series plus numerous additional works to the Museo Picasso in Barcelona, which had been founded with Sabartés's personal collection of Picassos. Shortly afterward, the artist embarked on his last major printmaking campaign, the creation of the 347 so-called erotic engravings. Many of these etchings seem to recreate the world of Don Quixote; the preoccupation with Spain and things Spanish reflected in them may well have resulted from Picasso's rumination over the Spanish past he shared with Sabartés. Although many of these prints demonstrate the most amazing new technical variations on the art of aquatints, they remain empty virtuoso performances demonstrating Picasso's mastery of all the tricks of the trade, here presented as a goal rather than a means to expression. Like so many of his late paintings and drawings, the style and content of these prints suggest that the artist's auto-critical abilities had suffered impairment.

> Too many people, relationships, events, works of art—his own as well as those of others—now crowded in upon the aged painter and threatened to swamp him. In these prints, allusions to the history of art from the time of the Etruscans to the present mingle with the most personalized references in a disorderly melange. In Picasso's final decade, then, chaos became the main quality of the self. Many critics, repelled by this chaotic quality, concluded that Picasso now tottered on the brink of senility. Not necessarily so. In his second wife, Picasso had acquired a helpmate who admired everything he produced. Entrapped with a loving misunderstander who held up a distorting mirror before him, the aged artist perceived only darkly—or not at all [Gedo, 1980, p. 248].

THE MIRROR OF LIGHT

Henri Matisse inaugurated his final phase in 1941, following a series of major surgical procedures to excise an abdominal malignancy and correct ensuing complications. The 71-year-old artist emerged from these experiences a semi-invalid; his weakened abdominal muscles could sustain his weight for only a few hours a day, so he had to spend much of his time in bed. Thereafter, he lived with frequent pain and insomnia. But he had not expected to survive at all, and he greeted each new day of the nearly fourteen additional years of his life with the radiance of the rising sun. He felt reborn, granted unexpected time, and he made the most profitable use of it imaginable. Working propped up in bed or from a wheelchair, employing young female assistants to carry out mechanical tasks, such as prepainting the papers to be used for the cutout compositions he now invented, Matisse generated a magnificent final opus before his death in November 1954.

Unlike Picasso, Matisse was no *wunderkind* resolved on a career in art from early childhood. Rather, he found his vocation suddenly, at the age of twenty, when he began to paint as an amateur. Interestingly enough, he initiated the earliest phase of his artistic career, like his last, while recuperating from abdominal surgery. To help him while away the hours of his convalesence, his mother gave him a box of colors. He discovered a whole new world through this gift. Within two years, he had abandoned his law training and enrolled in the studio of Gustave Moreau, who taught several of the most prestigious French artists of the following generation. Thereafter, Matisse never deviated from his dedication to his new profession, although the early years of his career and married life were filled with economic deprivation and struggle.

Unlike the art of Picasso, who practiced in so many disparate styles, the over-all oeuvre of Matisse possesses a kind of seamless quality. This is not to say that his manner and subject matter did not vary widely from one period to another. They often did, but certain qualities which characterize his earliest mature style can be found throughout his oeuvre. He began to achieve some success around 1905 as the leading inventor and practitioner of the Fauve artists, the so-called wild beasts, whose canvases were notable for their riot of unnaturally brilliant colors. Influenced by both Gauguin and the followers of Seurat, the Fauves alternated the broken brushwork of the Impressionists and Neo-Impressionists with areas of flat color broadly applied, à la Gauguin.

Matisse soon abandoned the unnatural hues of Fauvism, as well as its divisionist brushwork. As the greatest colorist of the twentieth century, however, he always favored compositions which permitted him to display a riot of colors and patterns. Also, his later canvases continue the emphasis on contrasting types of brushwork found in his Fauve work. In his later paintings, this contrast often reveals itself in the interplay of broad, flat, even passages of paint with those featuring springing arabesques and lively linear forms. Even his still-life compositions radiate such liveliness and verve that they refute the immobility implicit in the generic term, *still* life.

Many of Matisse's Fauve compositions reveal another enduring feature of his technical procedure: that of painting thinly, so that the white of the canvas shines through, lending transparency to the picture. He also often permitted small areas of naked canvas to surround each area of paint. He believed that this practice permits the painting to "breathe." Certainly, this technique contributes greatly to the luminosity and amplitude which characterize his art.

Each of his canvases thus constitutes a kind of dialogue between drawing and painting, between line and color, at once reaffirming the flatness of the picture plane and providing the illusion of a third dimension. The creation of this tension or "push-pull" remained one of Matisse's salient goals throughout his lifetime.

The chief subjects one discovers in his Fauve canvases likewise remained his favorites until his death: landscapes, still lifes, and, above all, depictions of the female face and form always constituted his primary motifs, and he often combined all three subjects in a single composition. He always worked from nature, from the most exacting study of the model or motif in the actual setting he intended to represent. He established the details of the composition via detailed preliminary drawings before starting to paint, although the process of evolution continued on the canvas. One can follow his typical procedure from a more naturalistic to a more abstract conception of the subject in surviving sequential drawings which reveal his progression from detail to essence. Photographs made during the creation of key canvases painted during the 1930s document the continuation of this process in his compositions of late maturity. Only in creating the cutout pictures of his last years did he sometimes condense this procedure; drawing on his lifelong practice of careful study from the model, he at last found himself able to perform these preliminary steps mentally, proceeding more directly to his ultimate conception of the theme.

Most Matisse canvases reveal obvious pentimenti, vestiges of this process of constant redefinition and refinement of the problem as the picture evolved. He made no attempt to disguise such pentimenti; rather, the conservation of this evidence permits the viewer to share the history of each canvas with its creator. Although willing to divulge such technical secrets to his public, Matisse, unlike Picasso, did not believe in communicating his private distress or anxiety to the viewer. Rather, he dedicated himself always to the creation of an art featuring *Luxe, Calme et Volupté*, to borrow the title he gave to one of his most beautiful Fauve paintings, a work named after a line in a poem by Baudelaire. Throughout his life, Matisse's stated—and achieved—goal in painting and drawing was to provide the spectator with the comfortable feeling of relaxation one gains from lolling in a good armchair.

Matisse created sculptures intermittently throughout his career; like his production as a painter and draftsman, his sculpted oeuvre concentrates on portraits of women and, above all, on depictions of the nude. He always insisted that he sculpted as a painter, not as a sculptor, and his two art forms constantly nourished one another. For example, the painting, *The Blue Nude* (*Souvenir of Biskra*), 1907, which depicts a sinuously reclining female nude, was born when a sculpture of a standing figure he was modeling collapsed as he worked, brought down by its too-heavy head. Matisse resurrected this wreck in his painted *Blue Nude*, then recomposed the sculpture in accord with the solution he had reached in the painting. His sculptures also reveal his lifelong preoccupation with moving from the more realistic to the more essential conception of the face and figure. His series of larger-than-life-size reliefs of a female back illustrate this process; actually executed over a long time-span, they work very effectively as an unbroken series, revealing the continuity of his artistic interests over the intervening years.

During his long career, Matisse produced hundreds of prints and book illustrations, as well as a significant number of tapestries and murals. His magical talents as a decorator made the artist a natural choice for commissions of the latter type. Among the earliest and most famous of his murals were the large-scale *Dance* and *Music* canvases commissioned by the Russian collector,

Sergei Shchukin. The sketch for *Music*, 1907, already reveals the artist's post-Fauve style and strongly influenced his subsequent production. The *Dance* commission proved equally stimulating. Matisse produced several variations of the theme, then utilized it as the background motif in two versions of the *Still Life with Dance*, painted in 1912.

Most of Matisse's pictures and prints portray a space as perceived by the artist and witnessed by the viewer. This technique draws the spectator into the life of the artist's composition. *Music* and *Dance*, however, omit this specific viewpoint, prefiguring the similar characteristics of the late cutout compositions, also presented from a nonspecific viewpoint. The brilliant colors and glorified treatment of the final version of the *Dance* mural also predict similar aspects of the cutouts of his final phase.

Between 1911 and 1913, Matisse traveled extensively, visiting Spain and Morocco. The impressions he collected on these journeys, as well as the artifacts he purchased, informed his entire subsequent artistic production. The achievements of the Moorish and Moroccan craftsmen delighted him, while the motif of the Odalisque lolling in her seraglio in a provocative state of near nudity became one of his favorite themes. (It has a time-honored position in French painting.) The Moroccan textiles, ceramics, and screens acquired on these journeys appear again and again in the backgrounds of canvases painted throughout the remainder of his life. Many critics also perceive allusions to Moorish painted tiles in the shapes and colors of the components of the artist's cutout murals.

During the years of World War I, Matisse's art became more severe and geometric, more preoccupied with elucidating problems of underlying structure. It is difficult to ascertain how much this change resulted from his reaction to the war, how much from his response to the challenges presented by Cubism. Canvases such as *Bathers by a River*, worked on for several years but completed in 1917, typify this more severe manner. The picture apparently started life as a much more sensuous depiction of nudes in a landscape; the contained foliage portrayed in its final form recurs in a slightly varied state in one of the stained-glass windows of the chapel at Vence (Cowart, Flam, Fourcade, and Neff, 1977, p. 23).

From 1917 on, the artist spent a good deal of time in Nice on the Riviera. In 1921, he moved there permanently. Most critics associate a noticeable relaxation in his style to this change of locale. Certainly, during the twenties, he produced some of his most masterful compositions, paintings which integrate the human figure, still life, and landscape into one harmonious composition.

During the 1930s, Matisse's interest in easel painting, formerly his core preoccupation, fluctuated. In a period of personal and artistic restlessness, the artist traveled widely, accepting many noneasel commissions to execute books, murals, tapestries, and even the decor and costumes for a ballet, *Rouge et Noir*. His painting procedures changed during this period, and he began to have canvases in process photographed systematically as they evolved. While creating the *Pink Nude*, 1935, he pinned cutout pieces of paper to the surface of the canvas as a compositional aid, a process which again anticipates the creation of the cutout works. This picture, along with *The Blue Robe*, represents a real change in his style and focus. These still, flat images, presented from a nonspecific point of view, anticipate many characteristics of his cutout compositions.

Always active as a draftsman, Matisse devoted himself more than ever to his drawings during the 1930s; he now felt uncomfortably aware of the conflict between his paintings and his drawings. As he expressed it, drawing and painting started to "come apart" for him. How much his deteriorating domestic situation contributed to Matisse's malaise remains an unanswered question, but during 1940, he formally separated from Mme Matisse, establishing a dwelling with Lydia Delectroskaya, who had been a favorite model since the early 1930s. Subsequently, she assisted him in creating *Jazz* and other cutout compositions. During this same period, Matisse's health became so problematic that it seriously interfered with his productivity, and he finally underwent surgery during the spring of 1941.

As soon as his health permitted, Matisse returned to full activity as a painter, draftsman, sculptor, and book illustrator. Alfred Barr notes that the canvases which Matisse produced during World War II show wide variations in subject and style; generally, however, they are characterized by a greater degree of abstraction, flattened space, and a darker palette.

He began his experiments with the paper cutout technique on a small scale, creating the illustrated book, *Jazz*, a project which occupied him intermittently from 1943-1947. This represented his first experiment with colored prints; previously, this brilliant colorist had limited his graphics to black-and-white work. He produced the maquettes for reproduction by cutting the shapes from papers previously painted with gouaches in bright tones. Matisse provided a text of his own invention to accompany the colored illustrations for *Jazz*, "writing" the lines like a Chinese calligrapher with a brush dipped in ink. The contrast between the black-and-white imagery of the text and the brightly colored illustrations would be invoked again in the decorative schemes of the chapel at Vence.

The cutout compositions immediately following *Jazz* were all small-scale, completely abstract works. As Matisse explored his new medium, he grew more expansive; during his last few years, he executed both enormous abstract murals and equally large-scale narrative works, such as *The Sadness of the King*, from 1952. Matisse employed several young women assistants to help him achieve his major cutout compositions. Under the artist's careful supervision, they painted sheets of paper with gouache pigments he designated. They also held and helped to guide the papers while he cut. (Typically, he cut by gliding the open scissors through the paper, rather than by snipping, an action he usually reserved for difficult angles.) Again following his directions, his assistants pinned the cutout designs to the walls of his apartment, rearranging the components until the artist felt satisfied with the composition.

Although Matisse gave up painting and sculpture during his last years, he continued to make large-scale drawings until nearly the end of his life. In addition to the sketches he made while standing, he also drew in bed. Assistants pinned sheets of paper to the ceiling, on which Matisse sketched, utilizing a six-foot-long stick with a charcoal tip. Some of his very late works combine drawing with cutout elements, such as the depiction of a sketched female nude surrounded by pieces of fruit executed from cut paper.

Matisse began his work on the chapel at Vence in late 1947. The project to build this structure, intended for the use of a group of Dominican nuns, came to his attention when one of their novices, Sister Jacques, consulted him about the designs she was trying to fashion for the chapel's stained-glass windows. Earlier, this young woman had been a nurse; assigned to tend Matisse during his illness of 1941, she became so devoted to the artist that she delayed entering the order to continue caring for him. In gratitude, he offered to help with the window problem only to become so immersed in the project that he ended by designing virtually every aspect of the chapel and its furnishings. He worked closely with the architect, and they decided upon a very simple L-shaped building; the long stem of the L would contain the nave; the short arm would function as a transept where the nuns could worship in privacy.

Matisse's designs for the chapel emphasize the color white within and without, with strong black accents provided by the mural paintings. He designed and executed all these murals himself; working from a grid scaled to match the finished wall, he painted each tile composing the murals with Chinese ink. Afterward, the tiles were glazed, fired, and fixed in place by artisans. The composition of the most complex mural, a condensed depiction of the Stations of the Cross, occupied Matisse for several years. Other paintings feature St. Dominic and the Madonna and Child.

The soft, pinkish-mauve color notes in the chapel come from the light which filters through the stained-glass windows, composed of rich yellow and blue panes. The artist designed these windows via his paper cutout technique; the compositions went through several evolutions until he arrived at the final predominant pattern, a very simplified so-called *Tree of Life* motif. As I already noted, this pattern recalls the lush plantings in the left margin of the *Bathers by the River*. Even the long, narrow format of each window section echoes the slender verticality of that area in the 1917 canvas. The beautiful pierced-wood confessional door recalls the many similar Moorish screens which appear in Matisse canvases through the years. Like Monet's *Nymphéas*, Matisse's chapel at Vence summarizes the work of a lifetime. As his final touch, the artist designed all the furnishings for the chapel, as well as the vestments and linens utilized there. The building was dedicated on June 25, 1951.

During his remaining three years, Matisse continued to explore the possibilities and limitations of his new cutout technique, which he now applied to major designs intended to be executed in painted-tile form, such as his murals for a swimming pool, or in stained glass, like *The Vine*. In one of his favorite compositions from this period, the artist portrayed himself as a plump little parakeet perching quietly in a colorful garden, watching a cavorting mermaid. Afterward he explained to a visitor: "I have made a little garden all around me where I can walk. In entering into the object one enters one's own skin. I had to make . . . this parakeet with colored paper. Well, I became a parakeet. And I found myself in the work. The Chinese say one must grow with the tree. I know nothing truer" (Cowart, Flam, Fourcade, and Neff, 1977, p. 233).

During his last year, Matisse's energy slowly drained away. But he never lost his creative zest. Until he drew his last breath, Matisse remained the man who carried the sun in his belly, as Picasso once described him, and he continues to shed the radiant light of his genius upon us all.

CONCLUSIONS

The elderly geniuses of the Renaissance epoch relied on a variety of institutional systems to help sustain their creativity and productivity at peak levels. Their religious convictions, atelier organizations, and enlightened patronage all promoted the continuing excellence and originality of the final phases of such artists as Donatello, Giovanni Bellini, Titian, Michelangelo, and Bernini. The aged artists of our epoch, deprived of such support systems, must either construct their own buttresses or rely on the supports provided by media exposure, gallery and museum exhibitions, and contemporary patrons, the latter often more fickle than their Renaissance counterparts and much more preoccupied with demonstrating their up-to-the-minute knowledge and sophistication than with developing true connoisseurship.

The late careers of Monet, Matisse, and Picasso reflect the varied reactions of three different artistic personalities to this dilemma. The fact that both Monet and Matisse succeeded in sustaining their former high level of quality to a greater extent than Picasso suggests that the two French masters found a more effective solution to these problems than the aging Spanish artist. Although one can do no more than speculate about the implications provided by this sample of eight artists, the available data support several hypotheses.

First: there seems to be a strong direct correlation between the development and maintenance of strong autocritical abilities and the continuing creation of works of the highest level. Both Monet and Matisse seemed to have more highly developed autocritical faculties than Picasso. In part, this difference probably reflects their individual approaches to artistic creation. Picasso was a "gut" artist, a creator whose instinctive responses always played a dominant role in his production. Matisse, by contrast, seems the quintessential cerebral artist, the man whose intellect exerted the strongest influence on his work. Such dichotomous descriptions oversimplify, of course, but the distinction does reflect a real difference in the working procedures the two men followed. Picasso claimed that an artist always paints to unload himself of feelings and visions. A walk through the Forest of Fontainebleau produces a kind of " 'green' indigestion" which can only be cured by creating a painting dominated by green (Ashton, 1972, p. 10). Although Matisse also emphasized the primacy of his "inner feelings" over his intellect in the creative process, he repeatedly emphasized that every person or object possesses an "inherent truth" which must be disengaged from the outward appearance of the object to be represented. "This is the only truth that matters" (Barr, 1951, pp. 561-562). This process of distilling the essence requires a conscious intellectual discipline, an approach radically different from Picasso's often repeated insistence, "I do not seek—I find."

Monet, too, seems to have initiated his career as a finder, rather than a seeker, but he steadily evolved toward a much more self-critical, self-doubting stance as he matured. As an elderly man, Monet might have echoed Matisse's statement: "[A]n artist has no greater enemy than his bad paintings, [so] I do not release a painting or a drawing before I have made every possible effort" (Barr, 1951, p. 562). The same type of unrelenting determination always to do his best led Monet to rework his paintings for months, even years, until some of them built up an encrusted surface so heavy it seems almost palpable.

The aging Picasso, by contrast, apparently grew more and more slapdash and careless in his compositional and technical procedures. During his final phase, he consigned very few pictures to the junk heap, and the Zervos *catalogues raisonnés* contain numerous sketches of such minor quality that another artist would have destroyed them, rather than insisting that they be catalogued and immortalized. Elevated to the status of a living monument of art so many years prior to his death, Picasso gradually assumed the mantle of papal infallibility; there were *no* bad Picassos—only good and still better Picassos. The partner with whom he spent his twilight years actively aided the destruction of his self-critical judgment, a condition seldom productive of the greatest art.

Second: the irreligious modern artist probably fares best when he can substitute some other type of magnificent obsession for the religious fervor so uniformly reflected in the late oeuvre of the Renaissance giants. In Monet's case, this ecstatic experience consisted of a kind of magical fusion with nature, a fusion in which the artist clearly assumed a Godlike role. During his final years, Monet concentrated almost exclusively on depicting *a world which he himself had created.* Like God the Father, the artist formed a universe from the void, separating the water from the land, and peopling his miniature world with the plants and other furnishings which made it a microcosm in miniature, the perfect subject for his brush. Just as our universe continually renews itself through constant change, Monet endlessly reconstructed his private world through his long series of *Nymphéas* paintings. Just as God condemned Satan and his fellow-rebel angels to eternal hellfire, Monet thrust his unfit works into the flames. Only his most beautiful and perfect creatures were destined to survive and illuminate our world with their glory.

Matisse enjoyed a similarly uplifting experience by surviving his series of life-threatening illnesses and surgical procedures. He viewed his survival as a kind of-miraculous reincarnation, an example of divine grace which could only be merited by the expenditure of extraordinary efforts on his part. Everyone who encountered him emphasized the serenity he radiated during his final years, a serenity unclouded by his growing weakness and frequent pain. Like one truly reborn, he looked at the world through fresh eyes and created a fresh art to express his joyous reactions for us.

Third: both Monet and Matisse gave themselves over totally to a vast final project of a completely selfless type. Picasso created a number of public monuments during his final years, some of them outright gifts from the artist; however, each of these works constituted a discrete, finite effort. None of them required the same type of dedication to virtually unending labor involved in the creation of the *Nymphéas* cycle or the Vence chapel. But this largess brought its own reward: Monet and Matisse surpassed themselves in the creation of a single, summary magnum opus. The ancillary works which both painters created during these same years were from their great self-generated commissions. Monet's studies and rejected panels for the *Nymphéas* cycle became magnificent works in their own right, capable of assuming an independent existence. Matisse utilized experiments which came to fruition in the Vence chapel design and decoration to inform his subsequent drawings and cutouts. Picasso, by contrast, neither cast so much artistic bread upon the waters nor reaped commensurate rewards.

As a kind of bonus, the relationship which Monet enjoyed with Clemenceau closely mirrored some of the durable partnerships which such great Renaissance masters as Titian and Michelangelo enjoyed with their most important patrons. The very nature of the tasks which Monet and Matisse developed also shows parallels with important Renaissance projects. Monet's plan to create a total environment reflecting his water-lily paradise might be compared with some of the great fresco cycles with which Renaissance artists decorated entire rooms or chapels in important public buildings. Matisse's action in assuming virtually total responsibility for the architecture and decoration of the Vence chapel probably most closely parallels certain activities of the great Baroque master, Bernini, who designed both the architecture and the decorative schemas for several complete churches, as well as for chapels within existing churches.

In summary, the evidence suggests that, in order to

enjoy an optimal final phase, an aged artist must be able to identify with some larger force outside himself. This identification—or, perhaps more properly, ecstatic merger—permits and encourages the elderly genius to view himself and his creations as small, imperfect works, thus heightening his autocritical abilities. This type of experience and self-detachment enabled Monet and Matisse to expand their previous artistic conceptions and invent a new late format and style. Picasso, lacking this type of objectivity, failed to achieve a comparable inventiveness.

We possess too little biographical data about seven of the eight artists discussed to enable us to speculate about the types of early experiences which permitted and promoted this type of final achievement. (Although Matisse lived quite recently, he preserved his privacy so rigorously that we possess few intimate biographical details about him.) We know much more about Picasso's past history. As I pointed out in my book (Gedo, 1980a), his entire history points to his absolute dependence on partnerships to maintain his integrity and creativity. Imprinted very early with the stamp of his fragile, yet controlling, mother, Picasso again and again chose women in her image. Far from liberating himself from this cross, the artist grew ever more dependent on the maintenance of such merger relationships as he aged; chained to the most fallible of mortals, Picasso failed to achieve a final cosmic fusion.

REFERENCES

Art News (1981), All of Michelangelo's work will have to be restudied. Vol. 80, no. 8, October.

Ashton, D. (1972), *Picasso on Art: A Selection of Views.* New York: Viking Press.

Barr, A. H., Jr. (1951), *Matisse: His Art and His Public.* New York: Arno Press for the Museum of Modern Art, 1966.

Boggs, J. S. (1973), The last thirty years. In: *Picasso in Retrospect*, ed. R. Penrose & J. Golding. New York & Washington: Praeger, pp. 197-242.

Corbett, P. (1982), After centuries of grime. *Connoisseur*, May, pp. 68-75.

Cowart, J., Flam, J. D., Fourcade, D., & Neff, J. H. (1977), *Henri Matisse: Paper Cut-Outs*. Published by the St. Louis Art Museum and Detroit Institute of Fine Arts. New York: Abrams.

Fisher, M. T. (1959), *Titian's Assistants during the Later Years*. New York: Garland Publishers, 1977.

Gedo, M. M. (1980a), *Picasso: Art as Autobiography*. Chicago: University of Chicago Press.

———— (1980b), Art as exorcism: Picasso's *Demoiselles d'Avignon. Arts Magazine*, 55:70-83.

Guillemot, M. (1898), Claude Monet. *Revue illustrée*, 13, March 15.

Heinemann, F. (1962), *Giovanni Bellini i Belliniani*. 2 vols. Venice: Pozza.

Herbert, R. (1979), Method and meaning in Monet. *Art in America*, 67:90-108.

Hibbard, H. (1974), *Michelangelo: Painter, Sculptor, Architect*. New York: Harper and Row.

Janson, H. (1963), *The Sculpture of Donatello*. Princeton, N.J.: Princeton University Press, 1979.

Mount, C. (1966), *Monet: A Biography*. New York: Simon and Schuster.

O'Brian, P. (1976), *Picasso: A Biography*. New York: Putnam's.

Seiberling, G. (1975), The evolution of an Impressionist. *Paintings by Monet*, ed. S. Wise, foreword J. Maxon. Chicago: Art Institute of Chicago, pp. 19-41.

———— (1976), *Monet's Series*. New York: Garland, 1981.

Spies, W. (1971), *Sculpture by Picasso*, trans. J. M. Brownjohn. New York: Abrams.

Stuckey, C. (1979), Blossoms and blunders: Monet and the State. Part 2, *Art in America*, 67:109-125.

———— & Gordon, R. (1979), Blossoms and blunders: Monet and the State. Part 1: *Art in America*, 67:102-107.

Tietze-Conrat, E. (1946), Titian's workshop in his late years, *ArtBull.*, 28:76-88.

Part IV

On the Epistemology of Psychoanalysis

Introduction: On Some Dynamics of Dissidence within Psychoanalysis

JOHN E. GEDO, M.D.

Credo in un Dio crudel che m'ha creato . . .
E credo l'uom gioco d'iniqua sorte . . .
Verdi/Boito, *Otello* (Act 2, scene 2)

The sources of dissidence within psychoanalysis probably transcend the arena of political and transference issues to which they have commonly been ascribed. Let me begin to illustrate this thesis by means of a personal example. Some of my work was recently reviewed by a number of distinguished colleagues, among others by Hanna Segal, the *doyenne* of the Kleinian school (Segal and Britton, 1981). In her characteristically perceptive manner, Segal commented at some length on the fact that my proposals possess an unusual degree of coherence and internal consistency. Needless to say, I was initially delighted by such a tribute from unexpected quarters, but my joy was destined to be short-lived! Segal did not look with favor upon such a tightly constructed conceptual edifice as mine: *in principle*, she prefers a more intuitive—dare I say a more romantic?—approach to the theoretical task. Apparently, Melanie Klein's cavalier attitude toward theoretical coherence actually attracted Segal to the work of her mentor.

But I must turn from this subjective viewpoint to a broader perspective. Some years ago, Ernest van den Haag (1965) called attention to the similarity in outlook about the human condition between Freud and St. Augustine. At first we may be startled by this comparison, for we are accustomed to emphasize the difference between psychoanalysis and our religious traditions. In my view, however, it makes sense to classify both religious and psychoanalytic orthodoxy as doctrines occupying middle-of-the-road positions between the extremes of philosophical pessimism and utopian optimism. The theological controversies to which van den Haag was alluding do find their echoes in contemporary psychoanalytic discourse. It is true that Freud simultaneously rejected views parallel to the Pelagian heresy, which was based on the concept of man's limitless perfectibility, and the Manichaean one, which reflected the notion of irremediable human wickedness. And it will cause no surprise that similar divergences in outlook have splintered the Moslem world (see Hodgson, 1974). I suspect that these fundamental differences about human nature may be destined to polarize every intellectual community.

At the level of competing clinical proposals, we have therefore all been guilty of dismissing the ideas of rival schools too readily. Yet our customary parochialism in these matters has not been justified by demonstrably superior results within our home parishes (cf. Gedo, 1980), so that we also tend to castigate ourselves for the unseemliness of the general dogmatism in our midst. How embarrassing it is! We turn out to be believers, like

Thomas Aquinas—except that we cannot match his insight that one is forced to have *faith* precisely because what one believes is absurd! And whatever we find unfamiliar can permanently be disregarded by pronouncing it anathema: it is "*not* psychoanalysis."

When a more ecumenical spirit prevails, most of us will grant the value of a wide gamut of clinical theories that have guided various groups of psychoanalysts in the bewildering task of processing their observational data. Each of these conceptual schemata encodes one or another of the primary meanings implicit in human existence —unfortunately, often to the exclusion of all others. Thus the view of man embodied in the libido theory, especially in the form it took prior to 1920, attributed primary significance to the satisfaction of the appetites. By contrast, Melanie Klein's psychoanalytic system is a doctrine that teaches the need to make reparation for man's constitutional wickedness—in other words, it is a species of psychoanalytic Manichaeanism! Recently, Heinz Kohut put forward views that give comparable emphasis to the unique healing power of empathy and acknowledge man's entitlement to an affectively gratifying milieu—a position that comes close to the optimism of the Pelagian heresy. Let me hasten to add that I am emphatically in agreement with the need for appetite satisfaction, for the curbing of destructiveness, and for the provision of a gratifying environment for our children. Isn't everyone?

Passionate declarations of commitment to reductionist formulations do not involve the real world of human transactions—the "green of experience," as Goethe called it—but only the arcane realm of psychological theory. How can we account for the fact that our community seems to regard the theoretical scaffolding around our collective enterprise as the crux of psychoanalysis, in spite of Freud's appeals not to do so? I would hazard the conjecture that this attitude harks back to the origins of the discipline within biology (cf. Sulloway, 1980). Freud's attempts at theory construction were explicitly based on the materialist postulates established by Descartes for the *res extensa*. Hence the "metapsychology" that developed on this Freudian framework was intended to be an explanatory theory that could meet the positivist criteria of early twentieth-century epistemology. In other words, psychoanalytic psychology aims to develop scientifically valid propositions. The fact that, by the current criteria of empirical science, Freud's metapsychology lacks *explanatory* value has introduced a Babel of confusion into our discourse—but most of us have persevered (or perseverated?) in searching for a theory that embodies biological Truth.

One of the most prominent ideological fissures among psychoanalysts has opened along this fault in our conceptual terrain. On the one hand, we have scientific Jeremiahs—I have to confess to being among them myself. The idols of our energeticist past must be overthrown, we cry! We cringe to hear respected colleagues render homage to false doctrines such as narcissism, the ego—sometimes even to that chief abomination, psychic energy! We feel that our sanity is being assaulted when traditionalists continue to adhere to these outworn rituals while they admit that the latter have no scientific standing. They tell us that, in using these terms, they are speaking metaphorically, yet we suspect them of continuing to claim possession of biological truth. Their attitude strikes us as scientific dadaism—or delinquency. On the other hand, I am reasonably certain that their indictment of our position could sound just as devastating—and, alas, just as persuasive.

From a historical perspective, the fate of Freudian metapsychology is a curious paradox, for its principal rationale was an effort to anchor psychoanalysis within natural science. Since its components have lost their connections with neurobiology, Freud's metapsychology can no longer lay claim to materialist foundations. To the contrary, its continuing use amounts to a return to the doctrines of vitalism and idealism Freud was trying to oppose by erecting energeticist theories in the first place. You will recall C. G. Jung's report (1963, pp. 150-151) that Freud enjoined him to cleave to the libido theory because it protects psychoanalysis from engulfment by a "black tide of occultism." Hence contemporary analysts who would make do with a theory composed of metaphors are reverting to a prescientific, idealist doctrine, very much in the footsteps of Jung! Like the latter, they tend to clothe these quasi-mystical attitudes in the noncontroversial outer garb of empiricism (cf. Stepansky, 1976). The most unequivocal example of this "heresy" on the current clinical scene is the mythology promulgated by the students of Melanie Klein, e.g., their insistence on the presence of primal envy in infants shortly after birth.

Needless to say, I regard the work of such biological visionaries as the opposite of true empiricism. Actual empiricists tend to view the mind as a *tabula rasa* that becomes filled as a consequence of external stimulation. Hence this viewpoint underlies a wide variety of nurture psychologies, including behaviorism. Although Freud's emphasis on the inborn patterns of behavioral disposition he called the "drives" has probably deterred most of his followers from embracing such views without reservations, the pragmatic bent and philosophical optimism of American intellectual life have pushed a substantial segment of the analytic community in their direction.

The most common form of nurture psychology within psychoanalysis at this time is a heterogeneous group of clinical theories centered on object relations. By and large, these hypotheses tend to pay a bit of lip service to the importance of some constitutional ground-plan for personality development, but they clearly look upon the nature of early transactions with the caretakers as the most crucial variable in this regard.

The decision to place object relations at the center of man's motivational system appears to elevate into a position of primacy in theory construction an issue that does not seem to be a matter of great import for pathogenesis in the majority of people. Can it have been forgotten by anyone that it is possible to create elaborate neuroses while being raised optimally by the best of parents? or that acts of God are just as likely to ruin a person's character as are the peculiarities of a caretaker? What makes certain theoreticians choose such an unlikely focus as object relations for articulating the universal crux of human psychology?

Before I hazard an answer to this question, let us note that the majority of those who advocate nurture psychologies actually disavow the fact that they are proposing an *alternative* for Freud's system, claiming the privilege of using several uncoordinated theoretical fragments simultaneously, even if they happen to be mutually contradictory. This incoherence is allegedly justified by appealing to the precedent of the coexistence of two valid theories of light. Needless to say, I regard this argument as a gross misuse of the concept of complementarity, for the physicists resorted to this desperate expedient only because a single explanation was unavailable—a situation that has not arisen in psychoanalysis. I *have* long espoused the principle (see Gedo and Goldberg, 1973) that we need a number of subsidiary hypotheses, each applicable to a different mode of the organization of behavior in the developmental sequence. Nonetheless, we have to have a consistent and unitary metapsychological framework into which we can fit each of the subsidiary concepts we wish to employ.

To return to the main thread of my discussion: If it is granted that theories of object relations actually give human relatedness primacy in their psychological system, what induces their proponents to do so? Perhaps we may be able to discern their motivation by reviewing the intellectual course of the most influential recent convert to a nurture psychology, Heinz Kohut. Kohut himself called his version of clinical theory "self psychology," but this designation is something of a misnomer. I would classify his theory as an approach centered on object relations, because his hypothesis about the formation of the structure he called "the self" involves only the activities of the caretakers.

With the passage of time, Kohut's discourse shifted its emphasis (see Kohut, 1975a, b), away from the accurate interpretation of structural conflicts involving primitive grandiosity and/or idealization. The rationale for this change seems to have been focused on the issue of empathy; Kohut apparently decided that the truth value of analytic interventions was much less important than their effect on the therapeutic relationship. In other words, he began to stress the healing power of the analyst's "empathic" behavior. In practice, this meant adherence to a therapeutic stance stressing the legitimacy of the patient's claims on the caretakers. With this step, Kohut's analytic system had crossed the continental divide into the realm of the nurture psychologies. Kohut was admirably clear about the fact that the basic point of difference between himself and analytic traditionalists was one of values (cf. Kohut, 1981)—he decried the exclusive commitment of the discipline in the past to the attainment of valid knowledge.

Most theorists who center their work on the issue of

object relations have failed to think through the logic of their position with Kohut's intellectual rigor. By and large, therefore, their proposals have created less of a threat to the cohesion of the psychoanalytic community than did essentially similar ideas when Kohut proclaimed them, with complete justification, as a new dispensation within our field. He really meant that one cannot be a Buddhist and a Shintoist at the same time, whatever the Japanese practice may be; his work forced us into making a choice. What a fanatic, we cry; he really *believes*! Of course, self psychology is by no means the only belief system extant on the current scene: as Michael Polanyi (1974; Polanyi and Prosch, 1975) has shown, every scientific theory is an expression of such beliefs. *Even our own.*

In recent years, it has become fashionable to disavow the necessity of a priori psychoanalytic commitments to one or another of these conceptions of human nature. This evasion generally takes the form of rigidly defining the limits of our subject matter in terms of the analysand's communications in the context of the basic rule of free association. If we do this, it follows logically that our therapeutic activities can only consist of deciphering the latent meanings of the analysand's messages, so that we do not have to concern ourselves with very much beyond language per se. Probably the most prominent contemporary exponent of such views was Jacques Lacan, but there are a number of American exemplars as well among those who have repudiated the need for a metapsychology.

Of course, the refusal of these advocates of a purely hermeneutic, structuralist approach to specify their a priori biological assumptions does not actually mean that they do not have any. The psychoanalytic hermeneuticists systematically ignore those aspects of the psychoanalytic transaction that do not conform to the model of an *explication de texte*; by doing so, they reduce the scope of psychoanalytic psychology to one specific area of mental life. In other words, they focus on derivatives of those phases of childhood development that follow the acquisition of language or of equivalent symbolic systems. Preverbal issues, if considered at all—and it is my impression that they are rarely taken seriously—are viewed as prehistoric *anlagen*. In a purely hermeneutic approach, the existence of these archaic dispositions as vectors that contribute to the specific configuration of later mental properties must be inferred through deductive reasoning. Direct observations of nonverbal behavior performed in the mode of a natural scientist (recently called the ethological mode) are allegedly never attempted. Of course, some of us remain skeptical of such claims and continue to insist that there is always more to effective psychoanalytic treatment than meets the ear—especially in instances where the communicative use of language is impaired.

If we attempt to articulate the presuppositions about human existence implicit in the hermeneuticists' restrictive viewpoint, it may be easiest to do so by noting that it leaves out of account the area of experience Freud (1920) believed to be under the sway of the repetition compulsion—"beyond the pleasure principle," as he put it in the title of his most profound monograph. In Freud's sober view, the area of man's mastery over his inner experience is severely limited. In contrast, the hermeneutic approach seems to imply that, instead of being lived by the demonic forces that Freud called "Thanatos," humanity regularly triumphs over them through the magic agency of words. Would it were so! In fact, the most fundamental discovery of psychoanalysis about mankind may well be that the Word is not our Beginning.

In terms of the polarity between philosophical pessimism and utopian optimism, however, the analytic hermeneuticists also belong at the optimistic end of the scale. How ironic! Visionary biologists, visionary culturalists, and visionary structuralists share only their utopian assumptions—or, if you will, their disagreement with Freud's therapeutic modesty. Can the center hold, contrary to the predictions of W. B. Yeats? Need I say that I look upon my own conceptual work as a last-ditch effort to save the Freudian acropolis from the assaults of the Persians? Of course, this is the claim of each and every competitor in the current free-for-all of psychoanalytic discourse: we all declare that our views have captured the viable essence of Freud's thought (cf. Gedo, 1972).

What, then, is my version of that essence? (For a full expositon, see Gedo, 1979, 1981.) I share the Freudian conviction that psychoanalysis is a biological discipline, so that our basic theories must be congruent with up-to-date knowledge in cognate fields such as neurophysiology and developmental psychology. I believe that the most essential of our therapeutic activities are those directed toward preverbal, even presymbolic issues, such as optimal tension regulation or the establishment of a stable hierarchy of biological aims and patterns, especially in the affective realm. I assume that this hierarchy, which I prefer to call the "self organization," is established on the basis of infantile experiences codetermined by constitutional factors and by the nature of the early milieu. These archaic dispositions are almost always assimilated within networks of subjective wishes of later origin, wishes that are encoded in verbal symbols that screen their primitive beginnings. At any rate, whenever the archaic self finds no acceptable pathway to expression in later adaptation, its effects are destined to be experienced subjectively as alien forces that overwhelm the individual as an autonomous agent. As sentient beings, we are indeed passive victims of the demonic within us; this is, I believe, what Freud meant when he kept repeating that the Unconscious is truly unknowable.

David Rapaport (1974) once showed that Freud's insistence on giving equal weight to nature and to nurture in his developmental propositions attempts to reconcile the antithetical approaches of empiricists and of rationalists. These simpler alternatives to his complex position represent polar opposites along the continuum of philosophical possibilities, whereas Freud occupied the middle ground. But we might put these different viewpoints just as well in the terms proposed by van den Haag, as the alternatives considered by theological anthropology 1500 years ago—those of Augustine, Pelagius, and Mani.

Claude Bernard succeeded in ejecting vitalism from the biological study of mankind only one generation before Freud began his investigative work. We may reasonably postulate that this achievement was contingent on the omission of the psychological vantage point from the study of the organism—if you will, on the continued relegation of the soul or human spirit to the realms of religion and of the arts. Viewed from the perspective of general intellectual history, Freud's accomplishment was the reintegration of psychology into natural science. It should therefore cause little surprise that, in a regression to pre-Freudian ways of thought, many psychoanalysts through the years have clung to the concept of mind-body dualism. This position, in turn, permits an integration of their clinical data about mental functions on the basis of a variety of vitalist notions: Jungian archetypes, psychic energy active in a nonmaterial matrix, the Unconscious as a "language," etc. I see no hope of reconciling these dualist theories with psychoanalytic hypotheses built on monistic, non-Cartesian foundations.

If we accept that the right wing of psychoanalysis consists of reactionaries who wish, consciously or unconsciously, to revert to prescientific conceptions, such as that of the soul, how can we characterize the psychoanalytic Left? Insofar as these opponents of metapsychology are neither dualists nor monists, it is scarcely a pun to call them "nihilists," the name given to those who lose belief in any Sacred Order—many of them explicitly deny the need for a philosophical framework, after all. From an epistemological point of view, they are probably "naïve realists," observers who believe that their perceptions capture the essence of things without further thought processing. What do they care about the soul or the brain? Their psychoanalysis concerns itself only with the behavioral output of that black box, "the psyche." This position is not merely prescientific; it takes us back two-and-a-half millennia to undo the genesis of Western thought.

REFERENCES

Freud, S. (1920), Beyond the pleasure principle. *Standard Edition*, 18:7-64. London: Hogarth Press, 1955.

Gedo, J. (1972), The dream of reason produces monsters. *J. Amer. Psychoanal. Assn.*, 20:199-223.

―――― (1979), *Beyond Interpretation*. New York: International Universities Press.

―――― (1980), Reflections on some current controversies in psychoanalysis. *J. Amer. Psychoanal. Assn.*, 28:363-383.

―――― (1981), *Advances in Clinical Psychoanalysis*. New York: International Universities Press.

―――― & Goldberg, A. (1973), *Models of the Mind*. Chicago: University of Chicago Press.

Hodgson, M. (1974), *The Venture of Islam*. 3 vols. Chicago: University of Chicago Press.

Jung, C. (1963), *Memories, Dreams, Reflections*. New York: Vintage Books.

Kohut, H. (1975a), The future of psychoanalysis. *The Annual of Psychoanalysis*, 3:325-340. New York: International Universities Press.

———— (1975b), The psychoanalyst in the community of scholars. *The Annual of Psychoanalysis*, 3:341-370. New York: International Universities Press.

———— (1981), Introspection, empathy, and the semi-circle of mental health. Presented November 7 at the Conference on The Vital Issues, Chicago Psychoanalytic Society.

Polanyi, M. (1974), *Scientific Thought and Social Reality* [*Psychological Issues*, Monogr. 32]. New York: International Universities Press.

———— & Prosch, H. (1975), *Meaning*. Chicago: University of Chicago Press.

Rapaport, D. (1974), *The History of the Concept of Association of Ideas*. New York: International Universities Press.

Segal, H., & Britton, R. (1981), Interpretation and primitive psychic processes: A Kleinian view. *Psychoanal. Inquiry*, 1:267-278.

Stepansky, P. (1976), The empiricist as rebel: Jung, Freud, and the burdens of discipleship. *J. Hist. Behav. Sci.*, 12:215-239.

Sulloway, F. (1980), *Freud, Biologist of the Mind*. New York: Basic Books.

van den Haag, E. (1965), Psychoanalysis and utopia. *Bull. Phila. Assn. Psychoanal.*, 15:61-78.

12

One Theory or More?

ARNOLD GOLDBERG, M.D.

INTRODUCTION

Pioneers in psychoanalysis, as in any field of scientific inquiry, are few and far between. In fact our science may still be too young for us to determine who the significant leaders are, since it is often only in retrospect that one can assess the meaningful contrbutions in the history of a science. So many of the seemingly great chemists and physicists of their time have faded into obscurity that it will be little surprise to our future historians to note that the many, to us, meaningful figures of today will have contributed little of lasting significance to our science of psychoanalysis. As regards our own pioneers, only the future will reveal if their contributions will continue to take hold on our minds as the edges of psychoanalysis are further explored. This essay will be directed toward examining some facets of the reception of new ideas before history can make a more reasonable assessment.

A different version of this paper originally appeared in *Contemporary Psychoanalysis*, 17:626-638, and we are grateful to the William Alanson White Institute for permission to publish it in this volume.

One of the very great difficulties in the establishment of new ideas in the field of psychoanalysis, perhaps more so than in other scientific pursuits such as physics and mathematics, is the heritage of our ideas from one man, Sigmund Freud, and a form of trusteeship of his ideas that seems to carry on from generation to generation. Trustees are usually assigned the role of guardianship, and at times they feel a necessity to decide issues of truth or falsehood in terms of the reigning ideas. I have been particularly interested recently in the impact of the new ideas of self psychology on the overall field of psychoanalysis, and I have often been struck by the wave of responses which these new ideas have evoked. Although some of these responses are quite challenging and provocative, a number of them seem to fail to meet the minimum demands for scientific theory and inquiry. The most recent one that struck me was a statement in a book review in a psychoanalytic journal (Gediman, 1980) which said that Heinz Kohut's ideas were incorrect. I should like to expand upon that seemingly innocuous matter of opinion in order to pursue what I think is an erroneous form of criticism of scientific ideas, one that stems from a conviction that there is a "correct" theory and/or that one must protect and guard, and so judge new ideas in comparison to such correctness.

The criticisms of self psychology at times seem confined to a mere protest that all of these ideas are not very new or different; they are no more than every good analyst has adhered to all of the time and thus need no particular attention to be paid to them. I suspect this is more of a problem in sociology than in psychology since there seems to be no consensus among analysts as to the originality or popularity of the ideas. Some seem to feel them as revolutionary or deviant or dangerous; and this hardly squares with the old wine in new bottles thesis.

Of course the best example of such a criticism was the one that followed the publication of "The Two Analyses of Mr. Z." (Kohut, 1979)—which dismissed that report by saying these two inadequate analyses should have really been one adequate one. The fact that these analyses were at times contradictory and that the central dream was interpreted quite differently in the separate treatments seems to have escaped these readers (Rangell, 1980). But, more importantly, the question arises as to what guiding theory would allow one to see these two analyses as one, or would compel one to face the conclusion that the theories, though perhaps compatible, are really quite different.

Do we have one theory or do we have two or more? If we have one theory which is essentially the correct one, should we work toward translating supposedly new ideas back into the old language, and should we make minor changes or adjustments in our accepted theory in order to accommodate new findings? This, of course, is what Thomas Kuhn (1962) felt was the job of normal science. On the other hand we might have to face a problem of different theories which, by certain standards, are necessarily what some philosophers of science have called "incommensurable" or seemingly lacking in any basis of comparison. Karl Popper (1963) feels that any theory worth its salt would necessarily overthrow the old one because it must be, by definition, revolutionary and, thus, a really new finding cannot long exist in the confines of an old theory. Yet another school of philosophy (Feyerabend, 1975) believes in a multiplicity or plurality of theories which coexist for a time until the best survives. It is important for any proper evaluation of the pioneers of our field to try to determine whether these are political movements characterized by schools and personalities, whether they are significant additions within the realm of normal science, or whether they have presented us with a vision that challenges the basic "facts" of our old theory. But, especially in these evaluations, we should pursue as objective and scientific a course as is possible. I think we are now witness to such an inquiry into the theoretical status of self psychology, and I believe we can profit from relinquishing a preoccupation with correctness in favor of one of usefulness, i.e., that of the breadth, depth, and elegance of the explanatory yield of the theory.

THE CONTROVERSY

At a conference on self psychology several years ago, Heinz Kohut started a discussion of the "one theory or two problem" by likening it to that of the dim appearance of a figure of a man who approached the viewer from far away down a road. At first one could not make out whether it was the one or the other of two men. As the figure came closer there was more of a tendency to commit oneself to a decision; and, finally, as he came clearly into focus there would be no doubt as to who the person really was. So too, it was felt, most of the questions that confronted the either-or problems of psychoanalytic psychology could be likened to that stage in our scientific investigations at which a certain level of uncertainty necessarily dominated our perceptions. A resolution and an absolute conviction as to the one truth remained a bit beyond our ken. It is important to note that, at least at that point in our scientific study, most of the controversy seemed to be posited around seemingly rivalrous positions, i.e., either it was a problem of narcissistic pathology *or* it was one of a structured neurosis, either it was an oedipal or a preoedipal problem, either the analyst was a real object or a selfobject, etc., etc.

It is also important at the outset to realize that an

appeal to a resolution of any controversy can only fall on willing ears. If all of one's cases do well and there exists little or no sense of dissatisfaction with one's theory, then it is pointless to hope to enlist one even to consider a controversy. Recent literature has revealed such a posture wherein authors (Richards, 1981; Tyson and Tyson, 1982) attempt to demonstrate that they do just fine with their cases and the existing theory. They unfortunately tend to denigrate the supposed opposition by coining words such as pseudo-narcissistic (Tyson and Tyson, 1982) which are used to reveal a lack of fidelity to the correct theory. Other than a certain awe that one must necessarily feel toward analysts who have achieved such contentment, it is certainly the case that they are not to be disabused of that state.

I should like to take this opportunity to pursue this matter of supposed rivalry since I think there remains a good deal of ambiguity in these controversies. There are at least three different opinions which can be considered: In brief, they are:

(1) The view of one school of thought, best articulated by Robert Wallerstein (1980), states that it is not a question of either/or but of both/and. Essentially this orientation pays close attention to the deficits of developmental arrests but claims that analytic material is too fluid to make a sharp dichotomy between deficits and regression. It especially espouses what is felt to be a variant of Waelder's multiple-functions principle by stressing multiple vantage points in assessing clinical data. Although this approach seems most flexible and liberal it tends to evolve into its own either/or question, i.e., a question of the crux of pathology as being either due to deficit *or* due to conflict, and the latter does seem to win the day. Therefore, there remains a tendency to subsume the new findings of self psychology under the rubric of classical

findings and to stretch the umbrella a bit in order to define conflict as "any opposition of any kind involving any aspect of psychic functioning in any form." I think that is worth pondering.

(2) The second approach to the either-or problem takes a much firmer stand and seemingly divides the world of psychoanalysis into narcissistic pathology and structured pathology, and only occasionally allows oedipal pathology to have narcissistic features. There is a marvelous convenience to this kind of strict dichotomy in that one can even separate analytic practitioners into those who are treating narcissistic disorders and those who do not. But, in all seriousness, these somewhat political considerations stem from the early writings of self psychology, and they resist the encroachment of self psychology onto the area of classical psychoanalysis. They admit of a category of narcissistic disorders but they are strict segregationists. While the first position is all-inclusive, this one treats self psychology as an aberration of sorts.

(3) The third position is the most radical one. It posits self psychology as subsuming classical oedipal pathology as but one form of aberrant self development. It states that the natural culmination of normal self development is oedipal resolution, but that failures in such resolution always reflect underlying problems in the self-selfobject matrix. And although it allows for a focused concentration on the oedipal conflict in a neurotic, it always looks beyond this to a developmental defect. In a rather obvious way this is also the most radical point of view in terms of development since it states that oedipal problems are developmental ones that are not inevitable but are determined by the vicissitudes of normal development.

There are other positions to be sure. They range from an utter dismissal of the existence of any of the findings of self psychology to an equally absurd embracing of the primarily clinical material in every possible encounter whether psychoanalytic or therapeutic or social. Such severe stances which liken self psychology to a cult, or claim it to be some sort of gratification exercise, are probably best classified as nonscientific efforts which are, fortunately or otherwise, themselves only capable of being understood by a self-psychological approach. But leaving these exaggerated poles aside, I would offer these three positions as being at the heart of the controversy.

Now initially I want to sidestep these different stances to say a few more words about theories in general since the three positions of both/and, either/or, or entirely one are essentially three different clinical theories.

To begin with we must accept the fact that all scientific theories are underdetermined. That is to say that there is never a one-to-one correspondence between theories and fact; but rather we know that any given theory allows us to see some things and to miss others and to make of many things what we wish them to be. Our theories do pretty much direct our perceptions and, unfortunately, they probably belong in the category of "preconceived ideas". This is not so unfortunate as long as we retain a certain flexible capacity: that of recognizing a misfit when it occurs and of realizing that a theory is valuable only in terms of its usefulness, i.e., its utility as a kind of map or visual aid. The remarkable beauty of Freud's discovery of the Oedipus complex, a clinical theory in itself, was its enabling us to see, understand, and explain a host of disparate phenomena which had previously made no sense. The phobia of Little Hans is now revealed in a way that was not previously possible. And, of course, once one can and does see phenomena in a new light, then they will never be the same as before. In a similar sort of manner the theory of selfobjects makes for a perception of relationships and transferences that is also similar to a new map of foreign terrain, and this allows for a kind of explanation of patient-analyst relationships that was heretofore lacking.

The other point about theories that I want to emphasize is that they are always wrong and are waiting for a better one to come along. Any good and new theory should be revolutionary and should overthrow the old one. This certainly does not mean that rival theories do not coexist for long periods of time, but ultimately one of them manages to dominate because of the aforementioned points of simplicity, elegance, and explanatory yield. But theories that continue to live side by side are either explaining different phenomena or are waiting for a single theory to replace both of them. In the history of any scientific enterprise one sees periods of relative agreement about the value of a theory followed by the introduction of a new set of ideas. This is often accompanied by a form of social and/or political dispute until the practitioners of the science reach some sort of consensus on how they do their work. Naturally, this sequence need not be clearly demonstrated or easily observed, but a few salient periods do seem to stand out. One of these is the task of tampering with the old theory to incorporate the findings of the new one. I think we see this in the first position outlined wherein the usual and customary tenets of classical psychology are modified to accommodate self psychology. These efforts are praiseworthy since old theories should never be abandoned without extremely good reasons. However, ultimately there occurs an eroding of the old theories. Certainly Waelder's Principle of Multiple Function (1930) had nothing whatsoever to do with multiple vantage points of observation except in the most generous of interpretations. And if conflict theory is allowed to equal any sort of opposition that one experiences, including that of a conflict over developing further because of the lack of sufficient structure, then it probably can embrace just about everything and thus runs the risk of trivializing its original meaning.

Let us focus on the conflict issue. We all know that it enjoys a narrow definition, such as that offered by Brenner (1979), who confines it to the instinctual wishes of childhood, or a more broad and inclusive one, such as that of Anna Freud (1965), who includes conflicts between the child and his environment, between the ego and the superego, and between drives and affects of opposite quality. The latest to be enlisted in this stretching exercise is that of a conflict between ideals (Tyson and Tyson, 1982). The direction of the extension of a definition of conflict is certainly outward, since for Sandler (1976) it includes an adult use of a childhood defense in a particular circumstance.

My own thought is that of an analytic case, a homosexual, who for the first time was entering into heterosexual activity. I suppose one could say that he was filled with conflicts of all sorts. Perhaps one could say that he had a conflict between being homosexual or heterosexual. One of his major problems was a need for a reponse to his masculine strivings. He had had a childhood of ridicule in this regard, having been dressed in girl's clothing. His penis was an object of scorn for his sister and mother, and he had been ashamed of his body for all of his life. Much of the period in his analysis had to do with the emergence of exhibitionistic fantasis of his masculine self and the concomitant need for a reflecting selfobject. My own way of conceptualizing the new developmental achievement is that I am simply not able to consider this as much of a psychoanalytic conflict situation. It is a matter of ongoing new experiences being confronted. I have no doubt that some heroic stretching of classical theory could make it a conflict, but it seems at some point to have lost its moorings in Freud's original sense. This, I think, is a fine example of theory tampering and is probably cause enough to say that the theory really cannot do the task assigned it. To say that conflict should embrace what are essentially conscious *decision* problems i.e., a movement into a new state of affairs versus maintaining the old—should I do this or should I do that?—is, to my mind, no longer a psychoanalytic effort. Even the material of child and infant observation can remain on a descriptive and superficial level if one reports that the child departs and returns for refueling because of a conflict over separation. Psychoanalysts must ask exactly what the child communicates to the mother and vice versa. Of course going back and forth is a conflict of sorts, but it is not quite what Freud had in mind about the clashing of forces. If everything is "conflict," then conflict is nothing.

Another step in the historical sequence of theory ascendency is the attempt to isolate the new one by admitting its value but assigning it to a diferent domain of inquiry. Sometimes we see the development of new methods of investigation in this manner. At other times, however, these efforts are doomed to failure because new theores are, as emphasized, essentially incompatible and revolutionary. I think we see this dilemma in the field of self psychology in terms of the very concept of the selfobject. Either one grows out of such a relationship, leaves it behind, and advances to clear and permanent self and object differentiation, or else a whole new way of conceptualizing normal growth and development must be entertained in order to comprehend the existence of lasting and mature selfobjects.

Let us compare the clinical situation in terms of the data gathered and conclusions drawn to an analyst listening to a patient who is upset or concerned about a pending separation. If one listens with a theoretical assumption that normal development involves a movement toward individuation and gradual independence, then one would probably concern oneself with the struggle over such freedom and the conflict over leaving the libidinal object with whom one is attached. The typical sequence of behavior seen in separation-individuation conflicts and translated back into fantasies about the relationship with and the ties to the analyst or parent may or may not lead to different analytic results from those derived from an alternate theory. But a typical statement such as: "The analyst continued to sense the patient's need to evoke the hated and wanted intrusiveness in the transference, followed by resistive withdrawal" certainly sounds like the theory is dictating the kind of information one obtains from a patient (Selma Kramer, 1979). Other elaborations of the need for the patient to experience rage (Rothstein, 1979) insist that one will do a disservice to a patient by neglecting a consideration of the patient's sadism and aggressiveness. This seems to support the position of most philosophers of science that one cannot separate observation statements from theoretical statements (Grundy, 1973) and to confirm that we see what we look for.

If one contrasts this guiding theory with one that states that the individual wants and needs continuing relationships with his selfobjects and that individuation is not separation but rather a change in the nature (controlling versus being controlled) of the relationship, then a new and different form of data emerges. Rage is not a necessary condition of separation but rather a reaction to selfobject failures. Termination is not a working through of a particular individuation conflict but rather the attainment of empathic connections (Kohut, 1979). Much, if not all, of the material elicited sounds and looks different, and even the technical interventions become changed. But this soon is seen *not* as a matter of translating one theory back into the other, but rather as facts that are so theory-laden as to defy comparison.

The important and really only significant point about the lack of compatibility of the two ways of looking at separation is not that one is right and the other wrong. This is simply not the case with theories, and for any critic to show incorrectness by stressing incompatibility is merely to underscore the obvious. The question is a much more difficult one and has to do with a lengthy examination of the value of one theory against the other. Herefore if one examines a new set of ideas and finds them in conflict with old established ones, this is not an occasion to write a critique. It is a call for proper surprise and curiosity in order to ascertain if certain old unanswered problems may now lend themselves to better understanding. Of course all new theories are "incorrect." That is as they should be; or else one only relearns what one already knows.

This, of course, brings us to the final position of the three, the one that posits a psychoanalytic theory of self psychology that includes and replaces that of the primacy of the oedipal conflict. Again, without making a claim for its correctness, I can suggest what we must expect of it: it must encompass everything we already know, and more. If it fails to do this then it indeed is but a minor variation on a theme which will ultimately be absorbed into our existing views of psychoanalysis without any fundamental radical upheavals. This is where we are today, and that is the problem that confronts us.

To return to some clinical material, I would like to reconsider a point that we are all familiar with which demonstrates the seeming paradox of good analytic work followed by depression and despondency. A patient, for example, gains insight into a phobic avoidance and, instead of this resulting in feeling better, feels worse. There are many ways to talk of this: certainly as one variant of a negative therapeutic reaction. Either the patient felt guilty about getting better, or was afraid to get better, or the correct interpretation undid repressions which released aggression which was turned inward. And yet another way of seeing what happened is quite different. It is that the very act of interpretation takes place within a self-selfobject matrix and that one must subsequently respond to the patient to confirm him or her, to mirror an achievement positively, much like one must respond to the oedipal achievements of the developing child. Inasmuch as some analysts might agree with this technical advice it still is necessary to recognize that there is a significant theoretical difference between the insight alone making the change and the insight also serving as the expression of a developing self. There should be no question that one needs to interpret the need for confirmation in turn; but there is a distinct difference between the two clinical theories in terms of levels and breadth of the interpretive work. The introduction of so-called structure-building features in psychoanalysis is certainly not new or confined to self psychology.

There are two points to be made which might illustrate how the psychology of the self may go beyond what we know in this regard. The first is that the selfobject transferences enable one to conceptualize, literally to see the unfolding development of how the self as structure accomplishes such an increased capacity to be self regulating. This is a more congenial and more clinically relevant picture than an abstract concept such as one of "ego repair." The second feature that needs our careful consideration is the one that suggests that interpretations per se are structural alterations which proceed by transmuting internalization; and the interpretation of the meaning of an interpretation might therefore be a necessary activity of every analysis. Every interpretation is capable of eliciting a new feeling about one's self.

Since theories are undetermined as to facts and since alternative theories seem to handle the data equally well at a certain level of investigation, how are we to decide which one to follow? It is certainly not a case for an indiscriminate choice of theories, yet the answer (and there is one) may be hard for some to take. In order to decide which theoretical approach is of maximum utility one must commit oneself to it and use it in a nonprejudicial way for a period of time. Only a test of usefulness is worthwhile, and only a complete understanding of the theory will allow such a test. Unfortunately and incredibly so many of the criticisms of self psychology are based on those basically irrelevant comments which range from a claim to the nonexistence of selfobject transferences to the insistence that the conduct of these analyses is no different from what everyone has been doing all along.

The final acceptance of one theory over another is not arbitrary. No matter how long parallel theories may coexist, there are criteria for choosing one over another. Philosophers of science (Harre, 1972) sometimes suggest two poles of the epistemology of science: phenomenalism and realism. Some sciences like anatomy are more suited to realism, and some like physics more suited to phenomenalism. So, too, are some theoretical statements directed to real things and some to "fictions" which have a degree of plausability. But regardless of how we position psychoanalysis in our consideration these same philosophers list criteria for choosing one theory over another (Popper, 1963). Until we come to grips with the essentials of our analytic observations, with the true facts of psychoanalytic evidence we must content ourselves with criteria of comprehensibility and coherence in our selection of theories. But the first and essential step is to utilize the theory to see just what we can learn.

The person who claims never to have seen an idealizing transference must first learn what to look for. The person who claims he has known this all along and/or has been doing this all along, as in the typical critiques of Mr. Z., betrays both a suspect honesty and a glaring misconception of the basis of scientific theory. One can only wonder what would be the psychoanalytic explanation behind a statement of the need to confirm the patient's accomplishments in dealing with a phobia—one that would be capable of being communicated to others and is part and parcel of a classical approach. Niceness, kindness, support; those are not answers since even these social amenities are capable of being explained. The claims of doing what every good analyst does are both foolish because we simply do not all do the same things, and insubstantial because the next generation of analysts needs a framework for operations. I, for one, do not see a place in classical psychoanalytic theory for this particular kind of intervention except, perhaps, in the usual effort of expanding the theory.

It might be quite worthwhile to examine just what so many of the so-called pioneers in psychoanalysis do offer us. I think it is an opportunity: one that allow us a choice to see if our old map is as good as ever or if we can go further with a new one. Theories are never right or wrong. No theory can be conclusively refuted. No theory is absolutely acceptable (Hesse, 1978). The criterion of pragmatism is the single best guide to adopt; and this certainly calls for a maximum of tolerance and a minimal conviction of certain truths.

CONCLUDING REMARKS

Self psychology has presented psychoanalysis with a challenge by way of allowing certain observations to be made. This includes a theory of self development that uses the concept of maturing relationships with selfobjects. It is a holistic theory which posits an overall open system of the self and which suggests continuing viable relationships with ones' selfobjects. It likewise places the center of the treatment of many individuals at the development and resolution of the selfobject transferences.

Psychoanalysts must come to grips with these ideas of self psychology by testing their utility in the service of explanation. Such an inquiry involves an acquaintance and understanding of the working through of these selfobject transferences. Unfortunately most critics of self psychology seem to restrict their activities to citing deviation and difference. This is not the proper avenue for the critique of new ideas. On the other hand, to neglect a careful study of the contributions of pioneers is to rob ourselves and our patients of a chance at an advance of our science. This is hardly tolerable in any effort that aims to help and is equally unfair to our wish to know.

New ideas are not new paradigms. That unfortunate word has been so abused that its greatest popularizer (Kuhn, 1977) has now disowned it His intent seems to have been to describe an event in the sociology of knowledge. But pioneers who present new ideas essentially offer us epistemological tools, and the reactions to these changes in perception are not necessarily an accurate gauge of their value. To change a set of convictions is always an effort, but psychoanalysts should be *more* rather than less capable of this task. Sigmund Freud was as "incorrect" as Heinz Kohut (1979b) now is. We owe our gratitude to that pioneer who has the courage to be wrong.

REFERENCES

Brenner, C. (1979), The components of psychic conflict and its consequences in mental life. *Psychoanal. Quart.*, 48:547-567.

Feyerabend, P. K. (1975), *Against Method.* London: New Left Books.

Freud, A. (1965), *Normality and Pathology in Childhood: Assessments of Development.* New York: International Universities Press.

Gediman, H. K. (1980), The search for the self: Selected writings of Heinz Kohut. Special book review. *Psychoanal. Rev.*, 17:4.

Grundy, R. E. (1973), *Theories and Observations in Science.* Englewood Cliffs, N.J.: Prentice-Hall.

Harre, R. (1972), *The Philosophies of Science.* Oxford: Oxford University Press.

Hesse, M. (1980), *Revolutions and Reconstructions in the Philosophy of Science.* Bloomington & London: Indiana University Press.

Kohut, H. (1979a), The two analyses of Mr. Z. *Internat. J. Psycho-Anal.*, 60:3-27.

―――― (1979b), Concluding remarks at the Conference on Self Psychology, Los Angeles, October.

Kramer, S. (1979), The technical significance and application of Mahler's separation-individuation theory. *J. Amer. Psychoanal. Assn.*, 27 (Supplement):251.

Kuhn, T. S. (1962), *The Structure of Scientific Revolutions.* Chicago: University of Chicago Press.

―――― (1977), *The Essential Tension.* Chicago & London: University of Chicago Press.

Popper, K. (1963), *Conjectures and Refutations.* New York & Evanston: Harper & Row.

Rangell, L. (1981), From insight to change. *J. Amer. Psychoanal Assn.*, 29:119-141.

Richards, A. D. (1981), Self theory and conflict theory. *The Psychoanalytic Study of the Child*, 36:319-337. New Haven: Yale University Press.

Rothstein, A, (1979), Toward a critique of the psychology of the self. Unpublished manuscript.

Sandler, J. (1976), Actualization and object relationships. *J. Philadel. Assn. Psychoanal.*, 3:59-70.

Tyson, R. L., & Tyson, P. (1982), A case of "pseudo-narcissistic" psychopathology: A re-examination of the developmental role of the superego. *Internat. J. Psycho-Anal.*, 63:283-294.

Waelder, R. (1930), The principle of multiple function: Observations on overdetermination. *Psychoanal. Quart.*, 5:45-62.

Wallerstein, R. (1980), Self psychology and "classical" psychoanalytic psychology: The nature of their relationship. A review and an overview. Presented at the Boston Psychoanalytic Society and Institute Symposium on Psychology of the Self, November 1.

13

The Self as Fantasy: Fantasy as Theory

WILLIAM I. GROSSMAN, M.D.

The problem of the self in psychoanalysis stands at the intersection of many traditional philosophical and psychoanalytic issues which might be thought of as lying along two axes. The first axis, by far the older, joins the everyday personal experiences of self—that is, self-awareness, self-consciousness, self-observation, self-esteem, self-determination, and will—with the ancient philosophical dilemmas concerning the relationship between the self and the world of things, of mind and body, free will, and other variations on these themes. The other axis is the psychoanalytic axis with the concrete events of the clinical situation and the subjective experience of

Presented on the occasion of the 70th Anniversary of the New York Psychoanalytic Society and the 50th Anniversary of the New York Psychoanalytic Institute, New York, November 14, 1981. Some parts of this paper are taken from "The Self as Fantasy: Fantasy as Theory," presented at the panel on Psychoanalytic Theories of the Self at the fall meeting of the American Psychoanalytic Association, New York, December 1980, and published in the *Journal of the American Psychoanalytic Association*, 30:919-937, 1982.

the patient at one end, and its mosaic of systematic, theoretical concepts at the other end. The concept of the self joins these coordinates and the different perspectives they offer.

The poles of the two axes of the self, the philosophical-everyday-personal and the psychoanalytic-clinical-theoretical, might seem at first to represent the poles of abstraction and concreteness. However, this would not do justice to the difference between them. The issue here is rather one of the subjectivity and objectivity of the points of view taken at either pole of each axis. With this orientation, the examination of the concept of the self to follow is guided by a number of central propositions.

First, there is an essential tension in psychoanalytic theory between the subjective and objective points of view regarding patients' experiences. Second, this essential tension between subjective and objective is built into the experience of patients themselves; that is, it is inherent in personal concepts of the self. Third, this tension between subjective and objective cannot be avoided in the philosophy of the self or in any theory of the self. Fourth, any psychology that takes subjective experience as a starting point and as a communication from the patient will be involved in this tension between subjectivity and objectivity. The only points of view which can escape such a tension are those that are strictly behavioristic and treat patients' verbal statements not as communications about themselves but rather as reports to be correlated with other behaviors irrespective of their subjective meaning to the patient. Fifth, theories derived from direct infant observation may attempt to evade this tension between subjective and objective points of view by assuming that the behavior observed can be treated as equivalent to the mental activities of the infant and therefore unwittingly blur the distinction between subjective and objective by placing subjective meaning into behavioral observations. (For an excellent philosophical discussion of subjective and objective, see Nagel, 1979; for a clinical discussion, see Bach, 1980.)

Both the subjectively oriented clinical data on the self and the objectively oriented theory of psychoanalysis include the personal and philosophical ideas of the self. This will become apparent if we now talk about the sources and nature of this subjective-objective duality in psychoanalytic theory.

There are three sources of this duality. First, we have the views that Freud himself brought to his organization of his earliest psychoanalytic data. Among these are his idea that man has a dual orientation which serves both his species and himself. Freud (1914, p. 78; 1915, pp. 124-125) said this explicitly in discussing the sexual instinct, which serves the reproduction of the species and the pleasure of the individual, noting that these two aims were not always to be harmonized (1916-1917, pp. 413-414). Man's psychology, then, was also to serve his biological destiny. He is both a person and an organism. His psychology serves himself and his society. His hate and love are divided between himself and his objects. His consciousness faces both outward and inward.

In keeping with his views on man's dual orientation, Freud organized the data of the clinical situation with two kinds of concepts: those derived from a general theoretical orientation to psychology as a branch of biology and those derived from the categories of experience of conflict that his patients brought to him with their everyday language about their impulses and their values.

The second source of the dual subjective-objective orientation of analysis comes from the position of the analyst as analyst. On the one hand, in his clinical work he must take the point of view of the patient in order to understand something of the patient's experience and to understand the subjective experiences of childhood which are somehow contained in the present communications and reminiscences of the patient. In other words, he must recognize a unity in the subjectivity of the present and the subjectivity of childhood. At the same time, he must maintain a position of objectivity, being neither caught up in his own subjective reactions to the patient's subjectivity nor, on the other hand, absorbed in his own subjective preoccupations. He takes, then, an objective view of both his own subjective responses and the patient's subjective communications. We call the analyst's objectivity his "psychoanalytic neutrality."

The third source of this dual subjective-objective orientation of analysis comes from the data of analysis itself. That is, the patient's reports, deriving as they do from the personal-philosophical axis of the self, are bound to contain a double orientation. A subjective component expresses imagery, feelings, thoughts, emotions, sensations, urges, desires, tensions, wishes, and memories. A capacity for reflection on subjective experience introduces a more distant viewpoint, an objective mode or perspective (cf. Sterba, 1934; Loewenstein, 1963).

In other words, a patient reflecting, in addition to revealing himself, imparts objectifying constructs to his experience. His activity in this way parallels that of the analyst.

Thus Freud constructed a psychoanalytic theory of mind; the analyst constructs the mind of his patient; and the patient constructs his own experience in speaking about himself. That these three activities have a similar form, roughly speaking—that a person speaking about himself is in a situation similar to a theoretician—is built into the psychoanalytic model of mental activity according to which personal accounts and descriptions of self-experience are, in a broad but fundamental sense, theories. They are theories on the everyday-personal-philosophic axis. On that axis, personal theories have always informed philosophy as philosophy has informed personal theories. (See conceptual analyses of "the self" by Mischel, 1977 and Toulmin, 1977.)

When Freud took the self-reflecting patient and the observing analyst and placed them in the mind as the system Conscious-Preconscious, he viewed all mental products as being, in some sense, theories. For instance in his paper on "Screen Memories" (1899, p. 322) he said that memories are selected and formed with a purpose. For this reason, we have memories, not "*from* our childhood," but only "*relating to*" our childhood. Freud also referred to secondary revision as the first interpretation of the dream. For Freud, myths are theories and theories are myths (1913a, 1913b; 1933b, p. 211). In this sense he spoke of the theory of drives as "our mythology" (1933a, p. 95). Infantile fantasies are theories about sexuality. All mental products, then, are personal constructions. Theory and fantasy serve both subjective, conflict-resolving aims, and objective, reality-orienting aims. According to Freud, both theory and fantasy have a similar form. They are composed of elements of the infantile, the actual, and the contribution of regulating interests, goals, and values. Differences among various mental products result from the particular mixture and correspond to the uses for which they are constructed and their relation to reality.

In an open-minded spirit, Freud pointed out the similarity of structure between Schreber's delusion and the libido theory (1911, pp. 78-79). Freud was later to emphasize that even delusions have a basis in fact, and like constructons in analysis are "attempts at explanation" (1937, p. 268).

Both Schreber's delusion and Freud's theory are theories of Schreber's self-experience. They both postulate entities. Freud's are inner entities; Schreber's are outer entities. These entities are made to conform to subjective experience. The similarity of the forms of the two theories derives from the fact that they are both efforts to describe self-state and object relations.

If Schreber had described his state in terms of his self in relation to his world, if he said, as many patients do, that his world had collapsed and so on, his message would have been more intelligible but no less problematical. The self-state description is, according to our theory, constructed in the same way any mental product is constructed, in a manner similar to Schreber's delusion, screen memories, and dreams. That is, the self-state description renders feelings, impulses, and ideas in the form of a fantasy construction. In the case of the self-state, the language of this fantasy is everyday language about an everyday fantasy about a fantasized entity, "the self" (Schafer, 1968, 1976, 1978; Abend, 1974). The "self" is the term popularly used to provide a concretely conceived organizational point of reference for inner experiences (Spiegel, 1959). The "self," then, is a special fantasy with its own language and referrents. It is caught up in the popular discourse in the language of self-experience. It is anchored in and derives a sense of immediacy from the bodily experiences, activities, and emotional interactions with other people. The "self" as a part of daily experience *appears* to be both supremely subjective yet also an objective organization, an organismic property, discernible to others. This apparent objectivity of "the self" arises from the fact that a person and those around him may equate observable and characteristic behavioral organizations or traits with an internal entity, "the self."

In calling "the self"-concept a theory or a fantasy, I

do not wish in any way to diminish its importance in regulating behavior. It seems to me that our concept of fantasy at times is a rather static one, as though we thought of a fantasy as something like a TV picture. Perhaps the model from which the unconscious fantasy was taken, namely, the daydream, gives fantasy this connotation. However, fantasy has and has always had, a much more important role in our theories. That is, it organizes and directs behavior. Fantasies are complex structures which have an effect on mental organization as well. They are both an aspect of mental organization and have an effect on it. The relationship between fantasies, mental contents in general, and structure or organization of mental life was discussed by Rapaport. Starting from Hartmann's distinction between the "inner world" and the "internal world," Rapaport (1957) wrote:

> It is the *inner* world which regulates the orientation in the external world. It is an inner map of the external world. The *internal* world is the major structures—the identifications, defense structures, ego, id, etc.; . . . The inner map of the outside world has selective omissions and is shaped to the structure of the internal world, that is, of the psychic apparatus. . . . The relation between the inner world and the internal world is one of the very interesting systematic questions, which may turn out to be the crucial one in the problem of the self" [pp. 696-697].

For Rapaport, the inner world, the map, was a substructure of the ego. However, he considered the relationship between the contents of the inner world of fantasies, perceptions, and so on, and the internal world, the structures, to be one of complex interaction. In fact, he said, changes in the internal world, major changes in mental structure *could* certainly be initiated and occur under the influence of the inner world. Structural changes, alterations in defenses and identifications, could in turn change the over-all organization of the inner world, as well. I think he was correct in linking this complex relationship between the functions of mental content and mental organization with the problem of the role of self-experience in mental life. Rapaport's comments point to the dynamic and structural importance of fantasy structures. It is precisely when we are considering a fantasy structure with such wide-ranging organizational and dynamic importance as the "self"-concept used in psychoanalysis that the structure-content polarity becomes less relevant.

As a fantasy, the details of the "self" may be elaborated, distorted, rerepresented, repressed, and otherwise defended against. In short, it may be conscious or unconscious. As the mental representation of the person as his own object, the "self" includes some representation of the person's mind. To be one's own object, after all, involves recognizing one's desires (id), dealing with one's interests in reality—acting on one's own behalf (ego), being what one loves or criticizes (superego). Only in this sense does the self "contain" the mental apparatus.

So far, then, I've made the point that the concept of the self as a popular and philosophical concept is the source of the self-concept in analysis, which thus derives from the common experience of self-reference. If the self is a fantasy, what is the fantasy about? It is customary to speak of the self as referring to certain properties (Schafer, 1968, 1976, 1978), such as agency, that is, the source or the initiator of action. Self is usually treated as a place (Spiegel, 1959; Schafer, 1968) which would be the locus of experience. It is the object of reflection and self-reference, of the self-defining experiences of continuity or recognition of history. In some sense it is thought of as the initiator of self-control. The fantasy is essentially embodied in the idea of self-reference, reference to an entity separate from other people, at least in some sense. Along with separateness come the issues of connectedness, similarity, and difference so prominent in the fantasies of some patients. Other properties and issues could be mentioned, but those will suffice to make my point. Taken together, all such elements constitute the framework and dimensions of self-fantasies for all patients, regardless of diagnosis. Toulmin (1977) stresses the point that the effort to use the noun "self" in a technical theoretical way, apart from reflexive idioms, never escapes the link to everyday self-reference.

"Self" depends on a person's view of himself, which from a psychoanalytic point of view means it is a fantasy. In short, "the self" is a "personal myth" (Kris, 1956), a myth of which everyone has his own more or less original version.

In presenting the elements and dimensions of the self as a fantasized entity, it should be recognized that these are a kind of framework, the categories of experience of the self. Ordinarily these are not within awareness or a matter of concern. Like the framework of the analytic setting, they are taken for granted unless something happens to focus attention on them. It is precisely those borderline and otherwise narcissistic patients who are in one way or another preoccupied with defining, characterizing, and delineating themselves who are also extremely attentive to and concerned with the setting, the framework, and the details of the analytic situation.

The categories of self-experience are in part the categories used to classify events in the objective, physical world and are to that extent a cognitive classification. As cognitive capacities they can be studied systematically as can their development in the child. Bach (1975, 1976, 1980), exploring subjectivity and objectivity, has discussed clinical material relating to preoccupation with continuity and perspective. Clinical material of this type shows the patient's preoccupation with description and self-delineation and often has a static and lifeless quality. It is as though the narcissistic patients are preoccupied with finding an objective view of their boundaries. The act of describing those boundaries, in fact, immobilizes and excludes the auditor. What gives these preoccupations life again is the exploration of the object relations from which this effort springs.

The situation has its parallel in the hypochondriasis which expresses object-related conflicts through somatic preoccupations (Richards, in press). In both cases, a concrete and ostensibly objective anchor has been found for the projected inner conflicts from which consciousness of significant objects is excluded, except secondarily. Similarly, the patient's concern with the framework and details of the analysis displaces the conflict from the person of the analyst. The static quality of boundary preoccupations and hyperobjectivity contributes to the boredom that may be experienced at times with these patients. According to the view I am offering, the clinical appearance of the preoccupation with the dimensions of self-experience is the manifest content of unconscious conflict. The viewpoint that such phenomena are independent of conflict is based on an overly narrow conception of conflict.

The problem of dealing with material relating to the self in analysis is not resolved by accepting the patient's view that the fantasies about the state of the self, whether conscious or unconscious, in fact describe some actual entity or endopsychically perceived state. Nor, on the other hand, can such descriptions be analyzed by immediately reducing them to some sort of caricature of unconscious drive-related fantasy. The technical handling and interpretation of such self-descriptions is a rather delicate matter. The patients giving such descriptions are narcissistically invested in their accounts and in their particular point of view of themselves. The narration of elaborate "self-observations" often serves as means of relating to others. In other words, self-description may serve many interpersonal functions, such as appeal, reproach, revelation, gift, and so on. By no means the least important is the invitation to appreciate and approve the style, wisdom, and self-knowledge.

Any effort to explore such fantasies, especially in states of tension, may be experienced as an attack. Some interpretations that focus on anxiety, hostility, and conflict, as well as those focusing on issues of closeness and affection, may stir up anxiety in some patients. They may then be experienced as "disintegrating," because for the patient they increase self-doubt by introducing an alien or disapproving point of view into the mind.

Clinically, then, the issue is one of relevance and the way the patient perceives the process of interpretation. If the patient feels the need to control or use the analyst for support, self-esteem regulation, an opposing view of self and the world, need satisfaction, tension regulation, or narcissistic gratifications, he will understand interpretations as serving or failing to serve these functions. Clarification of the "use of the object" (in Winnicott's phrase) will then be of primary relevance.

This will also entail the careful exploration of the patient's point of view. However, his need to protect his way of seeing things may mean that he equates being understood with having his point of view acknowledged before exploration is possible. What is at issue is a fear that his perceptions and fantasies will be condemned and devalued with the valuable parts ignored or submerged by those of the analyst. The elaboration of these problems belongs to the subjects of transference—and character analysis.

These brief remarks on technique are meant only to indicate that the problem of the"self" in analysis is a matter of tactics and technique. Problems of analysis of self material have been mistakenly regarded as showing the inadequacy of Freudian drive and ego-psychological theory. Rather than a theoretical difficulty, the trouble was a lack of systematic consideration of what goes into the art of the analyst—what Loewenstein called timing, dosage, and tact and the careful exploration of the psychic surface. Many of the examples purporting to show the inapplicability of classical theory are really criticisms of timing, dosage, and tact. Mechanical, insensitive, or poorly timed interpretations of drive and conflict, sometimes "wild analysis," do not refute theory but expose its misapplications. However, the fact that such examples of technique are frequent points to a gap in the theory of therapy—the theory of how to apply the psychoanalytic theory of mind to psychoanalytic technique. The interest in problems of ego distortion and narcissistic personality disorders has stimulated the process of making the art of analysis the subject matter of a theory of technique.

This sketch of some aspects of the self-concept as an issue of technique points to the view that "self" is the name given to experiences of organization and therefore of unity as well as experiences of agency and purpose of the experienced organization. Pathology of "the self" involves experiences of disorganization, disunity, lack of agency, or purpose, and so on. The self-fantasy is in this sense the patient's personal theory of his subjective experience of organization, just as Schreber's delusion is a theory about his self-experience. Consequently, our genetic considerations would concern not so much the organization of a psychoanalytic theoretical entity "the self," but rather the way patients develop experiences and fantasies of their organization, that is, experiences and fantasies of "self" (Spruiell, 1981; Pine, 1982). We would recognize that these self-fantasies, conscious or unconscious, are not direct manifestations of some elementary entity "the self," if only because self-fantasies include so much of other people. To make the self-theory of the patient into a theoretical entity "the self" accounting for self-experience is to make the patient's theory into psychoanalytic theory, to the advantage of neither.

This having been said, the problem of the relationship between mental and behavioral organization and experiences of self-organization remains to be discussed. Let me remind you of the parallel I drew earlier between the development of psychoanalytic theory and of patient's constructions of experience, both built up from subjective and objective viewpoints. As psychoanalytic theorists in the manner of Freud, we construct our ideas of the development of self-experience from both objective child observation and the clinical data from adults. Clinical data provide objective observations and the subjective experiences already shaped by the capacity for reflection arising in development.

Reflection, like objectivity, carries the implication of looking at oneself, and one's experience, from some different perspective. The process of interpretation in psychoanalysis provides a new kind of reflection. In *this* sense, psychoanalysis renews and continues development, as conflict resolution provides new perspectives.

At the heart of the problem of the self is the question of how the capacity for reflection develops and how the dialogue of the self is engaged. Until language develops we know nothing about the capacity for self-reflection. It may not be simply the problem of method, that is, the ability to communicate the results of reflection on the self without words. It seems more likely that the full capacity for self-reflection and therefore a self-concept is dependent on the progressive development of language. Without language, only reflection in imagery derived from perception as provided by the smiling or frowning face of the mother, or by a mirror, is possible. The development of language provides for the possibility of refinement in conceptualization of distinctions between self and others and the simultaneous maintenance of the experience of similarity in the face of difference.

The observable behaviors of preverbal infancy generally considered to be indicative of the developing self are actually behavioral organizations necessary for and contributing to adaptation. That is, the discrimination among family members, initiation of different kinds of interaction, playfulness, mimicry, and so on serve social adaptation and may be observed in the family pet. The behavior so organized may well form a nucleus of behavior which can become a basis of later self-observation.

Both highly organized prelinguistic behavior, of the kind attributed to the functioning of the self, and the role of later reflection and memory construction may be illustrated by a brief clinical vignette. Let me tell you about my dog.

In what follows, it is *not* my intention to parody child observation. I wish merely to underscore the problems of interpreting rich and complex data in a most important area.

My dog behaves differently toward each member of the family. He shows discrimination. He initiates interactions of different kinds—playful, demanding, affectionate. He seeks me out, and if I am attentive and willing to follow, he will lead me to the kitchen where he will look steadfastly at the biscuit jar. He shows agency and initiative. When he bites my hand in play, he watches my face attentively and lets go if I mimic a painful expression. He distinguishes my discomfort from his, distinguishes self from other. He knows when he is being mocked. If I mimic him when he is whining a complaint, he barks and becomes agitated. Finally, I come up behind him when he is lying on the floor watching me in the full-length mirror as I approach. I raise my foot and bring it down behind his head outside of the range of his vision, never touching him. He cringes. Does he recognize himself in the mirror? My reason for telling you about my dog is not to brag about him or to set an example for you in my joyful and approving mirroring of his achievements. Rather, I am struck by the fact that perhaps some people would be willing to treat these achievements as a manifestation of a self and self-other discrimination, if I were describing an infant rather than a dog. Does my dog have a self?

In answer to this question, a friendly critic wrote: "I cannot say whether your dog has a self. The reason . . . is that I never was a dog. But I am a person and I was a child, and as far back as I can remember, I always had an experience of self." He added, "Furthermore, everybody I know (almost) would say the same thing." Of course, he is right. His reflection on his experience compared with my dog reveals that despite the apparent affiliations that I have suggested, he *is* different. His memory constructs a continuous self right back to the beginning. And everyone he knows—he might have said "has ever known"—says the same thing.

Adaptive behavioral and emotional interactions achieve a human significance because they are interesting to a mother and become a part of the story of the mother's relationship with her child. The scope of the organizing factors governing adaptaton has now broadened from preadapted behaviors to organization by meaningful human drama in the form of maternal fantasy. We are born into, as well as create, fantasy structures suited to adaptation, much as we are born into, and create, the language suited to our innate linguistic competence. I believe that the similarity of these processes rests on more than mere analogy.

However "self"-directed he may appear, the child whose behavior is thus organized need have no self-awareness or awareness of the fantasies that guide the mother-child drama. Only later will he discover some version of those fantasies in himself in some of their transformations. At that time, they become a matter for the reflection that creates the self as experience and the fantasy of the self.

REFERENCES

Abend, S. (1974), Problems of identity: thoretical and clinical applications. *Psychoanal. Quart.*, 43:606-637.

Bach, S. (1975), Narcissism, continuity and the uncanny. *Internat. J. Psycho-Anal.*, 56:77-86.

——— (1976), Some notes on perspective. Unpublished manuscript.

——— (1980), Self-love and object-love: some problems of self and object constancy, differentiation, and integration. In: *Rapprochement: The Critical Subphase of Separation-Individuation*, ed. R. F. Lax, S. Bach, & J. A. Burland. New York: Jason Aronson, pp. 171-197.

Eisnitz, A. J. (1980), The organization of the self-representation and its influence on pathology. *Psychoanal. Quart.*, 49:361-392.

Freud, A. (1954), The widening scope of indications for psychoanalysis: discussion. *J. Amer. Psychoanal. Assn.*, 2:607-620.

Freud, S. (1899), Screen memories. *Standard Edition*, 3:301-322. London: Hogarth Press, 1962.

——— (1905), Fragment of an analysis of a case of hysteria. *Standard Edition*, 7:3-124. London: Hogarth Press, 1953.

——— (1911), Psycho-analytic notes on an autobiographical account of a case of paranoia (dementia paranoides). *Standard Edition*, 12:3-84. London: Hogarth Press, 1958.

—— (1913a), Totem and taboo. *Standard Edition*, 13:ix-161. London: Hogarth Press, 1955.

—— (1913b), The claims of psycho-analysis to scientific interest. *Standard Edition*, 13:165-192. London: Hogarth Press, 1955.

—— (1914), On narcissism: An introduction. *Standard Edition*, 14:67-104. London: Hogarth Press, 195.

——(1915), Instincts and their vicissitudes. *Standard Edition*, 14:111-140. London: Hogarth Press, 1957.

—— (1916-1917), Introductory lectures on psycho-analysis. *Standard Edition*, 16. London: Hogarth Press, 1963.

—— (1933a), New introductory lectures on psycho-analysis. *Standard Edition*, 22:3-184. London: Hogarth Press, 1964.

—— (1933b), Why war? *Standard Edition*, 22:197-202. London: Hogarth Press, 1964.

—— (1937), Constructions in analysis. *Standard Edition*, 23:255-270. London: Hogarth Press, 1964.

Grossman, W. I. (1967), Reflections on the relationships of introspection and psychoanalysis. *Internat. J. Psycho-Anal.*, 48:16-31.

—— & Simon, B. (1969), Anthropomorphism: Motive, meaning and causality in psychoanalytic theory. *The Psychoanalytic Study of the Child*, 24:78-111. New York: International Universities Press.

Kernberg, O. (1975), *Borderline Conditions and Pathological Narcissism*. New York: Jason Aronson.

Klein, G. S. (1976), *Psychoanalytic Theory: An Exploration Of Essentials*. New York: International Universities Press.

Kohut, H. (1977), *The Restoration of the Self*. New York: International Universities Press.

Kris, E. (1956), The personal myth: A problem in psychoanalytic technique. *J. Amer. Psychoanal. Assn.*, 4:653-681.

Lewis, M. & Brooks-Gunn, J. (1979), *Social Cognition and the Acquisition of Self*. New York: Plenum Press.

Loewald, H. (1971), On motivation and instinct theory. *The Psychoanalytic Study of the Child*, 26:91-128. New York: Quadrangle.

Loewenstein, R. M. (1963), Some considerations on free association. *J. Amer. Psychoanal. Assn.*, 11:451-473.

Mischel, T. (1977), Conceptual issues in the psychology of the self: An introduction. In: *The Self: Psychological and Philosophical Issues*, ed. T. Mischel. Oxford: Blackwell, pp. 3-28.

Nagel, T. (1979), *Mortal Questions*. Cambridge: Cambridge University Press.

Piaget, J. (1971), *Insights And Illusions Of Philosophy*. New York: New American Library.

Pine, F. (1982), The experience of self: Aspects of its formation, expansion, and vulnerability. *The Psychoanalytic Study of the Child*, 37:143-167. New Haven, Conn.: Yale University Press.

Rapaport, D. (1957), A theoretical analysis of the superego concept. In: *The Collected Papers Of David Rapaport*, ed. M. M. Gill. New York: Basic Books, 1967, pp. 685-709.

———— (1960), On the psychoanalytic theory of motivation. In: *The Collected Papers Of David Rapaport*, ed. M. M. Gill. New York: Basic Books, 1967, pp. 853-915.

Richards, A. D. (in press), Self theory, conflict theory and the problem of hypochondriasis. *The Psychoanalytic Study of the Child*. New Haven, Conn.: Yale University Press.

Rubinstein, B. B. (1981), Person, organism and self: Their worlds and their psychoanalytically relevant relationships. Presentation to the New York Psychoanalytic Society, January 27.

Rycroft, C. (1966), Introduction: Causes and meaning. In: *Psychoanalysis Observed*, ed. C. Rycroft. New York: Coward-McCann, pp. 7-22.

Schafer, R. (1968), *Aspects of Internalization*. New York: International Universities Press.

———— (1976), *A New Language For Psychoanalysis*. New Haven: Yale University Press.

———— (1978), *Language and Insight*. New Haven: Yale University Press.

Spiegel, L. A. (1959), The self, the sense of self, and perception. *The Psychoanalytic Study of the Child*, 14:81-109. New York: International Universities Press.

Spruiell, V. (1981), The self and the ego. *Psychoanal. Quart.*, 50:319-344.

Sterba, R. (1934), The fate of the ego in analytic therapy. *Internat. J. Psycho-Anal.*, 15:117-126.

Stone, L. (1973), On resistance to the psychoanalytic process. *Psychoanal. Contemp. Sci.*, 2:42-73.

Toulmin, S. E. (1977), Self-knowledge and knowledge of the "Self." In: *The Self: Psychological And Philosophical Issues*, ed. T. Mischel. Oxford: Blackwell, pp. 291-317.

14

Two Modes of Psychoanalytic Thought

LEO SADOW, M.D.

The acquisition of knowledge in psychoanalysis is based on a study of the patient, most particularly the transferences; on the interaction of analyst and patient, what is generally referred to as technique; and on ever more detailed investigations of the psychological operations of the analyst within the analytic situation. Except for Leo Stone's (1961) important contribution to our understanding of the actual psychoanalytic situation, until relatively recently little attention has been centered on the psychological operations of the analyst except to consider the very fact of the intrusion into the analytic situation of such material as a manifestation of a countertransference, a pathological response. Within the last decade, the concept of countertransference appears to have broadened, stimulated in part by Kohut's (1971) seminal work with the narcissistic transferences. It is now understood that the analyst's psychological responses may be studied not only as a source of information about the patient but also with regard to the limitation they may place on the analyst's analyzing function.

It is not my purpose in this presentation to examine and extend our understanding of the psychological operations of the analyst in terms of either pathological countertransferences or information gathered introspectively by reflecting on emotional responses to the patient. My interest is in yet another way by which the psychological operations of the analyst profoundly affect the analytic situaton; and that is in learning how the cognitive set of the analyst, the analyst's mode of thought, affects what he looks for, what he sees, how he responds, and how all of these factors affect the course of the analysis.

Psychoanalysts have traditionally made the implicit assumption that the psychological operations of analysts in the clinical situation will differ from one another in relatively insignificant ways. The style of one analyst, then, might differ from that of another in some small matters of emphasis, timing, linguistic usage; but it is assumed that there is an "analytic" mode of thought which is common to all those working within the analytic paradigm to which most of us generally subscribe. This paper will argue that in at least one crucial area two quite distinct modes of analytic thinking can be discerned, and that these may complement one another and thus enhance the analytic process, or they may diminish the analytic process by creating confusion.

By "mode of thought" I mean the particular cognitive set which may, in general, distinguish one analyst from another. The term will also and more particularly be used in describing how the thinking of an analyst may differ from moment to moment in the analytic situation. It is my intention to focus on the two most common types of psychoanalytic thought. One is the intuitive, introspective, on-line creative mode which is most strongly involved with the moment-to-moment grasp of, and interpretation of, the productions of the patient. The other is a more organized cognitive mode: analytic in the more general sense of the term; most strongly associated with a theoretical approach to the patient's productions. The creative, empathic, introspective aspects of the analyst's psychological operations are more engaged in the first; the logical, rational, analytical, theoretical activities of the analyst are more engaged in the second. The vastly expanded meaning which has become associated with the word "empathy" makes me hesitate to use it. By empathy I refer to a highly evolved capacity to "feel one's way into" the affective life of another and not to what is therapeutically done with the information so acquired (Basch, 1981). I have elsewhere (Sadow, 1980) referred to psychoanalytic data as generative in the sense that it is an amalgam produced by contributions from both patient and analyst. It is the activity of the analyst in contributing to such an amalgam that corresponds to the first of our two modes, which, based on this kind of activity, I shall refer to as the *generative mode*. The second, more logical mode is that psychological operation which seeks to find or to impose a pre-existing pattern or theory on the productions of the patient and on the resonating, empathic responses of the analyst to those productions which together constitute psychoanalytic data. The major goal of this mode of thought suggests the name *patterning mode*.[1]

Both the generative and the patterning modes are concepts familiar to analysts under other names. Colleagues are sometimes described as being very intuitive in their clinical approach, or somewhat intellectual, pos-

---

[1] The word "pattern" was taken from Gedo (1979, p. 6) where it was used in a similar way.

sibly even obsessional in the benign sense of the term. These are generally accepted as differences in style or clinical tone which do not significantly alter the analytic experience. Only if these differences in tone tend toward the extremes of disorganization or "wild" analysis on the one hand, or of rigidity on the other, are they seen as pathological distortions of the analytic process. Within broad limits, the tendency of a given analyst toward a greater emphasis on the generative or on the patterning mode of thought will mean only that the analytic product will be a little richer and deeper in one direction or the other. Stone (1961) anticipated this view of the generative mode by pointing out that "our entire interpretative method involves the presentation of the analyst's *own* mental activity, which leads to the subjective transformation of what the patient has shown into something manifestly different, albeit latent or implicit in what was shown" (p. 26; emphasis added). This statement was an expression of disagreement with Freud's "mirror" simile in which he held that the analyst ought to have an attitude of emotional coldness which, like a mirror, shows the patient only what the patient has shown the analyst. In the discussion which follows I hope that it will become evident that the analytic stance which Stone rejects, correctly, is based on an excessively constricted understanding of the generative mode of thought. Freud's mirror simile does not adequately address the special quality of psychoanalytic data as an amalgam of elements which stem from the analyst as well as the patient.

A question might arise as to which mode of thought is most truly psychoanalytic. My response would be, of course, that both are psychoanalytic. This accords with Freud's (1923) tripartite definition of psychoanalysis: first, as a method for the treatment of neurotic disorders based on a number of technical rules that he designed; second, as a body of knowledge obtained by this treatment method which "is gradually being accumulated into a new scientific discipline" (p. 235). These two parts of the definition, as well as the third part—psychoanalysis as an investigative procedure—were, for Freud, interdependent (Sachs, 1979, p. 123). That is to say, clinical psychoanalysis cannot exist independently of the theory which is based upon it and which at the same time is guided by it; nor can either exist independently of the investigative methodology Freud evolved. But this does not suggest that the rules we use for thinking are the same no matter which of these aspects of psychoanalysis is being considered.

The concept of psychic determinism, so central to clinical psychoanalytic thought, may be used to illustrate how the mode of thought of the analyst changes as he relates to one or another aspect of the psychoanalytic enterprise. Psychic determinism is the major underlying assumption which explains the meaningfulness of free associations. We assume, correctly, I believe, that when the patient free associates he will quite spontaneously express thoughts which are emotionally linked. For example, a sequence of memories, both recent and remote, may be expressed as a consequence of the experience of an affect or need, the affect or need having been initiated by some interaction within the analytic situation, i.e., by the transference. The analyst responds, silently, to this sequence of psychically determined free associations by his own chain of associations. To the extent that his own experience and memories are of sufficient variability and richness and to the extent that he is able to identify with his patient, the analyst's associations will tend toward the same qualities of affect as the patient is expressing or toward associations which can be interpreted as responses to the patient's affect. The content of the analyst's associations consists of idiosyncratic memories or experiences as well as memories of what he has previously heard from his patient. The mode of thought of patient and analyst are so far the same: both are responding to intrapsychic experiences determined by a particular affect which arose out of the patient's unconscious responses to the analyst or to the analytic situation. The "work" of free association and interpretation results, it is hoped, in ultimately bringing that unconscious affect to consciousness. This is the generative mode of thought and activity. It is expressed in action by free associations. These are linkages of memory and experience based on emotional contiguity. The underlying psychological law upon which this whole concept rests is psychic determinism.

When, on the other hand, the analyst seeks to impose an order, to explain, to discern a pattern in the combined productions of his patient and himself which corresponds to some part of his theoretical repertoire, he is engaged in the patterning mode of thought. Such a pattern, or theory, is not based on a claim of free association, but is seemingly extrinsically imposed. The rules which govern this activity are logic, issues of probability, comparisons to the available store of propositions—secondary-process thinking generally. Psychic determinism is important only insofar as the products of free associations are the data which are utilized in theory construction or patterning.

A comment on the idea of the "spontaneous unfolding of the transference" is in order at this point. My description about the generative mode of thought suggests that a reconsideration of this important tenet of psychoanalysis is in order, because what unfolds "spontaneously" in the view of one highly creative observer might appear quite forced to another. The difference results from the special qualities of each generative observer; each perceives a somewhat, or markedly, different transference. The vantage point of each observer is both important and idiosyncratic. The value of the specific kind of transference each such creative observer develops is determined by whether he or another observer finds it useful. I suspect that there are many analysts working effectively in their own offices who, on the basis of their generative mode of thought, create new and therapeutically helpful clinical theories based on perceived transferences which they do not communicate to others. They may be issues relevant to that one case or they may be potentially applicable to many. But they are based at their inception on the qualities of that patient and that analyst engaged in their mutual work.

The kind of thinking called for in these two basic analytic modes of thought is so distinctive, and the rules governing them are so different, that their confusion will very likely result in an inadequate or pathological psychoanalytic experience.

Ideally, there is a smooth synchrony between generative and patterning modes of thought as the analysis progresses. The analyst immerses himself in the feelings and thoughts of the patient and listens as well to his own responses. He may be relatively silent or overtly responsive at this stage. The response, whether silent or verbalized, is very close to the patient's experience. That is, the response is essentially atheoretical. There can be no doubt that the theoretical knowledge of the analyst, no less than other aspects of understanding and experience, informs his response. But the analyst's response is guided mainly by his spontaneous rather than his considered reaction to the feelings expressed by the patient and is not an interpretation of those feelings in some more abstract sense. At some point, which I shall not at this time attempt to define, the analyst actively removes himself from this immersion experience to formulate an interpretation based on his understanding of the generative experience and on a theoretical generalization or pattern which he believes fits the situation, gives meaning to it, and places it within a larger, more experience-distant context. This activity provides the patient with a set of references, an anchor, which enables him to fix the experience more usefully and permanently than the more amorphous generative mode allows. If the interpretive, patterning work has been successful, a new and perhaps deeper cycle of generative and then patterning activity takes place.

So much for the ideal: the real-world analytic situation frequently deviates from the ideal in a number of ways which serve both to highlight the analytic process and to extend our understanding of that process by enabling us to study its details more focally. In the remainder of this paper I shall try to detail some of the specific characteristics of each of these modes of psychoanalytic thought and describe some of the problems which are frequently encountered in exercising them. Then I shall take up certain crossover issues, problems which arise when the rules for one mode of thought are misapplied to the other mode. All of the material which follows is based on self-observation, that is, on my own work as an analyst and on the observations of analytic candidates under supervision by myself and others.

The qualities which define the generative mode can be loosely described as empathy and introspection; and the goal of the generative mode is to produce an amalgam of information from patient and analyst which is, in effect, the data of psychoanalysis. What, then, are the specific attributes or characteristics of this mode of thought, and what tends to promote such thought? First, the analyst needs to be able to immerse himself deeply in the painful (or other) affect of the patient, to tolerate it, to experience it, sometimes for prolonged periods of time—perhaps over many analytic sessions—without undo defensiveness. Sometimes the affect is not so much painful as pleasurable. Either way, the analyst's task within the context of the generative mode of thought requires considerably more capacity to tolerate and experience the psychic pain of another human being than is needed for any other kind of professional activity. Some analysts, of course, are limited by neurotic conflict which has been inadequately analyzed; the solution for them is obvious. For most analysts, however, the limiting factor will not be so much a matter of incapacitating conflict as of relative incapacity resulting from a relative absence of those experiences which promote the capacity—specifically, the absence of the experience of mastering psychic pain of sufficient depth. Analysts differ widely in respect to this capacity. What are the experiences which influence and help develop the capacity to immerse oneself in the pain of another? It has been my observation that some degree of early maternal depression may be one such experience. That is, the analyst who had to experience his mother's pain and had to relate to her in her painful state, and who nonetheless was able to master this, is possibly best able to immerse himself in the pain of the patient. Too much maternal pain tends to result in avoidance and insensitivity. Too benign an experience may leave the analyst relatively disinterested.

Another significant characteristic of the generative mode is also closely involved with the very earliest experiences of the analyst. The very act of allowing oneself to touch another psychologically so as to produce an amalgam of one's own thoughts and feelings with his thoughts and feelings implies the formation of a microscopic merger of sorts. To accomplish this with some degree of comfort, or at least with no incapacitating discomfort, the analyst must be able to "hear" his patient—i.e., he must have the capacity to give up or surrender his total investment in self, in the primacy of his own standards, thoughts, and feelings. To put this another way, he must be reasonably free of the fear that if he gets very close to his patient he will, so to speak, psychologically lose his own sense of self, his core of initiative, to the patient. Or, again, he must be able to make use of the mechanism of identification to empathize with the patient. For our purposes these statements are all equivalent; they are merely expressed in different theoretical idioms. On the other hand, while the analyst must surrender his total investment in self, he must be able to resist being pulled too deeply into the patient's frame of reference without undo defensiveness. The capacity to enter very deeply into the patient's emotional life while yet retaining a firm sense of self depends on the analyst's being free of pathological archaic transferences or on his having resolved them. Problems in this area appear to spring from the need of the child to establish excessively powerful and impenetrable defenses against an excessively intrusive mothering figure at the point in development when the core of self is being established. Details will vary depending on whether the personality was allowed some freedom to develop to the point of firm differentiation of self from other, and on the intensity of intrusiveness, complicating physiological problems, specific areas of maternal intrusiveness, capacity of the child to respond, presence or absence of father or others as ameliorating factors, etc., etc.

Still another important ingredient of an effective capacity to utilize the generative mode of thought is a reasonable freedom from fear of the unknown, of novelty. I believe that this is a very widespread problem in learning generally. For the analyst this may be a particularly disturbing issue, because the analyst, by virtue of the large number of novel variations to which he is routinely exposed, is continuously beset by destructuralizing experiences which challenge his established sets and structures. Gunther (1981) has described patients with certain types of archaic transferences who develop rather frightening acting-in crises when subjected to destructuralizing, unempathic responses on the part of the analyst. It is my impression that, in mild but nonetheless therapeutically destructive form, such destructuralizing experiences may affect the analyst at the moment when the generative mode of thought would be most active. The typical response to such a situation is to respond defensively with an established more-or-less obsessive intepretation which preserves the analyst's established set but which fails generatively to engage the patient. In effect, such an interpretation imposes a restatement of the analyst's established theory in place of the data whose generation is prevented by the anxiety of the analyst. From our present frame of reference the analyst has prematurely shifted out of the generative mode due to the destructuralizing effect of the press of a novel state. Rather than move along with a patient, generatively developing a common form of amalgam, the analyst stops the process by an abrupt and defensive shift to a patterning mode which interrupts the analytic process and thereby spares him from pain.

An example might help to illustrate how an analyst responds to an incipiently destructuralizing analytic process. The patient described a series of hopeful but ultimately unfulfilled relationships in which there were increasing difficulties in communication. The analyst experienced the patient as unable to express his longings within the transference and responded in two ways. First, the analyst interpreted the contents of the stories told by the patient in either oedipal or self-psychological terms. When these interventions failed the analyst grew increasingly angry and interpreted the patient's silences and flat, affectless tone as resistances to the analysis. The analyst understood transferences as affect displaced from external or early objects to the analyst, and repeatedly fell back on this standard paradigm whenever the patient attempted to express his actual analytic experience by reference to external events. Unable to maintain the generative mode adequately until there was sufficient data to establish what was a somewhat unsettling pattern—in which the patient could feel strongly about the actual functioning of the analyst—the analyst repeatedly interrupted the generative mode with less than adequate patterns which served only to intensify the frustration of the patient at not being understood.

It might be asked, isn't all of this subsumed under the term "regression," and is it not, therefore, that the generative mode is in essence the capacity to regress? The "capacity to regress" when so used is, I believe, a simplistic and misleading term. It is true that the contents with which patient and analyst work may be part of a regressed area of the patient's mental life. However, the generative mode of thought requires that the analyst has satisfactorily resolved those archaic issues from which this mode of thought derives. Either (1) the regressed analyst feels the patient's pain so deeply that he is paralyzed; or (2) he is so captivated by his patient's drive derivatives that his effectiveness is compromised by excessive excitement; or (3) his capacity to self-soothe is so damaged that he is unable to tolerate the possibly necessary prolonged immersion in the painful affect experienced by the patient. But this we recognize as pathological.

The resemblance of the generative mode of thought to Freud's primary process should be clear to any reader. Moraitis (1981) has proposed that the primary-process, or generative, mode of thought as I use it, and the secondary-process, or patterning, mode may be seen as "filters" which are ways of dealing with thought. He suggests that the primary and secondary processes differ in speed of thinking and in degree of linearity. The primary process is very rapid thought and is circular; the secondary process is slower, more material is filtered out, and the thinking can then be more linear and connected. This way of discriminating between the modes of thought in terms of formal characteristics corresponds closely to my own observations.

I am aware that, while I have spoken of the particular characteristics and limitations of the generative mode in terms of their early psychogenic origin, the true state of affairs may be more complex. For example, there may also be some genetic components that contribute. However, thus far, the psychogenic explanation appears sufficient.

The characteristics of the patterning mode of thought are closely related to those generally described for the secondary process: logical thought, reason, etc. This mode of thought enables the analyst to select those bits of data which can be organized into a definite pattern which is replicable. At the very least, knowledge of known patterns or theories is essential. Given the wide variability of character structures, genetic predisposition, and developmental patterns, the availability of a large number of organized clinical theories or methods for organizing patterns, based perhaps, on developmental models is essential if the analyst is to avoid the pitfall of forcing his data into one or two major molds (see Gedo and Goldberg, 1973, for a very useful developmental approach). The possibility that simply ignoring highly significant data that fails to fit neatly into an excessively circumscribed theoretical package will create serious distortion is very great.

Of vital importance for adequate functioning within the patterning mode of thought are highly developed verbal and metaphoric skills. The translation, so to speak, from the affect-action-laden, generatively derived contents to the pattern which the analyst and patient must work with requires such skills at a high order of competence. Their absence may result in a stilted, dull, obsessional recitation of a theory in the form of an interpretation which fails to capture the special richness and tone of that particular patient or the uniqueness of his experiences. These essentially cognitive skills are, of course, not peculiar to the psychoanalytic situation.

What is of more central psychoanalytic interest is the problem of disengaging from what can become a pathologically pleasurable sharing of the patient's thoughts and experience. For in order to engage his pattern-finding skills, the analyst must establish the necessary distance. When the analyst fails to do so, the analysis develops an amorphous, unstructured quality which the patient may find pleasant, but which is ultimately without much therapeutic gain.

The inability to *stop* using the generative mode of thought and the resulting failure to achieve closure are among the class of difficulties in the process of conducting an analysis which may be termed crossover problems. These are analytic-process errors that result from the inappropriate use of one mode of analytic thought when another mode is indicated. An example of such an analytic process error can be seen in the case of an analyst whose patient rather enjoyed the freedom to express whatever came to mind, a freedom which is certainly optimal for analytic progress. The analyst was easily able to accept and was very comfortable with any and all associations and was able with a few words here or there to facilitate the flow of associations. Interpretations were almost never made, however. The specific reasons are not central here; but it is clear that in the example just cited the process error results from the strong preference for the generative mode, whatever the motive, and the inability to cross over to the patterning mode.

Another crossover problem is the premature and obsessional imposition of a pattern or theory without an adequate base line of data derived from the generative mode. This sort of process error can result from an ideological belief on the part of the analyst in one or another theory and the need to impose that theory on the patient. It has a venerable history in psychoanalysis, there being evidence that Freud was no less subject to such crossover problems than a great many analysts since his time (Sadow, Gedo, Miller, Pollock, Sabshin, and Schlessinger, 1968). An interesting and less frequent variant of this problem occurs when an analyst of unique patterning capacities is able to piece together an interpretable pattern based on so little generative data that it comes across as magical to the patient. The interpretation based on such great cognitive skill may be correct, but the analytic process is subverted because the patient has hardly begun to participate in the process. The interpretation is experienced as an infantalizing voice from on high.

The patterning mode of thought has thus far been discussed in terms of the refinding of a known pattern in the data of the analysis. There is a second usage which is less common, but no less important—that is, the discovery of a pattern in the data which had not been previously identified. While the problem of pattern construction is clear, the solution and the etiology are anything but clear. In the most general sense, three ingredients seem critical: (1) Great effort and energy are required to overcome the much easier and more parsimonious task of making a bad fit of data to an established theory. To learn a new theory in the absence of some significant gratification such as the great pleasure some find in the idealization of a gifted teacher or idealized leader is difficult enough. To give up all old patterns and find an entirely novel one requires even greater effort. (2) Enormous courage is needed to leave behind the security of the known, as illustrated by the understandable need of some who have been pattern finders to establish supportive groups of loyal followers. Freud's distribution of special rings to his small band of loyal early followers comes to mind in this connection. (3) The motive or driving force, as it were, behind the finding of a new pattern may be related to the need to solve a deep psychological difficulty or to fill an important structural gap in oneself. I will not attempt an elaboration of this very important issue at this time.

SUMMARY

Two modes of psychoanalytic thought have been described: The generative mode makes use of the introspective, empathic, more or less creative qualities of the analyst. The patterning mode makes use of the logical, rational, organized, and organizing qualities of the analyst. Both are essential to the psychoanalytic process, and both are essential ingredients of the psychoanalytic situation. The organization of the cognitive activities of the analyst in this manner appears to offer a convenient and systematic approach to the detailed study of how the analyst works and how certain errors of the analytic process occur and how they might be corrected. Errors of the analytic process can be caused by the improper use of either of the two analytic modes of thought or the cross-over problems that result from the erroneous substitution of one mode for the other.

REFERENCES

Basch, M. F. (1981), Empathic understanding: Review of the concept and some theoretical considerations. Unpublished manuscript.

Freud, S. (1923), Two encyclopedia articles. *Standard Edition*, 18:235-259. London: Hogarth Press, 1955.

Gedo, J. E. (1979), *Beyond Interpretation*. New York: International Universities Press.

———— & Goldberg, A. (1973), *Models of the Mind*. Chicago: University of Chicago Press.

Gunther, M. S. (1981), Archaic transferences: A prototype. Unpublished manuscript.

Kohut, H. (1971), *The Analysis of the Self*. New York: International Universities Press.

Sachs, D. M. (1979), On the relationship between psychoanalysis and psychoanalytic therapy. *J. Philadel. Assn. Psychoanal.*, 6:3-4, 119-146.

Sadow, L. (1980), Psychoanalytic data. Unpublished manuscript.

———— Gedo, J., Miller, J., Pollock, G., Sabshin, M., & Schlessinger, N. (1968), The process of hypothesis change in three early psychoanalytic concepts. *J. Amer. Psychoanal. Assn.*, 16:245-275. Also in: *Freud: The Fusion of Science and Humanism*, ed. J. Gedo & G. Pollock. New York: International Universities Press, 1976, pp. 257-285.

Stone, L. (1961), *The Psychoanalytic Situation*. New York: International Universities Press.

Index

Compiled by Glenn E. Miller